Social Structure and Culture

Editor: Hans Haferkamp

Social Structure and Culture

Editor
Hans Haferkamp

Walter de Gruyter · Berlin · New York 1989

Hans Haferkamp †
former Professor of Sociology at the University of Bremen, Federal Republic of Germany

Angelika Schade
Dipl.-Soziologin, wissenschaftliche Mitarbeiterin am Zentrum für Europäische Rechtspolitik (ZERP) Bremen, Federal Republic of Germany

The contributors and the publisher express their gratitude to *Angelika Schade* who supervised the editing of the work patiently and competently.
Angelika Schade thanks Anne Dreyer and Gitta Stender for their support during the various stages of the editorial work.

Library of Congress Cataloging in Publication Data

Social structure and culture / editor, Hans Haferkamp.
Includes bibliographies and index.
ISBN 0-89925-362-8 (U.S.)
1. Culture. 2. Social structure. I. Haferkamp, Hans, 1939–
HM 101.S69345 1989 89-33149
306--dc20 CIP

Deutsche Bibliothek Cataloging in Publication Data

Social structure and culture / ed. Hans Haferkamp. – Berlin ;
New York : de Gruyter, 1989
ISBN 3-11-011310-4
NE: Haferkamp, Hans [Hrsg.]

Typesetting and printing: Tutte Druckerei GmbH, Salzweg-Passau. Binding: Dieter Mikolai, Berlin. Cover design: Johannes Rother, Berlin. – Printed in Germany.

Contents

Hans Haferkamp: In Memoriam (Shmuel N. Eisenstadt) 1

Introduction: Culture and Social Structure in Recent Sociological Analysis (Shmuel N. Eisenstadt) 5

Part I Social Structure and Culture – A Tenable Differentiation?

1 The Cultural Foundations of Society (Friedrich H. Tenbruck) 15
1.1 Culture and Society: About the History of Concepts 16
1.2 The Concept of Culture: A Preliminary Review 20
1.3 Representative Culture 22
1.4 Some Remarks on Weber and Parsons 27
1.5 A New Type of Culture: Modern Culture 29
1.6 The Culture of Everyday Life 31
1.7 About the Significance of Culture for Sociology 33
Notes 33

2 Structures, Cultures, and Knowledge: A Historical and Comparative Exploration (Richard Münch) 37
2.1 Introduction 37
2.2 An Intercultural Comparison of the Development of Modern Scientific Knowledge 38
2.3 The Development of Modern Scientific Knowledge: A Theoretical Explanation 39
2.4 An Intracultural Comparison of the Development of Special Characteristics of Knowledge 42
2.4.1 Great Britain: The Scientific Communities, the Enquiry, and the Normative Binding Power of Knowledge 42
2.4.2 France: The Salon, the Café, the Essay, and the Expressivity of Knowledge 43
2.4.3 Germany: The Private Study, the University Seminar, the Academic "Work", and the Abstraction of Knowledge 44
2.4.4 The United States: The Meeting, the Periodical Article, and Rapidly Changing Knowledge 46
2.5 Concluding Remarks 47
2.6 Summary 47
References 48
Appendix (Figures 2.1–2.23) 50

3 Symbolic, Institutional, and Social-Structural Differentiation: A Selection-Theoretical Perspective (Bernhard Giesen and Michael Schmid) . 67
3.1 Introduction 67

3.2 Three Views on Culture 68
3.2.1 Culture as Language and Constitution 68
3.2.2 Culture as Value-Orientation and Tradition 69
3.2.3 Culture as Product and Consumption 71
3.3 Institutions and Social Structure 74
3.3.1 Selective Factors for the Reproduction of Modes of Culture 74
3.3.2 Everyday Action: Life-World and Community 75
3.3.3 Organization: Social Inequality and Social Control 76
3.3.4 Public Situations: Inclusion and Mass Communication 78
Notes 82
References 83

Part II Culture and Modernity

1 Sociology and the Crisis of Western Culture (Johannes Weiß) 89
Notes 98
References 99

2 Differentiation and Culture: Sociological Optimism under Scrutiny (Hans Haferkamp) 101
2.1 Differentiation and Pattern Maintenance by Culture 102
2.2 Change toward and within Modern Culture 108
2.3 Sociological Optimism 119
References 121

3 The Cognitive Representations of Social Inequality: A Sociological Account of the Cultural Basis of Modern Class Society (Klaus Eder) 125
3.1 The Discourse on Social Inequality 125
3.1.1 Inequality: Social Fact or Interpretative Scheme? 125
3.1.2 The Universality of Vertical Classification 125
3.2 Class Position and Social Inequality 128
3.2.1 Four Forms of Classificatory Struggles 128
3.2.2 The Theoretical Construction of the Concept of Class 130
3.3 Beyond Class-Specific Subcultures 133
3.3.1 A Critique of the "Discourse on Class" 133
3.3.2 The Cultural Reproduction of Class 135
3.3.3 Class-Specific Schemata of Social Experience 138
3.4 A Social Critique of Morality 140
Notes 141
References 143

4 Towards a Sociology of Postmodern Culture (Mike Featherstone) ... 147
4.1 Introduction: Postmodernism in Sociology 147
4.2 The Development of Postmodernism within the Cultural and Intellectual Fields 155
4.3 The New Cultural Intermediaries and the Centers of Postmodernism 162

4.4 Postmodernism and the Aestheticization of Life 166
Notes 167
References 168

Part III Culture and Social Action

1 Choice and Culture: The Behavioral Basis of Cultural Impact on Transactions (Siegwart Lindenberg) 175
1.1 Introduction 175
1.2 The Parsons-Shils Solution 176
1.2.1 The Value Theory of Action 177
1.2.2 Evaluation of the Parsons-Shils Solution: The Plasticity Paradigm of Choice 178
1.3 The Scarcity Paradigm of Choice and SEU Theory 180
1.4 Reason and Rationality: Stinchcombe's Social Agency Theory ... 182
1.5 Prospect Theory: Kahneman and Tversky's Alternative 183
1.5.1 Prospect Theory 184
1.5.2 Some Problems with Prospect Theory 186
1.6 The Discrimination Model of Probabilistic Choice and Framing . 187
1.7 Culture and Rational Choice 190
1.7.1 Social Production Functions 190
1.7.2 Culture, Social Norms, and the Avoidance of Loss 192
1.8 Summary and Conclusion 194
Notes 195
References 198

2 The Interplay of Culture and Social Structure in the Mind: The Social Actor as a Tangled Decision-Maker (Luciano Gallino) 201
References 214

3 The Role of the Game between Culture and Social Action (Carlo Mongardini) 217
Notes 226
References 227

4 The Cultural Construction of Social Identity: The Case of Scotland (Josef Bleicher) 229
4.1 Introduction: Social Identity and Nationalism 229
4.2 Culture, Nation, and the Absence of Political Nationalism 229
4.3 Culture, Modernity, and Social Identity 230
4.4 The Construction of Scottishness 231
4.5 From Cultural to Political Nationalism 234
4.6 Some Implications 237
Notes 239
References 240

Part IV Culture, Ideology, and Science

1 The (Re)Colonization of Science by the Life-World: Problems and Prospects (Ullica Segerstråle) ... 245
1.1 The Problematic Relationship between Science, Culture, and the Life-World ... 245
1.2 Possibilities and Problems of Practical Discourse in Natural Science 247
1.3 Disagreement among Scientific Experts: A Case Study ... 249
1.4 Cognitive Differences among Scientists and the Permeability of Scientific Discourse to Life-World Thinking ... 251
1.5 Strategical Action in Scientific Discourse ... 253
1.6 "Coupled Reasoning" and the Prevention of True Communicative Action ... 255
1.7 The Role of Moral Argumentation for the Cognitive Content of Science and the Short-Circuit of Practical Discourse ... 257
Notes ... 262
References ... 265

2 Subjective Rationality and the Theory of Ideology (Raymond Boudon) 269
References ... 287

3 Sociology and the Professional Culture of Philosophers (Richard Kilminster) ... 289
3.1 Introduction ... 289
3.2 The Culture of Philosophers ... 290
3.3 The Sociological Revolution ... 293
3.4 Sociology and Philosophy Today ... 298
3.5 Conclusion: Philosophy as a Culture of Defense ... 301
Notes ... 307
References ... 310

4 Legislators and Interpreters: Culture as Ideology of Intellectuals (Zygmunt Bauman) ... 313
References ... 331

The Authors ... 333

Index ... 337

Hans Haferkamp: In Memoriam

Shmuel N. Eisenstadt

Hans Haferkamp was one of the most outstanding representatives of the second generation of post-World War II German sociologists – a generation that was able to forge anew several specific modes of sociological inquiry that could become not only an integral but also a distinct part of international sociology.

The first generation of post-World War II German sociologists faced the very difficult problem, after the ravages of the Hitler era, of reestablishing sociological teaching, research, and analysis. One of the most pressing problems was that of how to combine some specific tradition and orientation of German sociology, especially its philosophical and theoretical orientations, with what has since developed in international sociology, mainly the burgeoning of empirical research, as well as some of the major theoretical developments in American sociology, particularly, the structural-functional school.

This generation was divided between what René König – probably the scholar who has done most to bring about a growing *rapprochement* between German sociology and international sociology, especially American sociology – designated as those who were engaged in social theory, as opposed to those who focused on sociological analysis.

A crucial component of the background against which the second generation of German sociologists developed has probably been the Habermas-Luhmann debate. This debate which cannot, of course, be fully understood without considering specific German tradition, was at the same time guided by an orientation to empirical research, as well as to various theoretical developments, for example, those of system analysis, as well as the structural-functional school, and various developments in psychology (the work of Piaget).

The impact of this debate on second generation German post-war sociology was varied. Some of these debates have continued and even intensified the split referred to by René König and have given rise to the growing ideological sectarianism within German academic life, in general, and sociology, in particular.

At the same time, however, there has also emerged in this period in the German sociological community a group of younger scholars who have attempted to overcome this split and to combine systematically varied empirical research with theoretical and analytical orientations.

Hans Haferkamp has been one of the most outstanding of this second group and has made marked contributions to the development of this new type of German sociology – a sociology rooted both in the German tradition and in the developments beyond Germany, and with a view toward both theoretical and analytical orientations and empirical research.

Hans Haferkamp began his work in chemistry, and then moved on to social work and sociology, establishing a firm foundation in social analysis, theory, and research. He went far beyond this training, forging out a very distinctive direction of his own in the panorama of sociological work in Germany. It was characterized by a strong emphasis on interactional processes as the starting point of analysis of larger macro and systemic formations and was combined with strong emphasis on empirical research.

He was strongly influenced by Parsons' functional analysis and along these lines equally interested in the work of Luhmann. At the same time he emphasized very strongly the importance of the interactive aspects of social relations for the understanding of broader structures and combined these orientations with empirical research in several areas – criminal behavior, power relations, social problems and others – attempting to direct such research to problems that were significant from the point of view of more general theoretical and institutional analysis.

When I visited his department at Bremen I was struck by the richness of his theoretical orientations and his empirical research program, and its impact on both his colleagues and his students.

His training and the combination of theoretical and analytical interests with strong orientation to „meta-problems," a thorough background in empirical research and attempts to combine it with central problems of sociological theory and analysis, made it natural for him to be very open to, and interested in, international scholarly cooperation.

He participated actively in the first German-American theory conference on problems of the link between micro-macro levels in sociological analysis and his insightful paper expounding the nature of the micro-macro link from the point of view of his interactionist analysis made an important contribution.

It was at the second of these conferences – the one on social change held at Berkeley in 1986 – that I first made his acquaintance. From the onset, a very close rapport developed between us – a rapport that, for the most part, cemented when we drove together from Berkeley to the San Francisco airport. During this ride we were able to discuss, with great intensity, some problems of sociological analysis. We parted as friends.

In 1987 he invited me to Bremen to the meeting of the Theory Section of the German Sociological Society on Culture and Social Structure and to lecture at the University. During this visit it was not only his intellectual but also his personal generosity and warmth as host and guide that became apparent. He introduced me to the beauty of the landscape, the charms of Worpswede, the delicacy of East Frisian tea, and explained in detail and with great insight the vicissitudes of the urban reconstruction of post-World War II Bremen. He told me also about his love of sailing.

When we parted in late June it was with hopes and plans for further continuous meetings and cooperation; but it was not to be. Cruel fate has decreed otherwise.

The present volume is a fitting tribute to his memory and to the resolve of his colleagues, friends, and students to continue his work and make it a living part of the collective memory of the sociological community.

Introduction: Culture and Social Structure in Recent Sociological Analysis

Shmuel N. Eisenstadt

The present volume constitutes one very important indicator of the general dissatisfaction in the social sciences with the way in which the analyses of relations between culture and social structure have been undertaken in the last two or so decades.

These developments, which we shall analyze in somewhat greater detail later on, constituted a part of the so-called crises that have emerged in the social sciences and the broader intellectual discourse since the late 1960s or early 1970s.

At the roots of these crises were the growing criticisms of the structural-functional school, which developed from the early 1960s on, and the controversies to which they gave rise. These criticisms, gathering strength from the late 1950s through the 1960s and touching more and more on some of the most central problems of sociological analysis, have become transformed into the so-called crises of social sciences by virtue of the interweaving of these controversies with the far-reaching changes in the whole intellectual climate of the late 1960s – especially with the disappearance of the optimistic vision of history, modernity, and modernization, and of the belief in the progress of science that characterized the first two decades after World War II. This growing pessimism manifested itself among others with the growing disenchantment with the welfare state; a growing emphasis on the crises of "late capitalist" or of postindustrial society; with what was seen as the breakdown of modernization in the Third World. It was probably most fully epitomized in the student rebellions of the late 1960s and the closely connected revolt against the Vietnam War, at least in the United States, and in Europe with a growing disenchantment with the age of the "end of ideology" declared in the 1950s by many social scientists (Eisenstadt and Curelaru, 1976).

These discussions have raised questions about the analysis of the major substantive problems of social sciences, such as, the nature of modern society or societies, the perennial meta-problems of social sciences analysis, such as, the vision of man and history and the different modes of analysis and explanation in the social sciences, as well as the place of the social sciences in the modern and postmodern intellectual traditions, in general, and over the boundaries of different scholarly disciplines, in particular.

In conjunction with these trends and transformations, there have taken place far-reaching changes in the definition of the major concepts of social science analysis, the relations between the major explanatory models employed in the social sciences, and the consequent directions of research.

The major shift in the basic tenets of social science analysis (culture, religion and knowledge, social structure, and social behavior) which had far-reaching implications for several central aspects of sociological analysis, consisted in their conceptualization as distinct and "real" ontological entities, and not, as in earlier periods of sociological and anthropological analysis, as analytical constructs referring to different aspects or dimensions of human action and social interaction, that is, as constitutive of each other and of partners of social interaction.

Concomitantly, there has developed a shift with respect to the emphasis of different dimensions of culture and of social structure, particularly one that emphasized values and norms that had characterized the structural-functional school. One version of this shift, most evident among the structuralists and less explicit among the ethnomethodologists, conceived of "culture" as the programmatic principles or codes of human behavior espousing (to use Geertz' felicitous even if ironical expression) the view of man as a cerebral savage. In this view, culture is seen as fully structured according to clear principles, embedded in the very nature of the human mind, which, through the medium of a series of codes, regulate human behavior. The symbolic anthropologists (e.g., specifically, Geertz, 1973, 1983; Turner, 1947, 1968, 1974; Schneider, 1973, 1977, 1980) as well as, to some extent, the symbolic interactionists in sociology and many trends in the humanities, by contrast, displayed a growing shift from values and norms to the conception of culture as a set of expressive symbols of ethos – a "world-view" constructed through active human interaction.

R. Peterson has stated, "the focus on drama, myth, code, and peoples' plans indicates a shift in the image of culture. While it was once seen as a map *of* behavior it is now seen as a map *for* behavior. In this view, people use culture the way scientists use paradigms ... to organize and normalize their activity. Like scientific paradigms, elements of culture are used, modified, or discarded depending on their usefulness in organizing reality ... as nearly equivalent to the term ideology, but without the latter's pejorative connotations. ... Sociologists now recognize that people continually choose among a wide range of definitions of situations or fabricate new ones to fit their needs" (Peterson, 1979: 159f.). Finally, there was the view espoused by studies that started from individualist (or "rational" choice) modes of analysis, which viewed culture as the result of the aggregation of individual choices, reflecting differences of power or of individual choices (Hirshfeld, Atran, and Yen-goan, 1982).

The conception of culture, as constituted through some process of negotiation, was shared by the "symbolic" anthropologists and symbolic interactionists with those schools who concentrated on the analysis of patterns of behavior and social organization, from the point of view of "rational choice." The nature of such negotiation was, however, conceived in radically different ways by these two approaches.

The "rational choice" viewed culture as resulting from the aggregation of individual choices, reflecting differences of power or of rational choices. In this they were often close to the Marxist view which sought the manipulation of symbols for narrow class-ends or the one which studied processes of symbol production.

The concept of culture espoused by "symbolic anthropologists," mainly Geertz, and implicit in most of the hermeneutical works, implied a radically different point of view, aptly summarized by J.B. Bruner (1986: 65f.).

> It would not be an exaggeration to say that in the last decade there has been a revolution in the definition of human culture. It takes the form of a move away from the strict structuralism that held that culture was a set of interconnected rules from which people derive particular behaviors to fit particular situations, to the idea of culture as implicit and only semiconnected knowledge of the world from which, through negotiation, people arrive at satisfactory ways of acting in given contexts. The anthropologist Clifford Geertz likens the process of acting in a culture to that of interpreting an ambiguous text. Let me quote a paragraph written by one of his students, Michelle Rosaldo: In anthropology, I would suggest, the key development ... is a view of culture ... wherein meaning is proclaimed a public fact – or better yet, where culture and meaning are described as processes of interpretive apprehension by individuals of symbolic models. These models are both "of" the world in which we live and "for" the organization of activities responses, perceptions and experiences by the conscious self. For present purposes, what is important here is first of all the claim that meaning is a fact of public life, and secondly that cultural patterns – social facts – provide the template for all human action, growth and understanding. Culture so construed is, furthermore, a matter less of artifacts and propositions, rules, schematic programs, or beliefs, than of associative chains and images that tell what can be reasonably linked up with what; we come to know it through collective stories.

Parallel shifts have also taken place, starting in the mid-1960s, in the concept of social structure. Here there has been a growing reification of social structure, manifest in the definition of social structure and of institutions, especially the "State" or various interest groups, as "real" and "autonomous" agents or actors (see, e.g., Wallerstein, 1974–1980; Skocpol, 1979).

At the other end of the spectrum of sociological analysis, closely related to the rational-choice approach, social structure was viewed as networks or organizations arising from the aggregation of the patterns of interaction, with almost no autonomous characteristics, except for some emergent qualities of such structures often described as primitive effects. In many of these studies, the tradition of structural analysis represented by the work of Simmel, Merton, Blau, or Boudon (Wolff, 1950, 1957; Blau, 1964, 1964a; Boudon, 1981; Merton, 1963) which has stressed the analysis of the formal characteristics and emergent properties of social structure, was often neglected.

This shift in the definition of culture and social structure, and in their analytical or logical status, was accompanied by a preference for exclusive deterministic, reductionist, "idealist," or "materialist" interpretations of social action or cultural creativity.

The conceptualization of culture, personality, and social structure as distinct ontological entities, and the concomitant development of the mutually exclusive deterministic, materialistic, or idealist approaches, were in their turn closely linked with the nature of the relations between the major explanatory models prevalent in the social sciences. The most important of such models were, to follow d'Andrade's (1986) distinction, the "positivistic" models taken from the physical sciences as represented by the behavioristic approaches that seek universal causal relations between different social or behavioral phenomena; models borrowed from the natural sciences, which view social entities as living systems; and semiotic models, which analyze patterns of social life and cultural creativity in terms of systems of signs and their meaning. Each of these modes of explanation was energetically implemented in continuously expanding processes of research, but with some exceptions there were few attempts to link them together.

At the same time there has been a growing emphasis not only on the importance of hermeneutical interpretations – a mode of analysis that can be seen as one of the strongest variants of the semiotic approach and considered the most appropriate mode of analysis in the social and behavioral sciences and in the sciences humaines – but also on the closely related importance of contexts of different activities for the understanding of their meaning.

The new mode of conceptualizing culture, social structure, and behavior was connected with a profound neglect of those aspects of social life that, in the classical as well as in the structural-functional approaches of sociology and anthropology, provided the major links between personality, social structure, and culture, defined as different analytical dimensions of human action. The most important of these neglected aspects were rules and norms, as well as new modes of the closely related problem of the distinct emergent qualities of social structure, particularly the possible systemic tendencies of patterns of social interaction and "functions" of such systems. None of these various approaches came to grips with the problem of the extent to which patterns of social interaction evince systemic qualities or tendencies, or whether these qualities or tendencies can be analyzed in better ways than were used by the structuralist-functionalists.

Among the structuralists à la Lévi-Strauss, and to some extent among some of the Marxists, it was assumed that, insofar as they address themselves to these problems, such rules, as well as the systemic tendencies of social formations, are derivable from the structure of the human mind (or of the "forces of production") and that these structures or forces provide the specification of the appropriate rules and take care of the organizational systemic problems of such formations.

In both these approaches the processes through which such general, possibly universal, structures can be translated into – necessarily changing – specifications of concrete patterns of social interaction and of systemic qualities or functions of social formations have not been posed or analyzed.

At the same time, these approaches, which have stressed the dimension of negotiability in the construction of social interaction, have neglected to inquire, on the whole, with the partial exception of the ethnomethodologists about the rules according to which such negotiations are conducted or about the processes through which such rules are established.

These shifts in the definition of the basic concepts of sociological analysis also had very far-reaching effects on the directions of research that have developed in the social sciences in this period. One such very important direction, which spans all the social sciences – sociology, anthropology, political science – has been a growing dissociation between what has been usually designated as the study of culture and the study of social structure, that is, between, on the one hand, studies that have focused on "culture" (i.e., different types of symbols, their construction, their patterns and meaning, and to some extent also their relation to patterns of social interaction and behavior) and, on the other hand, studies focusing on the analysis of social structure and organization, of institutional or organizational formations, and of patterns of social behavior, as well as system analyses as applied to social sciences.

There has also taken place a growing dissociation between those studies of social structure that emphasized the impact of formal characteristics of social interaction and of their impact on social behavior, or the distribution of population among different social positions (such as studies of occupational mobility) and those studies that focused on the analysis of institutional formations.

Another closely related trend was the growing marginalization, in the panorama of social science research, of the major arenas of sociology of culture, namely, sociology of religion, knowledge, and the arts.

In consequence, of all these developments, most areas of social science research became characterized not only by a far-reaching dissociation between studies of behavior, structure, and meaning, but also by the inability to analyze how all these are interconnected and how such interconnectedness influences the formation of different patterns of social action and formations.

The combination of all these developments – the conceptualization of culture, social structure, and personality as "real" ontological entities, the mutually exclusive deterministic approaches, the neglect of analysis of rules, norms, or of the emergent systemic qualities of social structure – pointed to the inability of most analyses to address themselves to the central questions of sociological analysis which were, as we have seen, opened during this period, particularly, the relations between the different constituents of social order; of the ways in which culture is constitutive, as an inherent component of social order and structure, of such structure (even if it does not constitute it), and, conversely, the degree to which social structure is constitutive of culture.

Accordingly, all of these developments were also unable to resolve the classical problem of the order-maintaining as opposed to the order-transforming functions of culture, as well as the related problem of the degree to which social structure determines culture, or vice-versa – i.e., the extent of mutual determination of culture, social structure, and social behavior, or, as

Renato Rosaldo has stated, the degree to which culture is a cybernetic feedback control mechanism controlling behavior and social structure or whether there exists a possibility of choice and inventiveness in the use of cultural resources.

The various approaches surveyed here, and the studies that developed in connection with them, while sharpening the definition of these problems, always oscillated between viewing the relationship between "culture" and social structure as either static and homogeneous in any given society, or as entirely open.

The first view, typical of some structuralists and extreme Marxists, depicts the basic cultural orientations and rules prevalent in a society as relatively static with little principled change throughout the major period of the histories of the societies of civilizations in which they have become institutionalized, and as relatively uniform and homogeneous within the society, or no more than local variations. Such a picture does not seem to leave much room for reconstruction and change in the relations between "culture" and "social structure", beyond the initial institutionalization of the different "cultures", codes, or visions. It does not allow for or explain various aspects of praxis and of the construction of changing mentalities that have been stressed in the more recent anthropological, historical, and sociological literature. Neither does it explain the development of different strategies of choice, maximization, and possible innovation, as these are depicted in different rational-choice approaches. The second view, on the other hand, can be interpreted as implying that culture is merely a mirror or aggregate of continuously changing choices – rational or expressive – by individuals and groups.

In this approach culture has been viewed as an aggregate result of patterns of behavior, of structures, power or, as Ann Swidler (1986) states, as a tool-kit of different strategies of action, which can be activated in different situations, according to the "material" and "ideal" interests of different social actors, without seemingly having any distinct autonomous impact of its own.

It was against the background of all these developments that there has arisen meaningful attempts to reconnect these different stands of research and to reconstruct the analysis of the relation between culture and social structure. This volume constitutes an important contribution in this direction.

References

Blau, Peter M. (1964). *Exchange and Power in Social Life*. New York: John Wiley.

Blau, Peter M. (1964a). "Justice and Social Exchange." *Sociological Inquiry* 34: 193–206.

Boudon, Raymond (1981). *The Logic of Social Action*. London: Routledge and Kegan Paul.

Bruner, J.B. (1986). *Actual Minds, Possible Worlds*. Cambridge, Mass.: Harvard University Press.

D'Andrade, R. (1986). "Three Scientific World Views and the Covering Lae

Model." In *Methodology in Social Science*, ed. D.W. Wiske and R.A. Schweder. Chicago: The University of Chicago Press.
Eisenstadt, Shmuel N. and Curelaru, M. (1976). *The Form of Sociology, Paradigms and Crises*. New York: John Wiley.
Geertz, Clifford (1973). *The Interpretation of Culture*. New York: Basic Books.
Geertz, Clifford (1983). *Social Knowledge*. New York: Basic Books.
Hirshfeld, Laurence A., Atran, Scott, and Yen-goan, A. (1982). "Theories of Knowledge and Culture." *Social Science Information* 21 (1): 161–198.
Merton, Robert K. (1963). *Social Theory and Social Structure*. New York: The Free Press.
Peterson, R. (1979). "Revitalizing the Culture Concept." *Annual Review of Sociology* 5: 137–166.
Schneider, David M. (1973). *Class Differences and Sex Roles in American Kinship and Family Structure*. Englewood Cliffs, N.J.: Prentice-Hall.
Schneider, David M. (Ed.) (1977). *Symbolic Anthropology*. New York: Columbia University Press.
Schneider, David M. (1980). *American Kinship*. Chicago: University of Chicago Press.
Skocpol, Theda (1979). *States and Social Revolutions*. Cambridge: Cambridge University Press.
Swidler, Ann (1986). "Culture in Action: Symbols and Strategies." *American Sociological Review* 51 (April): 273–288.
Turner, Victor W. (1947). *The Forest of Symbols*. Ithaca, N.Y.: Cornell University Press.
Turner, Victor, W. (1968). *The Drums of Affliction*. Oxford: Claredon Press.
Turner, Victor W. (1974). *Dramas, Fields, and Metaphors*. Ithaca, N.Y.: Cornell University Press.
Wallerstein, Immanuel M. (1974–1980). *The Modern World-Systems I, II*. New York: Academic Press.
Wolff, K.H. (1950/1957). *The Sociology of Georg Simmel*. Glencoe, Ill.: The Free Press.

Part I
Social Structure and Culture – A Tenable Differentiation?

1 The Cultural Foundations of Society*

Friedrich H. Tenbruck

In any language or country a volume on culture is likely to tread on uncertain ground, due to the ambiguity of the concept. But an intercultural volume on culture is fraught with additional difficulties which we should note beforehand.

"Die Kultur," "la culture," "the culture," "la cultura," "de cultuur" – these words still carry different connotations and denotations in the respective languages, as the dictionaries and encyclopaedias readily reveal, – the "Encyclopaedia Britannica" (1958) by not even listing such entry. Obviously, the selfsame word carries different meaning in various languages, occupies a different place in their cultures, and has played a different role in their histories. Of course, all these differences are being concealed, rather than removed, by adopting English as the only tongue for this volume. It would be an illusion to think otherwise. We find even that the pertinent sciences are all at variance about the meaning and standing of the concept. Considering this treacherous situation, we ought first to survey the ground on which we stand instead of trying for hasty constructions that are bound to remain lofty conceptions. If we want to avoid the risk of merely vindicating and elaborating received concepts, we must begin by looking into their intricate origin and history, before we later turn to the substantive problems.

This convention is another promising instance of a renascent interest in culture as a sociological issue. However, sociology has been shunning this issue for so long that we cannot build on the firm ground of common knowledge. We may expect to hear convincing reports which, by choosing some concrete case, will carry their own evidence. Yet wherever general questions about the nature and role of culture intrude – as they needs must do –, we are ill prepared to deal with them, since mainstream sociology has failed to provide us with a common concept of culture from which to start. And the use of the selfsame word must not invite the pleasant illusion of sharing a common concept or identical object, when in fact we are entertaining dim and divergent notions about culture such as we have received from nation-bound traditions of educated language. Besides, we are schooled in a professional terminology which, by tacit assumptions about society, is jealously prejudicial to a serious consideration of culture, unless domesticated into another variable of structure.

We cannot escape the predicaments by fiat of definitions which will merely land us in a ceaseless turnover of lofty conceptual constructs. But we must not

* For a more detailed account of my argument, see F.H. Tenbruck "Die kulturellen Grundlagen der Gesellschaft. Der Fall der Moderne." Westdeutscher Verlag, Opladen/Wiesbaden 1989.

proceed from our diverse and unreflected preconceptions about culture, either. Instead of immediately facing the substantive issues, we ought to begin, therefore, by noticing the historical contingency of our diverse notions about culture. In order to see the problems, we must first look into the genesis of the pertinent concepts on which we rely for identifying the problems.

1.1 Culture and Society: About the History of Concepts

As part of the classical legacy, the Roman words *cultura* and *societas* had securely survived in Latin, the learned language of Europe, almost unchanged for roughly two thousand years. Yet, around 1800 these two words rather suddenly acquired new and important meanings with which they came to pass into common use in the several European languages. Ever since, they have been – and still are – keywords of capital importance for both social discourse and private reflection, and certainly for science, too.

The sudden rise of "culture" and "society" to the eminence of key concepts marks a crucial event in the history of modern society[1]. Their emergence and acceptance indicated and proclaimed generally the suspension of all inherited notions about man, society, and history. While the new words stood for fundamental reorientation, they presented problems, rather than solutions. I cannot now detail the complex substantive issues involved in the emergence of the new words and will confine myself in the somewhat erratic history of the concepts, their meaning and function.

Of course, their appearance was not merely a semantical change. The new concepts were partly a reaction to objective transformations of social conditions, but not a strict reflection of them. There is a deplorable tendency in sociology to equate social change narrowly with objective alterations. However, even radical changes of social conditions depend for their social effect on when and how they are being perceived. Conversely, social change may occur under stable conditions if people come to see, for whatever reason, their situation in a new light. It is the subjective definitions of situations that translate into actions the objective conditions which an observer may note. For perceiving and defining situations, people regularly depend on a social vocabulary which every society provides. It consists of a number of characteristic concepts, notions, and images, mostly related, that allow people to perceive, order, and classify social phenomena by general categories, and to orient their actions accordingly. There is no society without a language, and there is no language without a social vocabulary. In the center of this vocabulary stand a few key concepts which embody a society's self-image, i. e. some notions about its characteristic order and cohesion, mostly linked to general images of the world. Apparently, radical changes in objective social conditions are likely to strain the traditional vocabulary to the point of obsolescence. On the other hand, a new social vocabulary is likely to change society by new definitions of the situation. Even radical changes in conditions must wait for their eventual social effects for the rise of a new social vocabulary.

Against this complex background we can understand the social significance of the emergence of "culture" and "society" as new key concepts of modern society[2]. Their adoption into the common language reflected the recognition of social change which had eventually produced a new type of society."Culture" and "society" replaced an obsolete vocabulary, because these notions conceptualized the two basic transformations in which people felt being involved, viz. the growing autonomy of culture and the growing formation of society by voluntary association. But the new words also lent expression to subjective ideals, expectations, and orientations. Formerly, social vocabularies had been tied to substantive identifications with some religion, group or conviction, thereby revealing some lasting normative order. By contrast, "culture" and "society" envisaged open situations, barely indicating the forces and processes at work. Indispensable though the new words proved, they were but expedient orientations which left the future open to the unforeseeable course of culture and society. Thus, these key concepts were bound soon to become social and intellectual issues that asked for clarification. Actually, both gave rise to new and prominent branches of knowledge, the cultural and the social sciences, respectively, thereby confirming their central role as key notions of modern culture.

Of course, the actual history of these concepts exhibits considerable national variations. In some countries, like France, *civilisation* was the term chosen instead of *culture*, the words being considered equivalent, though, for a long time. Even "culture" and "society" were originally used almost randomly like synonyms before they separated into distinct designations for different aspects of, and concerns over, reality. With that, they advanced to passwords in political conflicts over the priority of social or cultural concerns, respectively. Behind such controversies loomed questions about the ontological status of culture and society. From the two concepts grew characteristic ideologies and inclusive world-views. Socialist and liberalist thought proclaimed the historical and actual precedence of society in order to subject the state to the wishes and commands of people or parties. Thus, the concepts hardened into competitive programs and public alternatives. Moreover, they fared differently in different countries which forged their particular social vocabularies. Political representation, public opinion, and social forces largely decided on their meaning, use, and standing in particular countries or periods, sometimes establishing a definite and principal preference for one word over the other. In sum, the concepts came to bear, in any language, the imprint of their particular national histories. And there is overwhelming semantical, historical, and political evidence of those differences and the importance thereof.

This leads to questions about the role of science in the history of these concepts which rather suddenly originated in Western Europe at the end of the 18th century. They did not issue from the studies of scholars or were at least not the result of particular disciplines. Surely, scholars contributed to the invention and propagation of the new terms, but they did so in the company of poets, writers, philosophers, artists, and other cultured people, and not in their professional capacity. Besides, men of public affairs and ordinary people of public spirit found sufficient occasion to use the new words which arose in social discourse over public issues, in an effort to find common orientations, and therefore remained highly general ideas. By their ready adoption into the common languages, however, the new ideas bore witness to their consequence or at least to the role they were to play in Western culture, and subsequently all over.

Although science had not contrived the concepts, it soon had to attend to them. In any society, key notions are in the custody of some people who are expected to articulate and explain them. As "culture" and "society" rose to the eminence of key concepts, they became salient public issues asking for clarification. From such exigencies developed the cultural and the social sciences in an attempt to discover the truth about man, society, culture, and history by empirical investigation.

First developed and differentiated those disciplines which were later termed "cultural sciences" (*Geisteswissenschaften, humanities, sciences humaines*). Fascinated by man's capacity for producing culture, they investigated all the products thereof in their historical variety, complexity, and interdependence. Though sometimes overrating the role of ideas, the cultural sciences steadily advanced our knowledge of culture as a social reality by their factual, empirical studies on which Georg Simmel, Max Weber, and others later built their sociology. In all this, however, they relied on a generic concept of culture as a collective name for language, religion, art, law, state, history, society, craft, etc. In sum: the cultural sciences illustrated and demonstrated culture *in actu*, as a social reality, but cared little for elaborating it, conceptually and systematically[3]. For our heritage they collected an incredible amount of informed and reliable knowledge about culture and achieved a subtle, though implicit understanding of it.

The social sciences largely built on these foundations. Ethnology began as a study of culture, anyway, whereas "society" – though a word of intense public concern – struck people as a highly dubious and diffuse notion and remained a bone of contention in sociology, too. Suffice it to recall Max Weber's cutting remark about the term "social:" "Its 'generality' rests on nothing but its ambiguity[4]." Unhampered by such stricture, mainstream sociology developed on the basis of two fundamental assumptions that were simply taken for granted. There reigned supreme the belief that sociology could be nothing else but a generalizing discipline which, after the alleged model of natural science, must eventually produce a definite "theory of society." This professed formal ideal of sociology found its indispensable counterpart in a chain of massive, though mostly tacit ontological assumptions about the nature of society. To indicate briefly:

a) societies were regarded as existing entities (units, wholes, totalities, or systems, whether "open" or "closed");

b) they were seen as specimens and variations of a genus and therefore shared constitutive generic properties;

c) these common systemic components were considered as the essential determinants of all particular states of society and as the reliable warrants of general uniformities and regularities, so that
d) a generalizing science of society could be achieved by identifying the systemic components in question.

Obviously, none of these assumptions had a factual basis. They were merely requisite parts of a particular conception of sociology as a general "theory of society." The fascination of this design derived partly from the prestige of generalizing natural science, but mostly from the inherent promise of technical control over society by virtue of predictive knowledge. Such conception most easily prevailed in countries where public opinion, political institutions, and national traditions were little informed by, and about, the cultural sciences. Thus, sociology could develop as a search for a general theory of society, without ever noticing the underlying presumptions and, above all, the naturalistic presumption that societies were constituted and determined by some universal and ultimate elements[5]. Spell-bound by the idea of technical mastery over affairs, sociology sought for the ultimate determinants of societies that must form the requisite keystones of a general theory of society. Accordingly, when mainstream sociology began gradually elaborating the vague notion "society" by a set of structural concepts, these conceptual constructs, which did provide a useful heuristic chart for locating structural aspects of societies, were readily mistaken for the constitutive determinants of societies. Now bound to equate social structure with social reality, sociologists tended to consider culture a superfluous and fictitious notion which should be abandoned. They even came to regard the neat conceptual elaboration of "structure" as a corroboration of its presumed ontological quality, and conversely mistook the lack of conceptual classification for a confirmation of the presumed irreality of culture. The monistic ambition of an autonomous science with a general "theory of society" had forced on mainstream sociology a complete break from the cultural sciences, and this break became institutional practice with the professionalization of sociology. Lacking a firsthand knowledge of cultural facts, mainstream sociology fashioned its conceptual apparatus wholly from the notion of society, leaving no place for culture. And inasmuch as the cultural sciences specialized, the concept of culture became a derelict, to be had for the asking[6]. This explains why we all bring to this volume so many vague and diverse notions of culture.

Therefore, if we want to reconsider the case of culture, we must first discard the tacit premises of mainstream sociology. We must beware of the naturalistic fallacies of reification by which the notion "society" comes to pass for a systemic entity, and our conceptual constructs of structure in turn pass for an objective description of society. Our traditional trust that society is a clear, distinct, and given reality proves little more than our customary familiarity with the elaborations of the concept; it does not prove a manifest quality of society that we would observe. To think otherwise is a *naïveté*, though probably ineradicable. The professional training of our attention tempts us to overlook the fact that "society" actually is as messy a proposition as is "culture."

All that we can observe is an infinite number of concrete, individual actions and the products thereof. As such, these phenomena are neither social nor cultural. Only by selecting and ordering them do we fashion both concepts, "culture" and "society" which subsequently condition even our perception and apprehension. Accordingly, our mistrust of culture does result not from the irreality of culture, but from our lack of effort in the elaboration of the concept. It is not enough, however, to bandy the word "culture" around with various comments; we must first specify what we mean by culture so that we can then investigate its social relevance. This calls for a careful reconstruction of the facts from which the notion of culture must needs arise, rather than for an arbitrary or formal definition of the concept[7].

1.2 The Concept of Culture: a Preliminary Review

Culture is a word with a bewildering variety of meanings. Yet all these connotations derive from a common root, viz. the peculiar character of man as a cultural being. Unfortunately, the social sciences lost sight of this fundamental fact when they came to define man as a social being – a quality he shares with most animals. But man is set off from all animals by the fact that he "attaches a subjective meaning to his behavior[8]." Whereas animals behave in reaction to internal and external stimuli, man acts by virtue of his unique capacity (and necessity) of confronting reality by meaningful action. For us, reality is not a collection of sensory data, but a world of meaningful and significant objects. Short of our ability of creating a world of meanings and significations above and beyond the given perceptions, the variety and variability of human action could not be explained. Unlike the behaviors of animal species, our actions are not uniform because they rest on meanings and significations that we must create ourselves. Our actions are not a direct response to facts, but to our conceptions and representations thereof. The realities with which our actions are concerned are inevitably already interpretations of facts by virtue of meanings and significations that we attach to the otherwise chaotic variety of sensory data. The original and inexplainable capacity for creating meanings marks man unmistakably as a cultural being. For "culture," in the root sense of the term, comprises all that which originates by human action and consequently embodies meaning. All human actions and the products thereof – the material culture with its artefacts and techniques as well as the modes of social life, and the intellectual or artistic creations – are cultural phenomena, owing their existence to man's capacity for meaningful action. Whatever partakes of the world of meaning is a part of culture, regardless of how we choose to value those meanings. And unlike the social behavior of animal species, all human societies are cultural phenomena, too. To express itself, man's sociability has to wait for meaningful understandings which alone can explain the manifest variation and historical character of human societies.

Considering that all culture originates from human action, the concept has a very inclusive root meaning which excludes merely the pure work of nature. Throughout the last century, this inclusive concept of culture kept inspiring social thought, as can be seen, for example, from the famous definition with which E. B. Tylor opened his "Primitive Culture" (1871). He was not alone in proposing to draw up inventories of individual cultures, listing and classifying all their elements. However, all such programs failed since the sheer number of elements made it meaningless, if not impossible, to draw up inventories. Even later attempts to search for characteristic patterns and configurations of culture traits proved unsatisfactory, except for small, primitive societies. Thus, culture in its comprehensive connotation cannot be made an object of empirical investigation, which should be well noticed by all who now are ready to rely on an amorphous, and consequently unbounded, notion of culture. This limits the practical usefulness of the comprehensive concept severely, but does not diminish its fundamental import. Unsuitable as a specific tool for sociological analysis, it remains a crucial requisite for a general understanding of social phenomena and must not be displaced by the shallow notion of man as a social being, nor by the misleading notion of a self-sufficient society. A thorough grasp of culture, as originating from meaningful action, is a safe bulwark against many rash and superficial explanations of social phenomena, as for example, behaviorism, biology, basic needs, interests, or adaptions[9]. In fact, the naturalistic fallacies of reification, from which mainstream sociology has been suffering all along, have mostly resulted from a disregard for the cultural character of human action.

Anyway, the particular meanings of the term all derive orderly from the indicated root idea. There is first the fact that culture can but take place in society. Thus, while man is the creator of all culture, he is also the creature of a specific culture which is handed down from one generation to the next. Yet, if culture does not exist without a society, neither does a society exist without a culture. They refer to two different aspects of the same phenomena, rather than to two separate realms of different phenomena. When we classify some phenomena as social, others as cultural, our interest merely fastens on their presumedly predominant significance. It would be another case of naturalistic reification, however, if we thought of a hard and fast line, dividing those phenomena into separate realms. In principle, the observable phenomena in themselves are seamless facts that we can scrutinize from our perspective of either culture or society, be it on account of their actual predominance, or be it on account of our predominant interest[10].

All this explains why we can use the word "culture" as an alternate for "society." In this sense, the word draws attention to the fact that all societies possess an individual culture of their own. There are considerable drawbacks to the exclusive concern with the cultural aspects of the phenomena. But the exclusive concern with their social aspects encourages the erroneous belief that societies are self-sufficient systems. Against such blind faith in the omnipotence of the social components of reality we should insist on the legitimate use of "culture" as an alternate designation for "society," to remind us, at least, that we are dealing with our constructs of reality. Here again, we would become prisoners of our own constructs if we were to eliminate the notion of culture from the language of sociological analysis, where it reminds us of the cultural aspects and conditions of all things social and, by implication, of their historical uniqueness. When we designate societies as culture, the term denotes each individual culture in its totality. To study such a culture, however, we need have a more specific idea of what is important. This brings us to the different parts that we can discern in a total culture.

Perphaps an important distinction is that of material and immaterial culture, in spite of their constant interlocking. The cultural sciences can choose their respective objects from either area with little difficulty, none of them dealing with culture as such. But he enters the modern notion of culture as some web or pattern of meanings, significations, ideas, and values that are shared by people in a society. It was this idea that gave birth to the modern usage of the term in public language as well as in the cultural sciences. The modern concern with culture has been a concern with representative culture all along. Today, to point out the significance of the term, we need to make this explicit, by adding the adjective "representative." Anyway, it is representative culture that is of concern to sociology.

1.3 Representative Culture

Culture is a social reality in so far as it is representative culture. As such it is confined to those cultural phenomena that can be shown to have a representative character and significance. Representative culture includes those beliefs, understandings, images, ideas, ideologies, etc. which influence social actions, either because they are being actively shared, or because they are being passively acknowledged as valid, right, good, or the like.

Social science is not interested in the vast expanse of culture *per se*; but it ought to be concerned with representative culture. Except for strict behaviorism, sociology has always recognized indirectly the existence of representative culture, borrowing elements thereof for the construction of sociological theories. Durkheim's "représentations collectives" form a part of representative culture inasmuch as they are socially shared, respected, and valid. Parsons was forced to construe above the differentiated net of specific roles and positions a sphere of general norms and values which belong to representative culture. Durkheim and Parsons incorporated in their construct of "society" some elements of representative culture. Yet from their fear of culture as a productive and incalculable force sprang their policy of taming and domesticating culture. The "représentations collectives" and the "values" had to become anonymous products of "society;" further questions about their possible origins must not be tolerated. The same tendency has been characteristic of mainstream sociology, throughout. The key terms of social structure were another attempt of domesticating culture. Of course, socialization is not a mere learning of roles, norms, and values, with some deviations included; it is an exposure to culture. Even the few standard formulae for culture, which some sociologists occasionally employ, have a tame ring. "Tradition" is not a specific mark of culture, anyway. But he who presents culture merely as tradition, tames it by depriving it of its productive and imaginative capacity. Again, the phrase "shared culture" usually serves the purpose of preventing any questions about the reasons and origins of shared culture, and this holds true for the now preferred "symbolic code," too. In all these terms culture appears like a thin, static, airy, and disembodied mist that cannot be socially located, hanging anonymously over society, arising from mysterious origins, whereas in truth it is ultimately rather dynamic, unpredictable, and socially located. In other words, even the feeble survivals of the culture concept in the social sciences have long relinquished the idea of representative culture as a social force and reality[11]. I will therefore give a brief outline of this formerly familiar idea and its factual foundations. Inasmuch as modern culture requires some additional considerations, I will first present the outline with a view to premodern cultures.

To start where the misunderstandings begin: a science of "social facts" is a highly questionable project, unless instructed by the knowledge that human action is not identical with overt behavior, and that, consequently, society is not identical with "social facts," severed from the meanings of their constitutive actions. This, of course, is the central message of Max Weber's "verstehende" sociology which raises the problem how the meanings of social actions originate. Among other things, of course, actions are informed by the actors' understanding of the respective objects or situations, as Weber stressed throughout, too. Our actions are thus bounded by our understandings which rest on our interpretations of reality, however, because man does not live in a world of pure facts. The desire to understand and interpret (inner and outer) reality is not a whim or weakness that we can avoid. It is our essential constitution as cultural beings[12].

For us, reality is not a collection of separate facts, but a context of representations of objects. By selection and combination, we form from a mass of diverse and indifferent perceptions representations of meaningful objects and situations. Our actions are informed by this knowledge of reality which is not merely a knowledge of isolated facts. Separately, facts are but irrelevant or confusing items, that remain curious singularities and nondescript oddities, lacking any meaning. To acquire a meaning – and so to inform an actor – facts must fit into larger orders of references and concatenations. Therefore, actions depend on an interpretation of reality that cannot be restricted arbitrarily, since it must in some way account for the whole range of external situations and internal states with which human action is concerned.

Unfortunately, I cannot now detail this most important point. It follows, though, that man as an actor has a primeval practical need of incorporating all facts, external and internal, into a coherent interpretation of reality, that is into a sort of world-view. Since a reliable knowledge of objects requires some notion about their lasting order, man had to form his respective ideas about, for example, nature, society, man, and gods. Moreover, actors demand from an interpretation of reality forms for expressing symbolically their affective, emotional, valuative, and artistic involvements in objects and situations. For these reasons, man has been creating everywhere from times immemorial a culture above and beyond the practical techniques and social institutions. Obviously, this (so-called) immaterial culture is not a late and supplementary addition to material culture. It is as elementary a requisite of human life as is material culture. Myth, religion, poetry, music, art, or philosophy of some sort are ubiquitous ingredients of societies because they respond in their own way to practical exigencies of acting man, rather than merely to useless speculations or pleasant occupations. Against the modern prejudice that material culture could securely exist by itself – or that society could live by its practical techniques and institutions –, social science ought to recognize clearly that no culture – and no society, at that – could exist without an immaterial culture or, as I prefer to say summarily, without ideas, expressed verbally or symbolically[13]. As all interpretations of reality aim at some comprehensive viewpoint, they must all take the form of "ideas."

The ubiquitous existence of immaterial culture and the incessant role of ideas in social life are facts beyond that sociology must do overlook any longer. They raise the fundamental problem why men everywhere have developed surplus meanings which go beyond all concerns with practical techniques and social institutions, in fact beyond all practical interests, generally. The answer lies in man's peculiar constitution as a cultural being, that is as an actor. The universal conditions of human action involve him inevitably in an interpretation of reality beyond his immediate practical concerns, although mediately for these concerns. This explains the pervasive ubiquity and role of (so-called) immaterial culture in all societies. And it explains – now to proceed further – the representative character of culture as a social requisite.

I need not elaborate the basic idea of representative culture since it is more or less familiar. It has formed the core of the classical concept of culture, anyway. Roughly it denotes all those fundamental ideas of a society which are generally held to be right, true, and valid, or are generally so respected, at least. In the past, they have mostly taken the explicit form of myth, religion, world-view, moral, and the like, all informing people about the fundamental order of reality, in one realm or another. In this way representative culture is a relevant condition of human action. All individual action is informed by the actor's understanding of the situation. For this, however, the actors depend, among other things, on the basic understandings of reality which their own culture provides. Whatever their material or ideal interests are, on the one hand, and whatever the social controls and sanctions are, on the other hand, their actions will be conditioned by the fundamental interpretation of reality that their own culture holds on stock. Unable to invent anew the fundamental understandings of reality, individuals could not act, unless they could rely on the stock of respective ideas of their culture. Again, representative culture provides for some common interpretations of reality without which social actions could hardly gather force and continuity. Durable societies therefore emerge where they succeed in establishing a representative culture.

Since all this was generally known, social science could hardly avoid to reckon with representative culture, in one way or another. But the idea lost its force and significance when sociology, considering the self-sufficient nature of society as an inviolable axiom, treated the representative ideas of culture as anonymous products of social forces and mechanisms, as most notably Durkheim and Parsons did. Leaving no room for an active role of ideas, nor for their inherent logic and dynamic, this conception eliminated the distinctive characteristics of culture that so obviously emerge from all historical records. Again, I can only summarily indicate the most important points.

There is, firstly, the significant fact that all societies have possesed some representative interpretations of reality in excess of the exigencies of practical techniques and social institutions. It evidently follows that the cultural exigencies of social life have everywhere demanded a cultural division of labor, as we find it in the earliest societies. Considering their different inclinations and qualifications, people have regularly come to depend on the ability of intellectuals who could offer superior ideas.

Secondly, the ubiquitous cultural division of labor points to the social role of intellectuals, which is an original and elementary fact in all societies, revealing their cultural foundations. This is accentuated by the authority of intellectuals who are entrusted with the social task of interpreting the orders of reality, including the order of society. For such order to last, people need some common understandings and must therefore rely on an intellectual authority which can effectively claim to possess superior knowledge. The authority of intellectuals may be vested in (or distributed among) elders, sages, god-kings, magicians, or priests who may enjoy it by virtue of their own prestige or lean for support on political power which in turn asks for their advice and judgment.

Lastly, here is the fact that ideas are creations of individuals, though often resulting from a series of individual contributions. This is quite evident where we have historical records. But even primitive societies bear witness to the import of intellectual effort. Nowhere do we find a society to consist merely of structured relations, social interactions, plus common values. All primitive societies possess elaborate world-views, laid down mainly in myth, magic, religion, etc. which account for the origins of the cosmos, of society, of culture, and of morals. They have a knowledge of the forces of nature and of the nature of man. They have their cults and rites, linking the living to the dead, staging the meaning of life in face of devouring time, and giving expression to their unfathomable feelings and emotions. Very few elements of these beliefs can be chance products of anonymous social interaction. Serious inspection of these elaborate systems proves that they are the product of continued intellectual efforts of individuals. Even the common values and mores do not stand by themselves leading a separate life. They are part and parcel of a representative culture, linked up with its cognitive, religious, moral expressive, and emotional ideas. In their maintenance, intellectuals take a part and more so in their production. Even the tenacious persistence of their culture patterns over incredibly long periods, as may occur in exceptional cases, must not obscure their potential productivity and variability. When they persist, the possibility of unpredictable change by virtue of intellectual innovations persists too. Anyway, they must have evolved through a long line of intellectual efforts. Of course, I am not overlooking the inextricable linkage between "culture" and "structure," nor the pervasive force of the latter. Neither do I underestimate the ever present role of power or domination in any of their many forms. Even so, there is one thing which neither structure nor power can do: create ideas. For the past, at least, all these facts are in plain evidence in the historical records. The cultural sciences were familiar with the role of intellectuals, therefore, and found additional proof of it wherever they succeeded in reaching farther back into the past, as, for example, Eduard Meyer did in his famous "Geschichte der Alten Welt[14]." Likewise, Max Weber showed us, how intellectuals were at work from the earliest and throughout history. They all saw social life in many ways conditioned by ideas produced by intellectuals. And they all knew that the ideas of representative culture are highly fragile and can be easily challenged. It was Jacob Burckhardt who condensed his knowledge of representative culture into his memorable terse dictum: "Der Geist ist ein Wühler[15]." They were thinking of men's need of understanding and interpreting reality, and therefore were referring to the role of ideas and intellectuals as a regular feature of societies.

Culture is the concept which reminds sociology generally of the role of ideas and intellectuals in social action. Although the term by now asks for conceptual elaboration, it is sufficiently determinate when used in the sense of representative culture. It remains an empirical question, of course, in what manner and degree such a culture exists at a time, which ideas belong to it, and where the intellectual authority lies. Instead of considering culture a closed and static system, the term rests on an awareness for the potential conflicts and dynamics of ideas. The sociological study of a culture aims at

a) identifying the representative ideas,
b) locating their producers,
c) observing the means and channels of distribution, and
d) assessing the effects on social action, all this with a view to the formation or reformation of social groups, institutions, and movements by the impact of ideas.

Above all, the concept of culture is an indispensable antidote against the fallacious assumptions that societies are constituted by objective social facts whereas our actions depend on the representation and interpretation of facts. The notion reminds us that that even our interests are largely a matter of interpretation or, to exemplify, that political parties mostly gather their constituency by teaching the people what their interests should be. Here and elsewhere the concept of culture guides us to understand the meaning and significance of social action beyond its immediate concerns. The notion guards us against believing that ideas result anonymously from social interaction or naturally from social situations; even in capitalism and industrialism people had to wait for intellectual spokesman and leaders to find their stand. And generally the concept of culture saves us from the misapprehensions that sociology could and should become a technical science, and that society is a predictable system of social facts. The reawakened interest in culture demands from us a reconsideration of the aims and possibilities of an empirical sociology.

For the analysis of past societies, at least, representative culture has proved a viable and indispensable concept, resting securely on historical evidence. About its usefulness for an understanding of modern society I will later make a few comments.

1.4 Some Remarks on Weber and Parsons

Everywhere the formation of sociology occurred under the potent influence of general preconceptions about the nature and purpose of science and society. Whether sociology developed from some established science with a reliable stock of knowledge, or began as a lofty program, largely depended on the national and academic traditions and institutions. Due to these conditions, for example, American sociology could not, and would not, build on the empirical knowledge of the cultural sciences. It is interesting to notice that even Talcott Parsons gathered his knowledge about culture not from the cultural sciences, and his treatment of culture is the more revealing since he was not a narrow behaviorist. He acknowledged the existence of culture, at least, although readily forgetting about it on account of the self-sufficiency of the social system. He saw himself as "a cultural determinist, rather than a social determinist[16]." Yet, his very idea of culture is the emaciated version of a sociological theorist, anxious to reduce culture to a social mechanism for the generation of values. He does hardly suspect that norms and values are inextricably linked up with other elements of culture as a whole. By their isolation the values assume for him the appearance of a calculable and persistent entity. In this manner Parsons deprives culture of its productive and variable potential; what is left of it, can then safely be used as a building stone for "the social system."

Where did Parsons come by his domesticated notion of culture? Obviously not through a familiarity with the rich stores of cultural history. Rather, he borrowed it from cultural anthropology which at that time exerted considerable influence in America, enjoying a much higher reputation than sociology. Concerned with primitive societies, American anthropology conceived of culture as a set tradition. The concept was ahistorical and so is Parsons'. The anthropologists were content to start from the existence of culture patterns without asking about their origins. Likewise does Parsons take the social system for granted and is merely concerned with its functioning. At the time, the anthropologists (Ruth Benedict and Margaret Mead among them) were eagerly (and successfully) explaining the "Patterns of Culture" in terms of homogeneous value systems. In 1952 A.L. Kroeber and Clyde Kluckhohn, the leading anthropologists, opened their book on culture with the statement that "the idea of culture, in the technical anthropological sense, is one of the key notions of contemporary American thought" (1952: 3).

Clyde Kluckhohn, a leading anthropologist, was a member of the Harvard group whose discussions culminated in the publication of "Toward a General Theory of Action" (1951), to which Kluckhohn contributed the chapter on "Values and Value-Orientation in the Theory of Action." It is this static, ahistorical notion of culture as a value system, designed for primitive societies, which Parsons borrowed for his construction of society as "The Social System" (1951). For the formidable, far-reaching and long-lasting success of his book the Harvard Seminar had paved the way because this group of scholars from various fields – some of them publicly identified with large-scale research on national issues as, for example, S.A. Stouffer's "The American Soldier" – had agreed that the social sciences had finally come of age, viz. could now serve the U.S. as a technical instrument for planning the good society all over the world. It was in the wake of this confident belief in the technical maturity of the social sciences that sociology, late and suddenly, won public acclaim and recognition. Future historians will deal with this momentous event in which the political constellations at home and abroad played a decisive role[17].

All this is yet another illustration of the fact that sociology in the U.S. took for granted the ideal of a technical discipline, to be achieved by a strict "theory of society." On account of this tenacious preconception, Parsons could not understand Max Weber's concern with culture, although he was thoroughly familiar with Weber's works.

Max Weber had a realistic understanding of the power which social conditions, pressures, and interests exert on social action. He was a master in describing how anonymous social interactions generated new social processes and orientations. But throughout his work he did never loose sight of the role of "ideas," and, what is more, of intellectuals. There is little to be gained from reintroducing "ideas" into sociological theory without realizing that they are produced by "intellectuals" and therefore mostly can and must be traced to the unpredictable contributions of imaginative individuals. Even Parsons allowed somehow for the role of ideas. But he never made it a habit to identify their origins, authors, and histories as Weber did and not merely in his sociology of religion.

As of late, Parsons has been criticized for starting complacently from the existence of "culturally" ordered social systems, without explaining how the common understandings of norms and values ever came into being. Siding with the numerous critics, I find that their efforts remain, after all, within the fold of Parsons' tacit assumptions. The critics agree with Parsons in the belief that values and norms are bound to arise from the mutuality of social relations as a result of intersubjective processes. They continue Parsons' determinism, reasserting the strictly social origins of common values and orientations, hardly allowing for the role of culture.

Weber stressed the intellectual production (and social acceptance) of "Weltbilder." He shows how individual thinkers like Luther or Calvin created a new idea of man's ethical qualifications and thereby revolutionized his behavior. His curt critique of Lujo Brentano is applicable to modern sociology: "umso erstaunlicher ist, daß einzelne Forscher glauben, eine solche Neuschöpfung könne am Handeln des Menschen spurlos vorübergehen. Ich gestehe, das nicht zu verstehen[18]."

1.5 A New Type of Culture: Modern Culture

There remains the question whether representative culture is not a matter of the past since modern society proves its rejection of cultural authority by its manifest secularism and pluralism.

In this respect we must first note that "intellectual authority" is an observer's category of interpretation, but not necessarily a conscious understanding of the actors themselves. Even in the past intellectual authority often rested on the subjective belief of the actors to dispense or, respectively, to receive the obvious truth. It is a fallacy to impute our categories of description to the actors. There is no doubt that modern man prides himself of his independence; but this fact is besides the point for the question in hand.

It is true nevertheless that modern culture does not readily fit into the mould of past representative culture since it is a new variety of it. I have elsewhere described and explained the radical transformation of culture which began in the late 18th century[19]. From that transformation resulted a new type of representative culture, marked by its autonomy, its productivity, and its ever-increasing impact on society. In fact, the rise of this secular modern culture ("Bürgerliche Kultur") was a cause and condition for the emergence of modern society. However, this secular culture does not acknowledge an ultimate center of intellectual authority which is being dispersed and distributed over various sectors of limited and specialized competence. Modern culture is dynamic in constantly producing new, partial interpretations of reality, forcing people to keep up with the steady flow of cultural production. By multiplying the intellectuals and their public, it subjects ever larger sections of experienced reality to cultural interpretation and feeds on its own dynamics by subjecting its own products again to interpretations. The ubiquity of the mass media leaves everybody free to choose from the overwhelming plenitude what he likes. And the variety of opinions and convictions combines with the variety of life-styles and behaviors to form that pervasive pluralism of modern society which so obviously refutes the notion of representative culture. However, the apparent pluralism is rather deceptive.

Of course, there is no doubt about the facts, summarily described as pluralism. The term is misleading, nevertheless, by hiding behind an ostensible description, a tacit interpretation of the facts. By tacit assumption the observed plurality of behaviors evinces an original variety of opinions, convictions, and life-styles of the actors, and thereby visibly demonstrates the absence of intellectual authority and representative culture. The term thus secretly conveys the idea that pluralism is the normal condition and result of behaviors, once the actors are freed from social constraints. The apparently plain description actually puts a construction onto the facts that prevents any questions about the cultural nature and origin of pluralism. The unassuming term is a deceptively ambiguous notion which bears closer inspection.

To begin with, pluralism is an induced phenomenon which does less express an original disposition of the actors, than reflect their constant exposition to all sorts of messages, that is to interpretations of reality that range from plain information to imaginative exploration. Historically, it did not result directly from anonymous social processes, nor simply from concrete social interests. Changes of concrete circumstances are unlikely, anyway, of producing plural behaviors which typically rely on concerns with ideas and therefore spread first among the educated. But generally, conditions have to wait for their interpretations, to produce new behaviors. Even for the removal of restrictions intellectuals had to formulate, legitimate, and propagate the requisite ideas of freedom, involving ideologies of the good society far in excess of concrete interests. And yet, the removal of restrictions rarely sufficed for the actors to create plural behaviors without further instructions about the proper use of freedom. Even beyond that, modern intellectuals have been constantly inventing, exploring, propagating, and prescribing ever new behaviors in their efforts to interpret reality. To this extent, modern pluralism is above all an effect of the continual and steadily expanding production and distribution of ideas, and would soon shrink to normal size if the supply of messages were reduced. It is thus a characteristic product of modern culture and reveals both the influence of intellectuals on the actors' understanding of reality (and consequently on their actions) and the actors' dependence on the intellectuals' interpretation of reality.

Moreover, modern pluralism rests on a compact ideology which accepts the plural behaviors as proof of the actual consummation of freedom. Enjoying the sanction of legitimacy, pluralism is not merely a fact, but a mandatory idea of modern society. As such, it bears the unmistakable marks of representative culture and intellectual authority. Pluralism is surrounded by protective sanctions and taboos. Everybody is expected to praise publicly pluralism as an achievement and to demonstrate some active participation in it, regardless of this personal opinion. Actually, however, some opinions are being expected and some are not being tolerated at all. As any unprejudiced observer can notice almost daily, pluralism prescribes its own commandments and conversely proscribes and punishes certain opinions as heresies. Behind its profession of unbounded liberality, pluralism conceals a hard core of substantive ideology, that is a tacit interpretation of reality on which it does not compromise. On closer inspection, pluralism reveals its normative character, thereby displaying the characteristics of representative culture which provides binding interpretations of reality. Form and content of representative culture have radically changed. The representative ideas now issue from anonymous networks of intellectuals, rather than from identifiable authors. Modern society possesses a representative culture, nevertheless, which could not exist short of the authority effort of some intellectuals. For analyzing modern society, we need the notion of representative culture. Without this notion we would remain captives of anonymous modern culture.

1.6 The Culture of Everyday Life

Finally, I want to say a few words about the recent concern with everyday culture which is an understandable and legitimate reaction to mainstream sociology. It is an attempt to reclaim lived reality against the artificial constructs, complex abstractions, and aggregate data of a social science that indulges in the cult of facts. It is also an attempt to save one's identity from the inexorable stream of incoherent impressions, informations, and sensations to which we are being exposed in modern culture. In a manner, therefore, the concern with everyday life reflects the inability of modern representative culture to articulate itself explicitly.

The life-world concept has also proved helpful in dismissing the notion of over-socialized man who acts by merely carrying out roles, – even deviant ones. We again see the actor as he is taking an active part in the interpretation of his reality far beyond the mere specifications of norms and values for his roles. And this reopens the possibility for new values, new modes and views of life to develop, unpredictable in terms of the social system. The productive potential of man as a cultural being is in evidence, again.

But here the limitations begin. I forego repeating the obvious critique that everyday culture is hardly a suitable tool for the analysis of institutions. Rather, I want to criticize the failure of recognizing the existence and significance of representative culture as it is being produced by intellectuals. There is a tendency to reiterate, in a new form, the error of social determinism. As Parsons relied on structured interaction to generate lasting common values, so everyday life is now expected to generate new modes and understandings of life. Of course, such anonymous processes do occur. But for gathering momentum, they are mostly influenced by, often dependent on, or even initiated by representative culture as produced by intellectuals.

Our life-world is not a self-constitutive universe which freely arises in social communication and interaction. What we experience as our life-world is permeated by patterns and interpretations of representative culture which provides the mapping space for our aims and desires, our concepts and ideas, our problems and situations. As man has always been doing, we construct our life-worlds from the available stock of interpretations of representative culture.

Again, actual conditions may give rise to the slow and anonymous growth of new needs and orientations. Firstly, however, these anonymous and collective dispositions usually gather momentum and direction only when they are being made explicit through articulation which is a matter for intellectuals. And, secondly, such changes are often initiated by the propagation of ideas, in the first place. A fundamental weakness of mainstream sociology was its habit of considering changes of values as resulting from the average reaction of actors to their conditions, or from their social interactions. However, significant or marked changes in life-styles and convictions mostly come about by movements which in the name and wake of some idea lead people to associate or otherwise provide groups with new ideas and orientations. Marked changes in values rarely occur without intellectual articulators and spokesmen who may give vent to latent and widespread dispositions or may invent (as it were) and propagate new dispositions. We are putting a wrong construction on social facts by overlooking the crucial role which ideas play in the creation and formation of groups and associations, whose constitutive ideas are mostly direct or indirect products of representative culture, even if perhaps generated in its recesses. Even the counterculture of the 1960s was a web of groups and associations, formed in the name of new ideas, and created by intellectual propagators. The same holds true for the many alternative and post-modern movements. The well-known resistance of the working classes, their conservative bent of mind, results from their greater distance to representative culture.

In all this, representative culture displays its inherent capacity for innovation and, especially, the dynamics built into modern culture. Often the changes and movements spring from the free efforts of individuals propagating or accepting some new idea. Often they are a direct or indirect consequence of new ideas that had earlier been introduced by political decision, be it through the systems of education or other means of propagation, or that had come to dominate other sectors of representative culture. In a varying, but often very high degree the movements and changes of the last few decades have been the unintended consequences, implications, or extensions of new ideas that had come to dominate, one way or another, the systems of education, the media, or otherwise the representative culture itself.

The truth of all this could be established easily, but it is not being established since social science does not reckon with culture, being sworn in to the belief that social phenomena must originate from purely social facts. Caught in this social determinism we are constantly forgetting the role that representative culture – through ideas and intellectuals – is playing in the creation of social movements, values, and changes. Our very conception of value change as anonymous, collective, and inevitable outgrowth of social conditions is a mistaken notion with which we cannot get away forever.

It follows that we must not readily accept new movements, orientations, or values as the spontaneous actions and reaction of their adherents. We have to distinguish between what is due to the truly "collective" processes of interaction and what is due to efforts of intellectuals who create, comment, propagate, and legitimate the ideas of representative culture. Instead of confining our attention to observable social interaction, exclusively, we have to probe into the dynamic and productive constitution of representative culture, locate the typical origins of the dominant ideas, trace the lines and networks of their spread and reception, study the links between representative culture, political organization, social institutions, groups, and associations.

1.7 About the Significance of Culture for Sociology

Culture is an indispensable concept for sociology. In the first place it is crucial for a basic understanding of the nature of action, reality, and society, if only as a warning against the normal propensity for naturalistic reifications. In the second place, culture is an indispensable concept because it reminds us of the social significance of representative culture and thereby points to the role of intellectuals and ideas in all societies. This does not convert sociology into a study of culture, but it makes the study of representative culture an indispensable part of sociology. It does always depend on the kind of problem, whether or not, and to what extent, sociological research must consider representative culture. But to reach a proper decision requires the knowledge that representative culture is a constituent part of society. However, let us beware against the misunderstanding that culture and society are coextensive terms. While this is normally the case, a culture reveals its independence where it extends of several societies.

In sum, the concept of culture saves us from the misconceptions that a society is a social system and that sociology ought to develop a strict theory of society. A sociology which keeps entertaining the dream of becoming a strict theory – which always means: a technical science – will never admit the concept of culture. Conversely, when sociology now begins to reconsider the role of culture, it must critically review the tacit assumptions about its *raison de'être* and legitimation. It was Max Weber's idea that sociology, unable to become a strict theory anyway, had a very limited capacity for technical advice. For him, it was the foremost office of sociology to discover in the social phenomena their human meaning and cultural significance in order to assist us in becoming aware of our ultimate standards of values.

What is ultimately at stake in the issue over culture, is the concept and office of sociology.

Notes

[1] For most European languages the sudden emergence and subsequent fate of the concepts are fully documented. The rich materials have occasionally been used to advantage for studies in the history of ideas, whereas the social sciences on their preoccupation with social conditions have shown no interest in the key terms of modern social vocabulary. *Culture and Society, 1780–1950*, Harmondsworth/UK, Penguin 1962, by Raymond Williams is a rare exception.

[2] For a full account of the social significance of the two key concepts the reader is referred to Tenbruck, F., *Die kulturellen Grundlagen der Gesellschaft. Der Fall der Moderne.* Opladen/Wiesbaden, Westdeutscher Verlag 1989; especially to the Introduction and ch. 4.

[3] Wilhelm Dilthey's *Einleitung in die Geisteswissenschaften* (1883) Leipzig, Teubner 1922 was an attempt to develop a systematic understanding of culture without succumbing to the temptation of constructing a theory of culture. However, the book, which had a lasting influence on German sociology, suffered, among other things, from its predominant concern with the cultural sciences, rather than with culture.

[4] Max Weber, *Gesammelte Aufsätze zur Wissenschaftslehre*, 4th ed.. Tübingen, Mohr 1973: 166.

[5] Max Weber has laid bare the naturalistic presuppositions of most sociology, with little effect, though. These presuppositions already begin with the term "society" which regularly invites its own reification. Georg Simmel and Max Weber never used the term to suggest a unitary totality as mainstream sociology did from its inception. I have repeatedly drawn attention to the persistent role of fundamental tacit assumption in the history of sociology, generally in *Die unbewältigten Sozialwissenschaften oder Die Abschaffung des Menschen.* Graz, Wien, Köln, Styria 1984, and specifically in "Emile Durkheim oder die Geburt der Gesellschaft aus dem Geist der Soziologie." *Zeitschrift für Soziologie* 10, 1981: 333ff. and "George H. Mead und die Ursprünge der Soziologie in Deutschland und Amerika." In *Das Problem der Intersubjektivität. Neuere Beiträge zum Werk George H. Meads*, ed. H. Joas. Frankfurt/M., Suhrkamp 1985: 179ff.

It is encouraging to note that Michael Mann in his recent book *The Sources of Social Power*, Vol. 1. Cambridge, Cambridge University Press 1986, now rediscovers Max Weber's position, when he writes "Societies are not unitary. They are not social systems" (p. 1), and also arrives at my previous conclusion, when he continues: "It may seem an odd position for a sociologist to adopt; but if I could, I would abolish a concept of 'society' altogether" (p. 2).

[6] In common language, culture is now a term which can be applied indiscriminately to almost anything that allows for varying degrees of conscious performance or appreciation. The same tendency can be observed in the vocabulary of the social sciences.

[7] In 1952 A. L. Kroeber and C. Kluckhohn published *Culture. A Critical Review of Concepts and Definitions* (republished in 1963 by Vintage Books, Random House, New York). The book exemplifies the old standard of scholarship and erudition and can still prove helpful in some respects. But by its encyclopedic stance it exemplifies the futility of all attempts to search for a "true" definition. And yet it deserves respect for its insistent probing, when compared with publications that confidently rely on technically refined, but otherwise arbitrary definitions. It is quite true that definitions depend on the problems that we want to raise. But definitions lead to sham problems, unless informed by a thorough knowledge of the pertinent facts.

[8] This, of course, is the perspective from which Max Weber developed his "verstehende" sociology in opposition to a science of "objective" social facts. See *Economy and Society*, ed. G. Roth and C. Wittich. New York, Bedminster Press 1968: 4.

[9] All these approaches disregard the fundamental fact that societies are a complex net of meaningful actions. Even from the fact that human actions are partly determined by natural causes, the actors have to draw their own meaningful conclusions for their own actions. The same holds true for the unforeseeable consequences of social actions in which the actors regularly get involved. Here again they must decide how to react to the consequences.

[10] It is the legitimate prerogative – and even the constitutive condition – of any science to scan the facts from its predominant interest in some specified aspect. But every science must keep aware of the limitations of its peculiar perspective. Social science must needs dwell on the social aspects of the facts. But it must not go on the a priori assumption that the facts can be explained by their social aspects. Therefore, any social science must give a principal account of the role of culture.

[11] This happened in ethnology when social anthropology superseded cultural anthropology.

Except for the German tradition and most notably G. Simmel and M. Weber, sociology (as a "science of society") never cared to understand and study culture, anyway. It took scholars with a European background to venture onto this field like P. Sorokin (*Social and Cultural Dynamics*, Vol. 4. New York, American Book 1937–1941, and *Society, Culture and Personality*. New York/London, Harper 1947) and F. Znaniecki (*Cultural Sciences*. Urbana, University of Illinois Press 1952). But they remained rare exceptions and made no impression on professional sociology and neither did Alwin Gouldner's *Enter Plato*. New York, Basic Books 1965, although dedicated to Robert K. Merton. Likewise, attempts by anthropologists to use the notion of culture, for example, *The Interpretation of Culture*, by Clifford Geertz, New York, Basic Books 1973, have been little noticed by sociology.

12 For this I must refer readers to the previous characterization of man as a cultural being and generally to the rich literature on this topic in the German tradition of anthropology, so little known abroad. For now I simply want to remark that "reality" for us is not a collection of facts, but always a sum of interpretations of facts, as the development of children proves. To simplify, I have used the term "interpretation of reality", although it lends itself to misunderstandings.

13 "Ideas" is the traditional concept which refers generally to symbolic representations of meaning and is not restricted to verbalized doctrines.

14 Eduard Meyer, *Geschichte des Altertums*. Darmstadt, Wissenschaftliche Buchgesellschaft, Vol. 1, 1978, 8th ed.: 18. See my article "Max Weber e Eduard Meyer." *Comunità* 39, 1985: 150ff., the English version "Max Weber and Eduard Meyer." In *Max Weber and his Contemporaries*, ed. W. J. Mommsen and J. Osterhammel. London, Boston, Sidney, Allen & Unwin 1987: 234ff., German 3rd ed. forthcoming.

15 Jacob Burckhardt, *Weltgeschichtliche Betrachtungen* (ca. 1870). Stuttgart, Kröner Verlag 1978: 8. For a proper appreciation of Burckhardt's dictum, compare his general remarks on culture: "(Die Kultur) wirkt unaufhörlich modifizierend und zersetzend auf die beiden stabilen Lebenseinrichtungen ein, – ausgenommen insofern dieselben sie völlig dienstbar gemacht und zu ihren Zwecken eingegrenzt haben. Sonst ist sie die Kritik der beiden, die Uhr, welche die Stunde verrät, da in jenen Form und Sache sich nicht mehr decken" (p. 57).

16 Talcott Parsons, *Societies. Evolutionary and Comparative Perspectives*. Englewood Cliffs, N.J., Prentice-Hall 1966.

17 One of the rare comments about the impact of political constellations on the transformation of American sociology from a parochial perspective to global considerations is an article by Jose Casanova "Legitimacy and the Sociology of Modernization." In *Conflict and Control. Challenge to Legitimacy of Modern Governments*, ed. A. J. Vidich and L. N. Glassman. Beverly Hills and London, Sage Publications 1979.

18 Max Weber, *Gesammelte Aufsätze zur Religionssoziologie*, 6th ed., I. Tübingen, Mohr 1972: 72, note 1.

19 See F. Tenbruck, *Die kulturellen Grundlagen der Gesellschaft. Der Fall der Moderne*. Opladen/Wiesbaden, Westdeutscher Verlag 1989, especially the Introduction and ch. 4. For a brief account see F. Tenbruck, "Bürgerliche Kultur." *Kölner Zeitschrift für Soziologie und Sozialpsychologie*, special issue 27, 1986: 263ff.

2 Structures, Cultures, and Knowledge: A Historical and Comparative Exploration*

Richard Münch

2.1 Introduction

The formulation of human knowledge does not occur in a vacuum. It is a social undertaking organized in a particular way and taking place within a particular societal and cultural context. It is appropriate, therefore, to investigate what effects are brought to bear by differing social milieux and cultural contexts – that is, by certain forms of living and acting, and certain forms in which knowledge is formulated in practice – upon the development of particular characteristics of knowledge. Such an investigation is carried out in part of a comparative study from the perspective of the sociology of culture to which I should like to refer readers (Münch, 1986). My intention is to demonstrate that differing social milieux, working in conjunction with particular cultural forms (media) by way of which knowledge is formulated and communicated, lend this knowledge different characteristics accordingly. This will be elaborated in an intercultural comparison (see Figure 2.1).

The first step involves sketching out the social milieu and the form of knowledge formulation that are able to explain the special characteristics of knowledge generated by modern Western science when set against the differing characteristics of knowledge in premodern and non-Western cultures. I would like to show in what respects the context in which knowledge was formulated during the crucial phase of the Italian Renaissance in the fifteenth and sixteenth centuries was distinct from that of other cultures.

After this initial comparative step, I shall examine individually the societies that became centers for the development of knowledge during the following centuries (Great Britain in the seventeenth, France in the eighteenth, Germany in the nineteenth, and the United States in the twentieth centuries), again with a view to how particular social milieux and media for the formulation of knowledge affected and shaped special characteristics of that knowledge. This is not intended as an assertion that the social milieux and media of knowledge formulation worked to the exclusion of other effects in the countries mentioned. When viewed comparatively, however, they do occupy, nevertheless, a predominant position in those countries, and this allows us to use them to study the particular effects of social milieux and the media of knowledge formulation on an ideal-typical basis.

* I am grateful to Neil Johnson for translating this chapter from the original German.

2.2 An Intercultural Comparison of the Development of Modern Scientific Knowledge

Max Weber posed the question as to why it was only in Western cultures that economic relations arose that are rational and based on calculation, methodically ordered action, and reliability. He sought the answer to this question in his famous study on the connection between the inner-worldly asceticism of Protestant religion and the spirit of such rational economic action (Weber, 1972a: 17–206). However, Weber also stated that only the Western cultural area had given rise to what we term modern science. Weber did not bequeath us any study of his own in answer to this latter question. However, we are in a position to consider a number of Weber's remarks spread among his works and combine them in order to formulate an understanding of the unique nature of modern science and to explain its emergence.

Ancient China had extraordinarily highly developed technology. In this respect China remained vastly superior to the West up to the Renaissance. Conceptual and theoretical abstraction, on the other hand, were only weakly developed (cf. Weber, 1972a: 412–416, 435–443; Needham, 1969; Münch, 1984: 212–216). In ancient India we encounter abstract thinking, procedures of proof, and mathematics at a very high level of development. Extraordinary technical achievements also existed. The characteristic feature in this case is a pronounced specialization of subject disciplines (cf. Weber, 1972b: 146–147, 166–167; Münch, 1984: 216–219). No other culture achieved such progress in conceptual and theoretical abstraction as that of classical Greece, the originator of the logic of proof which retains its validity for us today (cf. Weber 1973: 596; Ben-David, 1971: 40–44; Münch, 1984: 219–223).

The immediate question therefore is: Why until the fifteenth century, had these cultures which had managed greater achievements in many fields of thought than the West, failed to develop science in the modern sense? When this question is examined comparatively one point, in particular, is directly apparent: What is lacking in these cultures is rational experimentation, which represents a conjunction of abstract theory, logical procedures of proof, experiential knowledge, and technical problem-solving. These different forms of knowledge remain separated from each other (Weber, 1972b: 439; 1973: 596–597; Münch, 1984: 224–226).

The rational experiment is the special invention of the fifteenth and sixteenth century Italian Renaissance. Furthermore, it was an invention with its own particular societal preconditions that were not provided in other cultures. What can be regarded as a decisive cause is the fact that scientific communities gathered for the first time in the Italian Renaissance – initially by virtue of loose contacts but then with increasing intensity – thus uniting representatives of different forms of knowledge on a cooperative basis: artists, architects, engineers, craftsmen, and scholars. This was an opportunity for craftsmanlike, empirical ability and rational abstraction to mutually penetrate the other (cf. Zilsel, 1976; Ben-David, 1971: 55–59; Münch, 1984: 224–226). An essential precondition for this was the decline of the barriers between social estates in the medieval city and the development of a general estate of the citizenry, a development furthered by Christianity's religious universalism (see Weber, 1976: 741–757). This was the first time that different societal groups had been able to freely associate and to cooperate with equal rights. This is the social context that only the Western cultural area was able to furnish for the emergence of modern science, whose unique characteristic is that rather than separating different forms of knowledge, it links them together on a new level. In modern science, a special union is formed out of theory, technique, logical procedures of proof, and experience. The relevant medium for the formulation of scientific knowledge is the scientific treatise, and the relevant social milieu is made up of rational experimentation and the scientific community (Münch, 1984: 233).

2.3 The Development of Modern Scientific Knowledge: A Theoretical Explanation

In order to gain a systematic grasp of the unique nature of modern Western science when compared with premodern and non-Western forms of knowledge, we can locate science within a particular field in an action space and then illustrate the relationships between it and the other fields in the same space. First, it is necessary to give an introductory description of the action space itself. We may conceive of action as a movement occurring within a space that has four extreme points: they represent closing, opening, generalization, and specification, and the area between them is termed the action space (cf., e.g., Münch, 1984: 11–71; 1987: 30–191) (see Figure 2.2).

Closing signifies that action is perfectly ordered, regular, and predictable. On the general level of action it is social action according to social roles – action oriented to social norms and motivated by social influence – that has this characteristic of orderedness and projects it on to the other fields of action. Actors can only conceive of a certain number of common norms limited by their life-world, and these norms place close limits on interpretation and make precise stipulations for action. For the scientist who is a member of a scientific community, certain methodological rules borne by that community have a binding validity. There is no alternative to the rules, which thus render the scientist's action predictable. This extreme combines low symbolic complexity and low contingency of action.

Opening signifies that action is highly flexible, can be varied over a broad spectrum, and is therefore barely predictable. On the general level of action, it acquires this characteristic and conveys it to the other fields of action from learning through the use of intelligence. Actors are able to conceive of an unlimited number of means that can be deployed for any action they like. The scientist is free to devise any hypotheses he/she chooses and to use them for any desired explanations of events in reality. In this case high symbolic complexity is combined with high contingency of action.

Generalization signifies that action maintains a general identity while, at the same time, the spectrum of variation remains broad. On the general level of action, this function is fulfilled by action's orientation to symbols and to general ideas by means of a universal definition of the situation. The most generally applicable idea for the scientist is that of the search for truth, an idea to which there is no alternative but which permits a broad spectrum of procedural methods. In this case low symbolic complexity is combined with high contingency of action.

Specification signifies that action is directed toward a particular goal even though a multitude of alternative goals are available. On the general level of action this orientation to goals is made possible when action is determined by personal dispositions and the utilization of personal decision-making ability. Every scientist has to select a concrete research objective from a variety of alternatives according to his/her own dispositions and decision-making capacities. In this case high symbolic complexity is combined with low contingency of action.

We can differentiate the action space more finely by again distinguishing the functions named before in each of the four fields of action also discussed, that is, social action, learning, cultural symbols, and personal dispositions (see Figure 2.3).

Social action is closed by communal association and commitments to norms, opened by markets and the use of money, generalized by communication and language, and specified by political authority and political power.

Learning is opened by situational learning, closed by regulated learning, generalized by thinking, and specified by purposeful learning.

Cultural knowledge is generalized by meaning constructions in works of philosophy, specified by expressiveness in literary essays, closed by norms in moral compendia, and opened by cognitions in scientific treatises. The scientific treatise, in turn, is generalized in the form of a theoretical treatise, specified in the form of a technical treatise, closed in the methodical enquiry, and opened in the empirical periodical article.

Personal dispositions are specified by personal goal-setting, generalized by personal identity, closed by personal morality, and opened by the personal variation of action.

The advantage of taking such a general frame of reference as our starting point is that we are able to approach our specific object of enquiry using general sociological statements derived from the basic assumptions set out here, which have also proved their worth in other fields of enquiry. In other words, we are not forced to discover everything on the basis of our specific object alone.

If one wishes to explain the development of modern science using this frame of reference, it is possible to distinguish three stages in that development.

In the first stage (see Figure 2.4), knowledge is still completely bound up within the limits set by tradition and the life-world of communities. The members of simple societies are closely linked with one another and have only very little contact with the outside world. All of them share the *traditional knowledge* of their parents and ancestors. Within the action space, knowledge remains confined to the sphere of closedness: It is controlled by norms and does not change.

The second stage (see Figure 2.5) is attained to a greater extent the more community members enter into contact with the outside world, whether it be in the form of economic exchange relations with strangers, political conflicts regarding the occupation of particular territories, or confrontation with the knowledge of other communities. This involves a differentiation of new spheres of social interaction, and of action in general, which are distinctly separated from communal action and take action into other fields within the action space. These spheres differentiated from communal action also allow new forms of knowledge to arise that are adjusted to the demands of the respective types of action. Economic exchange with strangers represents a sphere of utilitarianism that is the antithesis of communal brotherhood. The appropriate form of knowledge in this instance is useful experience, in the field of the openness of social action. Action attains still greater openness the more it departs from the confines of attachment to norms, is exposed to changing action situations, and has to rely upon learning. In this case, situational experience is the appropriate form of knowledge, and the relevant medium is the report of one's experiences. Political action with regard to strangers becomes a sphere of pure power politics. Here, the appropriate form of knowledge is practical technology in the field of the specification of social action, with the purpose of attaining collective goals. It is no coincidence that, throughout history, waging war has always been a substantial motivating force for technical development. Accordingly, a large proportion of technology is military technology. The more the individual pursuit of objectives becomes a self-contained activity, the greater the significance attained by personal techniques of self-realization (e.g., yoga techniques). The appropriate medium is technical instruction. Finally, dialog with strangers means that reflection about the world becomes a new sphere of intellectual discourse. In this case, knowledge takes on theoretical abstraction in the field of the generalization of social action. Self-contained reflection upon the world reaches its peak in the abstract meaning construction of a philosophical work.

As was shown by the review of the shaping of knowledge in the traditional societies of ancient China, India, and Greece, it is characteristic of these societies that, while they did achieve outstanding developments of knowledge in individual spheres, they were unable sufficiently to link these achievements together.

The third stage, modern science, occurred when blossoming of scientific communities of the Italian Renaissance produced the conjunction of individual forms of knowledge with the development of the rational experiment and the application of theory to technical problem-solving (see Figure 2.6). At this point, the medium of knowledge formulation is now the scientific treatise, an incorporation of the characteristics of those forms of knowledge that were formerly separated with their own specialized media. Useful and situational experience are now combined with meaning construction to form experiential knowledge, while practical technology and personal technique merge in technical problem-solving, and traditional knowledge and theoretical abstraction merge in formal method. Abstract meaning construction, once combined with experiential knowledge, technical problem-solving, and formal method, is specified into scientific theory, a system of empirically testable hypotheses.

The forces that, by virtue of their mutual penetration, have shaped the components of modern science can be summarized in the hypotheses set out in Figure 2.7.

2.4 An Intracultural Comparison of the Development of Special Characteristics of Knowledge

Following the development of scientific knowledge in the fifteenth and sixteenth century Italian Renaissance, the centre of the development of knowledge then shifted, century by century, sequentially to: Great Britain, France, Germany, and the United States.

2.4.1 Great Britain: The Scientific Communities, the Enquiry, and the Normative Binding Power of Knowledge

In the seventeenth century, Great Britain lead in the development of knowledge. The entities that can be accorded an outstanding significance in shaping knowledge were the scientific community as the social milieu and the enquiry as the medium for the formulation of knowledge (see, e. g., Hartley, 1960; Ornstein,1938; Stimson, 1948; Münch, 1984: 233–236; cf. also Hume, 1966; Toulmin, 1958).

The understanding of rationality characterized by this social and cultural context is far removed not only from philosophical abstraction, system, and deduction, but also from creative originality. This is already implicit in the concept of "reason" in the English language. "Reason" is more a matter of utilizing practical experience and of what can be commonly comprehended. The criterion under which it is examined is not the logical demonstrability of a thesis (an idea) and its capacity for being universalized but rather commonly shared experience within a community of communicating parties. This reason with an empirical bent finds its confirmation in the general agreement among the community members. If the binding validity of an idea is to be sealed, the agreement of the community needs to be found. The appropriate medium to serve this concept of reason is the enquiry. This is the form in which British philosophers and scientists have traditionally presented their ideas to the public. Enquiries are not unduly long, are formulated in language that is generally comprehensible, are made up of a sequence of separate reflections, and endeavor to present the ideas they have in such a way that the average citizen will be able to agree with them out of his/her own experience. The fact that a hypothesis is in agreement with usual experience and ought therefore to be accepted as valid is the argument most often used to win the assent of the reader.

Within the scientific community, members are bound primarily by common norms. These, together with the methodical procedures underlying an enquiry, lend knowledge a quality of being ordered by way of common rules of method or, in short, a quality of *normative binding power*. Because representatives of differing spheres of thought, experience, and practice are involved, the character of knowledge is also expanded in the direction of theory, experience, and technology. Taken in conjunction with the fact that it is shaped by common rules of method and the commonality of experience within the community, experiential knowledge thus gains the characteristic of *common sense*. Theoretical abstraction is enmeshed in the common horizon of experience and the prevailing common rules, and as such can never be more than the *systematization of common sense* or the hypotheses gained from experience. The involvement of practicians means that the purposiveness of knowledge is very significant, and this is manifested in *technical problem-solving* (see Figures 2.8, 2.9, 2.10, 2.11).

2.4.2 France: The Salon, the Café, the Essay, and the Expressivity of Knowledge

In the eighteenth century, the center of the development of knowledge shifted to France. The prime features that predominate in this case as far as the shaping of knowledge is concerned are the salon and café as social milieux and the essay as medium for the formulation of knowledge (see, e.g., Back and Polisar, 1983; Cunow, 1925; von Falke, 1977; Grana, 1964; von Jan, 1967: 101 ff.; Kreuzer, 1971: 202–216; Picard, 1943; Münch, 1984: 245–248).

The French concept of rationality assumed its characteristic form during the Enlightenment in the salon. This was the meeting place for scholars, writers, and men of the world: the salon of a society lady. In the contributions they made to the conversation, individual participants primarily gave of their own personalities. Self-presentation and the expressive nature of what any individual had to say, geared to presentation itself and to elegance, frequently received greater attention than the actual content. "He said that beautifully!," "How delightfully put!," "Wasn't that exquisitely formulated?" and "How wonderfully spoken!" are all typical reactions generated by a brilliant utterance.

Once the zenith period of the Enlightenment had passed, the salon lost its central role as the place of reasoning. Other locations then became more significant. The tradition of the salon was continued, under rather different circumstances, in a new arena: the café. Instead of a sophisticated party of people gathering at the house of a society lady, a group of intellectuals and artists would now assemble who wished to fashion their lives as works of art and to nurture a lifestyle running counter to the bourgeois norm. In this circle, too, then, a major part was played by expressive needs and the striving for self-presentation. Although the circumstances had changed, people wishing to gain recognition in this milieu had to develop similar qualities to their predecessors in the salon. In both places, a similar amount of credit was given to wit, originality, creativity, articulacy, the art of formulation, inspiration and astuteness.

The effects of the salon, and later of the café, did not remain confined to the sphere of conversation. The café shaped the style of literature that was generated in the salons. This is a phenomenon of which writers themselves were aware. Marmontel and Diderot believed themselves taught by the society ladies to present dry material with charm and clarity, to show flexibility in making readily comprehensible and humorous formulations, and hence prevent their audiences from becoming tired or bored. Philosophers and scientists cultivated an easily readable literary style. The appropriate medium to convey this "light" form of philosophizing is composed of philosophical narratives and essays. The author of an essay endeavors to participate in current discussions and assumes a particular stance with regard to current disputes. Such authors are oriented, therefore, toward a market for ideas, in which they compete with other authors.

The shaping of the intellectual scene according to market processes naturally also had its effect on the character of the knowledge produced. Markets accelerate the pace of social change. It therefore comes as no surprise that trends in French thought are dominated by a succession of intellectual fashions to an extent without parallel elsewhere.

In salon and café alike, a predominant part is played by the portrayal of one's own personality. Thus the formulation of knowledge becomes a means of self-portrayal. *Expressivity*, the art of presentation and formulation, is then the distinctive hallmark of knowledge. The latter tendency is given further support by the essay as the medium for the formulation of knowledge. In this instance, the need to adjust to changing situations also demands the further characteristic of *actuality* in knowledge. Speakers need to respond to rapid switches in interests and attention to issues. When it comes to generalizing knowledge in the face of such rapidly changing issues, only those will succeed, who are inspired by rousing and unusual ideas able to examine the matter concerned in a new light: This is *esprit* as the special characteristic of knowledge. In as far as thought is subject to the ordering influence of norms, the required quality in this case, as also carried by intellectual subculture, is *style* of presentation, or the rules of elegant formulation (see Figures 2.12, 2.13, 2.14, 2.15).

2.4.3 Germany: The Private Study, the University Seminar, the Academic "Work," and the Abstraction of Knowledge

In the nineteenth century the center of knowledge development shifted to Germany. Here, the predominant social milieu was provided by the private study and the university seminar, and the outstanding medium for the formulation of knowledge was the great work. Each of these has a special effect upon the characteristics of knowledge (cf., e.g., Fichte, 1971; also Dahrendorf, 1965: 175–191; König, 1970; Ringer, 1969; Schelsky, 1971; Münch, 1984: 248–255).

In this context, the concept of rationality as a comprehensive form of reason is closely associated with the solitude of the scholar. The embodiment of such a concept is the great work. The work must be sufficient in both depth and breadth if it is to even hold its own in a cultural landscape set out by giants. The scholar, if he/she is to find the truth, needs to withdraw from society in order to be free from other strivings governed by interests. His/her life must be devoted to the search for truth and nothing but the truth. Any other activity would divert the scholar from the proper path to that truth. It is not in the outward participation in action within society that the truth manifests itself to the scholar, but only in the release from the web of intricacy such action entails, in the perfect solitude of the private study and in the university seminar which is isolated from society as a whole. If the scholar enters into discussion, then this is not so much conducted with his/her contemporaries in the field, but with the great intellectual figures throughout the millennia. Whatever argument is put forward in the present, the scholar recognizes the thoughts that history has already produced. The only possibility available is to continue refining and deepening the thoughts of the past.

The private study and the university seminar isolated from society and its practical life-world interactions both serve, above all, to promote pure thought for its own sake, immersion in a question through to its logical conclusion, profundity and *abstraction* from all fortuitousness, and thrusting forward to the "essence" of things. These tendencies in thought are supported by the fact that the work is produced in solitude and freedom. Such thought is not socially anchored in the here and now, but beyond the bounds of time, and it is not regulated by the scientific community and society as they currently exist, but by the community of scholars stretching over thousands of years. This primarily lends *continuity* to thought, a long-enduring constancy in essential ideas, problems, and problem solutions. Thinking attains its orderedness far more from the most general rules of logic than from more specific methodical procedures. The links with reality gained by thought via learning processes do not so much arise out of the accumulation of experiential knowledge as out of theoretical constructs designed to cover the entire *truth* of the world, which are not intended to make do with the piecemeal collection of experience. Knowledge is not given a purpose by virtue of practical objectives being set – it is not directly intended to be practically useful – but by the fact that the scholar seeks to demonstrate the unique contribution made by his/her thought via the formulation and elaboration to its logical conclusion of a *specific idea* (see Figures 2.16, 2.17, 2.18, 2.19).

2.4.4 The United States: The Meeting, the Periodical Article, and Rapidly Changing Knowledge

In the twentieth century, the center for the development of knowledge moved to the United States. In this case, the prime influences on the shaping of knowledge emanate from the social milieux of the public meeting and competition and from the periodical article as the medium of knowledge formulation (see, e. g., Ben-David, 1972: 25–47; Caplow and McGee, 1958; Hirsch, 1968; Hofstadter, 1963; James, 1907; Kadushin, 1975; Lipset, 1963: 332–371; Smith, 1963; de Tocqueville, 1961; Webster, 1945; Wilson, 1976; Münch, 1984: 255–259).

Competition is an all-pervading feature of American society. Hence, it also characterizes the organization of *science*. This is already apparent in the way the universities vie with one another for the top academic reputation. They compete for financial support to fund both research projects and departmental expansion, for scientific discoveries, for able students, faculty members, and professors. The more such resources and achievements they are able to claim for themselves, the greater is their reputation and the more attractive they will be once again to the providers of funds, to academics, and students.

The competitive system offers greater rewards for the rapid publication of scientific findings in short articles than for scientific findings that have been allowed to slowly mature and attain greater depth before publication in a major work. The publication practice of leading periodicals also makes it clear how publishing results within the shortest possible time in article form favors a particular type of rationality. The field of enquiry must be a limited one, for if it is too broad, it will not be possible to treat it effectively in an article. For the same reason, the problem posed must be clearly formulated and delineated. Once again, this prevents any undue expansiveness. These are demands that are more easily fulfilled by formulating specific hypotheses and testing them using clearly defined empirical material than by making an exposition of theoretical developments; the latter is frequently too broad in its initial conception to fit within the framework of an article, or else it must be open to the criticism that reality in all its multifariousness is arbitrarily trimmed in order to concentrate on just a few aspects.

This tough competition and the compulsion to achieve short-term success in the scientific market naturally have both positive and negative consequences. For one thing, innovation is encouraged. For another, knowledge is subject to tremendoûsly rapid change, yet progress is not always clearly apparent because knowledge is lacking in theoretical orderedness. Scientists and academics are spurred on to immense productivity. On the other hand, the pressure of competition can also tempt ambitious scientists to manipulate or fake data for the sake of achieving appropriate or original results.

Public debate and competition mean that knowledge is under great pressure to perform. It is continually required to prove itself in the face of new criticism. Scientists have to hold their own in the marketplace against a stream of new alternatives. This promotes *rapid change* as the chief characteristic of knowledge. The article is the form in which such knowledge can best be packaged. A further feature applying to knowledge in this context is that of adaptation to external circumstances. It has to change rapidly to adjust to changing experience and to new data, while it must also *adapt to the objectives of the practical world* by serving a practical purpose. It must not be too out of the ordinary as it also needs to be in accordance with the tastes and conceptual horizons of its *public*, and this subjects knowledge to a particular normative control based on those points the members of the public have in common, which is liable to cyclical variation. This continual adjustment to suit new data, the objectives set in the practical world, or the tastes of the public places restrictions on theoretical abstraction. This may not proceed any further than to a *generalization of concrete experience*. Theory is no more than a collection of constantly changing experiential propositions (see Figures 2.20, 2.21, 2.22, 2.23).

2.5 Concluding Remarks

In conclusion, I would like to stress once again that the social milieux and media of knowledge-formulation examined in the individual countries concerned were not, or are not, alone in determining the development of knowledge. When a comparative view is taken, however, they are of such towering significance that it is indeed possible to elaborate the effects of given social milieux and media for the formulation of knowledge upon its characteristics, on an ideal typical basis. The differences in the extent to which social milieux and media of knowledge formulation have been present in individual countries provide an area of experimentation for general sociological hypotheses. Indeed, it is precisely the formulation and testing of such generally valid statements that is of interest to the sociologist. He/she must leave it to the historian to delve into the concrete complexity of the development of knowledge in particular countries at particular times.

2.6 Summary

This chapter examines the development of forms of knowledge by comparing both intercultural and intracultural bases. The development of modern scientific knowledge can be reconstructed in terms of a three-stage dialectic process. As long as human action remains contained within narrow communal boundaries, traditional knowledge predominates. In the ancient societies of China, India, and classical Greece, specialized forms of knowledge are differentiated from traditional knowledge: experiential knowledge, practical technology, and abstract meaning construction. The combined effect of the scientific communities, as the social milieu, and the scientific treatise, as the medium for the formulation of knowledge, draws together the differentiated forms of knowledge during the Italian Renaissance of the fifteenth and sixteenth centuries to produce modern scientific knowledge. In the centuries that follow, the nucleus of scientific development shifts successively to Britain, France, Germany, and the United States. If they are viewed comparatively, each of these countries sees its own particularly prominent social milieu and medium of knowledge formulation lending distinctive characteristics to knowledge. In Britain, the scientific communities and methodical enquiry primarily give knowledge normative binding power. In France, via the salon, café, and essay, the main quality transmitted is expressivity. In Germany, the private study, the university seminar, and the truth-seeking "work" give knowledge, and above all else, abstraction. Finally, in the United States, knowledge primarily attains rapidity of change because of the meeting, competition, and the periodical article.

References

Back, K.W. and Polisar, D. (1983). "Salons und Kaffeehäuser." In *Gruppensoziologie, Kölner Zeitschrift für Soziologie und Sozialpsychologie*, special issue 25, ed. F. Neidhardt. Opladen: Westdeutscher Verlag, pp. 276–286.

Ben-David, J. (1971). *The Scientist's Role in Society.* Englewood Cliffs, N.J.: Prentice-Hall.

Ben-David, J. (1972). *American Higher Education: Directions Old and New.* New York: McGraw-Hill.

Caplow, T., and McGee, R. (1958). *The Academic Marketplace.* New York: Basic Books.

Cunow, H. (1925). *Politische Kaffeehäuser. Pariser Silhouetten aus der großen französischen Revolution.* Berlin: Dietz.

Dahrendorf, R. (1965). *Gesellschaft und Demokratie in Deutschland.* München: Piper.

Falke, J. von (1977). *Der französische Salon.* Bonn: Keil.

Fichte, J.G. (1971 [1845/1864]). "Einige Vorlesungen über die Bestimmung des Gelehrten (1794)." In *Fichtes Werke*, Vol. 6, ed. J.H. Fichte. Berlin: de Gruyter, pp. 291–346.

Grana, C. (1964). *Bohemian versus Bourgeois. French Society and the French Men of Letters in the Nineteenth Century.* New York: Basic Books.

Hartley, H. (Ed.) (1960). *The Royal Society. Its Origins and Founders.* London: The Royal Society.

Hirsch, W. (1968). *Scientists in American Society.* New York: Random House.

Hofstadter, R. (1963). *Anti-Intellectualism in American Life.* New York: Alfred Knopf.

Hume, D. (1966 [1748/1751]). *Enquiries Concerning the Human Understanding and Concerning the Principles of Morals*, ed. L.A. Selby-Bigge. Oxford: Clarendon.

James, W. (1907). *Pragmatism: A New Name for Some Old Ways of Thinking.* New York: Longmans, Green.

Jan, E. von (1967). *Französische Literaturgeschichte in Grundzügen*, 6th ed. Heidelberg: Quelle & Meyer.

Kadushin, C. (1975). *The American Intellectual Elite.* Boston: Little, Brown.

König, R. (1970 [1935]). *Vom Wesen der deutschen Universität.* Darmstadt: Wissenschaftliche Buchgesellschaft.

Kreuzer, H. (1971). *Die Boheme. Analyse und Dokumentation der intellektuellen Subkultur vom 19. Jahrhundert bis zur Gegenwart.* Stuttgart: J.B. Metzlersche Verlagsbuchhandlung.

Lipset, S.M. (1963). *Political Man.* Garden City, N.Y.: Doubleday.

Münch, R. (1984). *Die Struktur der Moderne. Grundmuster und differentielle Gestaltung des institutionellen Aufbaus der modernen Gesellschaften.* Frankfurt: Suhrkamp.

Münch, R. (1986). *Die Kultur der Moderne* (Vol. 1: *Ihre Grundlagen und ihre Entwicklung in England und Amerika*; Vol. 2: *Ihre Entwicklung in Frankreich und Deutschland*). Frankfurt: Suhrkamp.

Münch, R. (1987 [1982]). *Theory of Action. Towards a New Synthesis Going beyond Parsons.* London: Routledge & Kegan Paul.

Needham, J. (1969). *The Grand Titration. Science and Society in East and West.* London: Allen & Unwin.

Neidhardt, F. (Ed.) (1983). *Gruppensoziologie, Kölner Zeitschrift für Soziologie und Sozialpsychologie*, special issue 25. Opladen: Westdeutscher Verlag.

Ornstein, M. (1938). *The Role of Scientific Societies in the Seventeenth Century.* Chicago: University of Chicago Press.

Picard, R. (1943). *Les Salons littéraires et la société française 1610–1789.* New York: Brentano's.

Ringer, F.K. (1969). *The Decline of the German Mandarins. The German Academic Community 1890–1933.* Cambridge, Mass.: Harvard University Press.

Schelsky, H. (1971). *Einsamkeit und Freiheit. Idee und Gestalt der deutschen Universität und ihrer Reformen*, 2nd ed. Düsseldorf: Bertelsmann Universitätsverlag.

Smith, J.E. (1963). *The Spirit of American Philosophy.* New York: Oxford University Press.

Stimson, D. (1948). *Scientists and Amateurs. A History of the Royal Society.* New York: Abelard-Schwan.

Tocqueville, A. de (1961 [1835/1840]). *Democracy in America.* New York: Schocken.

Toulmin, S. (1958). *The Uses of Argument.* Cambridge: Cambridge University Press.

Weber, M. (1972a [1920]). *Gesammelte Aufsätze zur Religionssoziologie*, Vol. 1. Tübingen: Mohr Siebeck.

Weber, M. (1972b [1921]). *Gesammelte Aufsätze zur Religionssoziologie*, Vol. 2. Tübingen: Mohr Siebeck.

Weber, M. (1973 [1922]). *Gesammelte Aufsätze zur Wissenschaftslehre.* Tübingen: Mohr Siebeck.

Weber, M. (1976 [1922]). *Wirtschaft und Gesellschaft.* Tübingen: Mohr Siebeck.

Webster, C.M. (1945). *Town Meeting Country.* New York: Duell, Sloane & Pearce.

Wilson, L. (1976 [1942]). *The Academic Man. A Study in the Sociology of a Profession.* New York: Octagon.

Zilsel, E. (1976 [1947]). *Die sozialen Ursprünge der neuzeitlichen Wissenschaft.* Frankfurt: Suhrkamp.

Appendix (Figures 2.1–2.23)

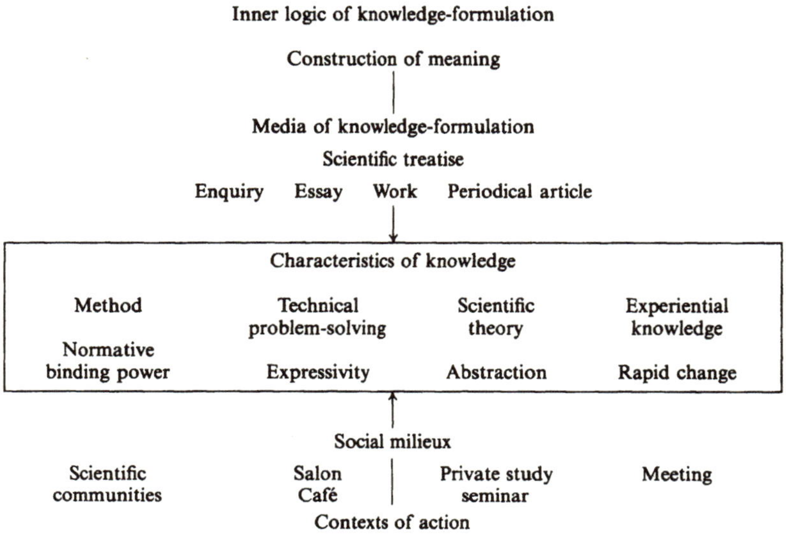

Figure 2.1 The Characteristics of Knowledge between the Inner Logic of Knowledge-Formulation und Varying Contexts of Action

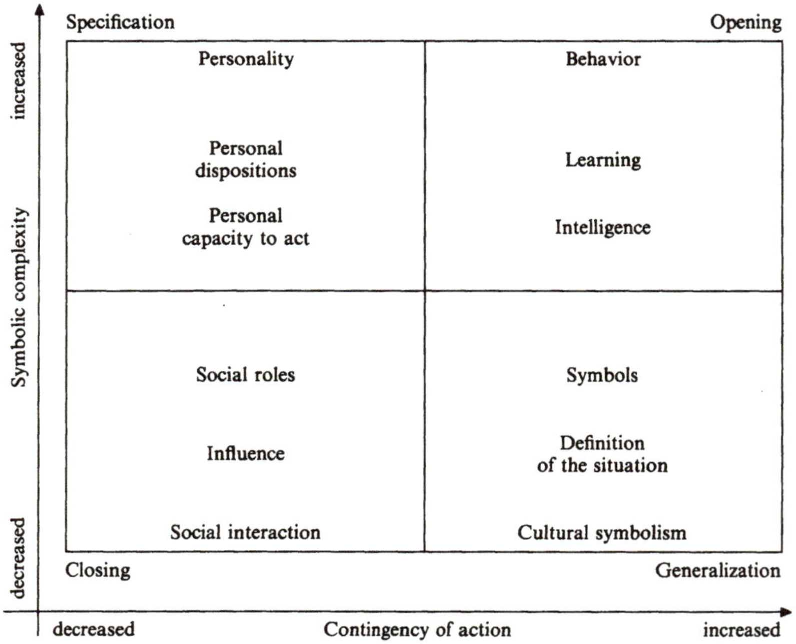

Figure 2.2 The General Action Space

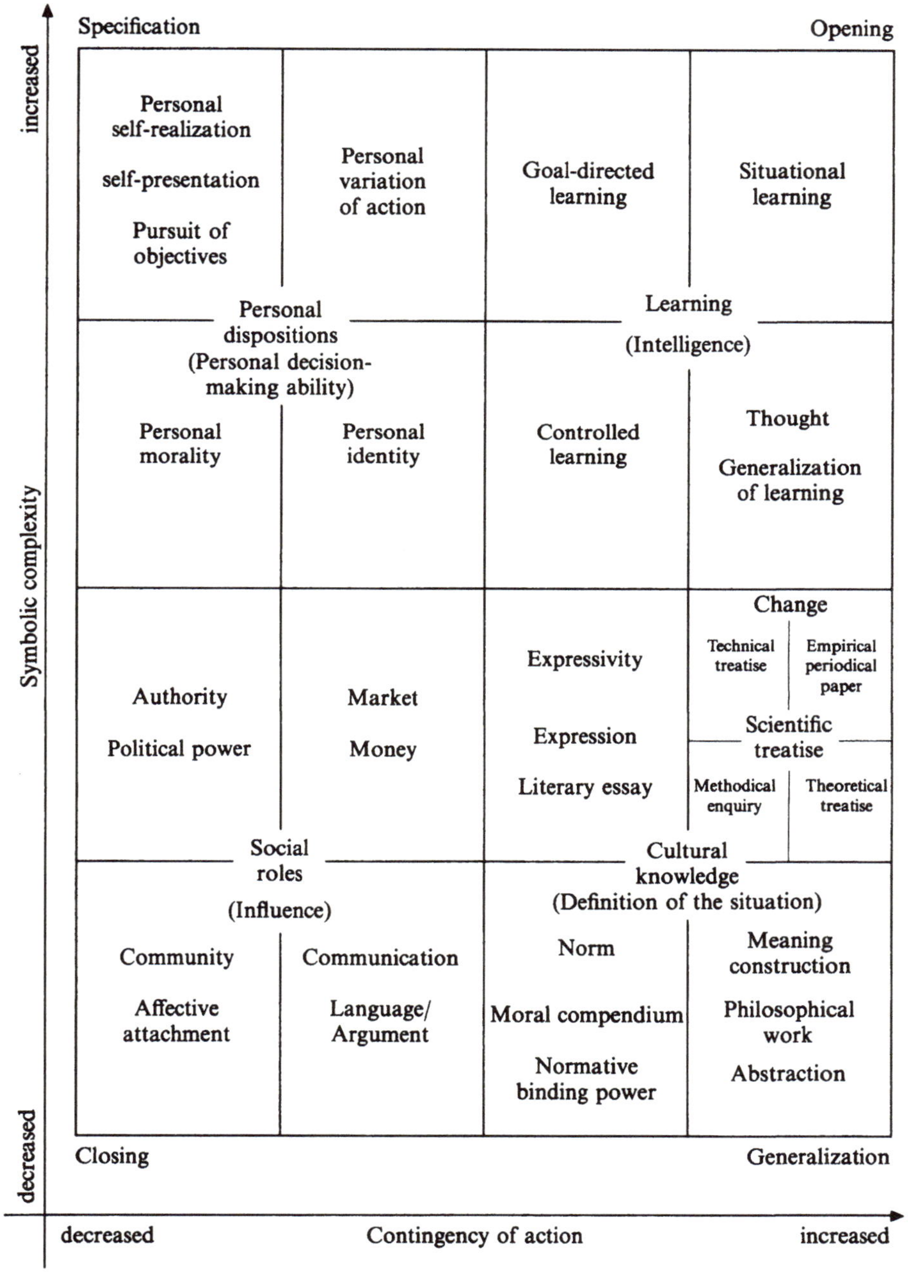

Figure 2.3 Cultural Knowledge in the Context of the Action Space: Its Inner Logic and External Interconnections

Figure 2.4 Traditional Knowledge

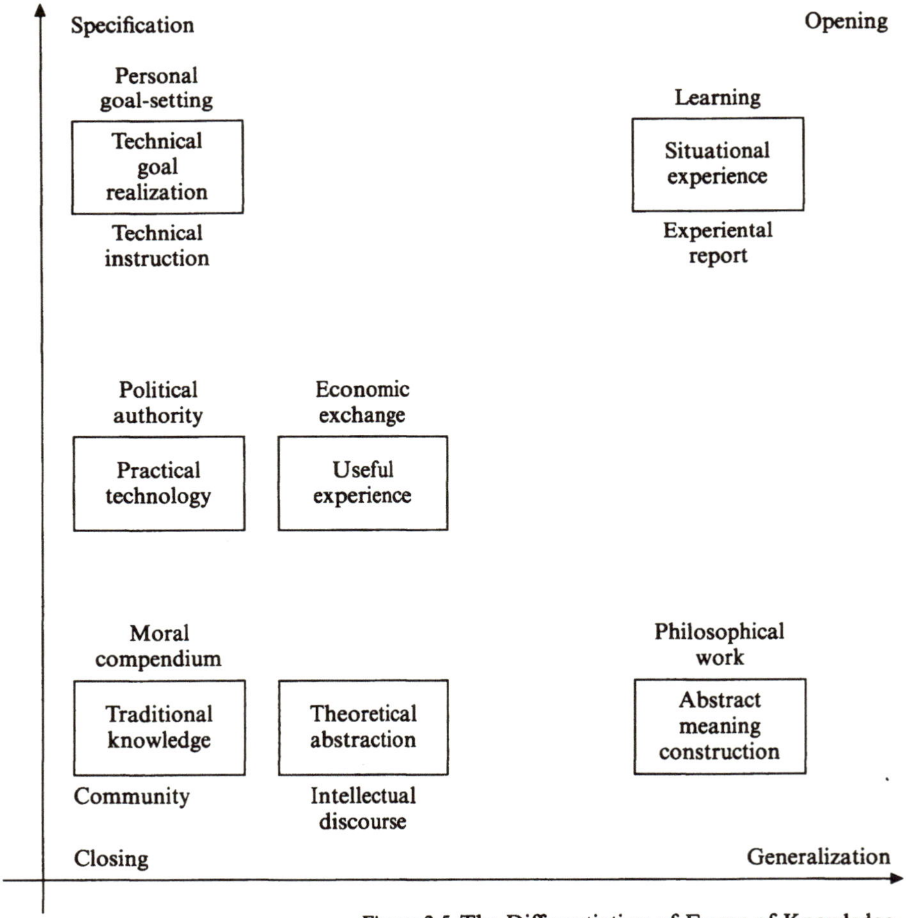

Figure 2.5 The Differentiation of Forms of Knowledge

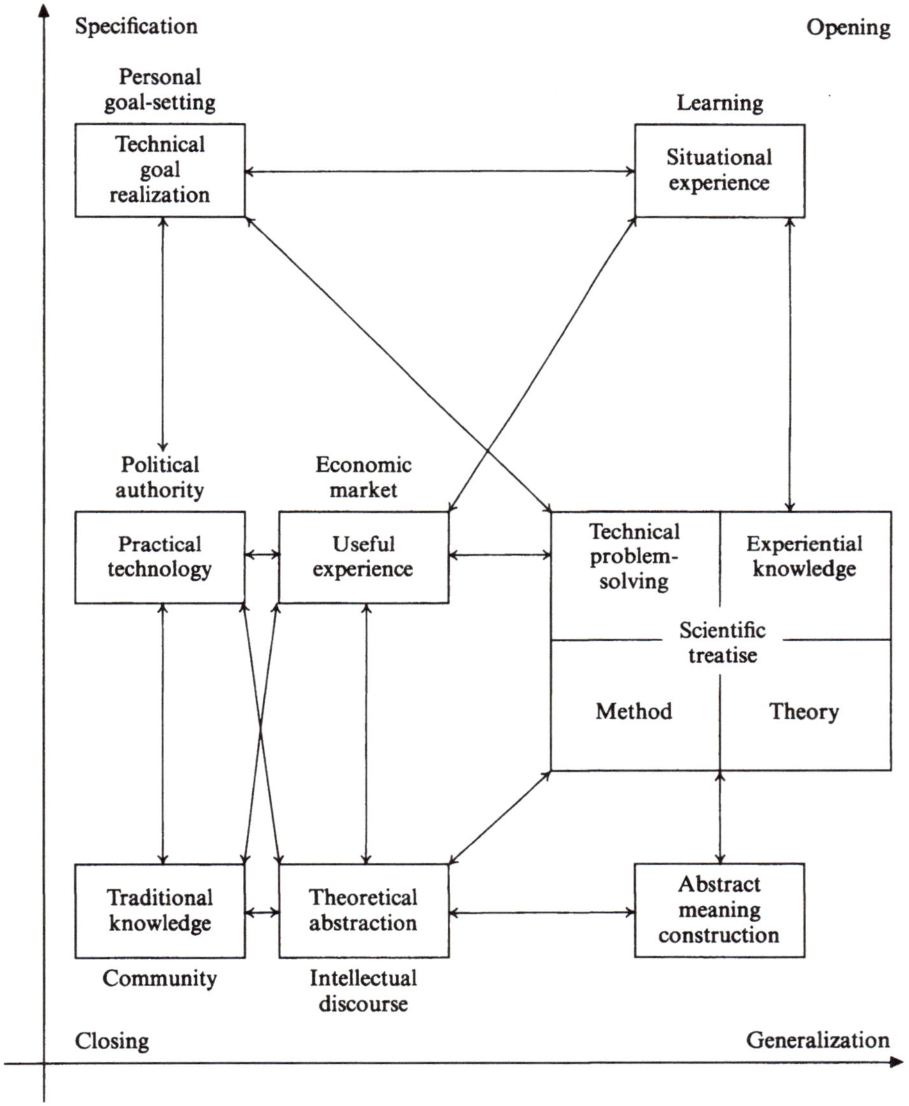

Figure 2.6 The Interpenetration of Forms of Knowledge within Modern Scientific Knowledge

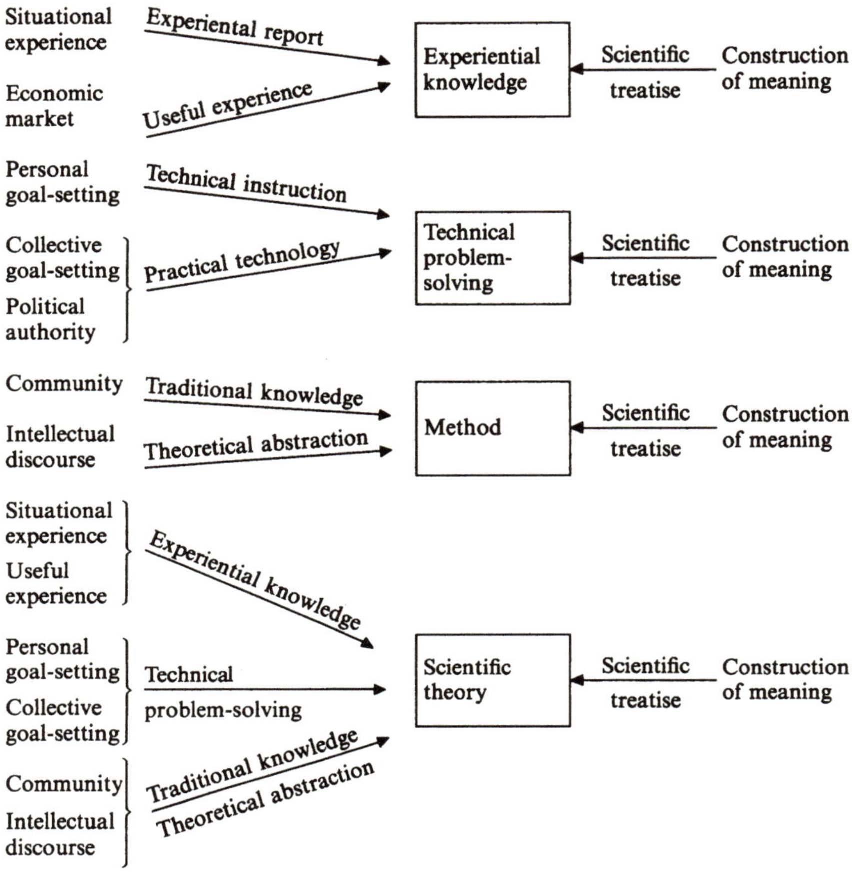

Figure 2.7 Hypotheses on the Shaping of Modern Scientific Knowledge

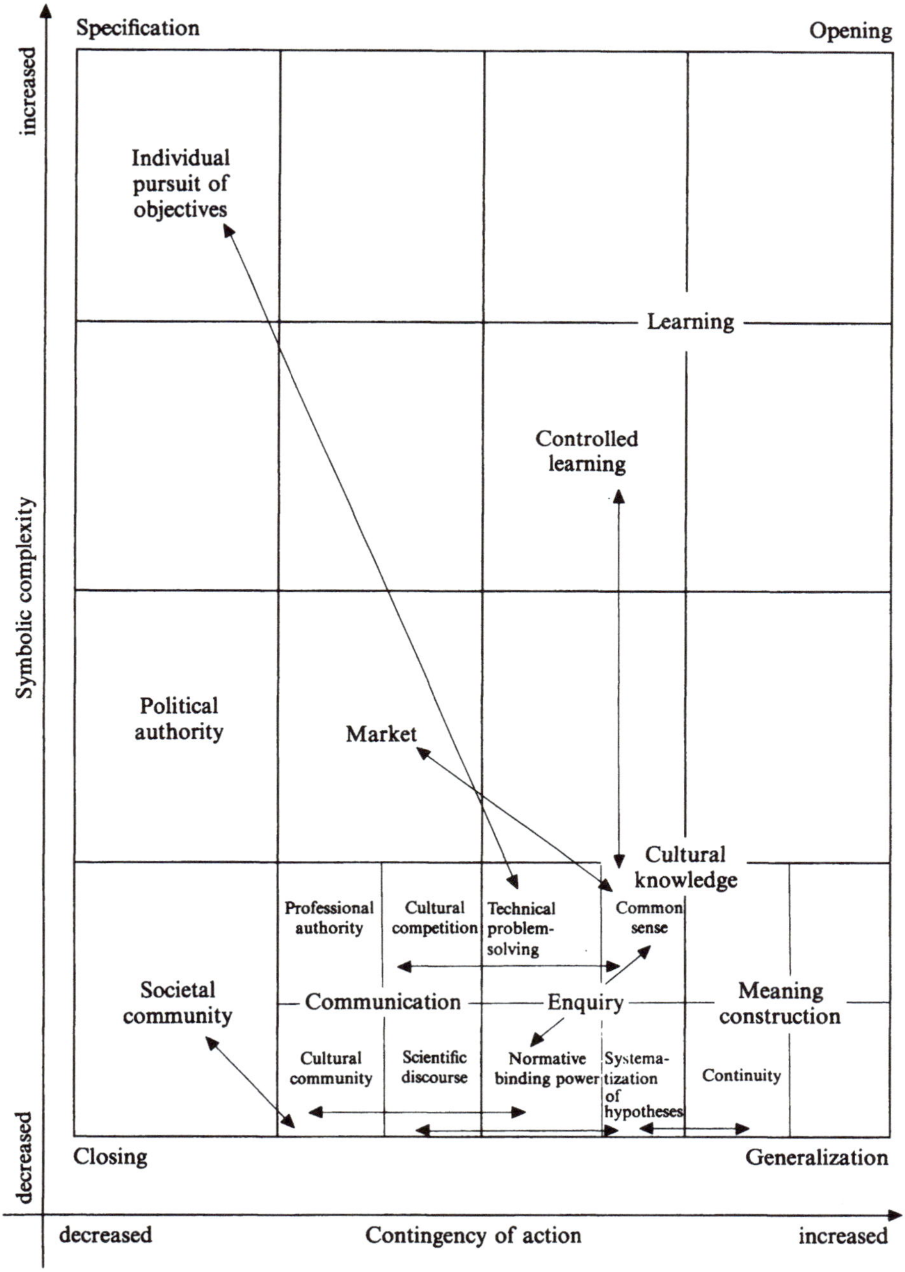

Figure 2.8 The Scientific Community and the Enquiry in the Context of the Action Space

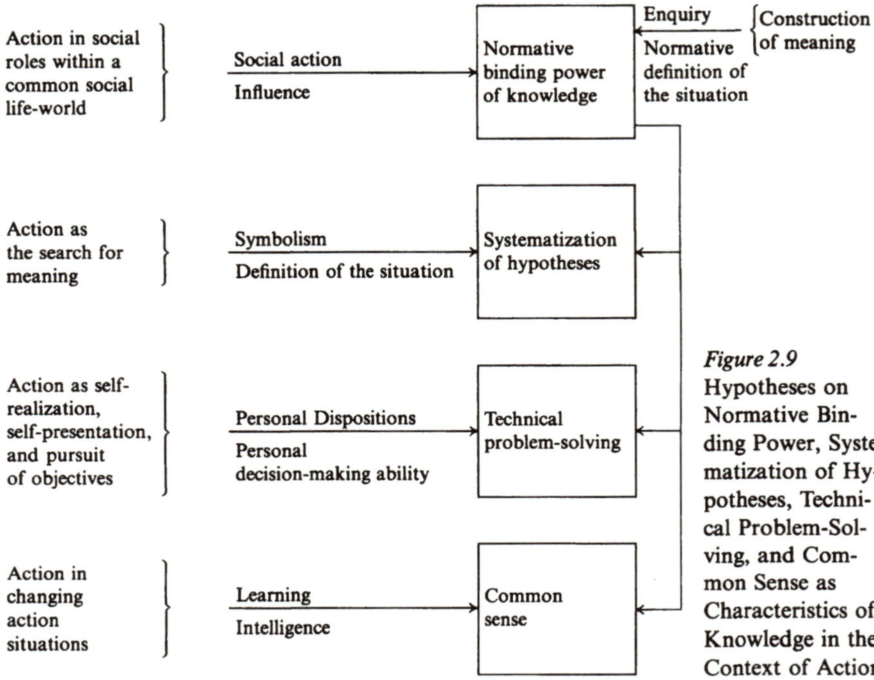

Figure 2.9 Hypotheses on Normative Binding Power, Systematization of Hypotheses, Technical Problem-Solving, and Common Sense as Characteristics of Knowledge in the Context of Action

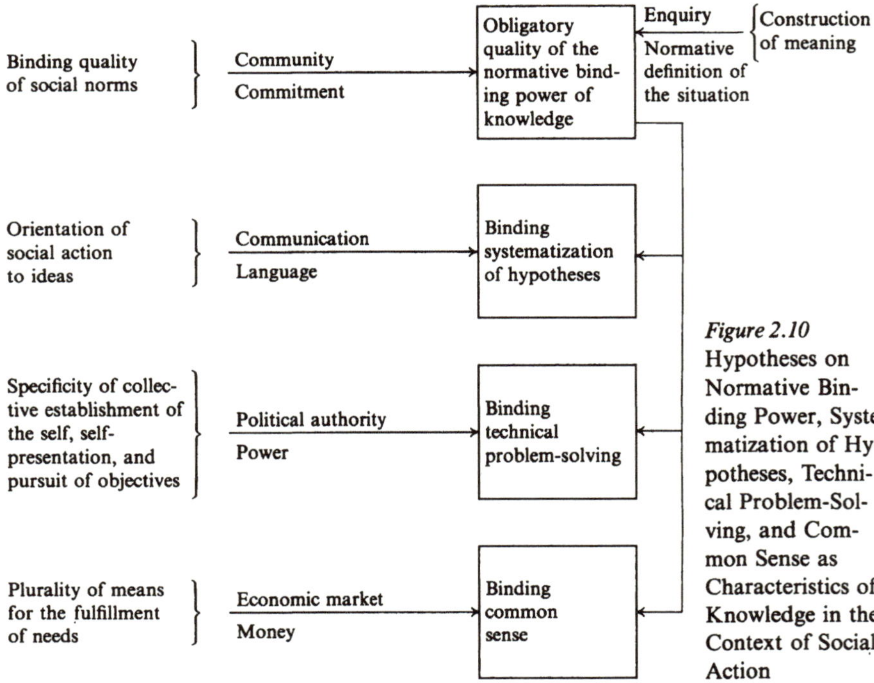

Figure 2.10 Hypotheses on Normative Binding Power, Systematization of Hypotheses, Technical Problem-Solving, and Common Sense as Characteristics of Knowledge in the Context of Social Action

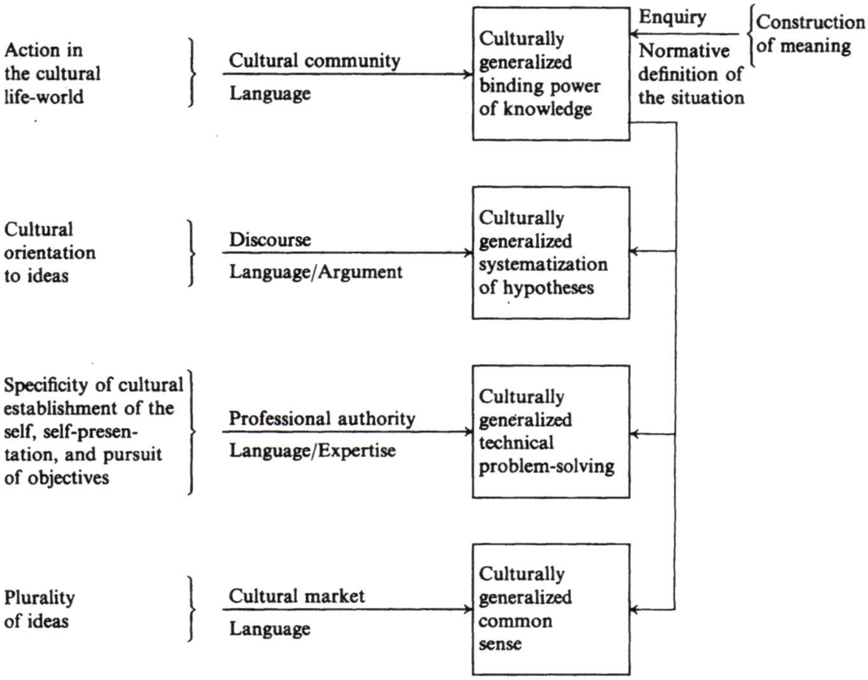

Figure 2.11 Hypotheses on Normative Binding Power, Systematization of Hypotheses, Technical Problem-Solving, and Common Sense as Characteristics of Knowledge in the Context of Communication

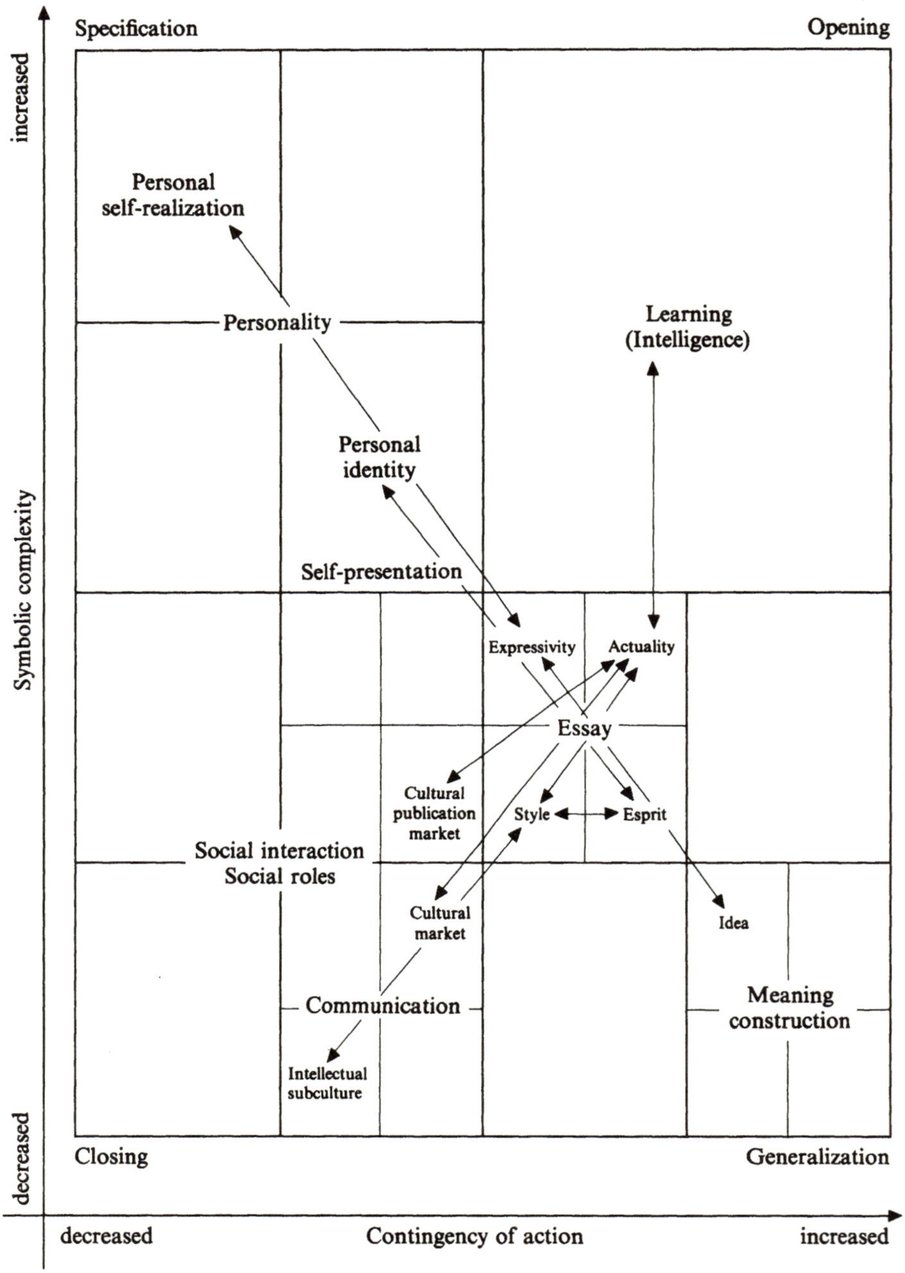

Figure 2.12 The Salon, Café, and Essay in the Context of the Action Space

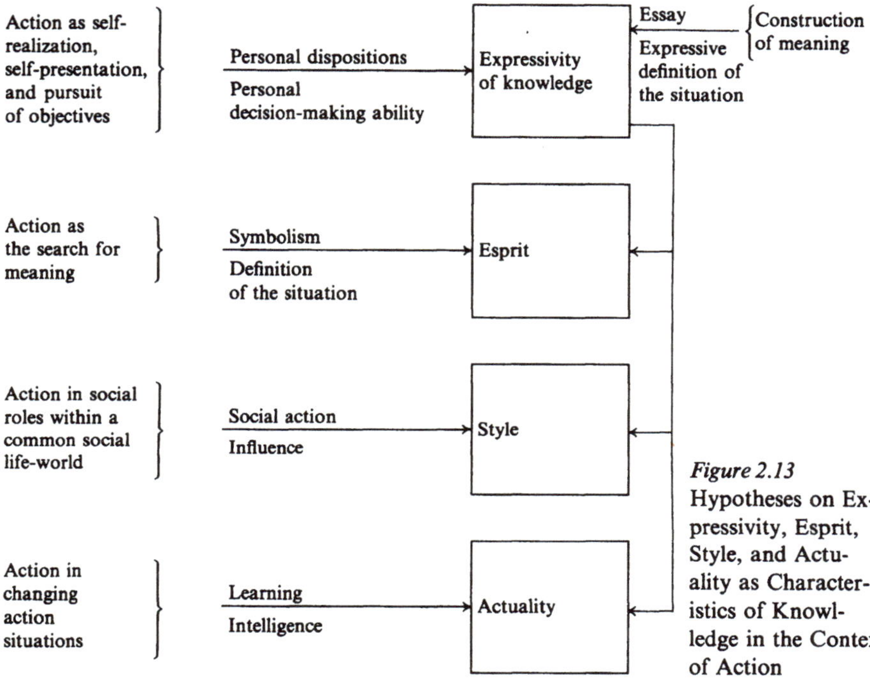

Figure 2.13
Hypotheses on Expressivity, Esprit, Style, and Actuality as Characteristics of Knowledge in the Context of Action

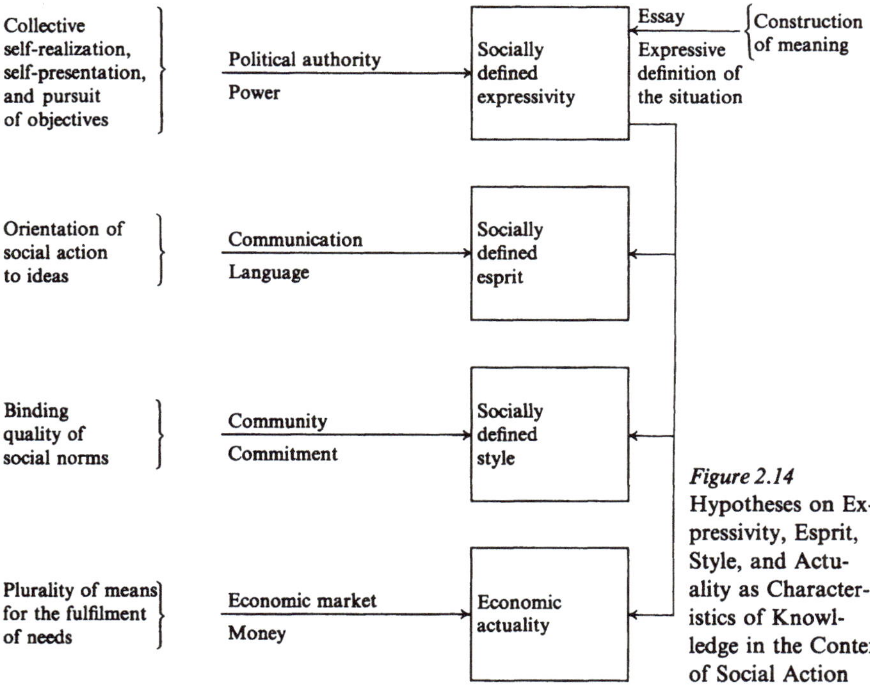

Figure 2.14
Hypotheses on Expressivity, Esprit, Style, and Actuality as Characteristics of Knowledge in the Context of Social Action

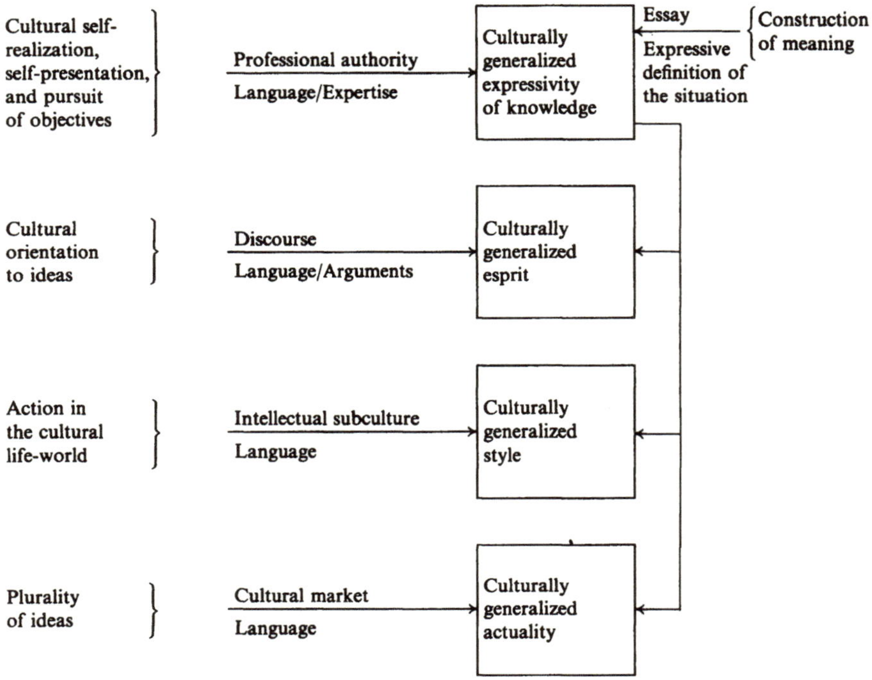

Figure 2.15 Hypotheses on Expressivity, Esprit, Style, and Actuality as Characteristics of Knowledge in the Context of Communication

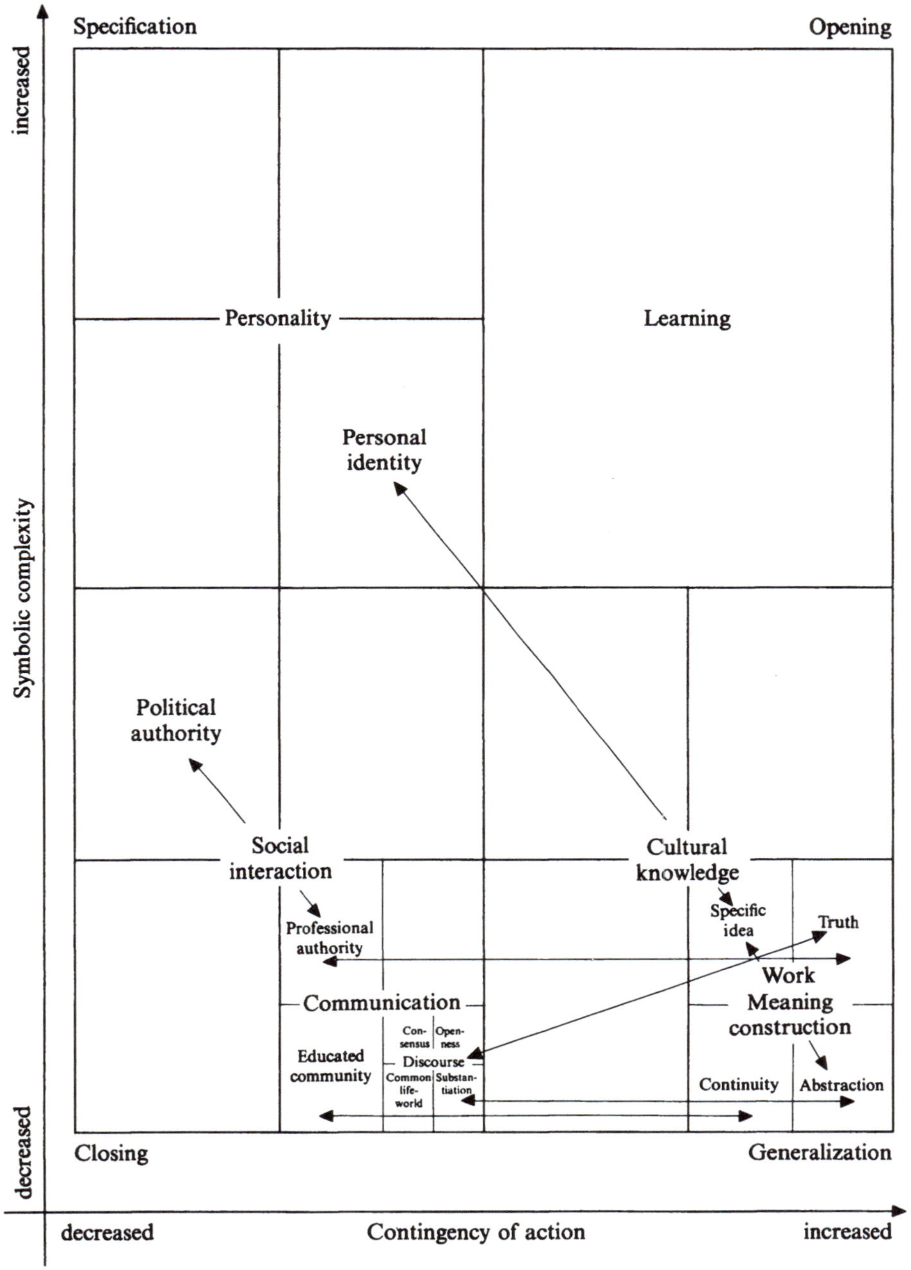

Figure 2.16 The Private Study, the University Seminar, and the Work in the Context of the Action Space

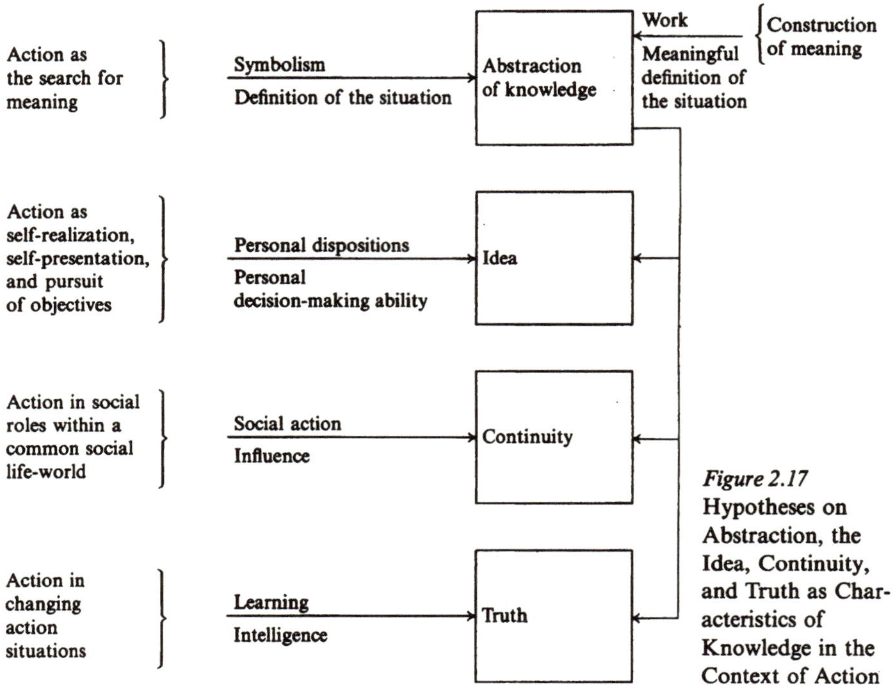

Figure 2.17
Hypotheses on Abstraction, the Idea, Continuity, and Truth as Characteristics of Knowledge in the Context of Action

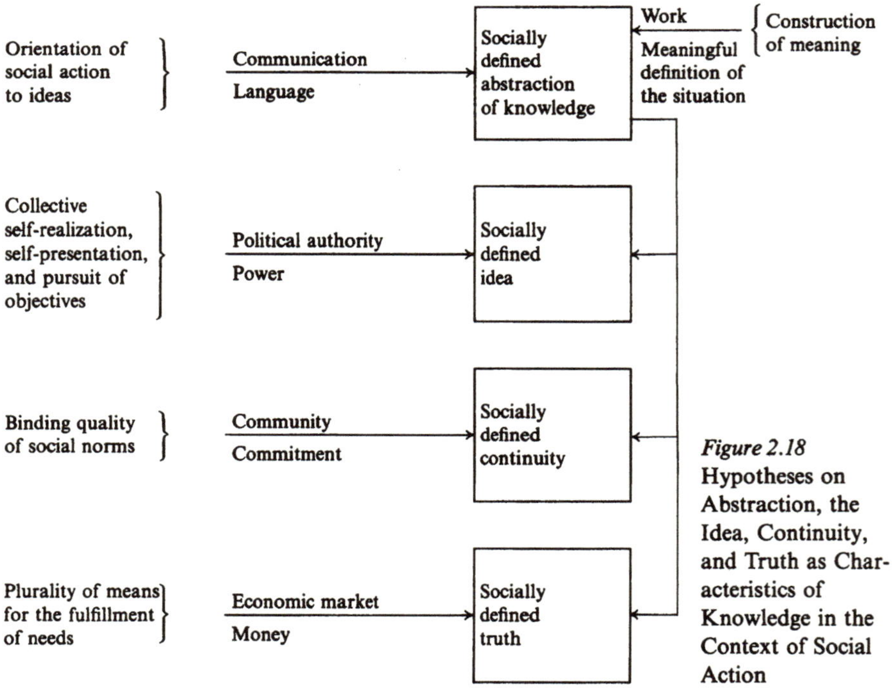

Figure 2.18
Hypotheses on Abstraction, the Idea, Continuity, and Truth as Characteristics of Knowledge in the Context of Social Action

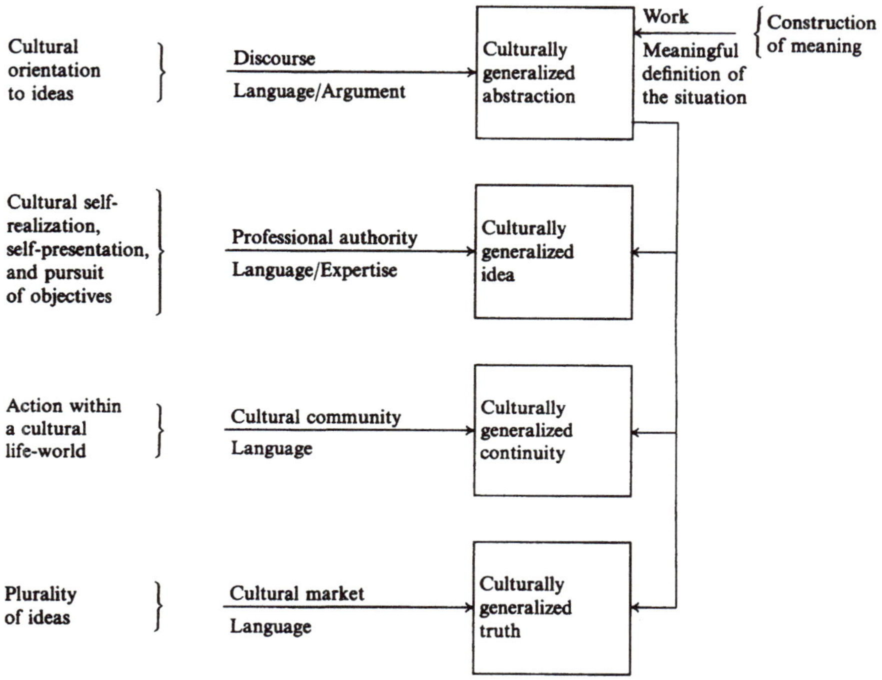

Figure 2.19 Hypotheses on Abstraction, the Idea, Continuity, and Truth as Characteristics of Knowledge in the Context of Communication

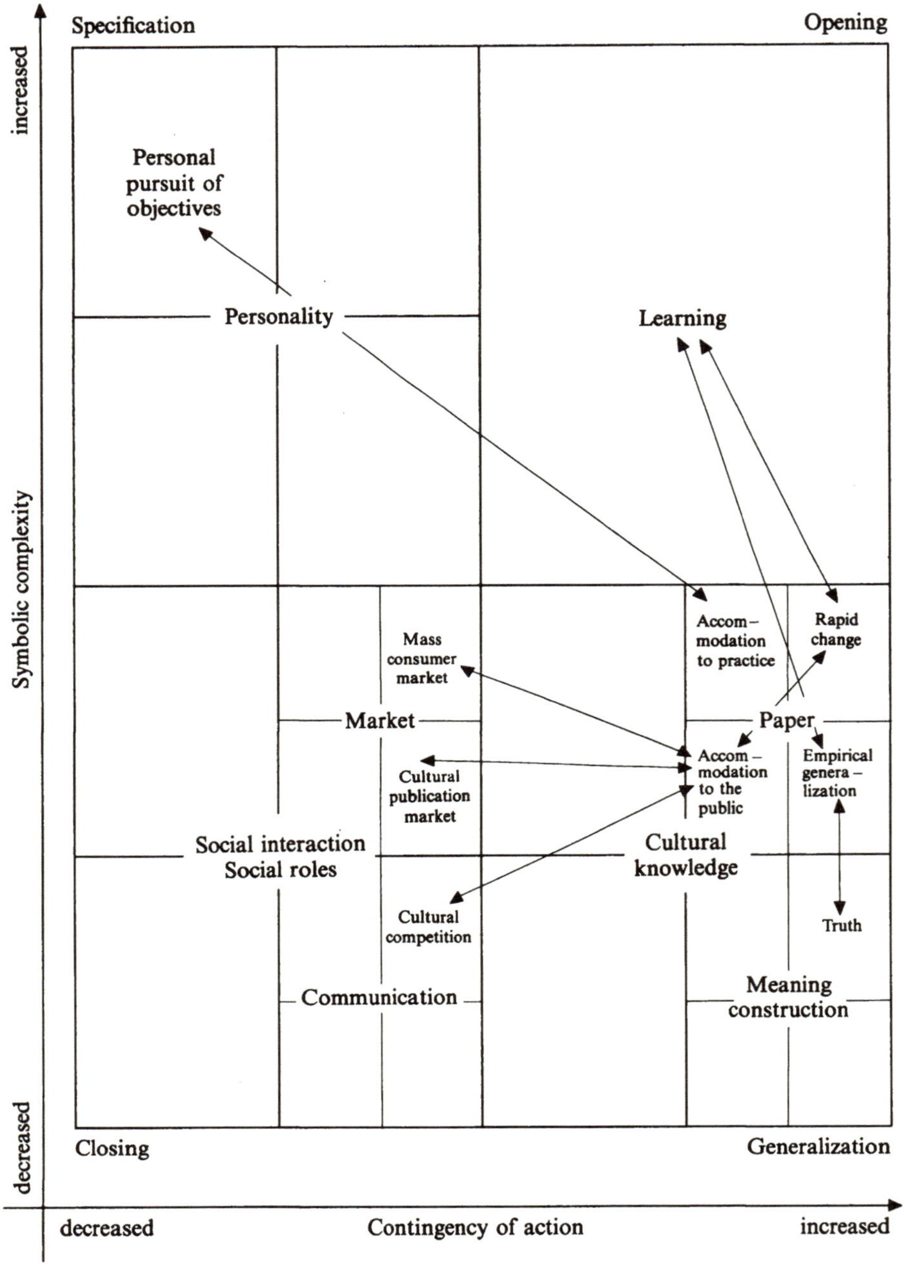

Figure 2.20 The Meeting and the Periodical Article (or Paper) in the Context of the Action Space

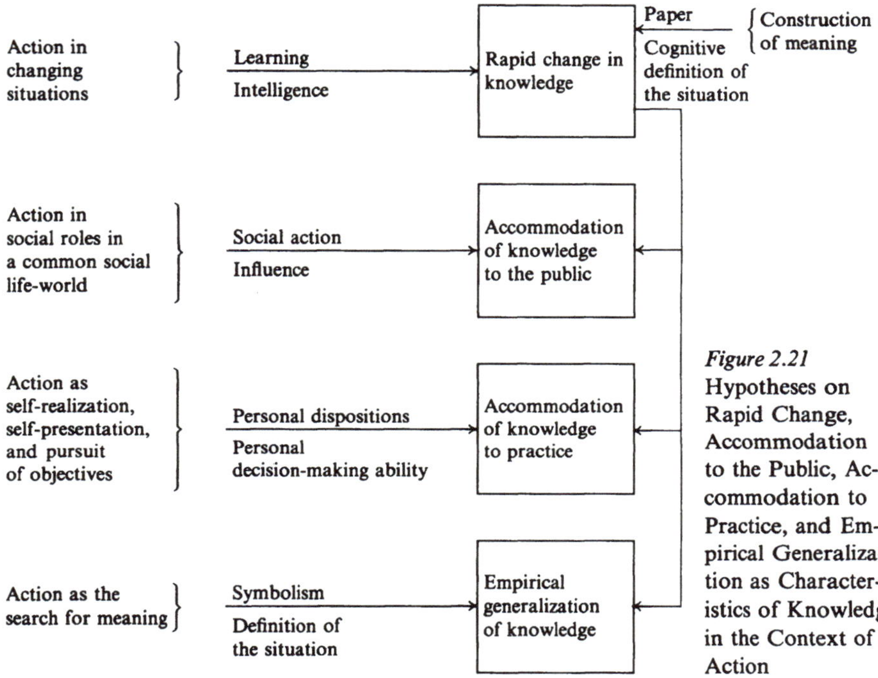

Figure 2.21
Hypotheses on Rapid Change, Accommodation to the Public, Accommodation to Practice, and Empirical Generalization as Characteristics of Knowledge in the Context of Action

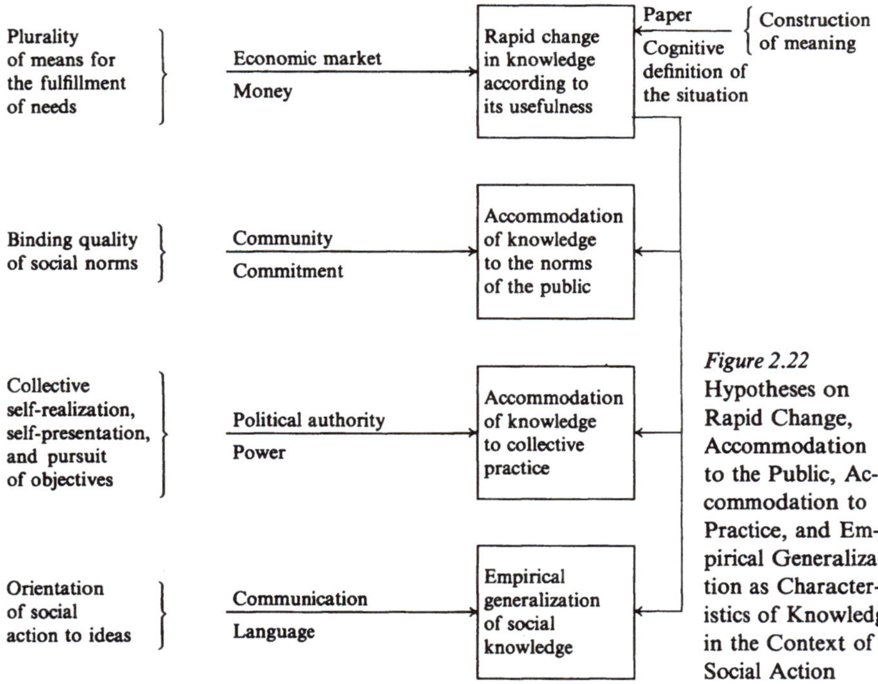

Figure 2.22
Hypotheses on Rapid Change, Accommodation to the Public, Accommodation to Practice, and Empirical Generalization as Characteristics of Knowledge in the Context of Social Action

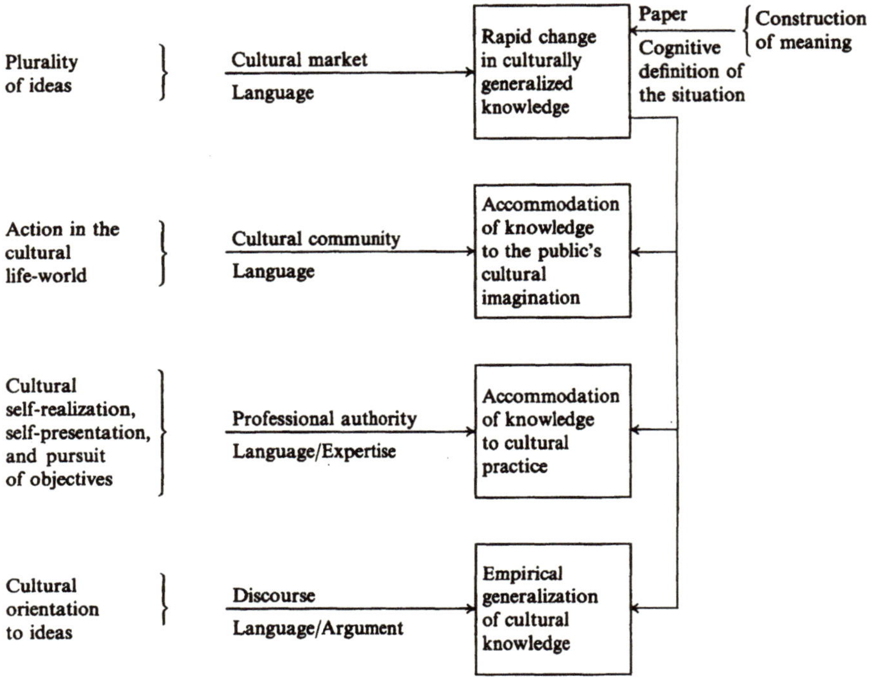

Figure 2.23 Hypotheses on Rapid Change, Accommodation to the Public, Accommodation to Practice, and Empirical Generalization as Characteristics of Knowledge in the Context of Communication

3 Symbolic, Institutional, and Social-Structural Differentiation: A Selection-Theoretical Perspective

Bernhard Giesen and Michael Schmid

3.1 Introduction

Sociological conceptions of the relationship between culture and social structure are usually based on a theoretical framework established by Marx and Durkheim. According to these conceptions, culture is analyzed as a function of social structure, as a reflection of particular social interests, or as a necessary prerequisite of societal integration. The Marxist or critical tradition considers culture to be the representation of social-structural differentiation: It is only by delusion and imposition that ideologies can provide a uniform and general interpretation of the world. In contrast to this, the Durkheimian tradition centers the integrative function of culture: It is precisely because of the diversity and multiplicity of social-structural differentiation that an embracing cultural interpretation is required to integrate different groups and to provide a common framework for interaction (cf. Barth, 1961: 66ff.; Durkheim, 1964, 1971; Parsons, 1951).

A third theoretical tradition may be separated from these mainstream perspectives on culture. This tradition imputes a dynamic peculiar to culture and assumes a particular "developmental logic" for symbolic structures. Here, the emphasis is not on the social-structural basis or on the empirical *causes* of culture, but on the symbolic or cultural *presuppositions* for social structure and social action: action is presented not as standing apart from culture but as deeply rooted in culture and impregnated with symbolic meaning. Consequently the focus is on the logic of change inherent in cultural symbolic systems (cf. Habermas, 1976).

The remarks that follow assume that these different perspectives on culture can be seen to be special applications of a general theory, which conceives *institutions* and rules of *practical action* as a mediating level between symbolic-cultural structures, on the one hand, and empirical social structures, on the other, and which emphasizes the process of *differentiation* between these levels. In particular we will argue that

1. the independent evolution of culture is rendered possible only to the extent to which the level of *symbolic meaning*, the level of *normative validity* and the level of *social structure* part company;
2. selective factors at the level of norms and *institutions* and at the level of *social structure* give way to this evolutionary process.

In order to articulate and illustrate this twofold thesis, we will distinguish basically between three views on culture (section 2); this distinction is followed by an analysis of the situational conditions for the adequacy of the three models of culture (section 3).

3.2 Three Views on Culture

3.2.1 Culture as Language and Constitution[1]

Structuralist analysis conceives of culture as a symbolic structure that is related to social action in the same way as grammar and semantics are related to speech acts. As much as language and speech act refer to each other, symbolic culture and social action, too, cannot be separated and put into mutual opposition: social action is social and meaningful only insofar as it is constructed and performed within the categorial framework of shared symbolic structures, and "meaning" and "reality" can be ascribed to a language only insofar as actions are performed. Thus culture and practical acting cannot be conceived of in a separate way and consequently cannot be viewed as opposed to each other. Both represent a unity that cannot be dissected, either with respect to symbolic structures or with respect to practical acting: Symbolic structures themselves do not as yet provide for a differentiation between language and speech acts, and the actors do not dispose of explicit knowledge about the rules they follow.

Simple speech acts refer to a tangible and present section of the world, to the situation in which they take place. Their meaning is perfectly *indexical* and the speech act itself cannot reflect the difference between itself and the world (cf. Garfinkel, 1967; Leiter, 1980; Cicourel, 1973).

In a similar way, practical actions and social relations are closely connected. Speech acts have to presuppose a propositional content, a "world" that they refer to. Likewise, social action has to presuppose a social relation between several actors, that is, a rudimentary social structure. Interaction is impossible without the actors referring to each other mutually and personally. *Ego* has to address *alter* and to be aware of third parties present in the situation. Hence action is occasioned not by a general conception of the situation or by the effects of the act on long-term and large-scale interdependencies but by a tangible vis-à-vis, a *present person*, to which a particular history of interaction can be attached. The meaning of action cannot be disclosed except by investigating the *interaction at hand* (cf. Luhmann, 1975: 21–38; Winch, 1958); obviously, it cannot be opposed to the social relations and the interaction to which it refers.

If the relationship between the culture and social structure of a whole society is shaped according to this model, the resulting pattern comes close to the reality of *primitive society* (cf. Lévi-Strauss, 1973; Service, 1962, 1966; Redfield, 1960; Radcliffe-Brown, 1952; Lenski, 1966: chapters 5–7; Lee and DeVore, 1968). Here the rules of practical actions are broadly fixed by the distinctions between different social groups, that is, by the social structure. Primitive norms are, above all, self-evident *positional rules* that are not changed intentionally and purposefully by specific institutional procedures, but unintentionally by alterations at the level of the social structure or the empirical situation. Because symbolic structure, practical action, and social structure mutually presuppose and specify each other, the analysis of culture is at the same time the analysis of social structure – and vice versa: Both simply represent different perspectives on the same object. Consequently, the meaning of symbolic utterances has to be perfectly indexical and cannot be separated from the social situation in which the utterance is made. Normative expectations are not yet effective "without respect of persons," as abstract and universal instructions, but remain closely tied to the expectations actually resulting from the social relations between the actors. These normative obligations, which are controlled by "the eye of others," cannot be questioned by appealing to higher authorities: Their self-evident claim emerges from the very reality of interaction.

3.2.2 Culture as Value-Orientation and Tradition

As soon as this self-evident connection between social relations, social expectations, and symbolic rules is dissolved, the relationship between culture and social structure is also changed (cf. Eder, 1976; Roberts, 1979; Parsons, 1951; Lenski, 1966: chapters 8–9; Fried, 1967). A tension-prone and unstable relationship between *social structure* and *normative expectation* can arise if the normative claims on validity are no longer tied to particular social groups or particular relations between individuals but cross the lines separating social groups. In this case, normative claims hold "without respect of persons" and can be extended to universal scope. They cease to be privileges or rights of particular persons but are *universal rules* applying to everybody and exhibiting a dynamic of differentiation disconnected from the differentiation of social structure. They appear as abstract rules disconnected from personal expectations and practical action and confront the acting subjects as commands from outside, from above, and from ancient times. Such normative expectations can provoke opposition and resistance on the part of those who are supposed to obey. Unlike the rules of language, they are not respected and followed in a self-evident way, but require specific efforts and regulations, sanctions, and arguments, acts of persuasion and decision as to which rules are to be valid and which are not.

This disconnecting of normative structures has to be prepared and supported by specific patterns of differentiation on the level of the *social structure*: Those who institute norms and are able to enforce their observance have to be distinguished from those who, instead of having access to the power of decision and control, are subjected to it. Thus hierarchical social structures not only *require* universal law in order to embrace the various groups and to create the unity of the total system, but also *result* from the very existence of this law (cf. Dahrendorf, 1961).

At the level of *normative structures*, claims have to be ordered hierarchically and their validity has to be grounded in universal principles: The basis and ground ensuring the general observance of norms is not the individual instituting the norm or his sanctioning power, but the universal necessity and justifiability of the norm, its consistency with other norms, and its deducibility from tradition. Rules can be justified only by deducing them from higher principles or by relating them to ancient and well-known traditions. The hierarchization of social structure corresponds to the hierarchization of normative structures, and the traditionalization of authority is in accordance with the traditional justification of norms.

This obligation to justify can be overridden by supreme principles of right conduct, values, and ideals of the "good life," which can be assumed without question or doubt because they have always been respected. In this case, culture appears as tradition and *value-orientation*, as principles and ideals, which claim validity unconditionally and without violence, and which can be proved to be in continuity and consistency with the claims of the tradition. If culture has to guarantee the unity of the normative system, then it cannot offer much space for functional differentiation at the level of symbolic structures. The perspectives of morality, truth, consolation, and aesthetics do not part company, but remain closely tied to each other. What is good is also true, beautiful, and consoling, and every attempt to regard one of these models of validation separately runs the risk of controversy and jeopardizes the precarious unity of society: Contradictory justifications of norms cannot simultaneously lay claim to validity. Because symbolic interpretations are tightly coupled to normative validity, culture appears as a "dogma" and shows a close affinity to morality (cf. Durkheim, 1964). The normative mode of validation penetrates culture, too.

In contrast to the close coupling of culture and norms, the relationship between *culture* and *social structure* reveals itself to be unstable and tension-prone (cf. Eder, 1973: 288–299). Value-orientations should be adopted without any recourse to violence but certainly cannot be chosen by individuals arbitrarily, nor can they rely on mere self-evidence. Instead, they are conceived as obligations justified by tradition and imposed on and inculcated in the acting individuals from above. Temporal continuity then guarantees the unity of society, and culture is passed on to individuals by specific acts of conviction, commitment and faith.

Particular institutions control this critical connection between culture and person[2]: Rituals of commitment and affirmation, on the one hand and on the other, elaborated procedures of socialization and education, sophisticated methods of interpreting and specifying the tradition with regard to the present actional situation. Even flagrant disobedience and disrespect shown towards moral commandments can be institutionally repaired by rituals of expiation and repentance.

Institutional methods also assume a prominent role when it comes to define the meaning of symbols (cf. Durkheim, 1969, 1971, 1973). Here, meaning is not available immediately and without presupposition by reference to the social situation at hand or to the relationship between the persons present; instead, meaning can only be determined by specific procedures and methods of coordination and mediation between symbolic structures and the world. It is only by observing the fixed methodical rules of interpretation and exegesis that meaning can be discovered and decoded. Truth is dependent on method, and the same holds for art and a morally perfect life. It is the rule that creates meaning and sense.

This uncoupling of rules from the social-structural substratum alters the modality whereby individuals participate in the realization of the morally good, the true, and the beautiful (cf. Weber, 1920: 181ff.). Not all individuals have equally access to morality, art, and knowledge. Instead, access is reserved for a few privileged positions or social groups. Knowledge is not public knowledge accessible to everyone, but secret; art is enjoyed by only very few; education is reserved for a small social group, the morally good life remains a desirable but distant goal; religious salvation is inaccessible and invisible – a secret that is disclosed only to the few and that requires complicated rituals of mediation.

3.2.3 Culture as Product and Consumption

A third model of culture emerges if particular *normative rules* are institutionalized (e.g., the institutionalization of criticism and the freedom of science) (cf. Popper, 1959; Merton, 1973: chapters 3–4), giving way to and increasing the *separation of symbolic processes from their normative substratum*. On the level of *social structure* this process of decoupling is supported by the differentiation of positions and groupings working at the production of cultural variation and change. In this case, culture no longer appears as the symbolic structures *presupposed* by any action or as an obligatory point of *reference* for stabilizing rules, rights, and norms, but as the everchanging *result* of the social production of culture[3].

If it is not only the case that the production of culture is controlled by institutionally and socially separated groupings and subsystems, but that the adoption and consumption of cultural interpretations is differentiated along these lines of social structure, although these culturally different groupings can interact and communicate effortlessly with each other – then culture has lost not only its "self-evidential" character but also its absolute validity. Instead, the validity of cultural interpretations has become temporally variable and socially differentiated: Several cultures, subcultures, or world views can *simultaneously* be implanted in various institutions or groupings of one society without creating any risk for the integration of the society; in addition to this social differentiation, which in principle is able to provide for stable orientations in a pluralistic and decentered society, the traditional continuity of cultural world views is gradually replaced by a fast turnover of theories, themes, and styles. Modern culture offers orientation only at the moment when it is new, and loses its fascination and power of interpretation as soon as it is considered oldfashioned, as soon as a new theme, a new idea, and a new orientation enter the stage to take its place (cf. Giesen, 1989).

Even more than in other areas of modern society, modern culture is determined by a tendency toward the dynamization and temporalization of structures (cf. Giesen, 1989; Lepenies, 1982: 285–300; Kosellek, 1978: 264–269). In its beginnings this fundamental process represented the secularization of eschatological conceptions transformed into the idea of progress, which gradually took control of all realms of social action (cf. Löwith, 1961). No longer is the paradigm of modern science the repeated exegesis of canonical texts with regard to a changing world; instead, the core of science is represented by the dynamic of theoretical development fostered and reinforced by the institutionalization of criticism and the premium set on discovery. The focus of modern art is not on following classical forms and motifs but on revealing the invisible, unusual, unknown, and even weird; artistic achievement resides in the contrasts between new and established ways of seeing and listening, whereas the repetition of classical patterns, however perfect, is disregarded as "academic" or even as mere "industrial art" (cf. Berendt, 1959: 228; Jost, 1982; Becker, 1963: chapter 6). At the level of fashion and "popular culture" the rapid turnover of styles and images has acquired a proverbial character: The need for differences that cannot be satisfied any longer by social privilege or economic advantage switches over to the temporal difference between the avant-garde and the old fashioned and conventional. To the extent that modern religion has not degenerated to a mere business of consolation and meditation, it can demarcate the realm of the sacred and the realm of the demonic only by continuously changing its definitions of impending catastrophes and promises of coming happiness and fulfillment. (Criticism of modernity deals with its rapid flux of symbolic interpretations under such headings as "erosion of cultural traditions," "cultural alienation," or "increasing demand on cultural interpretations" [cf. Spengler, 1963; Beck, 1986]). If culture is considered as a product and as mass communication, it has not only to open itself to temporal variation and social differentiation but also to protect the new arenas of discourse against alien controls: Arts, science, and religion are autonomous, and their arguments are only bound by criteria defined from within (cf. Simmel, 1912, 1923, 1984: 94–99). The relations between institutions or between symbolic structures are not patterned hierarchically but are defined by the distinction between different references and purposes. Differentiation by hierarchy or stratification is replaced by a functional differentiation providing for the underlying logic of cultural structures.

Obviously, *functional differentiation* can develop on the level of *social structure* even in primitive forms of association. Under the heading of the "division of labor" it refers to various activities of *acting individuals*[4]. However, functional differentiation as a *differentiation of norms* referring not to persons but to actions or spheres of action has to be distinguished from simple division of labor (cf. Parsons and Smelser, 1956). In this case, one sphere of action can, for instance, be controlled by economic norms, another by norms of solidarity, and a third by norms of scientific methods. If the unity and effectiveness of normative obligation is not to be endangered, two incompatible or even contradictory norms cannot be allowed to seek validity simultaneously and equally for a given action. This restriction disappears, however, if we refer by differentiation to the internal differentiation of symbolic culture[5]. Here functional differentiation presupposes that one fact or one social process can be considered from several points of view at the same time; functional references can be varied, and there is no prior arrangement as to whether a certain action has to be regarded solely by reference to the economic criteria of scarce resources, to the political criteria of binding collective decisions, or to the social criteria of solidarity and communal association. Within modern society culture makes it possible to have aesthetic views on technology, scientific perspectives on politics, and economic considerations about science, without thereby provoking critical consequences for technology, politics, and science. Such variation of possible references and meanings cannot be permitted on the level of normative validity with regard to *one* particular action at the *same* time: It cannot take place until the meaning of symbolic structures is released from its bonds to particular institutional procedures or social groupings.

By decoupling symbolic structures, on the one hand, and institutional and social structures, on the other, spatially, temporally, and socially distant facts can be put into often surprising relationships to each other, and the concrete manifolds of things can be reduced to comparable numbers. At the same time, moral, scientific, religious, and aesthetic questions can be separated and dealt with in ways appropriate to them. The unity of tradition and value-orientation is replaced by a plurality of perspectives and rationalities that are so distinct that they cannot contradict each other (cf. Simmel, 1922: 79–86). Thus functional differentiation of culture is closely connected to the differentiation between the level of symbolic meaning, the level of normative validity, and the level of social structure and group membership.

However, culture as a product is defined not only by functional differentiation and an increase in the speed of change but also by reference to the *social process of producing* culture (cf. Enzensberger, 1962; Benjamin, 1963: 7–43). The traditional conception of culture as a value-orientation had to conceal the social genesis of culture and the special interests implied in order to ensure that culture would constitute an embracing tradition and a universal value-orientation. In contrast to this, the modern view of culture can expose without risk the social bounds and genesis of symbolic-cultural structures. Modern culture differentiates between genesis and validity, between the production and the "consumption" of symbolic structures[6]. Social movements produce new cultural projects, scientists propose new theories, art directors create new mises-en-scène and feuilletonists write new essays about the present state of the world not because they want to translate morality into reality but because of quite profane interests, and nobody should reasonably blame them for doing so.

In modern contexts, culture is the product of a particular "industry."

Whether new ideas, theories, movie productions, or diagnoses of our time reach their audience and prevail in modern culture or not is decided not by the particular motives and interests of their producers but by the selective impact of competing symbolic structures and of the situation to which they refer.

This relationship of a theory to competing theories, of new orientations to old ideas, of aesthetic innovations to established styles determines and defines the meaning and importance of a symbolic element within the modern cultural system. Disconnecting symbolic-cultural processes from the level of institutions and norms in operation also bears consequences for the meaning of symbolic utterances. Meaning no longer emerges out of the self-evident and indisputable relationship between signs and things, nor does it result from the attempt to relate symbols and the facts of the world by presupposing fixed rules or methods of coordination; instead, *meaning refers to the relationship symbolic structures have with each other*[7]. The world that symbolic structures refer to is no longer to be considered as materially "at hand" or as definable by reliance on methodical procedures but as being itself *symbolically constituted* (cf. O'Malley, n.d.: 110–187). The evolution of symbolic structures thereby acquires a particular autonomy in the face of normative-institutional structures and of the social-structural basis. Given this autonomy, symbolic structures are able to undergo change more rapidly than a close coupling to the comparatively slow pace of legal norms or communal membership would allow. Those remain stable even if the turnover of symbolic structures can accelerate in a frightening way: Theaters incessantly present new plays, research institutes continue to produce new hypotheses, and television channels offer new shows, although the staff and the normative structure of the organizations remain the same.

3.3 Institutions and Social Structure

3.3.1 Selectice Factors for the Reproduction of Modes of Culture

Whether culture is dealt with as language, as morality, or as product depends not, or at least not primarily, on the theoretical perspective chosen but on specific situational conditions that are appropriate for a particular conception of culture, thus selectively fostering its adaptation. Traditional sociological evolutionism refers to these situational conditions mainly by means of developmental models of evolutionary stages (cf. Smith, 1973; Schmid, 1982; Boudon, 1986). Thus culture as value-orientation, for example, can be classified as a typical phenomenon of traditional societies, whereas culture as product can be seen as characteristic of modern societies. Such developmental classifications cannot be regarded as more than a first step. They remain inaccurate and schematic and cannot account for the fact that even in modern societies there are obviously situations where culture manifests itself as language or as value-orientation. Therefore a selectionist theory of evolution has to aim at investigating those general empirical conditions that foster, reproduce, and preserve specific forms and patterns of culture. Although the selective conditions for the reproduction of a particular model of culture are certainly manifold and complex, three ideal types of these situational conditions may be distinguished in order to approximate *roughly* the contingencies and manifolds of social reality: everyday action; organization; and the public.

3.3.2 Everyday Action: Life-World and Community

By "everyday" is meant situations of nonreflexive interaction between present individuals. Each of these individuals meets and addresses the others present by assuming reciprocity and authenticity; the exchangeability of perspectives and the equal disposition of knowledge about relevant action is presupposed even if the individuals actually differ with regard to age, gender, and biography as well as to social esteem and individual capacities (cf. Douglas, 1971; Berger and Luckmann, 1969; Goffman, 1969; Schütz and Luckmann, 1975).

In this respect everyday interaction requires a contrafactual presupposition of social equality: The contingent and natural differences between the actors are not regarded as relevant for the social level and are not reflected in an inequality of social positions[8].

Because individuals can participate in everyday interaction only if they are present in a locality and because this local presence is the most elementary line of demarcation, the social structure and the rules of practical action are also guided primarily by the inside-outside difference between the local community of present actors and the excluded nonpresent ones. Differences of social structure that cannot be accounted for by this criterion of locality and that differentiate *socially* between the individuals present are barely noticeable: Distinctions that cannot be overlooked are regarded as individual or natural – in any case, unalterable by everyday interaction. If this pattern of social structure is generalized, the resulting entity may be termed "the social community;" and if the corresponding rules of practical action are generalized they appear as norms of solidarity (cf. Münch, 1982). Communality and the expectation of solidarity apply without any social differentiation to all members of the community. This, too, points to the lack of an autonomous internal differentiation of social structure and norms in situations of everyday action or communality. Norms do not yet confront the actors as external expectations distinct from personal expectations. Distinctions between the actors are mainly differences between individuals rather than between social positions, which can be separated from the incumbents of these positions.

However important the "*spatial*" difference between inside and outside may be, however vague the contours of an autonomous *social* differentiation, a temporal differentiation of social interaction is not in question: We cannot speak altogether at the same time. Therefore rules of turn taking are of prime importance for the organization of everyday interaction (cf. Goffman, 1969; Sachs, Schegloff, and Jefferson, 1974: 696–735).

In a situational setting with no (or only incidental) social differentiation (speaker-audience), the symbolic culture fulfills a constitutive function for the process of interaction: Interaction can occur only if all individuals present partake of this culture equally and in a similar way. In addition, the competent use of symbols serves as a means of demarcation: Access to everyday interaction is gained not by simply adopting a symbolic system but by the gradual acquisition of praxis, by participating in interaction, by understanding the history of interaction, by the use of language. Only from the observers external point of view can the life-world of everyday interaction be analyzed as language on the one hand and as group or interaction process on the other. From the actor's point of view, language, cultural symbolism, and practical action appear as a unity difficult to dissect. Although the actors can apply the rules perfectly, they are usually unable to identify these rules.

From the point of view of everyday interaction we can hardly conceive of passing the borderline between one life-world and another or even of escaping the bonds of the life-world: Only horizons can be thought of, not borderlines; taking simultaneously several perspectives on the world seems to be impossible.

This absence of differentiation between the performance, practical rules, and symbolic interpretation of action, in other words, between community, norms and culture, does allow culture to be conceived solely as "language," as a self-evident presupposition that cannot be opposed to the praxis of action itself. The model of value-orientation assumes the existence of various social groups that are simultaneously committed to the same norms. However, it is this very difference between social-structural groups on the one hand and the obligation to the same norms on the other that is absent in everday interaction and social communities.

3.3.3 Organization: Social Inequality and Social Control

Action in organizational contexts differs from everyday action or community-type interaction in focusing on: (1) the distinction between social positions or social groups; and (2) the distinction between norms and social positions (cf. Blau, 1977; Aldrich, 1979; Pfeffer, 1981, 1982; Lenski, 1966; Luhmann, 1964).

Organizations enable social interaction to reach across the lines between communities and continue social relations in contrast to the transitoriness of everyday interaction. Of central importance for this social and temporal expansion of interaction is the emergence of a normative structure, which can be conceived of independently from the acting individuals concerned. The social scope of interaction is expanded if several communities and life-worlds are combined by and integrated into organizations, thus enabling interaction across the limiting horizons of life-worlds: The king enacts laws that have validity for the life-world of the peasantry, and the tributes exacted from the peasantry may limit the glamour of the royal court.

Most frequently this organizational integration of several communities exhibits a vertical pattern: Social-structural differentiation and inequality combine and unite communities of peers. In this case affiliation to a particular group ceases to be related to individual achievement but is based on birth, privilege, or other criteria that cannot be controlled by organizational interaction. Consequently, the inequality of social positions that is given at the beginning of a situation, and which cannot be altered within this situation, is fundamental to the situation of organizational interaction. This positional inequality of wealth and authority, power and prestige presupposed by organizational interaction results from decoupling the normative level from the level of practical action and individuals. The preexistence of inequality at the level of social structure has its equivalent at the level of norms: Norms cease to be mere practical regularities and situational expectations contingent on the process of interaction. Instead, they are fixed rules and instructions that exist prior to the particular situation; they claim validity independently from the expectations and approval of the actors concerned; they refer not to individuals but to social positions; and they are controlled by third parties (cf. Weber, 1985: 124–130, 387–513). These norms, disconnected from practical interaction and the consent of the actors, may be called "laws." As soon as the situation is legalized in this sense, procedures guaranteeing and enforcing the laws are required, and these procedures must be independent from the consent of the individuals to whom they apply.

Law can be guaranteed through sanctions by third parties (i.e., by special agencies of social control) or by deducing the law from universal value-orientations (i.e., from culture). This second way of guaranteeing legal norms also presupposes specialization and differentiation at the level of social structure. Interpreting value-orientation with respect to legal norm, deducing right conduct, and systematizing the law are regarded as the task of religious and legal specialists. Without this group of absent "third" individuals, the "legalization" of interaction and the evolution of culture as value-orientation are not possible.

The *temporal* scope of action is expanded by organization because the fleeting dynamic of direct interaction no longer limits the stability of social structures: Membership and not presence links individuals to organizations (cf. Luhmann, 1964). This membership is enacted and revoked by rule of law and refers to social positions instead of individual persons. Even the exchangeability of individuals and the succession of situations do not necessarily affect the positional structure of organizations and the legal norms of membership. Thus the organizational integration of various communities and life-worlds and the sanctioning control by third parties expand the scope of action beyond the temporal limits of interaction between present actors. Various successive or temporally unconnected situations are connected by a continuous normative structure.

If normative expectations and cultural value-orientations are recorded in writing, a tradition may arise embracing and incorporating the variety of stories of interaction recalled and narrated. This elimination of temporal differentiation is compensated for by the social differentiation of positions, and the "local" demarcation of presence is replaced by the social demarcation of membership rules.

In contrast to the horizons of life-worlds, these social borderlines can be crossed by individuals; they can choose to enter and leave organizations, or can be forced to do so. All encompassing organizations such as states or churches, however, usually do not provide for this opportunity of entering and leaving. Here, membership is most frequently permanent and not at the will of the members.

In these coercive organizations the tension between legal instruction and practical action, between integrative norms and differentiated social structure is increased to a critical degree: The problems of legitimation and of justification arise (cf. Habermas, 1973). If the problem of coping with this tension is not to be solved solely by sanctions, then, indeed, common value-orientations are required in order to justify law and to unify and integrate the organization by orientation toward ultimate common ends. Thus cultural value-orientations fulfill a central function in justifying organizational order. Culture as language, i.e. as the self-evident structure of a life-world, can by definition not contrast to this life-world and neither justify nor enforce the normative claims on practical action. Culture as changing social products cannot give additional stability to normative structures but will result in a dynamization of legal structures instead of stabilizing them. Furthermore the model of interests generating culture hampers the claim on absolute validity implied in the cultural value-orientations of organizations. Thus situations of interaction in organizations with permanent and nonvoluntary membership need the justifying potential of common value-orientations, if they do not want to make increasing use of coercion and force as integrating mechanisms.

However, the members cannot be allowed to dispose arbitrarily of value-orientations, if the unity, absoluteness, and obligation of these orientations are not to be jeopardized. In this case, a tight coupling of normative and symbolic structures turns out to be selectively superior. Culture adopts the face of the ecclesiastical dogma closely connected to legal structures and ensuring the unity in front of the worldly multifariousness of practical action (cf. Flasch, 1987: 129–131, 145). The tension between dogma and action is fundamental to this situation and can only be suspended in a timeless future (when any action has come to its end). Therefore, institutions for bridging this gap, like punishment and repentition or socialization and education, become extraordinary momentous for organizations.

3.3.4 Public Situations: Inclusion and Mass Communication

Situations with a predetermined structure of social differentiation and enforced membership differ from public situations as follows: (1) vertical social inequality between different groups, collectivities of social positions recedes in favor of the assumption of social equality and individual inequality; (2) participation in public interaction is organized on a voluntary basis and is open to everybody; (3) the differentiation and variation of symbolic contents are advanced and intensified by institutions and social structure (cf. Giesen, 1987:

171–194; Luhmann, 1986; Habermas, 1971; Parsons, 1980; Hauser, 1967: 574–575, 862–863).

Public interactive processes such as political debates, art exhibitions, television broadcasts or scientific discussions are basically distinguished by the fact that nobody is entitled on grounds of privilege, class membership, power or social status to receive more attention or consideration than any other individual. All participants in public interaction have a priori the same rights of access, and it is only by corresponding achievements during this interaction itself that they might win more attention than others. In this context any resulting inequality is justified by reference to the qualities of the achievement itself and not on the status and the power of its originator. That is to say: In scientific discussions, justifications are based on arguments, not on reference to the respect enjoyed by those engaged in these debates; television programs and newspapers are judged on the basis of their journalistic qualities and by the interests of the audience and not by reference to the preferences of editors and program directors; art peformances and film-productions are judged on the basis of standards of artistic or cineastic merit and not by reference to the reputations of artists and directors[9]. Even if the expectation that everybody has equal access to public interaction is often fulfilled only imperfectly, it is nevertheless regarded as a constitutive prerequisite of public interaction: Everybody is entitled to take the floor, everybody has an equal chance to be listened to. But such performances are risky, for the approval of the public is a quite uncertain factor. Free access and equal chances are balanced by the fact that during public interaction a social differentiation results according to success, i.e. audience numbers and level or response, frequency of publication and citations, etc. But this kind of inequality, which is not a prerequisite of public interactions but their *result*, is not allowed to be petrified, fixed, or socially transferred in order to avoid damaging the assumption of equality in public interaction. Thus, inequality is not so much related to social positions as to individual persons, or, more precisely, to the results of their actions. Film directors are judged by their films, scientists by their theories, television journalists by their broadcasts, and each new presentation is judged afresh. Thus, although public interaction constantly produces inequality, it at the same time prevents its social and temporal *stabilization*. In this context, differentiation does not mean unchangeable and life-long class membership, but momentary individual differences in respect of some specific performance that may vary from day to day. Hence public situations presuppose a social structure that allows for an individualization and temporalization of vertical inequalities.

But the assumption of an equal opportunity for access to public interaction applies not only to the *producers* of culture but also to the *consumers* of culture. Television and film, scientific education, and even art are no longer an esoteric pleasure of privileged groups but publicly accessible for all. The consumption of culture is no longer regulated by standards of exclusivity but by the idea that more and more people should be incorporated into the public. Like market exchange, public interaction depends on inclusion, growth, and expansion. As soon as this inclusion is visibly limited, as soon as there is no further prospect that the number of participants can be enlarged, the basis of public interaction becomes jeopardized. In this regard, public interaction evidently differs from everyday interaction, which, while sharing the idea of equality, also stresses a principle of exclusion.

In contrast to other types or situations, public interaction presupposes a differentiation between producers and consumers. It is true that in organizations we already find a preliminary differentiation of cultural specialists. In public situations, however, this differentiation gains incomparably in significance: In public situations the public decides whether a cultural product gets recognition, dissemination, and applause. Public interaction is not only based on equality and on requirements of inclusion but also on a continual confrontation between performances and audience.

Such a situation allows for two ways of growth and intensification: Either the supply of new cultural products is constantly enlarged, thus continuously giving rise to new decisions, or more and more social groups may be included into the public and thus confronted with new decisions. Both lines of development, intensification of cultural variation and change and enlargement of the public, are constitutive of public situations.

But, in consequence of this development, a set of new problems arises on the institutional, normative level. If public situations require an intensification of variation, change, and differentiation, then a similar development in the field of norms and rights should be expected only to a very restricted extent. For the special functions of rights and norms can be applied only if these stabilize social expectations socially and temporally by uncoupling them from changing situations of interaction (cf. Ullman-Margalit, 1977). Moreover, these stabilizing functions of normative-institutional structures acquire increasing importance as social-structural differentiations are dissolved, temporalized, and individualized. In addition, one has to take into consideration the comparatively slow tempo of variation and reproduction in social structure and institutions: A change of group membership, the passage from one form of status to another, or the institutionalization of a new rule of conduct take much more effort and time than inventing a new argument, redefining a field of problems, or reinterpreting a work of art. The extent of variation that public interactions are in need of is thus most easily satisfied on the level of symbolization. But this in turn presupposes that the level of symbolic meanings is uncoupled from any problem of normative validity, which means that rules of tolerance and liberality are firmly institutionalized (cf. Hauser, 1967: 714–717). In this case, the differentiation and variation of culture can take place on a fixed and permanent institutional foundation that allows for symbolic innovation and at the same time provides for the stable orientation of actions. And this is exactly what happens in modern culture: The institutional premium is on new ideas, new perspectives, new definitions of catastrophe, new promises of salvation. Attention and consideration are not given to the glance backward at continuity-preserving traditions or to the contemplation of unifying dogmas, but to the hectic production of cultural goods. In the course of this development, vertical social differentiation of the access to culture and tradition is replaced by temporal differentiation between fashionable and obsolete cultural products; but no longer can this kind of differentiation be reflected as a social-structural difference between avant-garde and mass or between center and periphery, for the production of cultural goods has now accelerated to such an extent that it can no longer be used as a strategy for stabilizing one's social status.

But this kind of institutionalization of symbolic-cultural change can avoid a loss of its efficiency (which in public situations means its public) only if two further conditions are fulfilled: (1) It must be possible quickly to present new symbolic interpretations to a public that is usually only mediately present; (2) the public must have at its disposal common and universal standards of evaluation that may serve to help it reach decisions immediately and without undue communicative efforts on cultural matters or that, at least, can shorten these decision-making processes. The first condition is met by most of the technical media of mass communication. The second condition aims at the institutionalization of interaction-media, which, analogous to money in a market-exchange system, facilitate and accelerate public communication. This process has been promoted by the institutionalization of functionally specialized standards of evaluation: judgments in modern art are not based on the idea of descriptive truth, moral validity, or existential consolation; the standards of evaluation is exclusively an aesthetic one. Any interference by moral or descriptive criteria is rejected. In modern science, instead, the validity of aesthetic or literary standards of evaluation has given way to the exclusive methodological criteria of truth[44], etc. (cf. Popper, 1959).

If the institutionalization of such standards proves to be possible in different fields of public interaction, they may help to reduce that multitude of perspectives and meanings originally introduced by functional differentiation within the symbolic domain. Thus it remains true that scientific theories may be regarded and judged from a moral, an aesthetical, or a consolational perspective; but within the everyday business of science, however, rewards usually are distributed in relation to descriptive-empirical achievements. Nobody, therefore, will object if material goods are judged on the basis of moral or aesthetic standards; but in the marketplace the decisive factor is their price in relation to costs.

At the same time, a successful institutionalization of functionally specialized standards allows for a coordination and coorientation of producers and consumers of culture, even if these never come into personal contact and even without external sanctions. As these standards are apt to abbreviate the process or evaluation, its results may help producers of cultural goods to improve or withdraw their production.

But the institutionalization of such functionally specialized standards has not succeeded in an equal degree in all kinds of public situations; and even if it does prove to be possible, there is no hope that such standards might be constructed in strict analogy to the economic medium of money (cf. Giesen, 1987: 183–194). Public situations should not be identified with markets in any technical sense of this concept, and symbolic interpretations do not allow for disposition and circulation such as material goods and property rights might do. Their value does not increase in relation to their scarcity but by a converse principle according to their propagation: The more individuals there are who accept a symbolic interpretation, the higher is its importance, status, and worth. The logic of public interaction is not determined by social relations based on scarcity and exchange, but by such temporal relations as innovation, actuality, and change of theme.

But, even if the market model is not adapted to the peculiarities of symbolic interpretations, both markets and public situations depend on a strong separation of two different social positions: (1) those who offer goods and those who demand (or decline) them and (2) producers of culture and the public. That is, in both cases we have producers and consumers. And this implies that culture can no longer be regarded as language or as value-orientation. It is true that public interaction cannot dispense with language and takes place under the shelter of certain universal value-orientation, but the relations between the acting individuals and culture is quite different from those obtaining with culture as value-orientation and culture as language. Culture is no longer the prerequisite or guideline for action but an "object" or theme; it is no longer a stable point of reference for social order but consciously produced variation and change.

The initially described differentiation between symbolic, normative, and social structure is impressively accelerated and selected by public situations that, in turn, greatly influence the process of social-structural evolution. To the degree that symbolic interpretations, normative validity, and social structure are separated from each other, there is a disjunction between the mechanisms of variation, of selection, and of reproduction: The evolution of evolution enters a new stage.

Notes

1 For this model cf. Charon (1979), Blumer (1969), Garfinkel (1967), Gebauer (1981), Giddens (1984), Hampshire (1969), Searle (1969), Shibutani (1986), and Winch (1958).

2 For the pervasive influence of rituals in modern societies cf. Douglas (1973) and Turner (1969).

3 This culture becomes an industry (cf. Benjamin, 1963; Adorno, 1981: 141–191).

4 In this sense the concept is originally used by Adam Smith (1789: chapters 1–3) and Schmoller (1890: 45–105).

5 This is the central thesis of the functionalist theory of modernization.

6 For the cognitive sphere, cf. Reichenbach (1968: 260–261).

7 This seems to be the focal point of Feyerabend's and Kuhn's criticism of empiricism.

8 Habermas stresses this presupposition (1981, vol. 2).

9 As to scientific debates cf. Ben-David (1971) and Merton (1973: 254–278).

References

Adorno, T. W. (1981). "Kulturindustrie-Aufklärung als Massenbetrug." In *Gesammelte Schriften*, Vol. 3, 2nd ed. Frankfurt: Suhrkamp, pp. 141–191.

Aldrich, H. A. (1979) *Organizations and Environments*. Englewood Cliffs, N.J.: Prentice-Hall.

Barth, H. (1961). *Wahrheit und Ideologie*, 2nd ed. Erlenbach/Zürich/Stuttgart: Rentsch.

Beck, U. (1986). *Risikogesellschaft. Auf dem Weg in eine andere Moderne*. Frankfurt: Suhrkamp.

Becker, H. S. (1963). *Outsiders. Studies in the Sociology of Deviance*. New York: The Free Press.

Ben-David, J. (1971). *The Scientists Role in Society*. Englewood Cliffs, N.J.: Prentice-Hall.

Benjamin, W. (1963). *Das Kunstwerk im Zeitalter seiner technischen Reproduzierbarkeit*. Frankfurt: Suhrkamp.

Berendt, J. E. (1959). *Das neue Jazzbuch*. Frankfurt: Fischer.

Berger, P. and Luckmann, T. (1969). *Die gesellschaftliche Konstruktion der Wirklichkeit*. Frankfurt: Fischer.

Blau, P. M. (1977). *Heterogeneity and Inequality. A Primitive Theory of Social Structure*. New York/London: The Free Press.

Blumer, H. (1969). *Symbolic Interactionism. Perspective and Methods*. Englewood Cliffs, N.J.: Prentice-Hall.

Boudon, R. (1986). *Theories of Social Change. A Critical Appraisal*. Cambridge/Oxford: Polity Press.

Charon, J. M. (1979). *Symbolic Interactionism*. Englewood Cliffs, N.J.: Prentice-Hall.

Cicourel, A. V. (1973). *Cognitive Sociology. Language and Meaning in Social Interaction*. Harmondsworth: Penguin Books.

Dahrendorf, R. (1961). *Über den Ursprung der Ungleichheit unter den Menschen*. Tübingen: Mohr Siebeck.

Douglas, J. D. (Ed.) (1971). *Understanding Everyday Life. Towards the Reconstruction of Sociological Knowledge*. London: Routledge & Kegan Paul.

Douglas, M. (1973). *Natural Symbols*. London: Routledge & Kegan Paul.

Durkheim, E. (1964). *The Division of Labor in Society*. New York: The Free Press.

Durkheim, E. (1969). *L'évolution pédagogique en France*, 2nd ed. Paris: Press Universitaire de France.

Durkheim, E. (1971). *The Elementary Forms of Religious Life*, 7th ed. New York: The Free Press.

Durkheim, E. (1973). *Moral Education*. New York: The Free Press.

Eder, K. (1973). "Die Reorganisation der Legitimationsformen in Klassengesellschaften." In *Seminar: Entstehung von Klassengesellschaften*, ed. K. Eder. Frankfurt: Suhrkamp, pp. 288–299.

Eder, K. (1976). *Die Entstehung staatlich organisierter Gesellschaften*. Frankfurt: Suhrkamp.

Enzensberger, H. M. (1962). *Einzelheiten. Bd. 1. Bewußtseinsindustrie*, 7th ed. Frankfurt: Suhrkamp.

Flasch, K. (1987). *Das philosophische Denken im Mittelalter. Von Augustinus zu Machiavelli*. Stuttgart: Reclam.

Fried, M. H. (1967). *The Evolution of Political Society*. New York: Random House.
Garfinkel, H. (1967). *Studies in Ethnomethodology*. Englewood Cliffs, N. J./New York: Prentice-Hall.
Gebauer, G. (1981). *Der Einzelne und sein gesellschaftliches Wissen*. Berlin/New York: de Gruyter.
Giddens, A. (1984). *The Constitution of Society*. Cambridge/Oxford: Polity Press.
Giesen, B. (1987). "Media and Markets." In *Evolutionary Theory in Social Science*, ed. M. Schmid and F. M. Wuketits. Dordrecht/Boston/Lancaster/Tokyo: D. Reidel, pp. 171–194.
Giesen, B. (1989). "The Change of Change." In *Social Change and Modernity*, ed. H. Haferkamp and N. J. Smelser. Berkeley: University of California Press.
Goffman, E. (1969). *Wir alle spielen Theater. Die Selbstdarstellung im Alltag*. München: Piper.
Goffman, E. (1969). *Behavior in Public Places. Notes on the Social Organizations of Gatherings*, 4th ed. New York: The Free Press.
Habermas, J. (1971). *Strukturwandel der Öffentlichkeit*, 5th ed. Neuwied/Berlin: Luchterhand.
Habermas, J. (1973). *Legitimationsprobleme im Spätkapitalismus*. Frankfurt: Suhrkamp.
Habermas, J. (1976). *Zur Rekonstruktion des Historischen Materialismus*. Frankfurt: Suhrkamp.
Habermas, J. (1981). *Theorie des kommunikativen Handelns*, 2 vols. Frankfurt: Suhrkamp.
Hampshire, S. (1969). *Thought and Action*. London: Chatto and Windus.
Hauser, A. (1967). *Sozialgeschichte der Kunst und Literatur*. München: Beck.
Jost, E. (1982). *Sozialgeschichte des Jazz in den USA*. Frankfurt: Fischer.
Kosellek, R. (1978). "Neuzeit. Zur Semantik moderner Bewegungsbegriffe." In *Studien zum Beginn der modernen Welt*, ed. R. Kosellek. Stuttgart: Klett-Cotta, pp. 264–299.
Lee, R. B. and DeVore, J. (Eds.) (1968). *Man the Hunter*. Chicago: Aldine Publishing Company.
Leiter, K. (1980). *A Primer on Ethnomethodology*. New York/Oxford: Oxford University Press.
Lenski, G. (1966). *Power and Privilege. A Theory of Social Stratification*. New York: Macmillan.
Lepenies, W. (1982). "Die Dynamisierung des Naturbegriffs an der Wende zur Neuzeit." In *Das Naturbild des Menschen*, ed. J. Zimmermann. München: Fink, pp. 285–300.
Lévi-Strauss, C. (1973). *Anthropologie structurale*. Paris: Plon.
Löwith, K. (1961). *Weltgeschichte als Heilsgeschehen*. Stuttgart: Kohlhammer.
Luhmann, N. (1964). *Funktion und Folgen formaler Organisation*. Berlin: Duncker & Humblot.
Luhmann, N. (1975). *Soziologische Aufklärung 2*. Opladen: Westdeutscher Verlag.
Luhmann, N. (1986). *Ökologische Kommunikation*. Opladen: Westdeutscher Verlag.
Merton, R. K. (1973). *The Sociology of Science. Theoretical and Empirical Investigations*. Chicago/London: The Free Press.
Münch, R. (1982). *Theorie des Handelns. Zur Rekonstruktion der Beiträge von Talcott Parsons, Emile Durkheim und Max Weber*. Frankfurt: Suhrkamp.
O'Malley, J. B. (n. d.). *Sociology of Meaning*. London: Human Context Books.

Parsons, T. (1951). *The Social System*. Glencoe, Ill.: The Free Press.
Parsons, T. (1980). *Zur Theorie der sozialen Interaktionsmedien*. Opladen: Westdeutscher Verlag.
Parsons, T. and Smelser, N. J. (1956). *Economy and Society*. London: Routledge & Kegan Paul.
Pfeffer, J. (1981). *Power in Organization*. Marshfield: Pitman.
Pfeffer, J. (1982). *Organization and Organization Theory*. Boston: Pitman.
Popper, K. R. (1959). *The Logic of Scientific Discovery*. New York: Basic Books.
Radcliffe-Brown, A. R. (1952). *Structure and Function in Primitive Society*. London: Routledge & Kegan Paul.
Redfield, R. (1960). *The Little Community. Peasant Society and Culture*. Chicago/London: University of Chicago Press.
Reichenbach, H. (1968). *Der Aufstieg der wissenschaftlichen Philosophie*, 3rd ed. Braunschweig: Viehweg.
Roberts, S. (1979). *Order and Dispute. An Introduction to Legal Anthropology*. Harmondsworth: Penguin Books.
Sachs, H., Schegloff, E. A., and Jefferson, G. (1974). "A Simplest Systematics for the Organization of Turn-Taking for Conversation." *Language* 50: 696–735.
Schmid, M. (1982). *Theorie sozialen Wandels*. Opladen: Westdeutscher Verlag.
Schmoller, G. (1890). "Das Wesen der Arbeitsteilung und der sozialen Klassenbildung." *Jahrbuch für Gesetzgebung, Verwaltung und Volkswirtschaft im Deutschen Reich* 14: 45–105.
Schütz, A. and Luckmann, T. (1975). *Strukturen der Lebenswelt*. Neuwied/Darmstadt: Luchterhand.
Searle, J. R. (1969). *Speech Acts*. Cambridge: Cambridge University Press.
Service, E. R. (1962). *Primitive Social Organization*. New York: Random House.
Service, E. R. (1966). *The Hunters*. Englewood Cliffs, N. J.: Prentice-Hall.
Service, E. R. (1975). *Origins of State and Civilization. The Process of Cultural Evolution*. New York: Norton & Company.
Shibutani, T. (1986). *Social Processes*. Berkeley/Los Angeles/London: University of California Press.
Simmel, G. (1912). *Die Religion*, 2nd ed. Frankfurt: Rütten und Loening.
Simmel, G. (1922). *Zur Philosophie der Kunst*. Potsdam: Kiepenheuer.
Simmel, G. (1923). *Philosophische Kultur*, 2nd ed. Potsdam: Kiepenheuer.
Simmel, G. (1984). *Das Individuum und die Freiheit*. Berlin: Wagenbach.
Smith, A. (1789). *Inquiry Into the Nature and Causes of the Wealth of Nations*, 5th ed. London: Strahan & Cadell.
Smith, A. (1973). *The Concept of Social Change. A Critique of the Functionalist Theory of Social Change*. London/Boston: Routledge & Kegan Paul.
Spengler, O. (1963). *Der Untergang des Abendlandes*. München: Beck.
Turner, V. (1969). *The Ritual Process. Structure and Anti-Structure*. Ithaca, N. Y.: Cornell University Press.
Ullmann-Margalit, E. (1977). *The Emergence of Norms*. Oxford: Clarendon Press.
Weber, M. (1920). *Gesammelte Aufsätze zur Religionssoziologie*, Vol. 3, Tübingen: Mohr Siebeck.
Weber, M. (1985). *Wirtschaft und Gesellschaft*. Tübingen: Mohr Siebeck.
Winch, O. (1958). *The Idea of a Social Science*. London: Routledge & Kegan Paul.

Part II
Culture and Modernity

1 Sociology and the Crisis of Western Culture

Johannes Weiß

The comment of René König that modern sociology originated as a "crisis discipline" (Krisenwissenschaft) can probably serve to express the consensus of opinion as far as the collective consciousness and the memory bank of our branch of social science is concerned. Now consenses of opinion are not always to be dismissed as mere prejudice or serviceable fictions, nor does a closer, unbiased scrutiny invariably lead to their destruction and to previously unexpected new insights. In this particular case, I do in fact believe that the traditionally received opinion has much to be said for it – not only so far as the historical origins of sociology are concerned, but also in regard to its context of justification: Sociology is not only to be seen as the actual consequence and expression of a deep-reaching encounter with crisis, but rather it quite explicitly derives and legitimizes both its own necessity and specific field of activity from an explicit reference to this very experience of crisis. Only by virtue of being a crisis discipline was it historically possible for sociology to gain acceptance, and this fact stands out irrespective of how the question is answered as to whether, in fact – and, if so, then to what extent – the purported crisis did actually exist and was not simply the fabrication of the social theoreticians themselves (either in its entirety or at least in its most radical and virulent expressions). Not merely in the early history of sociology but throughout the later course of its development right down to the present it has been possible to observe that both the self-image and the self-assurance of sociology as well as its public resonance and effectiveness have been pegged to the assumption that this discipline was needed to provide a reliable analysis of an ubiquitous "social crisis" and above all to help do something constructive about it. It is by virtue of conscious reference to this task that sociology derives its claim to recognition as the primus inter pares among the key disciplines of the late nineteenth and twentieth centuries; and it is obviously very difficult to preserve a dependable and permanent status for sociology as a branch of science in its own right on the basis of more modest and less dramatic claims and expectations. The often-mentioned "crisis" in sociology quite obviously has a lot to do with the fact that sociology can no longer be plausibly interpreted as a "crisis discipline" in this sense, either because it has somehow lost its old competence or because the crisis itself has lost its former actuality.

Thus the notion of a "crisis discipline" would refer to a "dialectical" state of affairs, though not merely in the sense that sociology understood in this sense tends to make itself progressively more redundant the more it fulfills its assigned task. Rather a closer scrutiny reveals that it is not so much the weathering of the alleged "crisis," but far more its comprehensive analysis and the resulting stance adopted toward it that constitutes (and this in principle, not merely in practice) a source of irritation as well as a danger for sociology. I shall elucidate and support this contention (inter alia) in the remainder of this chapter.

As is well known, the notion that European society is caught up in a deep crisis, or alternatively is drifting ineluctably into one, was not first conceived of by sociologists and then let loose upon the world. It was rather the political and historical philosophers of the eighteenth and early nineteenth centuries who were first responsible for making this their central theme. "We are caught in a crisis that will lead to either enslavement or liberty," stated Denis Diderot (Koselleck, 1973: 144); and Abbé Raynal seconded his thought, though without actually talking of a crisis, when he commenced his "Histoire philosophique et politique" of the year 1770 with the assertion: "Everything has changed and must change even more" (Koselleck, 1973: 148). Finally Thomas Paine, "who came closest to assuming the role of an Anglo-American Rousseau" (Adams, 1973: 171) with pithy brevity entitled his newspaper "The Crisis."

These scanty references (cf. Koselleck, 1973, 1982) serve to indicate that mention of a crisis existing was first made in the context of the progressive loss of power and legitimacy on the part of the traditional political authorities and of the closely connected, attending dissolution of the formerly dominant value and belief system that had been in large measure previously sustained by religious convictions. Indeed the system of social division of labor or social inequality (i. e., the social structure in the narrow sense) did not initially occupy the central focus of attention and controversy; thus the agitation of Paine, too, was primarily directed against the division of mankind into "kings and subjects" on the grounds that this could be justified neither by natural (i. e., empirical) nor by religious reasons (Adams, 1973: 172). On top of this, though, the political struggle of these theorists was waged throughout not in terms of power and interest but rather was portrayed as a *moral* struggle. Thus it came about, as Reinhard Koselleck has noted (1973: 133), that "the crisis was given moral overtones, its political nature concealed but not irradiated."

The moral perspective likewise dominated the historical and political thinking of Jean Jacques Rousseau. In his case, however, it is combined with a sharp, perceptive eye for the political nature of the crisis and for the fact that this political crisis was intimately bound up with society, meaning the system of social inequality and the conflicts of interest thus set up. This is indeed what gives rise to his conviction that what the crisis was finally speaking all about was not simply effecting a "grand changement"(Voltaire) – an admittedly painful transition to inhabiting the "beaux temps" of a better future – but rather was an integral structural feature of approaching sociopolitical upheavals: "We are drawing closer to a state of crisis and a century of revolutions" (Koselleck, 1973: 133).

In his treatise "On the Origins of Inequality among Men," published in 1755 (1971: 266f.), Rousseau asserts that "the spirit of society and the inequality thus created" is responsible for bringing about conditions that contradict the "laws of nature," since, among other things, they enable "an idiot to lead a sage and a handful of people to bask in plenty, while the starving masses are deprived of even the bare necessities." Not only "trade and money" but also "science" are for Rousseau parts of society, and indeed they are parts where society assumes its most developed form, being totally founded on private egoism and competitiveness. From science too – and indeed especially from science – nothing less is to be expected than a progressive breakdown of "morals and virtue," a complete erosion of morality and the "general will" (loc. cit.: 34.38.52; cf. Fetscher 1984: 46ff.).

It is well known that Rousseau with his radicalized and universalized conception of a "crisis" exercised a potent influence first on later philosophical developments, especially in Germany, and then on sociology, especially in France. None of his other contemporaries (with the possible exception of Johann Georg Hamann and then only with an incomparably lesser degree of influence) has given such memorable expression to the ambivalences and the costs of cultural and social progress; that is, to the set of problems that, above all in Germany, have found thematic expression as an antinomy existing between culture and civilization (or alternatively, between community and society).

Deserving of special note in our present context is the fact that the progressive decay of "morals and virtue" led Rousseau to undertake an investigation of society and its dynamics; thus cultural critique gives way to social critique. However, falling back on society by no means furnishes Rousseau with a way out from the crisis of morality and culture that he has diagnosed. Quite the contrary: The "logic" of society turns out to be directed in the final analysis toward the total dissolution of the "general will" – this as a result of the aggrandizement of a chronic hunger for prestige at the cost of virtue, of rationality at the cost of wisdom, and of pleasure-seeking at the cost of striving for happiness (Rousseau, 1971). Thus not only a condition of progressive dissociation is engendered but also one of cultural and moral regression, since the cultivation of man in both its inception and dissemination requires the "general will" as a growth medium.

The endeavor to achieve a scientific theory of society, which in the course of later developments proved an important factor in the establishment of sociology, appears to have originally been prompted by quite different expectations. This is all the more remarkable and striking because the theorists in question were constrained by a similar experience of crisis to that of Rousseau, and indeed this experience was often directly or indirectly influenced by Rousseau. In particular, we are entitled to conclude that early sociology inherited its central range of concerns from Rousseau (and not, indeed, as is often maintained, from Thomas Hobbes). The aim of these endeavors was to assess the possibilities for the inauguration of a new "general will," that is of a social order at one and the same time universal or all-encompassing and morally binding. Moreover, this was to be achieved while making full allowances for a differentiation and rationalization of society that was not only advanced but capable of advancing even further. Just like Rousseau, therefore, these social theorists assume the existence of a crisis of morality or culture. Where they differ from him, however, is in their conviction that an adequate thematic formulation of and also any possible solution to this crisis is to be found on the level of "society" (and indeed only on this level).

A classical formulation of this conviction and one that at the same time proved highly influential occurs in Claude Henri de Saint-Simon. In his work "Du système industriel" (1824) he states that "the social crisis" that had convulsed France and the whole of Europe owed its "fundamental cause" to the "complete change in the social system" (Saint-Simon, 1966, vol. 3: 3 [quoted in Koselleck, 1982: 631]; cf. Saint-Simon, 1973: 12). He goes on to conclude that only informed insight into the developmental and organizational laws of society would be able to point the way out of the crisis and pave the way for a transition from a society of the "critical" to one of the "organic" type[1]. Thus for Saint-Simon it is imperative to transfer "spiritual power" to the scholars, since they alone possess the necessary "intellectual force" (this would also extend to the representatives of industry, who dispose of "material force," their role being to discharge administrative functions). Only in this way would it be possible to organize society along the correct lines, namely to promote "progress in the sciences" and "prosperity in industry" (Saint-Simon, 1973: 33).

It was Auguste Comte (and then, above all, Émile Durkheim) who assigned to a new science – sociology – the function of providing the informed knowledge of the roots of the crisis and conditions for the reform of society that would be needed to accomplish this great task. "The achievement of a total reorganization, in whose power alone it lies to put an end to the great crisis of modernity, involves elaborating a sociological theory capable of providing an adequate explanation of the whole of the human past" (Comte, 1963: 92; cf. 82).

In Comte it emerges even more clearly than it does in Saint-Simon that the scientific theory of society is to surmount this "major crisis" by establishing itself as the socially dominant form of *knowledge*. The "reorganization of society" demanded, the setting up of the "positive society" (Comte, 1963: 119), is not conceived of as an exercise in social engineering on a large scale but rather, at least in the first instance, as involving a far-reaching process of learning and education, as requiring a "mental and moral" transformation, where "modern positivity" (Comte, 1963: 140) totally supplants traditional "speculative culture."

In fact the "major crisis" is for Comte, too, in the final analysis, moral and spiritual in nature. On the other hand, Rousseau, as has already been pointed out, relegated the sciences to the "ruinous system of egoism so widespread today" (Comte, 1963: 104) and had considered them to bear a large measure of responsibility for the dissolution of "morals and virtue." Comte, in contrast to this, holds the "positive spirit" to be "directly social;" its sheer universal character alone means that its dissemination will lead to a social consensus of the greatest possible binding force. Indeed the reason why he regards sociology as "the sole essential goal of all positive philosophy" (Comte, 1963: 133) is that it reveals the individual as an abstraction and society as being the actual reality (Comte, 1963: 106), as well as opening the door for the ineluctable persuasive force of the "positive spirit" to be extended to all matters of social organization. Moreover, the greatest readiness to undergo radical mental and moral transformation along the lines dictated by the "positive spirit" was expected by Comte to come from the proletariat, the reason being that of all classes this was the one that had been most left untouched and least corrupted by traditional "speculative culture." "If the celebrated *tabula rasa* of Francis Bacon and René Descartes ever were to be fully realizable, it would surely be among the proletariat of the present day who, especially in France, approximate more closely than any other class to the ideal type concerning possession of the requisite disposition that would pave the way for rational positivity" (Comte, 1963: 117f.).

It is precisely this idea of the existence of a specific role for the proletariat in overcoming the "great crisis of modernity" that would prompt one to focus on the figure of Karl Marx as being *the* particular theorist who quite pointedly and with the greatest decisiveness in the face of all "culturalist" or idealist approaches emphasized the social, indeed the "material," nature of this crisis. The accuracy of this widespread belief about the role played by Marx here – a belief that of course also fits in with his own self-perception – cannot further detain us at this point. It would be fair, though, to point out that the special role accorded to the proletariat in the Marxian theory of revolution is likewise very closely pegged to the alleged predisposition of this class for the formation of revolutionary consciousness (meaning of course also for Marx' own theory). Of greater significance, however, is Marx' recognition of an integrally constitutive function for religion in the class-structured societies of both the past and present as well as for science in the Communist society of the future. Beyond any doubt, it was Marx' opinion that class-structured societies can only survive in the long run when they draw on the ideological services of religion (in any of its manifold expressions)[2]. Still more interesting from the point of view of our present topic is his conviction that science (in particular here he means history and social science) will play a decisive role in the integration of the society of the future. It is clear for him that a throughgoing scientific rationalization process will regulate "the palpably rational relations maintained by men among themselves and towards nature" (Marx, 1958: 108) and the "deliberate and planned control" of the "social living process" that are to be characteristic of this coming society. This same conviction informs Marx' statement in his essay "On the Jewish Question" to the effect that only when men have finally emancipated themselves from religion will they stand "in a critical and *scientific* and in a human relationship" to one another: "*Science* will then represent their unity" (Marx, 1962: 453). There can be no doubt that Marx remained true to this conviction, despite all the many transformations and developments his "science" went through.

It would be easy to prolong ad infinitum these remarks and interpretations on the history and prehistory of sociological thought. Were we to do so, we would inevitably find ourselves focusing closely on theorists like Durkheim or Karl Mannheim, for example, who insist quite pointedly that the crisis or "pathology" of modern society can only be cognized and overcome by drawing on the resources of sociology – this to the extent that the crisis is manifested as a genuinely *social* state of affairs. But the more pointedly this conviction is insisted on, the more unmistakably there emerges a problem that is both structural and of great contemporary relevance and that is central to my range of concerns here. In what follows I wish to touch on several of its important aspects.

In all the conceptions adduced so far the notion of a crisis invariably refers to a state of affairs that is both basic and general. A sociological interpretation of the crisis so understood would therefore necessarily mean conceiving of it a menace in principle to the very order and stability of society *itself*, or as an expression of an advanced condition of breakdown in social integration. Yet the durable order and unity of societies in their entirety is grounded in a common, shared "knowledge" by virtue of which the ultimate commitments binding on every member of society in both a cognitive and a moral sense are specified and laid down in advance. This applies independently of how the nature of reality is further specified by and for a society; it would apply equally as much within the framework of a materialist conception of society as an "organism of production" (Marx), or for Saint-Simon with his depiction of society as "a veritable organized machine," but who goes on to add: "No society is possible without there being shared moral understandings" (Saint-Simon, 1966, vol. 2: 32).

Thus, for the social theorists and sociologists, too, this crisis is in its essentials a crisis of social culture and morality and not of the social system or social structure *as such*, this being so for the good reason that the unity or integrity of society sought after can only be identified in the unity of a "collective consciousness" or a "consensus." Social inequalities, even those of the crassest kind, only result in crisis when they no longer have any plausible theoretical and moral legitimations at their disposal; on the other hand, it is possible for societies to land in the gravest of crisis without external circumstances or changes in the social structure playing any kind of discernible leading role. Closely connected with this is the fact that, as Marx occasionally notes (Marx and Engels, 1956: 47), not only the dominant class of the time operates out of the (ideological) assumption that it represents the whole of society, but also the rising or revolutionary class.

Thus it is, to say the least, quite erroneous and misleading to maintain, as some have done, that those philosophers who have addressed themselves to the crisis of modernity (from Rousseau to Friedrich Nietzsche right down to even more recent thinkers) were at most concerned with the cultural crisis and that only later (in the context of the evolving theory of society) was the real (i. e., social) nature of, and causality underlying, this crisis stumbled upon. The truth of the matter is that the social theorists, too, were essentially concerned with a cultural crisis. With them, admittedly, this came to assume sharper contours in certain ways as well as a greater degree of inherent necessity, since the ideational and political-moral conflicts that occupy their attention are quite closely and explicitly bound up with economic and power-dictated *interests*. In my opinion, though, we are at most dealing with a difference of *degree* rather than of kind here. As has already been noted, Rousseau, for instance, addressed some considerable attention to the changes in social structure that were bound up with the cultural crisis; and in many of the other philosopher theorists of the cultural crisis (Nietzsche, for example) it is possible to find "sociological" observations that are more than worthy of note in this connection.

The seminal difference between thinkers like Rousseau and Nietzsche, on the one hand, and Saint-Simon, Comte, Marx and Durkheim, on the other, turns on the exact significance and role attributed to "society" – and above all the theory of society – for the task of elucidating the underlying causality behind the cultural crisis and eventually resolving it.

Those theorists who insist on interpreting the theory of society in general and sociology in particular as a "crisis discipline" not infrequently have recourse to a language that decidedly smacks of the rhetoric of social technology. This is especially so when a stabilization or restoration of the old order is not part of their practical ambitions (as with Louis de Bonald, for example; cf. Spaemann, 1959), but rather the creation of a completely new, rational society (as it was for Saint-Simon, Comte, Marx, or Durkheim). Still, as has been already remarked on, a closer inspection reveals that even then a reordering of social and cultural relations along large-scale "social engineering" lines is not envisaged. The new society is not intended to be installed over the heads of its members without their knowledge or approval; rather its inception is to be expedited and its actualization promoted through the dissemination of scientifically established truth. It is precisely for this reason that all these theorists ascribe such central importance to the reorganization and improvement of public education. Thus, the science of society is envisaged as unfolding its desired effects not indirectly and from without by means of some kind of scientifically derived social or mental technology, but rather, at least for the most part, by making possible the scientific rationalization of consciousness, intentionality, and motivation in the individual actors. The assumption is certainly operating here that the "positive rationality" of science would not only prove to be intellectually irresistible, but that its superior productivity and validity in normative and moral affairs would also come to be demonstrated. And so it would be incumbent on sociology itself to take on the role of the pacemaker in spreading the new "collective consciousness" on which the coming social order would be founded and permanently predicated. This expectation is by no means restricted to the theorists that can be regarded as "positivist" in the narrow sense; rather it represents a constitutive and persistent leitmotiv of the thinking of all the theorists (i.e., apart from Marx and Durkheim, for instance, also Mannheim, Leopold v. Wiese, and Charles A. Ellwood; cf. Ellwood, 1926: 201), in fact in all those who are at all ready to perceive for sociology a seminal and above all constructive role in the face of the "major crisis" diagnosed.

Hopes such as these for a saving intervention or revolution in culture proceeding from within sociology itself may well appear to most contemporary sociologists as being not just merely unfulfillable but also quite abstruse; this despite the fact that only a few years ago there was actually a renaissance of such conceptions, at least in West Germany. In point of fact, a conception not uninfluenced by the efforts of the philosopher theorists who have written on the crisis of Western culture is prevalent also within the "scientific community" at the present time, at least to the extent that here attention is still addressed at all to the crisis of culture or to the cultivation of this crisis (within sociology).

The most clear-sighted and radical of these philosophers is Nietzsche. His thinking, often mediated through the prism of "classical" German cultural sociology (Max Weber and Georg Simmel), has played a quite decisive role in contemporary sociological analyses of the crisis of Western culture. "Our whole European culture" according to the fragments from Nietzsche's last years (Nietzsche, 1964: 3) "has for some time been moving towards what looks like a catastrophe;" this catastrophe he identifies as "European nihilism." To Nietzsche it seems absurd to try and ward off or overcome the impending catastrophe with the help of modern science. It is true that in the first of his "Unzeitgemäße Betrachtungen" he asks: "What is the point of all this science if it doesn't lead to culture" (1980: 203)[3]. On the other hand, in his critique of David Friedrich Strauss' faith in science and the "philistine culture" that Strauss propagated and embodied, he states that the point of all science and rationality is highly relative (Nietzsche, 1980: 191, 197). Thus in his previously-mentioned later reflections he goes on to conclude that "European nihilism" achieves its fulfillment in modern science, revealing its true nature here, even if at first only unconsciously and reluctantly: "Since Copernicus man has been careering away from the centre into the blue beyond" (Nietzsche, 1964: 8). Categories handed down to us that vouch for the meaning of the world as a whole – "purpose," "unity," "being," and of course "truth" – prove in the end to be completely unfounded and unusable, "and now the world appears to be devoid of value" (Nietzsche, 1964: 15). According to Nietzsche these "after-effects of nihilism" are becoming more and more evident in all the sciences (and in art, too). And even sociology (which for him was represented above all by Comte and Herbert Spencer) will not remain free to them; indeed it will be affected all the more if it insists on defining not only the questions of domination but also cultural problems as problems of "society." For modern society with its dissolution of all binding hierarchical order, its logic of social levelling and mediocrity, is for Nietzsche only nihilism in practice, such as has found both its fitting expression and its theoretical high-watermark in "The Science of Society," even if the latter has proved disappointingly inadequate as a vehicle of criticism and overcoming.

These short comments are sufficient to show clearly the malaise sociology slides into if it insists on seeing the crisis of Western culture form a Nietzschean point of view. However unconvincing the wording and solutions of the problem along Comte's, Durkheim's, or Mannheim's lines are, these thinkers undoubtedly expressed not only great self-confidence of social science in its own powers, but also a high degree of conceptual rigor. Above all it was consistent in wanting to derive the new cultural ideals from the spirit of modern society and hence from the science of this very same society.

Over and against this, a sociology along post-Nietzschean lines is, to put it metaphorically, not only empty-handed, but rather, to the extent that it necessarily sees itself as a constitutive element of the "great crisis," greatly endangered in its confidence in and satisfaction with its own efforts, and even endangered in its intellectual and social identity. For to the extent that its efforts promote cognitive and technological progress (and, in this sense, the process of modernization or civilization) it proves in respect of the cultural problems (indeed the very same ones as were perceived by the sociologists mentioned) to be not only unproductive, but at least in as much as its findings succeed in gaining acceptance in the collective consciousness, also destructive[4]. It is therefore no accident (and a development not to be dismissed by falling back on political-ideological or psychoanalytical interpretations) that at present many sociologists (especially, it would seem, the renowned and respected ones – in West Germany above all but by no means only Helmut Schelsky and Friedrich H. Tenbruck) have found themselves making a very sceptical assessment of the cultural relevance of sociology. Self-criticism of this kind, however, is more calculated to deepen the current malaise than to point the way out of it. As a rule, it does not lead to a total break with the Durkheimian "god that failed" and with the sociological community; in any case a completely different kind of sociology that is, so to speak, culturally positive or at all productive is not exactly waiting in the wings, and indeed it is hard to imagine what form it would take. Though endeavors such as John O'Neill's (1978) "savage sociology"[5] or Dietmar Kamper's (1986) thoroughly postmodern sociology of the imagination[6] may serve to induce a sense of exaltation, uplift, and even moral edification amongst the cognoscenti, there can still be no question but that they pay for their success here by severing their links with even the most liberally defined semblance of scientific rationality.

There are, of course, other ways of dealing with the malaise induced in sociology by the crisis of Western culture: One is to deny in principle the existence of any such crisis (dismissing as a necessary fiction or ideology left over from early, prescientific sociology); a second possibility is to insist that, for the main part at least, it is *not* a crisis of culture[7]. A particularly elegant way of sweeping the crisis of culture under the carpet of nonrecognition would be to exclude the whole problem from the range of concerns of academic sociology by means of suitable conceptual and methodological devices.

Recourse to smokescreening or deadpanning tactics of this kind is neither convincing nor likely to be successful in the long run. One important reason for the present renaissance of such sociological theorists as Simmel and Weber lies in the fact that they have demonstrated in exemplary fashion on a high conceptual level how sociology can conduct itself in such a way as to maintain its identity and, of not least importance, be of some practical use in this situation. For Simmel and Weber neither sociology nor indeed any other discipline (not excepting philosophy) is destined or able to provide solutions to the conflicts and discontentments of modern culture. Still to the extent that sociology through its own specific devices is sensitized to these problems and admits them to consideration, this discipline is certainly in a position to make a decisive contribution not only to solving them outright but also to relaxing their hold on us by breaking them up into more manageable subproblems – in other words, to take the heat out of them. There is a price to be "paid" for this, to be sure: partly in the form of a permanent preoccupation with itself on the part of sociology but principally in its achieving a more modest view of its place in the general framework of modern culture. It is a price that must be borne, for there is no choice in the matter.

Notes

1 This terminology can be found in the "Doctrine of Saint-Simon" (exposé premier 1829), new edition Paris 1924, p. 127; cf. Salomon (1957), p. 34.

2 Cf. especially the well-known sentences from the introduction to the "Kritik der Hegelschen Rechtsphilosophie": "Mankind, that is the *world of man*, state, society. It is this state, this society, that produces religion, a *wrongheaded consciousness of the world*, because they are a *world stood on its head*: Religion is the general theory of this world, its encyclopedical compendium, its logic in popular form, its spiritual point d'honneur, its enthusiasm, its moral sanction, its ceremonial consummation, its universal groundwork from which solace and justification are derived" (Karl Marx and Friedrich Engels, 1958: 30).

3 In this piece Nietzsche defines culture as the "unity of artistic style in all the expressions of life emanating from a people" (p. 163). He employs this definition of culture to criticize the "fairground hustle and bustle" of contemporary and especially German cultural life, which the scholars had seized on as "modernity itself" and praised to the hilt. Astonishingly enough, it is this very "modernity itself" that today is dressed out as "postmodernity."

4 Cf. Salomon (1957: 12) for the contention that sociology exercises a destructive effect on the notions of the "inalienable worth and creative force inherent in man" and of "social and political liberty" crops up in the form of a censure directed against Saint-Simon and Comte. However, in its essentials our present problem is not addressed here.

5 O'Neill defines sociology as a "symbiotic science" whose purpose is "to give back to the people what has been taken from them (i. e., in the process of scientific and bureaucratic rationalization)" (p. 81 f.).

6 Here the task of the sociology of imagination is seen as "overcoming the impotence of thought through a forceful representation of the power of images" (p. 12). What is required is not seen as being a conceptually meticulous language that strives for precision and clarity, but rather an "optative, experimental language form" and a "rehabilitation of metaphor" (p. 20). So creating "images" of an emotionally or thematically intense type can and should be expected from sociology, for with their help it will be possible to sweep aside the "repressive tendencies" associated with the process of the disenchantment of the world and also the rationalization and differentiation of social relations. However, the sociology of imagination does not go so far as to strive for a "remythologization of experience," which is dismissed as naive or – even worse – as being pre- rather than postmodern.

7 Thus Niklas Luhmann (1986: 149) sees the real "catastrophe of the modern age" in the way

the "form type of social differentiation has been recast from being one of vertical stratification to being one of horizontal, functional differentiation." Noteworthy is the fact that Luhmann's work is itself an example – and in its own way an impressive one at that – of an attempt at constructing sociological concepts and theories, one which distances itself quite explicitly and as a matter of principle from the cultural "self-descriptions" that society makes of itself; cf. here especially Luhmann, 1985: 33–41, esp. 40).

References

Adams, W.P. (1973). *Republikanische Verfassung und Bürgerliche Freiheit*. Darmstadt/Neuwied: Luchterhand.

Comte, A. (1963). *Discours sur l'esprit positif*. Paris: Union Générale d'Editions.

Ellwood, Ch.A. (1926). *Unsere Kulturkrise, ihre Ursachen und Heilmittel*. Stuttgart: Kohlhammer.

Fetscher, I. (1984). "Kulturbegriff und Fortschrittskritik bei Jean Jacques Rousseau." In *Naturplan und Verfallskritik. Zu Begriff und Geschichte der Kultur*, ed. H. Brackert and F. Wefelmeyer. Frankfurt: Suhrkamp, pp. 46–68.

Kamper, D. (1986). *Zur Soziologie der Imagination*. München/Wien: Hauser.

Koselleck, R. (1973). *Kritik und Krise. Eine Studie zur Pathogenese der bürgerlichen Welt*. Frankfurt: Suhrkamp.

Koselleck, R. (1982). "Krise." In *Geschichtliche Grundbegriffe*, Vol. 3. Stuttgart: Klett-Cotta.

Luhmann, N. (1985). "Die Soziologie und der Mensch." *Neue Sammlung* 25: 33–41.

Luhmann, N. (1986). "'Distinctions Directrices'. Über Codierung von Semantiken und Systemen." *Kultur und Gesellschaft*. Kölner Zeitschrift für Soziologie und Sozialpsychologie, special issue 27, ed. F. Neidhardt, M.R. Lepsius, and J. Weiß. Opladen: Westdeutscher Verlag.

Marx, K. (1958). *Über Religion*. Berlin/DDR: Dietz.

Marx, K. (1962). *Frühe Schriften*, vol. 1. Stuttgart: Cotta.

Marx, K. and Engels F. (1956). *Werke*, vol. 3. Berlin/DDR: Dietz.

Nietzsche F. (1964). *Der Wille zur Macht*. Stuttgart: Kröner.

Nietzsche, F. (1980). *Sämtliche Werke*. Kritische Studienausgabe, vol. 1. München: dtv/de Gruyter.

O'Neill, J. (1978). *Revolution oder Subversion?* Reinbek: Rowohlt.

Rousseau, J.J. (1971). *Schriften zur Kulturkritik*, 2nd ed. Hamburg: Meiner.

Saint-Simon, Cl.-H. de (1966). *Oeuvres*, vols. 2, 3. Paris: Anthropos.

Saint-Simon, Cl.-H. de (1973). *Oeuvres choisis*, Vol. 3. Hildesheim/New York: Olms.

Salomon, A. (1957). *Fortschritt als Schicksal und Verhängnis. Betrachtungen zum Ursprung der Soziologie*. Stuttgart: Enke.

Spaemann, R. (1959). *Der Ursprung der Soziologie aus dem Geist der Restauration*. Studien über L.E.A. de Bonald. München: Kösel.

2 Differentiation and Culture: Sociological Optimism under Scrutiny*

Hans Haferkamp

It is possible for theories to run ahead of reality: The propositions they contain may be false at the time they are formulated yet may become more fitting over time because changing societal reality approaches the theory. Given that theories are composed of a number of propositions, it may be that this belated verification only occurs for a portion of them, while other propositions are wrong initially and remain so. The theories themselves need not actually have contributed to the changes occurring in reality that confirm the propositions. Self-fulfilling prophecy does not always come into play. Significant portions of Talcott Parsons' theory of culture formulated during the period 1937–1975 were wrong for a long time, and some of these have remained false to this day. However, there are other propositions that are correct for contemporary societies, or that are currently beginning to be proved correct. Indeed, it may be that Parsons' propositions as a whole have yet to reach the peak of their confirmation in reality, and that we should be prepared for one or two surprises in the future.

Changes over time in the extent to which a theory is confirmed do not need to be recognized or anticipated by its author. Talcott Parsons quite naturally believed that his theory did provide a correct description of past and present societal and cultural developments. The proposition will be put forward here that Parsons was undoubtedly incorrect in this judgment. He was unable to satisfactorily explain neither European developments between 1933 and 1945 nor those in the postwar United States and Western Europe until about 1960. And these time periods are, after all, those in which he actually formulated the most substantial parts of his theory.

These observations prompt a number of interesting thoughts on the relationship between theory and reality. Karl R. Popper, to my knowledge, only ever expected the future to provide falsifications of theories formulated earlier. However, refutation is not a negative matter in his theory of science but is in fact what a theoretician should expect – if he is lucky. If things do not turn out so happily, competing theoreticians or methodologists may find that the theory is not even capable of being falsified. Such a fate places "*paid*" on the theoretician's reputation, and he then joins the ranks of the speculative philosophers and poets. In this chapter, I would like to call into question this

* Thanks to Neil Johnson for translating this paper from the German original. The quoted passages from other German authors are also his translation.

rather unhappy choice supposedly facing the theoretician, between being found beyond doubt to be in error and being denied the very ability to be in error. Theories that are wrong today may be verified tomorrow, and this without exerting any particular influence of their own over the factual developments with which they are concerned; more and more confirmations of this are now coming to light. This, then, is the favorable position in which a number of important propositions from Parsons' theory of differentiation and cultural change now find themselves.

2.1 Differentiation and Pattern Maintenance by Culture

The cultural system of values, norms, regulations, and expectations is especially relevant to human action. This is the system that ensures "pattern maintenance" (cf. Parsons, 1971a: 98f.). If one recalls that Parsons' action theory begins with the situation of double contingency, that is, the double improbability that social action will be mutually coordinated, then pattern maintenance will not be valued too slightly, for the values, norms, regulations, and expectations that make up culture are the factors that, once they are specified in common orientations, ensure that all interactions take place in a mutually coordinated way. Thus Parsons' designation of the relationship between culture and the other systems of action comes as no surprise. He does not judge the role of culture differently from the way Max Weber did: While Weber had credited ideas with setting the course for the realization of interests, Parsons' formulation is that

> in the sense, and *only* that sense, of emphasizing the importance of the cybernetically highest elements in patterning action systems, *I am a cultural determinist*, rather than a social determinist. Similarly, I believe that, within the social system, the normative elements are more important for social change than the 'material interests' of constitutive units (1966: 113; the first emphasis is the author's, the second is my own).

Parsons also continued to adhere to this assessment of the role of culture, or of values, norms, regulations, and expectations, in later work.

Parsons does not simply treat the existence of culture as a prior assumption. The fact that culture controls other partial systems and determines other action does not rule out the idea that it, too, is attributable to another system or another process. The process Parsons takes to be responsible for culture is that of *differentiation*. However, Parsons does not treat the relationship between differentiation and culture, values, norms, regulations, and expectations on an overall societal level particularly differently from the relationship between double contingency and common orientations on the level of interaction. Social units become differentiated, that is, two different units are formed (the equivalent to this on the microsocial level is that "ego" and "alter" act differently and possibly uncoordinatedly, or at least that this will be the actors' reciprocal fear). If society is to continue to exist, effort must be made to achieve integration, and this must be rendered durable by pattern maintenance. Since Parsons did repeatedly observe the continuing existence of societies, his conclusion reads that these societies must also possess a pattern-maintaining culture. Pattern maintenance occurs if certain preconditions are fulfilled, that is, if the elements of culture perform certain operations as defined by Parsons: *The inclusion of roles, coordination of collectivities, differentiation of norms*, and *generalization of values* integrate and preserve the structure of differentiated segments.

Parsons' antimaterialistic thesis that culture is the supreme controlling unit, and that the system of adaptivity and other subsystems are subordinate to it, is a disputed one. Critics counter this with propositions of their own. What might be more productive, though, than setting thesis against thesis might be to specify the conditions under which particular approaches are empirically convincing, for empirical plausibility and a limited amount of empirical confirmation can be claimed for vastly differing theses. Parsons' theory of culture probably is correct in a constellation in which physical survival and life in general are secure for a society, and in which it is immaterial to the continuance of pure survival and of life whether actors and groups behave in one particular manner or in some other quite different one. "Societal options" are available involving widely differing patterns of action. When societies are in this type of situation, values and norms have a high priority, although material interests, coercion, and other factors do still have their part to play. Parsons is quite aware of this, but what he does not see is that his attribution of a high level of relevance to values really does not remain valid in all societal situations. If survival and life are precarious, certain actions intended to secure survival will assert themselves, independently of value relationships (contrary to Parsons, 1966: 11) and will mean that actors disregard existing values, norms, regulations, and expectations. Ample evidence of this is provided by public behavior in the event of accidents, in emergency situations, during wartime, and in the aftermath of war. Parsons seldom has situations of this kind in mind, and when he does, his analyses are not very convincing. In the societies he deals with, it is assumed that survival and life are secure. Values become established in these societies, and it is these values that determine how the adaptive system is organized – whether on a capitalist or socialist basis, for example. However, the assertion can be made with regard to Parsons' theory that a situation of relative security of survival and life in general has existed for decades in those societies where he claims values have a strong binding power. In these societies, Parsons' thesis that culture represents the significant determinant is not a false one. For a long period of time, though, the thesis was not correct. It is hardly able to explain the events of World War II in Western Europe and postwar developments, while the thesis of relative cultural determinism is remarkably unworldly when faced with genocide and mass emigration. From the 1960s onwards, on the other hand, there are many empirical observations that speak in its favor as far as modern Western societies are concerned.

Furthermore, Parsons' view that pattern maintenance by culture – that is, by values, norms, regulations, and expectations – is interlinked with a process of differentiation is often properly reflected in the results of covariance analysis. However, it remains questionable whether differentiation does constitute the cause and whether, when differentiation occurs, it is invariably accompanied by the necessary general values.

Parsons is only able to formulate his proposition that, in general, differentiation must be followed in sequence by integration and pattern maintenance on the precondition that he has already observed the continuing existence of society. Systems that are still in existence truly must have overcome the consequences of differentiation. Yet this is an ex post reflection and not an ex ante projection. Before the latter could be made, it would be necessary to carefully determine the initial position from which such developments occur. However, differentiation is not the most general of social facts from which a general theory could start out. It represents no more than a special case of multifariousness, the superior might of existing facts that actors, groups, and societies cannot handle *in their immediate state*. To make them more manageable, they reduce them by selecting and interpreting from among them. Obviously, though, there are several possibilities as to how these processes of selection and interpretation take place, and these cannot be reduced to a single process before the event:

1. Hierarchical control of the selection and interpretation of facts by special actors and groups
2. Conflicts among actors or groups due to differing interpretations
3. Unattached coexistence of different selections and interpretations
4. Revocation of selections and interpretations
5. "Peaceful and frictionless integration and pattern maintenance" via the widespread acceptance of selections and interpretations (Parsons' solution).

As you will be aware, the first four of these possibilities have also been elaborated in various different theoretical suggestions. Max Weber, and others such as Gerhard Lenski (1966) and Helmut Schelsky (1965) following on from him, have regarded authority as the basis for cultural development. Just recently, Dieter Claessens (1987) put forward "Stepping out to perform an image-shaping act in the cultural space" as the starting mechanism for the "motors of societal development" (these all apply to Alternative *1*). Conflict theory's treatment of the link between differentiation and culture is just as classical as Parsons' approach. Drawing on the work of Karl Marx, it was formulated by Ralf Dahrendorf (1957), David Lockwood (1956), and has more recently been returned to from a different perspective by Jeffrey Alexander (1986) (these apply to *2*). In the theory of "loosely coupled" system elements, it is thought possible that many units may coexist without any bonds between them, and without a common culture (cf. Weick, 1976, applying to *3*). Finally certain selections and interpretations can also be made too early. Michael Schmid (1982) gives a very instructive account of how, in Greece for example, democracy was differentiated "too early" and was therefore revoked. This represents dedifferentiation (applies to *4*).

In light of these alternatives, it must not be our concern to play off one of the five possibilities against all the others. It is this type of conception in which the standard critique of Parsons has become bogged down. One version of this maintains that power differentials need to be built into Parsons' theory, as *structural preconditions* for and *permanent determinants* of cultural change, given that it is possible to make the implicit assumption that all actors have equal power. However, the extent that Parsons does continue to work on such an implicit assumption, his theory is excessively simplified on the level of overall societal culture. There are just as many advocates for a radical conflict-based approach. This is made the central point in Jeffrey Alexander's new critique (1986) of Parsons which, though it recognizes that peaceful differentiation and cultural change do also exist, finds that conflict, struggle, and war – which can be seen to be pursued far more frequently than peaceful means – are just as *significant* or are *more important*. This critique is able to mobilize on its side innumerable arguments, ranging from Dahrendorf and Lockwood to Marx.

A point we may immediately establish as a counter to these objections from power and conflict sociology is that Parsons did by all means take power differentials into consideration, in several respects. As early as 1937, when Parsons wished to use Weber to dynamize Emile Durkheim, he analyzed the role of leadership and power in processes of differentiation and subsequent pattern maintenance. However, power is not given the *rank of determinacy* that Parsons attributes to the integrative faculties of cultural values and norms, consensus and integration.

Parsons' assertion that culture is not simply enforced from above is not implausible. Today at least, one would expect the enforcement of culture to be less and less in evidence, for even those who are stronger need to negotiate with those who are weaker if they intend to get anywhere with them. Ultimately, everyone must at least be prepared to accept culture. Factors that stand in favor of the idea that the stronger party has the intention of seeking the approval of his weaker counterpart are the advantages the stronger party will gain if culture is adopted by the weaker (this statement naturally harbors the empirical proposition that actors seek their own advantage). It is only if the stronger actor does not pursue this intention that he will not negotiate with the inferior one and will seek no agreement at all. Nor does the establishment of culture exclude the previous or continuing existence of conflicts. Even class subcultures are often overarched by a national culture that includes opposing classes. Investigations into life in prisons and similar total institutions demonstrate that, here too, a subculture is thrashed out to achieve a minimal degree of integration. One can then conclude that a different interest situation as far as the holder of power is concerned would provide for a considerably greater proportion of negotiation: When the actors are free, then, considerably more negotiation occurs. There are a great many empirical examples in history of abstention from the use of force and of conflict being allowed to rest in favor of the effects of negotiation, even when the potential for using force and the ability to engage in conflict did obviously exist. Naturally, there is a similarly long list on the other side of the picture of the superior wielding of authority and of long persisting conflicts – both within and between societies – that are preceded by the enforcement of culture. It is very important that the ratio between these contrasting outputs of differentiation should be empirically determined. The impression we have is this: In proportional terms, peaceful, frictionless negotiation on culture is increasing at the expense of the assertion of power or of conflict. The whole spread of empirical material displayed by symbolic interactionists under the heading of "negotiations" (Strauss, 1978; in summary: Fine, 1984) represents a strong empirical argument in favor of Parsons' conception of the peaceful emergence of culture. To this extent, then, Parsons' theory which builds on reasonableness, consensus, integration, and pattern maintenance, is becoming ever more correct.

This judgment would be a safer one if Parsons were to offer process and sequential analyses showing how, on a societal level, the gap between differentiation and pattern maintenance by culture is actually bridged. If those of Parsons' works (1966, 1971a) that were most markedly influenced by evolutionary theory are examined with this problem in mind, a process-theoretical viewpoint will indeed be found:

> A process of differentiation proceeds in a temporal sequence of "from-to." In the process it brings about differences among parts of the system which did not previously exist ... that the differentiated parts are comparable in the sense of being *systematically* related to each other. ... The term "systematically related" as used above of course needs to be defined. Here my assumption is that *function* is the master concept for analysis of the organization of living systems. As such it is superordinate to both "structure" and "process" (1971a: 100).

The following points of criticism arise out of this frame of reference for process analysis:

1. Although, programmatically, Parsons does keep processes in view, it is also a programmatic point for him that he relegates such processes to second place. He does not have an interest in differentiation as an open process: What he is interested in is the outcome and its location in functional terms, which then also allows comparisons to be made between initial and final situations, or between the nature of differentiation and pattern maintenance *in different societies*. If he were to confine his interest to the process actually occurring – without any comparative intent – he would have to work with the thesis that every element is able to develop in its own particular way, and that the developmental principle involved need not necessarily be differentiation – it could, for example, be exactly the opposite, namely dedifferentiation – and the outcomes need not necessarily exhibit functionality, but could also be dysfunctional or nonfunctional. Furthermore, it is also an open question as to what finally emerges: Is it pattern maintenance or its dissolution, "loose coupling" or its intensification? If one follows such an approach, every culture can be unique in its development; every culture is a special case. One will then

encounter cultural relativism. Parsons, however, rejects this viewpoint (cf. 1971a: 102). As he sees it, everything has a genealogical tree, and the products within it can be compared at each fork. Zygmunt Bauman, in his contribution to this volume, presents an explanation for the emergence of the comparative sociology of culture based upon the experience made at the beginning of the modern age that certain cultural styles belonging to individual classes could be problematical from other classes' points of view and could give rise to attempts at change. Thus Parsons' theory of culture – if we follow Bauman – might be a substantial contribution to continuing modernization in as far as the point of reference in his comparisons is the functionality of individual cultures and cultural elements for the development of modern societies. Still today, therefore, he would be helpful in establishing which culture has the highest functional value for the most modern of contemporary societies.

2. A complaint that has frequently been made (cf. Dahrendorf, 1955; Lockwood, 1956; Alexander, 1986) is that Parsons does not satisfactorily conduct even the deprioritized process analysis. Everything continues to be dealt with according to the pattern, by now familiar, of comparative-static or covariance analyses. No sequential descriptions are made. Even the process of value generalization that follows on from differentiation processes is given this treatment by Parsons:

> The basic proposition is this: The more differentiated the system, the higher the level of generality at which the value-pattern must be "couched" if it is to legitimate the more specified values of *all* of the differentiated parts of the social system (Parsons, 1971a: 126).

In the end, Parsons does also investigate the further requirements of system development, namely role inclusion, the coordination of collectivities, norm differentiation, and value generalization, but once again these are not linked with differentiation by means of process analyses. All of these processes are described in a manner very distant from the actors themselves, and the teleology that had already characterized his treatment of the double contingency situation largely continues to prevail here. In Alexander's view, the fact that positive effects and consequences of differentiation are simultaneously used as causes draws an "ideological patina" (1986: 23) over Parsons' theory.

The fact that Parsons' work *per se* does not block out the possibility of process analysis is demonstrated by various moves to dynamize his theory by viewing structural characteristics from a process perspective (cf. Devereux, 1961; Damm, 1976; Willke, 1976). Michael Schmid (1982: 149f.) comes to Parsons' aid by conceiving of the "functional preconditions" for societal evolution as processes of selection. In work published by Neil J. Smelser (1959), the necessary process categories were set out and then applied to an extensive range of material. However, another point becomes clear if one closely examines Smelser's analysis of the momentous upheaval in the British system of commerce and production in the late eighteenth and early nineteenth centuries, transforming the entire living situation of the weavers, a significant occupational group: The realization is that comprehensive processes involving newly emerging cultures do not occur so frequently as the transmission of culture. It is, therefore, quite plausible when Parsons devotes a lesser measure of attention to the birth of culture than to its transmission. This then places the criticism surrounding the lack of process and sequential analysis in a relative light. Nevertheless, the following problem remains for Parsons' theory of culture:

As a large, comprehensive symbolic entity, culture incorporates many striking details, the genesis of which certainly can be analyzed. Examples that might come to mind are a new artform, a new approach in academic science, or a new life-style (cf. Cohen, 1955; Fine, 1979, 1983; Haferkamp, 1985). It hardly seems acceptable to refrain across the board from investigating the emergence of details of this kind. If this were simply allowed to rest, it would amount to blindly accepting, *in toto*, Parsons' technique of deferment. There is all the more reason to take exception to this in that, from no later than 1966 onward, Parsons' macrosociological work is explicitly presented as drawing upon evolutionary theory, and the tradition among evolutionary theories is that the emergence and propagation of individual cultural elements is also dealt with as well as entire cultural complexes.

A general view on this theory, therefore, may be summarized as follows: Parsons' emphasis on peaceful and frictionless pattern maintenance has quite a lot in its favor in empirical terms. His relative cultural determinism can also be accepted, but only under restrictive conditions. A deficient aspect of the theory, on the other hand, is Parsons' explanation of the birth of culture, which in fact is only rarely in evidence. Given that it is not only new orientations that occur and are relevant to interaction, but also momentous new cultural elements and major partial cultures, this is a deficiency in Parsons' theory of culture that needs to be firmly grasped. The net outcome to date is not unequivocally clear – the credit side is counterbalanced by a number of debit items. How much store we should set by these evaluations does not become apparent until the Parsonian theory has been applied to processes of change both toward and within modern culture. I shall therefore work out the suggestions I have already made on this in more detail in the following part of this chapter.

2.2 Change toward and within Modern Culture

The first thing that makes an immediate impression if one wishes to appreciate and criticize Parsons' theory of change toward and within modernity is his overall vision of the system of modern societies. It is fascinating to see how Parsons establishes connections between widely differing developments in Europe – if indeed these are correct. It is difficult, for example, to follow Parsons' thinking when he allocates different societies to different functional systems. What are we supposed to understand when he promptly ascertains that the Soviet Union carries out the adaptive function today within the system of modern societies (cf. Parsons, 1971a: 108f.)? This has very much the air of superficial analysis about it and verges on sheer nonsense. Indeed, this type of analysis as a whole is applied too much "from the top down," and it is too far removed from the processes and structures with which it deals. In Parsons' work, we find that generalizations are made in grand style, and that precise details are not focused upon.

Another question that needs to be asked is whether – in present-day societies particularly – modern culture does have the priority in determining action that Parsons continued to give it. In common with many other critics, Zygmunt Bauman believes that the state no longer has any need of legitimation by culture so long as it is in possession of adequate political technology (cf. p. 324) with which it can carry out "surveillance, 'correction,' welfare supervision, 'medicalization,' or 'psychiatrization.'" Against the thrust of this criticism, and in Parsons' favor, it can be established that, even today, those in authority strive to motivate intellectuals to support a culture that can be reconciled with the aims of the state. Friedrich H. Tenbruck's evidence of culture's relevance to action, that is, the fact that "cultural domination was, and indeed had to be, at least as important to National Socialism as were social and political (domination)" (1979: 411), together with numerous facts taken by Helmut Schelsky to support his thesis of the ruling priesthood of intellectuals, can now be extended with current examples from national cultural policy. These are indications that the relevance to action that culture has been said to have is indeed persisting.

Many criticisms levelled at Parsons' relative cultural determinism by interaction theorists also have obvious empirical weaknesses. The idea of modernity – one that was taken seriously from Weber to Parsons – is regarded as a "continually failing project" (Knorr-Cetina, 1986). The notion of one subsystem controlling the pattern maintenance of the other systems, including the life-world, is treated as an untenable assertion. What these interactionists maintain is that the actors "down below" see to it that "diverging perspectives on work, *montage*, fiction, misunderstandings, confusion, errors and conflicts" (Knorr-Cetina, 1986: 8) generate the life-world in a form that could never be prescribed by a system of pattern maintenance. Karin Knorr-Cetina is therefore of the view "that the failing project (of modernity, my note) turns our attention to comprehensive and far-reaching characteristics of routine in reality as it is lived" (1986: 10). A "double articulation of social forms" exists or, to put it in Parsons' terms, takes place by pattern maintenance from above and by the routinization of the societal community from below. Between the two – so Knorr-Cetina formulates it – there is a relationship of mutual underestimation.

In fact this and other interaction-theoretical criticisms overlook the fact that Parsons, of all people, places a high value on the life-world even in his theory. The subsystem of the societal community (his concept for the life-world) is one of the four systems of action. Although it is subject to control by culture, it for its own part – together with culture – controls the systems of goal attainment and adaptation, and it is from it and the latter systems that culture actually derives its energy. It could hardly be too benevolent an interpretation of Parsons to maintain that a provider of energy also has some influence over the entity it energizes and helps to shape.

Another point many interaction theorists disregard in their empirical work is that – when related to their judgment – a great deal "actually works" and functions in accordance with cultural patterns, and hence that values are very extensively realized, that conformity to norms is still *the* pattern of action, that collectivities act in a sufficiently coordinated way for it to be possible to rely on them relatively well in everyday life, and that role inclusion, too, is widespread. Many interactionists are therefore in danger of mistaking the deviations, embellishments, and distortions in social processes for their very essence.

Beyond that, it is not logically necessary, even from an interaction-theoretical perspective, to equate interaction, life-world, mundane structure *solely* with willfulness which will then cause grand cultural projects to end in chaos, failure, and loss of dignity. Actors are quite well able to reach agreement on ordered sequences that are successful (and, every now and then, are even magnificent). The way social and technical projects are dealt with – examples being landing men on the moon, constructing giant ships, realizing social and cultural projects such as the creation of democracy or the foundation of companies or associations that achieve their purposes – indicates that we would do better to raise more confident expectations of the culture created by actors as part of the project of modernity (cf. Haferkamp, 1987a: 79ff.).

Another point regarded as problematical is Parsons' concentration on Europe. He has frequently been accused of "Eurocentrism." This, however, is not a sustainable objection. Whatever research has been conducted on this at a later date has come, again and again, to the rather unsurprising conclusion that Europe is especially significant for modernity and backed up the evidence of how it has spread from there to other parts of the world. A good deal of work has these findings in common – whether it be Shmuel N. Eisenstadt's demonstration (1986) that the societies of Europe have broadcast several European civilizations across the globe, whether it be Edward A. Tiryakian (1985) in his view that modernity is moving inexorably westward, having wandered from Israel to Europe, crossed the Atlantic, and now on the move again to a new "West" in Japan, Korea, and China, or whether it be Dieter Senghaas' recommendation that we should learn from "The European Experience" (1985). In material terms, these and other researchers put it beyond doubt that "Eurocentrism" is a criticism that cannot be taken seriously but represents an inadmissible foreshortening, with critical excess, of absolutely correct observations on Parsons' part.

Parsons' blanket explanation for the emergence of modernity as a result of differentiation, peaceful integration, and undisrupted pattern maintenance has also aroused critical judgment. Let us take a closer look at the two phases of cultural development Parsons cites as being vital to the formation of modernity, namely the Renaissance and the Reformation. These did not come into being according to a pattern of differentiation generating harmonious consequences. The emancipation of science and the arts, and of secular culture in its entirety, from their ecclesiastical bonds (this was a process of differentiation in which relations between those able to select and interpret existing facts were marked both by conflict and by hierarchical control) left masses of casualties behind, of whom Giordano Bruno and Galileo Galilei were only the most famous. The precursors of Martin Luther were burned, and their followers too, almost as soon as they had declared their unconventional selections and interpretations. It was not until Luther's time that the cultural climate in central Europe had changed sufficiently strongly that Luther was able to cleave off and to mobilize his own social movement "down below," a movement which, in terms of sheer numbers, was so widespread that the old approach of burning and execution could initially no longer be used against it; instead, the mobilization of the movement led to open conflicts that persisted for centuries. Before Luther could assert his ideas for changes within the Catholic church (in other words, he intended a further variation, and not differentiation), he needed to gain the support "up above" of holders of power, of princes, and their own interests probably led more strongly than Luther had intended to the differentiation of the church and to a deepening of the schism. The picture of peaceful differentiation and harmonious consequences is contradicted still more by the Counter-Reformation – enforced using fire, on the one hand, and baroque splendor, on the other – even if this did only affect parts of Europe. Only recently, Jeffrey Alexander (1986) drew attention to this phenomenon which not only has been underexposed frequently by sociology but also has unleashed wars and renewed oppression.

Furthermore, if one examines the industrial and political revolutions in England and France that are repeatedly singled out by Parsons, one will be reminded that neither of these revolutions took a nonviolent course. Even the peak of modernity, the educational revolution, has by no means been a differentiation free from the wielding of power or from upheaval. The enforcement of equal educational rights for the Black population in the United States would have been inconceivable if the police and national guard had not simultaneously been deployed. Still today in Federal Germany, legislative guidelines on education, schemes for comprehensive schools or "fast streams" are objects of dispute that also generate conflicts.

However, what we cannot overlook is that the share taken up by peaceful consequences of differentiation is dramatically increasing; indeed, even France and Prussia's adoption of the results of the industrial revolution claimed relatively few victims in these countries. This applies even more to the adoption of the results of the French Revolution, where the number of victims in the adopting countries was very slight when compared to the number of victims in the phenomenon's country of origin. The observation is valid most of all for the educational revolution. In comparison to the tribute of bloodshed claimed by the Reformation and Counter-Reformation and, in the societies in which they occurred, by the two great revolutions, the number of victims mourned as a result of the disturbances in the United States is extremely small, and in Federal Germany this is an almost negligible quantity. This trend of increasingly peaceful differentiation also arouses doubts with regard to Alexander's thesis that the Counter-Reformation still exerts its influence on the wars fought in the current century. Rather, one can join Parsons in opposition to Alexander's criticism by still maintaining that power and conflict, despite their significance within the process of modernization, must not be overestimated and hence regarded as having been "*rendered more permanent*." Parsons did in any case recognize that authoritarian rule and conflict were also involved in the modernization process, but he set out from the proposition that structuring society by means of power and authoritarian rule, conflict, and destruction is too inefficient and thus too expensive for the structuring forces. Under such circumstances, societies continue to perform below their potential, the actors show signs of protest and of withdrawal behavior, and the upshot is that achievements that could be generated are not. The structuring of societies, therefore, can normally take place substantially more efficiently with the aid of "positive processes;" a prime example of such a process occurs when the consequences of differentiation are negotiations and compromise. These are indeed mechanisms that are gaining in significance, as can be seen in the case of modern societies (Strauss, 1978; Fine, 1984; Haferkamp, 1987b). This, once again, is the reason that we should concentrate on "positive processes" of this kind, just as Parsons did, with the result that theories of power and authoritarian rule, of conflict and destruction, really did begin to lose significance.

In this sense, we are now able to ascertain empirically that, in the present-day societies of North America and Western Europe, the differentiated entities have continued to be integrated, and pattern maintenance has continued over a period of 30 years. This alone is a strong argument in favor of Parsons' theory of culture. The other possible outcomes did not come to realization. Although it is true that there have been retrograde developments, notably fascism and Stalinism, in the history of modernity's development, and that the threat of such retrograde developments is always with us, it is nevertheless the case that, as long as they do not occur – let alone endure for any longer period – then Parsons' theory, or at least a diagnosis of the present derived from it, remains superior.

There is no disputing that risks continue to exist. We find, for example, that modern societies in the East and West confront one another, both sides bristling with weaponry. One could hardly fail to be aware of the dangers of a war fought with atomic weapons. On several occasions – and this is a fact that is gladly overlooked by the critics because it does not agree with their image of him – Parsons drew attention to this peril in which modernity is placed (cf., e.g., Parsons, 1971b: 140f.). The risk of atomic warfare is often conceived of as a central proof that conflicts are persisting. Norbert Elias, who for decades has been an analyst of the civilizing process the world has undergone and the prophet of its continuation in the future, has been devoting his thoughts more strongly since 1980 to the "double-bind" situation in which the superpowers of the United States and the Soviet Union are locked, and he believes it is conceivable that this conflict could represent the end of the line for the development of humanity (cf. Elias, 1985: 68). The sceptics who agree with

Elias are many in number. Parsons, on the other hand, has had the empirical situation on his side to date: Despite all the threats they have made, leaders in the West and the East have refrained from using atomic force since Hiroshima and Nagasaki. This should not in any way be seen as securing the developments over the next 40 or more years; however, detailed descriptions of decision-making processes at the head of one of the two current superpowers demonstrate that, when conflict situations have arisen, the view has so far always prevailed that the use of weapons of mass destruction with the consequences that could be seen to entail could neither be reconciled with one's own conscience nor with one's responsibility before the human race (cf. Kennedy, 1968; Ball, 1982/1983). What that means as far as the system of modern societies is concerned is this: The differentiation of the two superpowers has been accompanied, for more than 40 years, by a sufficient amount of integration and pattern maintenance. Critics ought not simply to brush aside the process of value generalization as totally bizarre in the context of peace between the superpowers. A careful reading of Robert F. Kennedy's description of the Cuba conflict provides ample evidence of value generalization. The protection of human life is being extended to more and more actors. Even the life of one's potential enemy is covered by such values. In this sense, analyses of the speeches made by powerful politicians from the two superpowers ought to lead to the conclusion that the importance placed by their values upon the life of their opponents is on the increase.

Let us now turn to a systematic examination of the preconditions for pattern maintenance, that is, to the current levels of value generalization, norm specification, coordination of collectivities, and role inclusion.

The claim Parsons makes with his value generalization thesis is that values are becoming ever more generally applicable and thus that they legitimate an ever greater number of particular actions. This is true in purely definitional terms. The meaning of generalization is: A definition that covers certain details becomes broader. Concepts and notions encompass more and more characteristics and states, whether of actors or situations, that are regarded as desirable. On the other hand, the circle of those subscribing to the values concerned can be enlarged. Collectivities or societies that have not so far pursued certain values do adopt them and also regard them – as has just been shown – as applying to their opponents. Finally, value generalization may also mean that the priority ordering of different values is accepted by more and more actors, collectivities, and societies. However, pattern maintenance and value generalization are by no means the only theoretical possibilities. Parsons himself draws attention to the fact that, apart from value generalization, *value eclecticism* and *value antitheses* can also come into play. Apart from these, consideration must also be given to *the change in values*.

Parsons hastily rules out both the first two alternative occurrences as he believes that even value eclecticism is irreconcilable with a society's continuing existence, whereas value antitheses would be especially incompatible with it. Hence Parsons holds an opposing view to Max Weber, who is widely known to have spoken of the fight to the death, like the struggle between God and the devil, between different values (1964a: 272). Weber, however, believed this conflict was in any case present in every actor, and hence also in every collectivity. In day-to-day living, though, individual actors, collectivities, and societies have to make compromises on values. In this sense actors are able to make different value relationships compatible with one another. The classic example of this is having to balance out the differing consequences of either pursuing the value of "security of the family and care for one's dependents" or that of "freedom and independence." Just as Weber showed that religious value conceptions had to be carried into everyday action, so too both of these values need to be brought into everyday life to make following one of them compatible with following the other. The net effect of this, then, is to establish a more comprehensive value compromise. One then can interpret, in this light, a value system such as that which was found to exist for the United States by Milton Rokeach (1973) as a compromise. Hence value compromises following on from value antitheses do not contradict Parsons' value generalization thesis. Other value antitheses also exist that cannot be eliminated in this way. The differentiation process harbors the risk that subcollectivities may not be involved in the generalization of values, either actively or passively; that is to say, more and more subcultures may emerge that have their own controversial values. Weber's proposition of the struggle between values thus addresses a momentous state of affairs. *One* person, "somehow or other," has to reconcile the differing values in his person and his action with one another, whereas a number of different subgroups do not necessarily have to do so. They also have the option of coexisting and severely restricting their interaction. Within American society, for example, ethnically determined subcollectivities can be found that have very limited contact with the society around them. Accordingly, one encounters a lot of middle-range theories in North American sociology treating the matter of countercultures with countervalues (as early as Yinger, 1960). In the Federal Republic of Germany, too, countervalues are occasionally found to exist. An example of this is that the Turkish minority, for reasons that begin with its religious convictions, does not share the value system of West German society. Social movements, too, are carriers of other values to some extent. The on-going dispute between established parties and new social movements runs to the extent of it being said of the new social movements that they are striving for a "different kind of republic;" those who say this are not referring solely to forms of politics. A striking point, however, is that a good many of the "countervalues" are attributed to the movements not by themselves but from outside. What is also apparent is that, for decades, whatever groups have exhibited "countervalues" have been reintegrated, and structures have been preserved. Another reason for this could be, as pointed out by Richard Münch in 1985, that the "countervalues" propounded by, for example, the new social movements, "also to a substantial extent provide fresh interpretations of the modern pattern of values which points the way beyond present-day society as the cultural code of modernity" (Münch, 1985: 459).

Thus, by extending the process of interpretation, the new social movements are doing no more than generalizing old values in a new way, and their action does then conform to those values. If one follows Münch's analysis, Parsons' statement on value generalization is factually correct as far as the new social movements are concerned. Especially imposing evidence to fit this analysis is provided by the willingness, stretching right into these movements' camp, to carry out "*repressive universalization*" (Parsons would have substituted generalization for universalization) "of the post-material value hierarchy, especially in the legal sphere and, within that, primarily in the specialized area of criminal law" (Scheerer, 1986: 135). (We shall return to this question when it comes to dealing with norm specification.) So far, then, modernity in Federal Germany has spread out its value canopy to continue to cover almost all the "deviant" or "antithetical" values represented by social movements.

In addition to this, it was already clearly evident in Max Weber's time that values also change. Value systems undergo adjustments along with the culture to which they belong, along with the "very ideas which dominate men" (Weber, 1964a: 226). Such processes of change comprise

- The appearance of new values (sometimes with old values simultaneously continuing in existence)
- The return of old values thought to be defunct
- Neglect of and disregard for certain of the existing values
- The disappearance of values (on this, see Bollnow, 1958).

These are all processes that cannot be subsumed under the term value generalization. However, if, with regard to present-day societies, one investigates what lies hidden behind the changes in values that are empirically observed, one will rarely encounter an instance of any of the four elements of change I have just listed; what comes to light instead is a *change in the relative importance of values*. In Federal Germany, for example, the change in values has moved in the following direction: The values of individualization and participation have gained in significance, whereas values of duty and acceptance have become less important (cf. Klages, 1984). Yet, what have we here other than a raised appreciation of those generally applicable values that stood at the beginning of modernity and were first manifested during the time of the Reformation? Such processes, when viewed over the short term, do represent genuine change. Taking Parsons' "long view," though, they can by all means be covered by the concept of value generalization.

One thing should not be overlooked however, namely, that value generalization can be found neither in relation to all ethnic minorities nor in relation to all marginal groups. It certainly *is* possible to observe genuine countervalues and unequivocal change in values in individual groups: Examples where this applies in Western Europe are criminal marginal groups, terrorist and separatist movements. In these cases, there are absolutely no indications of value generalization. Nevertheless, factors that are of great significance for the sociologist of crime and deviant behavior because his immediate concern is with thematizing these particular actions and he has focused attention on these particular groups (i.e., factors that might spur the sociologist of crime and deviant behavior to develop a new explanatory program) are of lesser significance in general sociological terms. In this wider view, the observation that value generalization is occurring continues to predominate.

A second precondition for pattern maintenance is *norm specification.* Norms either prescribe or prohibit certain actions, the latter function being carried out especially by the norms of criminal law. Norms lend precision to those paths of value realization that either are positively commanded or are forbidden. Once values have been generalized, more possibilities then exist for values to be realized. Before this potential for action can be exploited, more specific norms are required, some of them commanding and others prohibitive. It is occasionally disputed whether such a process really does occur: Some, as an alternative, note the coercion to conform to *general* norms. Whereas priests, the nobility, and (for a particularly long time) soldiers all used to be subject to norms of their own, today the law of the public at large also applies to them at all times. Similarly, the spreading application of the law (or "juridification") is counteracted by an opposing trend of dejuridification (cf. Voigt, 1983). Those norms that remain in force are then those that are generally valid and binding. The vast majority of empirical objections to norm specification, however, tend to be more modest. The prevailing trend is too plainly obvious: Occupational groups, organizations, and institutions are all experiencing normative regulation, or, in other words, juridification is occurring. Frequently, the trend is equated with diminution of the freedoms to act. Yet if it is seen in conjunction with other processes in the sequence of value generalization, the formulation of additional norms is more or less a socially necessary consequence of value generalization and the increased potential for action it entails; *juridification therefore only dampens this increase in the potential for action to some extent.*

It is by no means a certainty that the socially necessary specification will take place and will succeed. Values can be left "generally hovering," and the norms needed to provide precision may be absent. Durkheim named this state of affairs "anomie." Nor is the specification of norms always necessary for individual actors. Undisputedly, a certain amount of norms is necessary, as anthropological sociology has shown us, to stabilize the behavior of individuals, but beyond certain limits the actors have no further reliance on norms. Rather, the requirement for increased regulation comes from action contexts, groups, organizations, or societies in order that interaction should prove successful. This brings the questions of the internalization of norms and the setting of norms back into the picture.

It continues to be vital that norms, once specified, should be handed down by tradition and should be internalized. Once again, this is something that is not guaranteed as a matter of course. Families, schools, or groups of friends may fail in this task. In such circumstances it is not possible for the actors involved to realize values in a norm-conforming way. All empirical investigations do show, however, that these functions have so far been fulfilled to a sufficient extent in Western societies.

An important factor for processes by which specific norms are set in present-day Western societies has been an increase in the significance of the value of self-development and self-realization (cf., e.g., Klages, 1984). This increase in significance should be understood not only in terms of the value being accorded more importance by individual actors, but also as implying that the realization of the value will also now be granted, in diluted form, to those actors who had previously been denied the right of self-realization (e.g., prisoners). In this sense, having once established that the value of self-realization has been accorded a greater significance, one may take this to explain the norms governing the humanization of the penal system, especially improved legal protection for prisoners and the extended use of suspended sentences. Similarly, the increased significance attached to the value of "nature's beauty" or "a world of beauty" (Rokeach, 1973) has probably contributed directly to the creation of prohibitive norms in the criminal law as it relates to the environment. Many newly determined specifying norms in penal law have broad public backing, which also includes social movements working toward a new life-style. Even those who profess to be "anti-authoritarian" or "nonviolent" are happy to be counted along with those who wish to give impetus to the generalization of certain of the values of modernity using the "truncheon of the penal law."

The relationship between value generalization and norm specification is often a complex one. For example, the value of equality has also seen an increase in the significance attached to it. This process then encouraged the setting of norms to ensure equality in the educational field and to give equal treatment to men and women. However, this was then followed by additional, deliberate specifications (of the specification that had already been made) with the aim of continuing, nevertheless, to legitimate the stratification of society: Those at the head of the political system set a good deal of store by the perpetuation of a "performance elite" and of "peak performance" in business, science, and sport. By carrying out an analysis of speeches, Anne Dreyer (1985) has shown that, for example, Helmut Kohl, the Federal Chancellor, draws together the values of equality and of performance or achievement, as well as ways in which they might be realized through legislation:

> However, equality of opportunity for all, and admission to higher education for many, undoubtedly best serve the common good if, at the same time, we do not lose sight of the duty to give special encouragement to the highly gifted (Kohl, 1984: 481).

Generalized values and specified norms mean that more permitted actions are carried out. This then, in turn, generates problems with regard to the coordination of action and the success of interaction. Specifying norms that are valid within different *collectivities* are not necessarily *coordinated with one another*. The resulting disharmonies between actions guided by norms and taking place within different norm and regulation complexes may stand alongside each other, and the consequence may, to some degree, be disintegration and the dissolution of structures, which is a contradiction of Parsons' view. This is the sense in which many symbolic interactionists claim that the links between collectivities operate in quite a different way from that thought of by Parsons. Modern organizations (clinics, public authorities, industrial organizations) develop their own perspectives for producing the results they are aiming for and for dealing with their clients (cf. Knorr-Cetina, 1986; Strauss, 1978; Fine, 1984). Thus, still today, the demands made by work in one's occupation, the fulfillment of family duties, and how one would like to spend one's leisure time often remain unintegrated. Depending on the action context involved, sometimes duties at work will be neglected, sometimes members of the family will be disappointed, and sometimes leisure activities that one had been hoping to indulge in will be given up. All in all, however, the collectivities' normative and nonnormative regulation of action does appear to be sufficiently well coordinated.

In the case of the fourth structural precondition, too, this can be empirically shown to be fulfilled as a rule. *Inclusion of roles* signifies that both the role expectations that have been differentiated and those making the expectations are embraced by society. This again cannot be taken for granted by any means, and when Parsons claims that it has always been the case, he is making an ex post judgment based on the situation in productive, integrated societies. For, apart from inclusion, exclusion is also always conceivable, and these very processes of exclusion are regarded as typical of modern societies by many critics. In publications on processes of stigmatization in the United States and Federal Germany using the labeling approach, not only are "criminals" discussed (in fact whether they qualify as role-carriers is questionable as they have illegal and illegitimate role expectations), but also psychiatric patients, the poor, and prostitutes; the actions of the latter certainly can be analyzed using the role concept. Such studies frequently claim that these roles are excluded. Similar diagnoses have been made by analysts in Federal Germany who have found that a "two-thirds society" exists from which long-term unemployed and those who are dependent upon welfare benefits are excluded.

Since Weber's time, studies made on "social closure" (Parkin, 1983) work on the basis that social circles restrict the access they grant to privileges and chances of success. Competitors are excluded (Weber, 1964b: 260f.). In any one of these cases, it is role exclusion and not role inclusion that is claimed to follow on from processes of differentiation. Yet again, though, empirical observations run in Parsons' favor, for inclusion is found to be widespread. Moreover, this takes place not only voluntarily when viewed "from above," but also partly in response to demands and pressure from those who have been excluded and now insist on being included or integrated (and hence, frequently, not simply pursuing closing strategies of their own as Parkin [1983] believes[1].) Agreement is sought with extreme marginal groups, with the idea of also tying them into society. One can speak of a veritable triumph of the welfare state with its attempts to tie in the most varying groups, even its own opponents. This process involves widely differing strategies. Deviants, even if there is no role concept by which their action can be grasped, are offered legal protection and resocialization, the poor and unemployed are offered a suitable subsistence income, and political opponents are offered freedom of thought, a fair hearing, and their own spheres which they will be left to shape autonomously. It is by no means only in Western Europe that this applies, for this process of inclusion can also be observed on a grand scale in the United States, where it is also pursued – contrary to their declared objectives – by conservative governments.

2.3 Sociological Optimism

If we consider the processes of cultural change as a whole, there are a great many signs that the processes of cultural change in modernity posited by Talcott Parsons actually are still under way: value generalization, norm specification, the coordination of collectivities, and role inclusion are all taking place. Parsons is also widely known to have used these factors as the justification for his "relatively optimistic" (1971 b: 141) prognosis for the future of modern Western societies. Having established this, it would be possible to leave the analysis at that, regarding Parsons' theory of cultural change toward and within modernity – albeit theoretically unsatisfactory because of the chronic lack of process analyses – as nevertheless empirically supported in many of its aspects, and indeed supported to an increasing extent, which would also effectively mean sharing Parsons' optimism. One would then arrive at a perspective representing the antithesis of "typically" German and French analysis of society. The German theory of culture in modern societies is, if not pessimistic throughout, then at least predominantly so. Only Georg Simmel might be said to be an important proponent of another viewpoint similar to Parsons' perspective. Weber believed, on the other hand, that as cultural beings, actors were in danger of imprisoning themselves in an "iron cage." Arnold Gehlen recognized the roots of the downfall of the institutions in the ascendancy of subjectivism. Helmut Schelsky, in his last great work, sensed a recurrence of priestly delusions. Niklas Luhmann has a similar perception of reality when he speaks of the widespread "no" to society. French societal analysis, too, is pessimistic to a great extent. Emile Durkheim saw the danger of anomie, whereas Pierre Bourdieu now writes about the persistence of class cultures which harden everything into habit. Michel Crozier attributes the immobility and closed future of French society to French culture in particular. In both these traditions of societal analysis, the future of modern society and of its culture are given very sceptical treatment.

With Parsons behind one, it is impossible to share these fears. Modern mass society, which is becoming a society of individuals as differentiation progresses, has so far managed to cope quite well with the consequences of advanced differentiation. New occupations, new areas of activity, new political activities, and also new subcultures and new value weightings are all coming into being.

These are differentiation processes that, like all such processes, initially involve release. They release workers into the black economy, citizens to voice protest, and others to become members of new sects and alternative communities. Actors give up their parts in previously existing entities to found action contexts that open up more concrete freedoms of action for them. These processes of release are, without any doubt, always risky. Differentiated subsystems can disturb neighboring systems, just as they can destroy their own presuppositions. So far, however, these dangers have been counteracted by value generalization, norm specification, the coordination of collectivities, and role inclusion. These processes, though, should no longer be conceived of too firmly, as they always were by Parsons himself. For example, loose integration and supple pattern maintenance are often sufficient. It is enough if the actors can come together to establish an adequate level of conjunction between the various subgroups and subcultures. An example of such loose coupling among collectivities is provided by those members of the black economy who, first, do not reject the notion of also working for entities that are well integrated into the economic system and who, second, do pay over a minimal amount of taxes and duties. The relationship many actors now have to the Christian churches is characterized by general, diffuse agreement with ecumenical values, but without any personal involvement. Television reports of a papal mass may be watched with interest, but without even a thought of going to church oneself the following Sunday. Even so, people do not stop paying church taxes or engaging in baptisms, marriages, and funerals according to the Christian ritual. Values are not taken so seriously, yet action is still value oriented. Within political culture, the relationship between the parties with long traditions and the new social movements is a manifestation of integration that, though limited, does still function.

There is an approximate balance between exclusion and inclusion. A similar situation also applies to values, norms, regulations, and role expectations in the life-world. The latter is itself more diversified, and multifariousness and coexistence are both in evidence. Because actors who were previously dependent have now become strong, they are developing partial cultures of their own: They have their own neighborhood cultures in the cities and alternative "scenes;" meanwhile the general public which had previously tended to conform is developing an increasing interest in these cultures and beginning to consume them too. So far, then, it has still been possible to achieve loose integration within the society of the mass of individuals.

Parsons had opened up an optimistic view into the future for modern Western societies. I have endeavored to show in this chapter that it was not until the societies of the present day that this perspective proved to be justified. Further evidence that this is not merely a wanton statement is provided by the Parsons renaissance now gathering momentum. Theoreticians sense that there is more involved in Parsons' analysis than was assumed during his own lifetime. This does not in any way alter the fact that significant revisions to his theory are required nonetheless; it has only been possible to sketch a number of these here.

These revisions ought to be undertaken from the perspective of the theory of interaction which, for all that it is frequently in danger of underestimating the *formative power* of values, norms, collectivities, and roles, can then describe their *birth* all the more aptly.

Note

[1] I am grateful to Angelika Schade for suggestions on the relationship between the themes of inclusion and closure.

References

Alexander, Jeffrey (1986). *Durkheim's Problem and Differentiation Theory Today.* Contribution to the Conference "Social Change and Modernity" of the Theory Sections of the ASA and the DGS, Berkeley, 21–23 August 1986.

Ball, Desmond (1982/1983). "U.S. Strategic Forces. How Would They Be Used?" *International Security* 7: 31–60.

Bollnow, Otto Friedrich (1958). *Wesen und Wandel der Tugenden.* Frankfurt: Ullstein.

Claessens, Dieter (1987). *Gesellschaftliche Organisation und Repräsentation als Verstärker von Ungleichheit: Die Problematik des "Heraustretens."* Lecture at the Meeting of the Section "Sociological Theories" in the DGS, Düsseldorf, 12–14 February 1987.

Cohen, Albert K. (1955). *Delinquent Boys. The Culture of the Gang.* Chicago: Free Press.

Dahrendorf, Ralf (1955). "Struktur und Funktion. Talcott Parsons und die Entwicklung der sozialen Theorie." *Kölner Zeitschrift für Soziologie und Sozialpsychologie (KZfSS)* 7: 491–520.

Dahrendorf, Ralf (1957). *Soziale Klassen und Klassenkonflikt in der industriellen Gesellschaft.* Stuttgart: Enke.

Damm, Reinhard (1976). *Systemtheorie und Recht. Zur Normentheorie Talcott Parsons'.* Berlin: Duncker & Humblot.

Devereux, Edward C., Jr. (1961). "Parsons' Sociological Theory." In *The Social Theories of Talcott Parsons. A Critical Examination*, ed. Max Black. Englewood Cliffs, N.J.: Prentice-Hall.

Dreyer, Anne (1985). *Parsons' These der abnehmenden Ungleichheit in der Moderne, die Entwicklung von Belohnungs-, Ressourcen- und Machtverteilungen in der Bundesrepublik und den USA und ihre Reflexion in Reden von Makroakteuren.* Manuscript, Bremen.

Eisenstadt, Shmuel N. (1986). *A Reappraisal of Theories of Social Change and Modernization.* Contribution to the Conference "Social Change and Modernity" of the Theory Sections of the ASA and the DGS, Berkeley, 21–23 August 1986.

Elias, Norbert (1985). *Humana conditio. Beobachtungen zur Entwicklung der Menschheit am 40. Jahrestag eines Kriegsendes (8. Mai 1985).* Frankfurt: Suhrkamp.

Fine, Gary A. (1979). "Small Groups and Culture Creation: The Idioculture of Little League Baseball Teams." *American Sociological Review* 44: 733–745.

Fine, Gary A. (1983). *Shared Fantasy. Role-Playing Games as Social Worlds.* Chicago/London: University of Chicago Press.
Fine, Gary A. (1984). "Negotiated Orders and Organizational Cultures." *Annual Review of Sociology* 10: 239–262.
Haferkamp, Hans (1985). "Mead und das Problem des gemeinsamen Wissens." *Zeitschrift für Soziologie* 14: 175–187.
Haferkamp, Hans (1987a). "Autopoietisches soziales System oder konstruktives soziales Handeln?" In *Sinn, Kommunikation und soziale Differenzierung. Beiträge zu Luhmanns Theorie sozialer Systeme*, ed. Hans Haferkamp and Michael Schmid. Frankfurt: Suhrkamp.
Haferkamp, Hans (1987b). "Beyond the Iron Cage of Modernity? Achievement, Negotiation and Changes in the Power Structure." *Theory, Culture & Society* 4: 31–54.
Kennedy, Robert F. (1968). "Thirteen Days. The Story about How the World Almost Ended." *McCall's Magazine* XCVI (2).
Klages, Helmut (1984). *Wertorientierungen im Wandel. Rückblick, Gegenwartsanalyse, Prognosen.* Frankfurt: Campus.
Knorr-Cetina, Karin (1986). *Zur Doppelproduktion sozialer Realität: Der konstruktionistische Ansatz und seine Konsequenzen.* Lecture at the Symposion "Mikrosoziologische Revolution" at the 23rd German Bi-Annual Meeting of the German Sociological Association (Soziologentag), Hamburg, 30 September–2 October, 1986.
Kohl, Helmut (1984). *Reden 1982–1984.* Bonn: Presse- und Informationsamt der Bundesregierung.
Lenski, Gerhard E. (1966). *Power and Privilege. A Theory of Social Stratification.* New York: McGraw-Hill.
Lockwood, David (1956). "Some Remarks on 'The Social System.'" *British Journal of Sociology* 7: 134–146.
Münch, Richard (1985). "Wege der Moderne. Zwischen Tradition und Modernität, Partikularismus und Universalismus, Routine und Revolution, Konformität und Entfremdung." In *Soziologie und gesellschaftliche Entwicklung. Verhandlungen des 22. Deutschen Soziologentages in Dortmund 1984*, ed. Burkart Lutz. Frankfurt: Campus.
Parkin, Frank (1983). "Strategien sozialer Schließung und Klassenbildung." In *Soziale Ungleichheiten, Soziale Welt, special issue 2*, ed. Reinhard Kreckel. Göttingen: Schwartz.
Parsons, Talcott (1937/1968). *The Structure of Social Action*, 2 vols. New York/ London: The Free Press.
Parsons, Talcott (1966). *Societies. Evolutionary and Comparative Perspectives.* Englewood Cliffs, N.J.: Prentice-Hall.
Parsons, Talcott (1971a). "Comparative Studies and Evolutionary Change." In *Comparative Methods in Sociology: Essays on Trends and Application*, ed. Ivan Vallier. Berkeley: University of California Press.
Parsons, Talcott (1971b). *The System of Modern Societies.* Englewood Cliffs, N.J.: Prentice-Hall.
Rokeach, Milton (1973). *The Nature of Human Values.* New York/London: The Free Press.
Scheerer, Sebastian (1986). "Atypische Moralunternehmer." *Kritische Kriminologie heute, Kriminologisches Journal, special issue 1*: 133–156.

Schelsky, Helmut (1965). *Auf der Suche nach Wirklichkeit*. Düsseldorf/Köln: Diederichs.
Schmid, Michael (1982). *Theorie sozialen Wandels*. Opladen: Westdeutscher Verlag.
Senghaas, Dieter (1985). *The European Experience. A Historical Critique of Development Theory*. Leamington Spa: Berg Publishers.
Smelser, Neil J. (1959). *Social Change in the Industrial Revolution. An Application of Theory to the British Cotton Industry*. Chicago: University of Chicago Press.
Strauss, Anselm (1978). *Negotiations. Varieties, Contexts, Processes and Social Order*. San Francisco/Washington/London: Jossey-Bass.
Tenbruck, Friedrich H. (1979). "Die Aufgaben der Kultursoziologie." *Kölner Zeitschrift für Soziologie und Sozialpsychologie* 31: 399–421.
Tiryakian, Edward A. (1985). "The Changing Centers of Modernity." In *Comparative Social Dynamics*, ed. Erik Cohen, Moshe Lissak, and Uri Almagor. Boulder/London: Westview Press.
Voigt, Rüdiger (Ed.) (1983). *Gegentendenzen zur Verrechtlichung*. Opladen: Westdeutscher Verlag.
Weber, Max (1964a). *Soziologie, Weltgeschichtliche Analysen, Politik*. Stuttgart: Kröner.
Weber, Max (1964b). *Wirtschaft und Gesellschaft. Grundriß der verstehenden Soziologie*. Köln: Kiepenheuer & Witsch.
Weick, Karl E. (1976). "Educational Organizations as Loosely Coupled Systems." *Administrative Science Quarterly* 21: 1–19.
Willke, Helmut (1976). "Funktionen und Konstitutionsbedingungen des normativen Systems der Gruppe." *Kölner Zeitschrift für Soziologie und Sozialpsychologie* 28: 426–450.
Yinger, Milton J. (1960). "Contraculture and Subculture." *American Sociological Review* 25: 625–635.

3 The Cognitive Representations of Social Inequality: A Sociological Account of the Cultural Basis of Modern Class Society*

Klaus Eder

3.1 The Discourse on Social Inequality

3.1.1 Inequality: Social Fact or Interpretative Scheme?

Social inequality is one of those issues that simultaneously mobilizes moral outrage, political engagement, and social analysis. The discourse on social inequality understandably functions as a receptacle for all expressions of disadvantage, repression, desire, and hope in our society. Sociological theorizing on social inequality is nothing but a special contribution to this discourse, adding empirical data that give scientific backing to one or another opinion. Yet even scientific discourse on social inequality does not escape the social function of this discourse: to produce a cognitive representation of social inequality. A sociological analysis trying to take into account this implication thus treats social inequality not only as a *social fact*, but also as an *interpretative scheme* of social reality and asks for the function of this scheme in social reality.

The sociological "objectification" of the concept of social inequality presupposes a theoretical perspective that locates the discourse on social inequality within the social reality that produces it. My thesis is that the modern discourse on social inequality is shaped by the collective experiences and perceptions of the social world that emerge with the bourgeois classes in the eighteenth century and that today are culturally dominated by the middle classes. The actual research and theorizing about social inequality (Kreckel, 1983) thus can be explained – to use a provocative formulation – as an outcome of the dominance of the middle classes in modern sociological thinking[1].

3.1.2 The Universality of Vertical Classification

The sociological "objectification" of the concept of social inequality will be described in two steps. First, the existence of social classes in society will be identified as the objective base underlying the discourse on social inequality. Second, the subjective conditions of reproducing social classes will be examined. We will show that with the emergence of the bourgeois discourse on

* Special thanks are due to Barbara Young who not only undertook the hard work of correcting the English version of this paper but who also made helpful critical comments that I did my best to take into consideration.

equality the discourse on social inequality starts to assume a central role in the reproduction of the class structure.

Social inequality is, as many theorists propose, a universal social phenomenon (Tumin, 1967), equally present in simple, traditional, and modern societies. But what is the reality represented by the concept of "social inequality?" What is the "signifié" that belongs to this "signifiant?" The facts that underlie the discourse on social inequality are the social differences between social actors, differences in hair color, income, aggressivity, attractivity, taste, etc. What we must first explain is why some of these differences are used by people or those doing research about them (or both) for separating social classes of people. This is the classical question concerning the origins of class society. Then we must explain why class differences are perceived by these people as inequality[2].

Thus to speak of social inequality involves making use of two types of cognitive operation. The first is to classify differences vertically. The second is to describe the classified social world as a deviation from an ideal of equality. *Vertical classification* is universal (Schwartz, 1981)[3]. All societies separate people vertically. In simple societies the classification is based on sex, age, and lineage. Traditional societies add estates and castes as criteria. Modern societies substitute individual achievement. What really distinguishes modern societies in this scheme, however, is that they are the first ones to specifically call themselves class societies. They interpret themselves as unequal societies. This shows that the concept of social inequality is an evolutionary specific interpretative scheme (Giesen, 1987) bound to the emergence of the discourse on equality that is characteristic for modern culture.

In simple societies the socially significant differences are the differences between age, gender, and lineage groups. The principles underlying this type of class formation are based upon ascriptive criteria. An extreme example would be the Australian tribe where older men can marry as many women they can handle. The younger men have to wait until the old men die before gaining the advantageous positions within this wife-distribution system. Practically speaking, this means waiting until they are 40 years old. "Membership" in an age class therefore is the specific basis of social class in this society[4]. As outsiders we might feel that such practices would have to produce the idea of social "inequality" between the old and young men (apart from that produced between men and women). Tribe members, however, actually experience and interpret this social inequality as part of the order of nature. But the conclusion drawn by diverse theorists of simple societies – that because there is no conception of social inequality there is no social inequality – is wrong. Although social differences are perceived as representing an order inherent in nature there is real social inequality.

In traditional societies differences that can be made the basis of vertical classification increase. Class formation is no longer strictly dependent upon "natural" indicators (age and sex), but upon indicators that are the result of an increasing division of labor. Additional differences, such as those between peasant and craftsman, between craftsman and lord, emerge. In such societies social inequality is perceived as part of the divine order. The principles of vertical classification are represented in a specific theory of social inequality: in the theory of a "hierarchy" of estates or castes. An extreme example is the Indian caste system (Dumont, 1967). And the literature about its modernization shows to what extent the notion of hierarchy contributed to preventing the caste system from being seen as an expression of an unjust social inequality (Béteille, 1965; Meillassoux, 1973).

Modern societies enlarge even more upon the differences between social actors (as any opinion poll or the official classifications of occupations show). To the extent that these societies insist on the "individualization" of life chances social actors become more different and at the same time more unequal (Beck, 1983; Berger, 1986, 1987). Life chances can be seen as the result of manifold and crosscutting classificatory strategies (Bourdieu, 1984). But statistical analyses show that these individualizing traits "cluster;" they show that there is a hidden class structure behind the image of an individualizing society. This image rather helps to represent class differences not within the model of hierarchy, as traditional societies have done, but within the model of equality. At times the modern bourgeois classes engaged in the discourse on equality have difficulties harmonizing the reality of class structure in modern society to this discourse. Such difficulties lead to descriptions of those forms of social inequality that proceed from modern class structure as being legitimate forms of social inequality and to the theories of social inequality. Then, as these theories take hold, they gain a paradoxical function: They have to legitimate social inequality and at the same time uphold the idea of equality. This paradoxon has been resolved by individualizing social inequality; inequality is represented as the outcome of individual achievement and competence. Thus theories of social inequality in modern society serve the function of representing the class structure of this society. Once done, the only problem left is whether we should or should not undertake some affirmative action on behalf of those who lose in the struggle for the better social positions. This allows for reducing social inequality to a political issue.

The more modern society advances the more the forms of representing the class structure within theories of legitimate social inequality gain importance. At the same time the idea of equality remains a latent source of critique of these theories. The discourse on social inequality therefore becomes a very dynamic force in modern society. The critique can manifest itself in the form of questions as to the justice of existing social inequality and pleas for redistribution bringing about a closer approximation to the ideal of equality. This approach treats social inequality as a temporary phenomenon. Another manifestation of the critique accepts the functional importance of social inequality but pleads for the equality of changes within it. A third manifestation of the critique acknowledges social inequality with regret that the world is not such as it should be and explains social inequality as the outcome of human nature. The sociological theories of social inequality express these variants according to their epistemological bias. These representations serve as a mechanism of the cultural reproduction of class positions in modern societies similar to the way representation as estates or castes allowed for it in traditional societies. Just which theories are used by what social groups or classes is an empirical question to be treated later.

To summarize my hypothesis developed so far: Social inequality is an interpretative scheme produced for a specific cognitive representation of modern society and then projected upon other societies[5]. The discourse on inequality is a specifically modern form of the cultural representation of class divisions in modern society. The discourse on social inequality is nothing but the legitimation for continuing strategies of classifying and reclassifying existing differences in society. It is rhetoric, apology, and rationalization at the same time. A sociological theory that simply continues this discourse of representation takes part in the legitimating discourse in society instead of analyzing its origins and functions.

3.2 Class Position and Social Inequality

3.2.1 Four Forms of Classificatory Struggles

In order to analyze the cognitive representations of social differences (social classes) the specific classificatory practices characteristic for modern society have to be examined. Any critical understanding of the theories of social inequality must be preceded by an analysis of the real social differences, i. e., of *social classes*, to which these theories refer. Thus we do not dismiss the concept of class as suggested by diverse theoreticians (Luhmann, 1985), but feel it needs to be theoretically constructed in a more adequate manner.

With the evolution of advanced modern societies, a shift in emphasis of the dominant dimensions of class can be shown. The theoretical problem resulting from this shift away from income as the standard of class can be formulated as follows: What are the effects of new classificatory practices on class structure? The key to explaining class positions is – and Bourdieu (1984, 1985) especially has stressed this point – understanding the strategies of reproducing existing classifications, viz., mutating strategies of classification and declassification, the struggle of the classifiers to classify the social reality to their own advantage[6]. The starting point for an empirical treatment of social class in advanced modern societies is to generate a typology of classificatory struggles that define the relevant dimensions of social inequality.

The struggle for income belongs to the type of conflict bound to the institutionalization of the antagonism between capital and labor. To some extent this struggle has smoothed out differences in income, but it has not equalized them (Bellmann, Gerlach, and Hübler, 1984; Schmid, 1987). More important is the fact that some groups, especially those involved in practicing alternatives to conventional work and business (Benseler, Heinze, and Klönne,

1982), have withdrawn from this struggle and now wage their classificatory struggles in noneconomic fields. The fact that their alternative economic practices have been described (and thus classified!) as self-exploitation already points to changes in what counts in classificatory struggles.

Today, new types of classificatory struggles complement the classical struggle for income. The following three can be distinguished: (1) the struggle for formal qualification; (2) the struggle for taste; (3) the struggle for moral excellence. Such struggles change the class structure of modern society in a fundamental way. They are at the core of what has been called "new social inequalities[7]."

The struggle for formal qualification has dramatically altered the differences, both qualitative and quantitative, between the middle and the lower classes. The key figure in this new struggle for status is the skilled worker who, having acquired new formal qualifications, has distanced himself from the normal unskilled worker and joined the ranks of the old lower middle classes. His struggle, made possible by the expansion of the educational system, has become one of the central types of struggle in advanced modern societies (Blossfeld, 1985). The working class is going to be separated into the core workers and marginal workers. Upward qualification and downward qualification are the result of new ways of constructing occupational roles in the labor system (Kern and Schumann, 1984).

The struggle for taste, the central topic of Bourdieu's analysis of social distinctions (Bourdieu, 1984), is tied rather closely to the struggle for formal qualification. The positions gained in this struggle often are described as being the result of the struggle for informal qualification, where symbolic capital (like the intuitive knowledge about the right behavior in a situation) is used to stabilize or ameliorate an actor's position in the class structure of society (Wippler, 1987). Informal qualifications crosscut income differences in the same way as formal qualifications do.

The struggle for moral excellence is an attempt to mobilize the moral weight of a group against that of other groups. The petite bourgeoisie, both old and new, is the group that has most promoted this type of struggle (Gusfield, 1966, 1981; Eder, 1986), thereby attracting much public attention and succeeding in organizing their moral claims in "new" social movements. The struggle for moral excellence is – beyond its mobilization into a social movement – part of a larger system of moral classification and declassification. It denotes a specific classbound moral life-style. Against the morality of the petit bourgeois life-style other types of moral life-styles are directed: those pleading for a utilitarian morality (the neo-liberal life-style), for obedience, duty and order (the traditional life-style), and for moral principalism (the intellectual liberal life-style). Because they tend to be the best explanatory variables for forecasting voting behavior, such classifications of moral life-styles have become a favorite topic in sociology.

The result of these different types of struggles are vertical classifications that redefine class differences in modern society, dividing social classes according to the quantity of material and symbolic resources of which they dispose. The dominant classes can be distinguished from the middles classes and the dependent classes by differences that refer beyond differences in income to claims of a "higher" moral consciousness, to a "higher" judgment of taste, and to a "higher" formal qualification[8]. The combination of income and qualification on the one hand and of moral and aesthetic competence on the other hand allows us to identify two types of social position making up the class structure as it developed in advanced industrial societies.

The first type is the social position related to work. Here we have to take into account the changes resulting from the increasing relevance of formal qualification for the distribution of work among the work force. This distributive process produces losers and winners (i.e., those who lose or win social status when rationalization changes the social and technical organization of work). The measure "control of the forces of production" has lost its classical relevance. The power accumulated in occupational positions via strategies of social and cultural closure has rather become the basic mechanism in the formation of social classes and class relations in advanced modern societies. This also draws a sharp line between those having an occupation (i.e., those who are not unemployed) from those who do not have an occupation. These phenomena show that the social construction of an occupation has become the most basic mechanism of changes in the modern class structure. And they show that occupation (and no longer the position in the social relations of production) has become the most important measure of the modern class structure.

But an actor's occupation is not yet sufficient as a class marker. There is a second type of social position becoming a class marker: the relation to culture. But the indicators of such culture, defined as secondary characteristics of social classes complementing the primary characteristic denoted by the occupation, also have changed. Nowadays, to have culture means to have opinions. Opinions related to politics and morals or to art and nature now tend to be the marker replacing the classical indicator of distance from the sophisticated high culture. For an actor to have opinions allows for his vertical classification according to a criterion of cultural competence[9]. It allows us to distinguish among those with opinions, to approve of those who know what opinions to have (which only a few people can know), and to pity those who do not. Ultimately we defer to those who create opinions and define what the right ones are from those who can not.

3.2.2 The Theoretical Construction of the Concept of Class

Thus there are two categories eminently suited for the statistical construction of social classes in advanced modern societies: *occupation* and *opinion*[10]. Both are achievements of modernity where one's occupation and one's opinions characterize one's social existence on a basic level. The proposition to see occupations and opinions as the central indicators of class positions claims not to be a universally valid description but a historically specific theoretical construction of social classes. The concept of social class that we can construct starts with characteristics that are themselves the results of the modern discourse on equality. The prominence of formal qualification in determining professional or occupational status can be seen to be the result of an educational system under democratic pressures. The differentiation of society along the lines of differences of opinion can be seen to be the result of a democratic political culture. The effects of an egalitarian culture, occupations and opinions, are equally the constitutive elements of the class structure of these societies. Occupations and opinions have become the privileged object of vertical classification.

The class structure of modern society becomes the more abstract the more social classes are defined by individual differences. Clearly visible differences, based for example on gross differences in income and consumption patterns, tend to dwindle in importance. Eventually, the class structure can be made visible only by measurement procedures and statistical analysis, the description of classes as statistical clusters of individual characteristics, becomes the privileged instrument. Classes tend to have a mere statistical "existence" (Bourdieu, 1985). Thus we are forced to conceptualize the notion of class beyond its existence as a concrete entity into a logical category.

But what constitutes the standard that allows us to assign status with respect to occupations and opinions? Who defines what is high and what is low? There is no standard that is not in itself the result of a class-specific perspective. Outside the class structure there is no criterion of inequality. There is no standard of inequality that escapes the context within and for which it is formulated. And even the most complex indicators offered by the techniques of empirical social research cannot neutralize the sticky fact that even researchers have to commit themselves to normative criteria that define some difference as inequality.

How then do we identify the criteria that underlie the vertical classification by occupation and opinions? What is the specific logic of this process? The traditional theory of class does have a criterion that works when the primary struggle is for income: the criterion of the degree of exploitation. This criterion is also expected to explain the logic of vertical classification in modern capitalist societies. But this criterion no longer suffices. We propose what will function as a workable standard for vertical classification derives from the logic inherent in the idea of *competence*. Competence is a criterion that allows for the transformation of quality (i.e., cognitive, aesthetic, or moral quality) into quantity (i.e., cumulation of first-level competence as against second-level competence and so on according to the number of levels of competence that are distinguished).

Thus vertical classification in advanced modern societies tends to become dependent upon the logic of "having culture." The measure of such vertical classification is the quantity of competence. To have an occupation presupposes a cognitive-instrumental competence (Beck and Brater, 1978; Bourdieu, 1984; DiMaggio and Mohr, 1985). To have an opinion presupposes a moral-aesthetic competence (Bourdieu et al., 1981; Wippler, 1987). Evaluating the immanent logic of these competences allows us to explain the class structure made visible by statistical analysis. What distinguishes among people is a differential amount of competence. Defining these differences solely in terms of "capital," of "market value," a solution proposed by Bourdieu (1983), is unsufficient. It is rather the "use-value" attributed to cultural qualities that counts. In fact to conceptualize the dimensions that determine life chances in an adequate manner we need a notion of culture that neither reduces culture to what people want to buy and have nor reduces culture to what philosophers think about the world.

The distinguishing characteristic that such attributions of quantities of competence have is an implicit criterion of value. To have greater or lesser competence can then be said to render a person or a group of persons better or worse. To the extent that "stages" of the development of competence (in the sense of Piaget and others) are theoretically distinguished, classes of people can be distinguished in a legitimate way. And the more society distinguishes people according to their amount of competence, the more this standard of competence (itself legitimized by scientific theories of stages of competence!) becomes the principle underlying a theoretical construction of social classes. This point will be elaborated on later.

To summarize we would like to distinguish two dimensions of competence that can combine and be transformed into each other and that together determine the quantity of competence, this specifically modern parameter of vertical classification. The relevance of the cognitive-instrumental competence is self-evident. The idea of a meritocratic social order as a realization of the modern principle of equality separates social classes according to quantities of cognitive-instrumental competence. The second dimension of competence, the moral-aesthetic one, has to do with orientations that have characterized modern society since its beginnings and that have gained new meaning within the moral and aesthetic protests of the rising new middle classes and the social movements these new middle classes have formed (Eder, 1986).

A system of vertical classification can be constructed using these two indicators. The quantity of competence is the result of specific combination of these two dimensions of competence. Such a model of vertical classification representing the class structure of advanced modern societies is a modified version of the model developed by Bourdieu (1984). Whether this class structure develops into the direction of a preponderance of the cultural element in constituting and reproducing the class structure of advanced modern societies is left open. It has to be treated as an empirical question. The decisive point is that in order to explain this class structure the recourse to material production and the material economy has become insufficient. We have to take into account more and more the phenomenon of cultural production as the mechanism of vertical classification. Only such a theoretical perspective gives us some theoretical tools that hinder us to see in advanced modern societies nothing more than individualization everywhere. There is no "beyond status and class" (Beck, 1983) in modern society.

Vertical classification according to quantified, value-designated competence thus characterizes a new evolutionary level in the realization of a class society. This means analyzing the mechanisms that attribute positive or negative competence; this means generating a typology of classificatory struggles in terms of "recognizing" and "decognizing" competence.

Defending the proposition that in advanced modern society a class structure based on the quantity of competence develops a central problem of class analysis has remained open. As long as we have to deal with, in sociological analysis, theoretically constructed and statistically identified classes ("Klassen an sich") the question remains open whether these classes can become "real" classes ("Klassen für sich"). This question leads to the old problem of "subjective" conditions of the existence of social classes, a problem that will be considered in the following, taking into account the objective changes in class structure described previously.

3.3 Beyond Class-Specific Subcultures

3.3.1 A Critique of the "Discourse on Class"

The first example of an influential theory of class trying to identify a "real" class is the Marxian one. But it is tied to social conditions that no longer exist and maybe have never existed. The Marxian concept of a "real" class ("Klasse für sich") starts with two assumptions that have been seen as constitutive for modern society: first the separation of labor from its traditional bonds and its transformation into wage labor and second the social and cultural homogenization of wage labor constituting a proletarian life-world. These assumptions explain a first stage in the modernization of the class structure of society. But further modernization has not generated this transition from the abstract individual worker to a class unity based on a common life-world (class solidarity, class consciousness). It rather has generated the contrary. The cultural reproduction of social class has been decoupled from its structural basis[11].

Concepts of classes today can no longer be projected upon traditional life-worlds nor can their putative unity be explained by taking recourse to such traditional life-worlds. Culturally classes have been dissolved. Modern culture in fact stigmatizes them as premodern. With the repudiation of old, class-bound life-worlds the direct experience of class has been, especially within the working class (Mooser, 1983, 1984), destroyed and illegitimized. The eclipse of the visible class distinctions that characterized class interaction in early modern society also destroyed the illusions that were tied to class concepts. Class as a world of homogeneity, solidarity, and communication, as a "Klasse für sich," has been debunked. The illusion derived from treating the working class as a "real" class (Bourdieu, 1985). The demystification consists in treating it as theoretically constructed.

But the demystification process is still incomplete. The old illusions about "real" class are replaced by new ones. The theory of class formation has been replaced by the theory of stratification. The new illusion is that classes no longer exist. But this secondary "substantialization" of the notion of class as status only reproduces the old problem. Status groups are nothing but theoretically constructed social groups. There is no concrete life-world that stands for a status group. There are no "real" status groups.

A necessary condition for solving the problem of the relationship between theoretical and real classes, between class position and class existence, consists in substituting sociological theories of social inequality for a theory of classes. It requires us first of all to construct the concept of class outside the notion of inequality. For this notion still presupposes living and concrete social entities, be they classes in the traditional sense or status groups in a more modern sense. Statements about increasing or decreasing social inequality (Haferkamp, 1987) are statements that have to do only "indirectly" (i.e., in a way that has to be clarified theoretically) with changes in the class structure of society. These statements are themselves the product of a class structure. They are the symbolic strategies of social groups trying to change the conditions of class existence and thereby change the given class structure of a society. Descriptions of a class structure as one of inequality is the result of a practice of symbolic classification that antagonistic social groups in advanced modern societies engage in in order to produce and reproduce their social position vis-à-vis other groups. It is in such descriptions that we have to look for the mechanism of transforming objective class position into real classes (which does not however imply classes with class consciousness[12]).

A sufficient condition for solving the problem of the relationship between theoretical and "real" classes in societies in which traditional class cultures no longer exist requires the sociological analysis of subcultural differences that serve as their substitute. The place of traditional class cultures (like the well-known "moral economy" of the English working class described by Thompson) is taken by new class cultures. The claim of getting a just income is going to be replaced – and this is a correlate of the thesis of the quantity of competence as the parameter of vertical classification – by claims that are inherent in the idea of a cultural competence. Those who enter into such a system of vertical classification (and the modernization of society seems to draw all into it) accept uno actu the idea of a highest stage of morality, of a highest stage of taste, of a highest stage of intelligence. The highest class then is the class with the highest competence. Class cultures tend to be differentiated by criteria of lower or higher cultures. Education rather than income mark barriers between social classes. What separates "real" classes of people is the ability to justify the legitimacy of one's own culture. In a "disenchanted" social world, those who can justify better have the better chance of prevailing.

This formulation points to a fundamental change of the logic of class struggles. Class struggle is transformed into a struggle that uses the medium of claims of competence. Class struggles become struggles to justify whatever it is.

And in these struggles all reasons are legitimate as long as they allow for the rationalization of one's own cultural superiority.

This structural transformation of class cultures invalidates the traditional cultures that previously made social classes "real" classes. Attempts to defend the class culture of the "Bildungsbürger" (Conze and Kocka, 1985) and the defense of working-class culture (Mooser, 1984) are nothing but defensive reactions of their demise. These subcultures are being supplanted. But by what?

3.3.2 The Cultural Reproduction of Class

What are the class-specific subcultures beyond the traditional ones that allow for the transformation of a potential class into a real class in advanced modern societies? What are the mechanisms that generate genuinely modern class cultures?

One answer to these questions – and this answer is typical for much empirical research on social class – is to correlate "subjective" variables that indicate cultural orientations with "objective" variables that indicate class position. Such "subjective" variables include attitudes toward society and politics, toward one's own person or group (self-classifications), attitudes that can easily be taken from opinion polls. This approach is connected with the theoretical assumption that a real class would emerge only through the covariance of objective and subjective aspects of class. A real class would be defined by the homogeneity of objective and subjective conditions of social existence and empirically proved by their statistical covariance. But because tests for such homogeneity usually show that classes in the traditional sense no longer exist in modern society the conclusion is that they no longer exist. Thus, when groups with significant correlations are found they are described as "milieus" that substitute for traditional real classes (Bolte and Hradil, 1984; Hradil, 1987).

Such a way of testing for the homogeneity of objective and subjective aspects of class has some serious flaws[13]. For what is called "subjective class" is itself a theoretical construction of objective class position. What these tests examine is the covariance of two types of theoretical construction. For the attitudes people have indicate nothing but class-specific cultural differences. These cultural differences are generated by the fact that people adhere or oppose one or another norm or value. But these norms differ in their degree of legitimacy. There are more legitimate and less legitimate norms and values. And there are differences in the knowledge of the legitimate norms and values. To prove that one has an opinion (e. g., to tell an interviewer that one knows about the right way to educate children which is nothing but the way defined by professional educators as the right and legitimate one), is only another dimension of objective class. This merely allows for a more complex theoretical construction of social classes in modern society (Hurrelmann, 1985).

But how then to identify real classes? An alternative answer to this question consists in describing class cultures on a *structural* level as generated by *class-specific schemata of experiencing, perceiving, and interpreting the world.* Such schemata do not emerge at random; they are rather logically derived from the culture dominating a society. Two examples will help.

First, if we ask anyone in traditional societies, be he a peasant or an aristocrat, about his religious ideas and his religious practices we get answers verifying the assumption of a unitary and collectively shared religious world view. And yet we know from actual historical and social anthropological research (Leach, 1968; Schindler, 1984) that there are competing religious subcultures: that of the peasants and that of the lords. The popular religious culture shares the religious world-view defined by the religious high culture. Yet it lives this religion in a different way. It is the specific *use* made of the religious culture that generates religious subcultures. The analysis of religious praxis thus allows us to identify religious subcultures.

The second example refers to the modern society. A survey on the quantity of journals and books consumed would certainly support the assumption of a generalized culture of reading. Everybody reads books and magazines (or at least buys them). But a glance at specific examples shows differences built into this culture of reading. It is a classified culture, divided between "Kickers" and "Scientific American," between "Quick" and "Freibeuter," between "Bild" and "Süddeutsche Zeitung," between "National Enquirer" and "The New Yorker." These examples indicate a sharp (and certainly not unique) division between (sub)cultural worlds. What counts is not that people read but what they read. Literary culture is classified objectively by the *use* made of it. The analysis of the different types of literary praxis allows us to identify literary subcultures.

To grasp subcultural differences the social scientist thus has to look for the interpretative schemata determining the cultural praxis in a society. To identify class-specific subcultures the following hypothesis can be formulated: Class-specific subcultures are defined by schemata of experiencing, perceiving, and interpreting the social world that thematize the vertical classification of social relations in a society. This hypothesis suggests locating the structure of modern class cultures in schemata thematizing social (in)equality.

The problem of the relationship between practices, interpretative schemes, and culture can be clarified using an analogy from Leach (1976). Interpretative schemes are like musical scores. Scores regulate performances like interpretative schemes regulate cultural practices. Scores thus can be seen as systems of rules governing a performance. Thus to understand and explain a performance we have to have access to the musical text. Whether the performance is good or bad, depends on the circumstances. But the score remains the same. To understand a score it is unsufficient to listen to a performance; one also has to know the musical text. One has to be able to read musical texts.

This analogy can be extended further. For musical scores can be read only by those who know the musical language and can read its notational system. Transporting this analogy back to the social field it becomes clear that the ability to explain cultural practices presupposes the observer's "reading ability" in cultural specifics. The ability to read modern interpretative schemes implies a reading knowledge of modern culture. We would defend the thesis that the rules for reading modern interpretative schemes can be reconstructed from texts articulating what has been called "Enlightenment[14]."

The "civil society" derived from the Enlightenment has given rise to an interpretative scheme claiming moral universalism and using this interpretative scheme for the legitimation of its praxis[15]. Opposed to the proletarian culture that practiced another version of the cultural logic of modernity, civil society – at least in Western societies – has succeeded in dominating the cultural practices. The possessive bourgeois culture, the interpretative scheme of possessive individualism (Macpherson, 1967), has become the dominant principle of a genuinely modern social and cultural praxis. In the last century the intent of the bourgeois class to "cultivate" the lower classes and teach them the higher civil morality can be seen as an attempt to integrate them into the possessive bourgeois culture. It succeeded quite well (Eder, 1985). The idea that the proletarian culture has a higher morality lost all its legitimacy. The discourse on equality characteristic for the possessive version of the logic of modernity destroyed the idea of a proletarian culture and at the same time promotes the illusion – typical for this discourse – that acquiring competence will minimize class differences.

Since the last century the "scores" of modern practices have been changed, amended, or newly invented in the class struggles. The different performances resulting have modified the boundaries between the real social classes, leading to revisions of social and cultural practices. Once flourishing practices have become outmoded. The most striking revisions are tied to the rise of the service sector: the new technocratic elites and the new petite bourgeoisie committed to the service industries. The ethos of the aristocracy and the higher bourgeoisie has been revised by the groups of professionals and managers. The ethos of the "Bildungsbürgertum" (e.g., the professors) has been revised by the new intellectual groups (critics, journalists, etc.). The "protestant" ethos of the old petite bourgeoisie has been replaced by the narcissistic ethos of the new petite bourgeoisie who base their "score" on "self-fulfillment" and "self-realization." And the "proletarian" ethos of the lower classes remains dominant in some groups. These actors are radicalizing the proletarian ethos into an ethos of consumption that imitates the sophisticated consumption patterns of the middle and upper classes[16]. But this hedonism is being forceably restructured by the increase of unqualified workers and of nonworkers. In the course of these changing strategies class-specific interpretative schemata emerge that allow for analyzing class-specific practices. New forms of a class-ethos, as Bourdieu (1984) put it, are generated.

The proposition made for identifying empirically real classes has been to introduce, instead of tests for the homogeneity of objective and subjective aspects of class, a third level of analysis: namely, differential interpretative schemata of the social world which, on the one hand, generate subjective attitudes and which, on the other hand, are the product of objective class positions. These differential schemata "transform" objective class positions into subjective class positions. To the extent that this transformation succeeds the theoretical construction of social classes can claim to have identified real classes.

In the following an attempt will be made to reconstruct such a process of transformation with respect to class positions that have been constructed theoretically as being defined by differential amounts of quantity of competence. Three propositions will be defended. First, what distinguishes modern culture from traditional cultures is the ideal of equality. To know the discourse on equality constitutive for modern culture is to dispose of the reading ability of modern cultural interpretations of social reality. As soon as this discourse has to be accommodated to the objective class positions the problem emerges to explain the fact that social reality deviates from this ideal. Theories of social inequality – and this is the second proposition – try to "explain" these deviations. The interpretations of social inequality vary with the objective class positions from which one's own position and the position of others are seen. Theories of social inequality – and this is the third and decisive proposition – are class-bound forms of interpreting the ideal of equality between men[17].

3.3.3 Class-Specific Schemata of Social Experience

What are some of the characteristic schemata used to justify social class positions? One is that material inequality between actors is the outcome of their differential cognitive competence; their relative social positions are deserved. A complementary idea is that cultural inequality manifests itself as the differential moral-aesthetic competence of actors; their cultural rank is well deserved. Both ideas advance the illusion that those who populate the lower positions and those who populate the higher positions are where they should be. Such arguments are strategies for transforming the factual into something normative. They are, to use a philosophical term, the result of a specific type of a collectively practiced naturalistic fallacy: an "ecological fallacy." Those using such a fallacy claim for themselves the highest form of moral and aesthetic consciousness, of professional quality, and economic value. The specific effect on the subjective level is the interpretation of low social status as the result of incompetence.

This type of a class-specific schema of experiencing and perceiving the social world can be distinguished from that based on an individualistic ethos, where social inequality is seen as the result of differential individual achievements in society. This is a pattern common among those who, thanks to their economic and cultural wealth, can afford such an ethos. The formal structure underlying this ethos consists in not acknowledging the fact that such individualism and universalism can only be realized by a few, can only have a particular empirical relevance in society. This ethos therefore can be characterized as another type of a naturalistic fallacy: an "idealistic fallacy." By those who share and practice the idealistic fallacy, social inequality is seen as what is functionally necessary in order to make sure that the best enter into the higher positions. To fulfill this function the principle of achievement is best suited. Anyone who has reached a position is there by right.

A third schema is based quite simply on the ethos of consumption. It emerges where material interests dominate everyday life[18]. The imagery of this ethos is also based upon a specific formal structure, one that reduces the representations of status positions in society to the material resources they are tied to. This can be interpreted as a third type of a naturalistic fallacy: a "materialistic fallacy." Those who share this fallacy relate social inequality to external forces that cannot be changed by individual will, to pure chance, or to the preserve or lack of attention. The lower positions are occupied by those who were hindered from rising: by a bad father, a lack of fertile contacts, or an untimely war or depression. Had education been otherwise these actors would surely have done better.

These three images of the social world are all based upon the formal structures of *naturalistic fallacies*, deducing what should be from that which is. They can be structurally described in the following three dimensions: (1) the underlying interpretative schema; (2) the cognitive form; (3) the types of life-world (Table 3.1).

The three fallacies each allow a perception of the social reality such that the discourse of equality can be accommodated to the facts of class position. The result of such strategies of accommodations are class-specific theories of equality that are, in fact, the base of theories that legitimate the social inequality that is the reality of modern society. These theories are strategies of systematic self-deception. These interpretative schemes of social reality can thus be defined as those collectively shared and practiced fallacies[19] key to the analysis of the subjective side of objective class positions in modern society.

Table 3.1 Types of Class-Specific Cultures

Interpretative schema	Cognitive form	Types of life-world
The individualistic ethos of personal identity and of the potential equality among men	Idealistic fallacy: what counts is the quality of culture one has	Predominance of life interests in the cultural, political, and public spheres
The ethos of achievement; recognition of inequality between men	Ecological fallacy: what counts is the culture one has achieved	Predominance of life interests in the private sphere (family)
The ethos of maximizing the chances of consumption; recognition of the division of society into social classes	Materialistic fallacy: what counts as culture is the goods one has	Predominance of life interests in the sphere of work, especially the work place

3.4 A Social Critique of Morality

Theories of social inequality are the key to defining real classes in modern societies. They are suited to this task because of their function of representing the class structure and because they are set up to organize the representation of this reality in a class-specific way. Such theories are part of the cultural reproduction of objective class positions. Yet the dominant theoretical discourse on social inequality is nothing but a translation of everyday discourses on social inequality into language that supports and strengthens the everyday discourses. The theoretical discourse on social inequality produces the illusion of its own validity. It is a discourse that reproduces the systematically distorted discourses legitimating factual social inequality (Miller, 1989). And as long as the theoretical discourse fails to thematize this context of application it contributes to the reproduction of the argumentative fallacies that lie at the base of everyday discourses.

No theoretical discourse on social inequality can escape this dilemma. The normative implications built into the concept of social inequality force integration of the effects of the theory into the theory of social inequality, force cognitive reflexivity with regard to how these theories correspond to class-specific schemata of interpreting the world and to what extent they are an expression of the class structure of society.

A possible effect of such a reflexive form of theorizing is the theoretical conclusion that the morality of the upper classes is the highest morality or even the highest developed morality[20]. One could derive a normative conclusion from this theoretical statement: Only those who have reached the highest stages of morality should enter the highest positions in society. This has a consequence that is fatal to morality. For the highest morality appears to be the morality of the dominant class. This, as we know, corrupts morality. We would like to propose a different conclusion. The class cultures analyzed here could serve as preconditions for new moral and political learning processes. The dynamics of such learning processes would consist in dissolving the specific fallacies at their bases. The conditions for generating "real" classes would then no longer have to be sought in the philosophical critique of the ideals of modern culture but in the social critique of the ideals modern society claims to represent.

Modern society made the moral universalism of modern culture part of a culture that was open only to a few. While it noticed this, it hoped for a compensating effect from the educational system which was supposed to trigger moral and political learning processes. But in placing hope here it denied its own class structure. The result of the expansion of the educational system was to reproduce the modern class structure not only on the level of material needs but also on the level of culture. For it is possible to say that stupidity excludes from power. Modern moral universalism did not hinder the reproduction of the class structure. And its philosophical refinement and sophistication as discursive morality has intensified this effect.

Only sociological analysis generating a social critique of modern culture can destroy illusions about the reality of social inequality. As long a theory of class is formulated without any reflection on its effects and functions it becomes merely another part of the classificatory struggles that regulate the production and reproduction of class differences in modern society. As a theory of social inequality it remains tied to its class-specific base. A way out is moralistic theorizing: be it elitist identification with the upper classes, avantgardistic engagement for the underdogs, or the urge to be a mediator between upper and lower classes. A sociological theory of inequality can escape such temptations by relating inequality to the class structure and analyzing the discourse on inequality as a way of perceiving and interpreting this class structure. My proposition is simply to formulate a sociological theory of social inequality as a theory of the cultural reproduction of the class structure of modern society.

Notes

[1] Nothing is more opposed to sociological thinking than attempting to explain the origin of social inequality through human nature. Yet this approach is still implicit in modern economic explanations (Elster, 1986). These are logically unsatisfactory because changes toward social equality would have to entail changes in the nature of man. But we assume that human nature does not change. Thus the context of human nature becomes the central explanatory variable. A sociological reformulation of the problem to be explained is: What are the mechanisms contributing to the definitions and redefinitions of the "context?" The sociological answer is: Permanent classificatory activity is the mechanism of defining the context that is described as social inequality.

[2] Social inequality can refer to a wide spectrum of conditions. So many different things are called "unequal" that we can with reason begin to doubt the thesis that it is universal. And its wide distribution forces us to specify the cultural dimension of this term. Social inequality is not only a social fact, but also a cultural representation of social facts (Giesen, 1987).

[3] The simultaneity of universality and specificity of social inequality that is implicit in the discourse on social inequality makes distinguishing between them difficult. Schwartz' (1981) approach, taken from the sociology of knowledge, avoids the difficulty by restricting the discussion to vertical classification as a cognitive operation.

[4] This difference has even been named by some authors as the fundamental determinant of class in simple societies (Meillassoux, 1976). Other authors, using other examples from social anthropological research, perceive the division of labor between women (collectors) and men (hunters) as the primary mechanism (Moscovici, 1972).

[5] That class divisions are not described as social inequality sometimes leads to the conclusion that there is no inequality in simple societies, more exactly: that there are no classes in simple societies. This is obviously erroneous. In this sense social inequality is also a sociocentric category.

[6] This assumption obviously draws heavily on Bourdieu (1980, 1984, 1985).

[7] The issue "new social inequalities" has been a fashionable topic in the last years. It has been treated theoretically in very divergent forms. The range of interpretation is going from "continuity of capitalist class structure" through "new middle class society" to "individualized society." See among many others Beck (1983), Berger (1986), Bischoff et al. (1982), Hradil (1987).

[8] This distinction corresponds to the one Bourdieu makes between cultural and social capital (see Bourdieu, 1983).

[9] The success of market-dominated relations, even in those subsystems or fields to which a specific internal logic (art, religion, science, or political culture) has traditionally been

attributed, transforms culture into something that can be measured and therefore classified. It is moreover not the market that dominates but the model of communication that it makes possible. This model establishes a standard that allows for aggregation, but the place of money is increasingly taken over by competence which thus becomes the new medium of communication (Jensen, 1984). For this reason culture becomes "countable" as if it were economic goods. This underlies the sociological meaning of statistical analysis: to correspond to the reality that it tries to measure and to represent.

[10] Research on occupations and professions and opinion research belong not by chance to the best developed strands of social science research. They measure the two central types of competence that generate and reproduce social inequality in advanced modern societies. These competences can be substituted for each other. Someone who has no occupation or a bad one might emphasize his culture. And vice versa: Someone who does not have culture seeks a better classified occupation. It is possible to compensate. Combining occupation and culture thus seems to be an adequate measure for identifying the class structure of advanced modern societies. Such a theoretical construction of classes contains at first glance very different groups (e.g., social workers and programmers). What makes them part of one class is the net amount of competence they have.

[11] For some of the consequences of this "modernization" of the concept of class (see Eder 1989). To modernize the concept of class means to take into account the increasing relevance of culture for the objective as well as the subjective side of class.

[12] The problem of class consciousness involves more than what suffices to identify real classes. It addresses the capacity of collective action and is a problem beyond the context of this discussion.

[13] Similar problems arise in research on value change. The claim of a change toward postmaterialist values does not take into account changes in class structure that might explain changes in attitudes better than the theory of a general cultural change in society. Such changes might primarily have to do with the emergence of the new petite bourgeoisie. See as an overview of that type of research Klages (1984).

[14] Such structures therefore cannot be observed through direct observation. They have to be analyzed by reconstructive procedures, by a process of distilling the schemata that organize the present-day social world. Thus we have analyzed the political discourse of early modern German society using philosophical texts, pamphlets, and statutes in order to identify the cultural logic of the bourgeois classes. The "score" of these practices is the discourse of enlightenment (Eder, 1985).

[15] In early modern society the bourgeois class could not yet superimpose its version of the cultural logic of a modern social order, its class-specific practice upon the whole society. For it still had to share economic, social, and political power with the traditional elites on the one hand and had not succeeded yet in destroying the traditional world of plebeian culture on the other hand.

[16] This difference can be shown in consumption patterns that are organized as imitations of the higher culture. This has been described in detail by Bourdieu (1984).

[17] This means that the class-specific world view, the cognitive schematizations of the world, and the judgments of taste, the aesthetic schematizations of the world, will be excluded from the following discussion. This does not imply the assumption of their insignificance concerning the constitution of a real class.

[18] From the perspective of the workers this logic leads to a dichotomic world view. This world view differentiates between high and low, between good and bad, between freedom and necessity. This imagery of the lower classes has been described by Bourdieu (1984) as constituting an ethos of "necessity."

[19] Behind such fallacies a new types of mechanism that produces a distinctive class culture can be located. It is the prestige tied to belonging to a class that counts. Prestige is concurred, however, only when a group is closed, its quantity limited (maximizing its market value), and its ethos controlled (to integrate the group). Thus it is the prestige usually used to represent social inequality that becomes the most significant indicator of class (Wegener, 1985), not only with respect to cultural consumption, but also with respect to some

occupations of central importance for modern society. Those occupations that are the more highly classified, that are made more difficult to enter, and are rendered more exclusive through the development of a strict, even eccentric, professional behavioral code (Beck and Brater, 1978) become the more prestigious. The mechanism of forming real classes best adapted to the new way of the cultural or symbolic constitution of real classes then is closure of objectively classified groups by attributing prestige to them. This hypothesis of a new mechanism generating class cultures requires concrete analyses of practices that reproduce class-specific interpretative schemes. The aspects enumerated in Table 3.1 give only some general hints. Historical research, especially historical social anthropology, is one field of research that has so far most productively developed this mode of analysis.

[20] In the sociological analysis of a class-specific morality (and of a class-specific taste and class-specific cognitive qualifications as well) one runs into the problem of which morality is the better one. The form of a moral judgment has normative implications that there are higher or lower forms. This problem has been transformed into a psychological theory by treating the different social forms of morality as steps or stages of a moral learning process. Piaget calls the telos of this learning process the competence to produce an autonomous moral judgment. In the same vein, Kohlberg speaks of a postconventional moral judgment being the telos of the moral development of human beings. But here we find no way to go beyond the individual to the level of society. Treating such theories of moral development as a medium of the cultural reproduction of society, as done in this chapter, is intended to open up a perspective beyond moral psychologism.

References

Beck, U. (1983). "Jenseits von Stand und Klasse?" In *Soziale Ungleichheiten. Soziale Welt*, special issue 2, ed. R. Kreckel. Göttingen: Schwartz.

Beck, U. and Brater, M. (1978). *Berufliche Arbeitsteilung und soziale Ungleichheit. Eine gesellschaftlich-historische Theorie der Berufe*. Frankfurt: Campus.

Beck, U., Brater, M. and Daheim, H.J. (1980). *Soziologie der Arbeit und der Berufe, Grundlagen, Problemfelder, Forschungsergebnisse*. Reinbek: Rowohlt.

Bellmann, L., Gerlach, K. and Hübler, O. (1984). *Lohnstruktur in der Bundesrepublik Deutschland. Zur Theorie und Empirie der Arbeitseinkommen*. Frankfurt/New York: Campus.

Benseler, F., Heinze, R.G. and Klönne, A. (Ed.) (1982). *Zukunft der Arbeit*. Hamburg: VSA.

Berdahl, R.A. (Ed.) (1982). *Klassen und Kultur. Sozialanthropologische Perspektiven in der Geschichtsschreibung*. Frankfurt: Syndikat.

Berger, P.A. (1986). *Entstrukturierte Klassengesellschaft. Klassenbildung und Strukturen sozialer Ungleichheit im historischen Wandel*. Opladen: Westdeutscher Verlag.

Berger, P.A. (1987). "Klassen und Klassifikationen. Zur 'neuen Unübersichtlichkeit' in der soziologischen Ungleichheitsdiskussion." *Kölner Zeitschrift für Soziologie und Sozialpsychologie* 39: 59–85.

Béteille, A. (1965). *Caste, Class, and Power. Changing Patterns of Stratification in a Tanjore Village*. Berkeley/Los Angeles: University of California Press.

Bischoff, J. et al. (1982). *Jenseits der Klassen? Gesellschaft und Staat im Spätkapitalismus*. Hamburg: VSA.

Blossfeld, H.-P. (1985). *Bildungsexpansion und Berufschancen. Empirische Analysen zur Lage der Berufsanfänger in der Bundesrepublik*. Frankfurt: Campus.

Bolte, K.-M. and Hradil, St. (1984). *Soziale Ungleichheit*, 5th. ed. Opladen: Leske & Budrich.
Bourdieu, P. (1980). *Le sens pratique*. Paris: Minuit.
Bourdieu, P. (1983). "Ökonomisches Kapital, kulturelles Kapital, soziales Kapital." In *Soziale Ungleichheiten. Soziale Welt*, special issue 2, ed. R. Kreckel. Göttingen: Schwartz.
Bourdieu, P. (1984). *The Distinction. A Social Critique of the Judgment of Taste*. Cambridge, MA: Harvard University Press.
Bourdieu, P. (1985). *Sozialer Raum und "Klassen." Leçon sur la leçon. Zwei Vorlesungen*. Frankfurt: Suhrkamp.
Bourdieu, P., Boltanski, L., Castel, R., Chamboredon, J.-C., Lagneau, G. and Schnapper, D. (1981). *Eine illegitime Kunst. Die sozialen Gebrauchsweisen der Photographie*. Frankfurt: Europäische Verlagsanstalt.
Conze, W. and Kocka, J. (1985). *Bildungsbürgertum im 19. Jahrhundert*. Stuttgart: Klett.
DiMaggio, P. and Mohr, J. (1985). "Cultural Capital, Educational Attainment, and Marital Selection." *American Journal of Sociology* 90: 1231–1261.
Dumont, L. (1967). *Homo Hierarchicus*. Paris: Presses Universitaires de France.
Eder, K. (1985). *Geschichte als Lernprozeß? Zur Pathogenese politischer Modernität in Deutschland*. Frankfurt: Suhrkamp.
Eder, K. (1986). "Soziale Bewegung und kulturelle Evolution. Überlegungen zur Rolle der neuen sozialen Bewegungen in der kulturellen Evolution der Moderne." In *Die Moderne – Kontinuitäten und Zäsuren. Soziale Welt*, special issue 4, ed. J. Berger. Göttingen: Schwartz.
Eder, K. (1989). "Jenseits der nivellierten Mittelstandsgesellschaft. Das Kleinbürgertum als Schlüssel zu einer Klassenanalyse in fortgeschrittenen Industriegesellschaften." In *Klassenlage, Lebensstil und kulturelle Praxis. Beiträge zu Pierre Bourdieus Klassentheorie*, ed. K. Eder. Frankfurt: Suhrkamp.
Elster, J. (1986). *Subversion der Rationalität*. Frankfurt: Campus.
Franz, H.-W., Kruse, W. and Rolff, H.-G. (1986). *Neue alte Ungleichheiten. Berichte zur sozialen Lage der Bundesrepublik*. Opladen: Westdeutscher Verlag.
Giesen, B. (1987). "Natürliche Ungleichheit, soziale Ungleichheit, ideale Gleichheit. Zur Evolution von Deutungsmustern sozialer Ungleichheit." In *Soziologie der sozialen Ungleichheit*, ed. B. Giesen and H. Haferkamp. Opladen: Westdeutscher Verlag.
Gusfield, J. R. (1966). *Symbolic Crusade. Status Politics and the American Temperance Movement*. Urbana: University of Illinois Press.
Gusfield, J. R. (1981). "Social Movements and Social Change: Perspectives of Linearity and Fluidity." In *Research in Social Movements, Conflict and Change*, vol. 4, ed. L. Kriesberg. Greenwich: JAI Press Inc.
Haferkamp, H. (1987). "Angleichung ohne Gleichheit." In *Soziologie der sozialen Ungleichheit*, ed. B. Giesen and H. Haferkamp. Opladen: Westdeutscher Verlag.
Haller, M. (1983). *Theorie der Klassenbildung und soziale Schichtung*. Frankfurt: Campus.
Hradil, St. (1987). *Sozialstrukturanalyse in einer fortgeschrittenen Gesellschaft. Von Klassen und Schichten zu Lagen und Milieus*. Opladen: Leske & Budrich.
Hurrelmann, K. (1985). "Soziale Ungleichheit und Selektion im Erziehungssystem. Ergebnisse und Implikationen der sozialstrukturellen Sozialisationsforschung." In *Die Analyse sozialer Ungleichheit*, ed. H. Strasser and J.H. Goldthorpe. Opladen: Westdeutscher Verlag.

Jensen, St. (1984). "Aspekte der Medientheorie." *Zeitschrift für Soziologie* 13: 154–164.
Kern, H. and Schumann, M. (1984). *Das Ende der Arbeitsteilung. Rationalisierung in der industriellen Produktion.* München: Beck.
Klages, H. (1984). *Wertorientierungen im Wandel. Rückblick, Gegenwartsanalyse, Prognosen.* Frankfurt: Campus.
Kreckel, R. (1982). "Class, Status, and Power? Begriffliche Grundlagen für eine politische Soziologie der sozialen Ungleichheit." *Kölner Zeitschrift für Soziologie und Sozialpsychologie* 34: 617–648.
Kreckel, R. (Ed.) (1983). *Soziale Ungleichheiten. Soziale Welt*, special issue 2. Göttingen: Schwartz.
Leach, E. (Ed.) (1968): *Dialectic of Practical Religion.* Cambridge: University Press.
Leach, E. (1976). *Culture and Communication. The Logic by which Symbols are Connected.* Cambridge: University Press.
Luhmann, N. (1985). "Zum Begriff der sozialen Klasse." In *Soziale Differenzierung*, ed. N. Luhmann. Opladen: Westdeutscher Verlag.
Macpherson, C. B. (1967). *Die politische Theorie des Besitzindividualismus. Von Hobbes bis Locke.* Frankfurt: Suhrkamp.
Meillassoux, C. (1973). "Y a-t-il des castes aux Indes?" *Cahiers Internationaux de Sociologie* 54: 5–24.
Meillassoux, C. (1976). *"Die wilden Früchte der Frau." Über häusliche Produktion und kapitalistische Wirtschaft.* Frankfurt: Syndikat.
Miller, M. (1989). *Systematisch verzerrte Legitimationsdiskurse.* Einige kritische Bemerkungen zu Bourdieus Habitustheorie. In *Klassenlage, Lebensstil und kulturelle Praxis. Beiträge zu Pierre Bourdieus Klassentheorie*, ed. K. Eder. Frankfurt: Suhrkamp.
Mooser, J. (1983). "Auflösung der proletarischen Milieus." *Soziale Welt* 34: 270–306.
Mooser, J. (1984). *Arbeiterleben in Deutschland 1900–1970.* Frankfurt: Suhrkamp.
Moscovici, S. (1972). *La société contre nature.* Paris: Union Générale d'Editions.
Niessen, H.-J. and Ollmann, R. (1986). *Schattenwirtschaft in der Bundesrepublik. Eine empirische Bestandsaufnahme der sozialen und räumlichen Verteilung schattenwirtschaftlicher Aktivitäten.* Köln: Leske & Budrich.
Schindler, N. (1984). "Spuren in der Geschichte der 'anderen' Zivilisation. Probleme und Perspektiven einer historischen Volkskulturforschung." In *Volkskultur. Zur Wiederentdeckung des vergessenen Alltags (16.–20. Jahrhundert)*, ed. R. Van Dülmen and N. Schindler. Frankfurt: Fischer.
Schmid, K.-P. (1987). "Die Kluft wird immer kleiner. Die Umverteilung von unten nach oben hat nicht stattgefunden." *Die Zeit* – Nr. 10 – 27. Februar 1987.
Schwartz, B. (1981). *Vertical Classification. A Study in Structuralism and in the Sociology of Knowledge.* Chicago: University of Chicago Press.
Touraine, A. (1985). "Klassen, soziale Bewegungen und soziale Schichtung in einer nachindustriellen Gesellschaft." In *Die Analyse sozialer Ungleichheit*, ed. H. Strasser and J. H. Goldthorpe. Opladen: Westdeutscher Verlag.
Tumin, M. M. (1967). *Social Stratification. The Forms and Functions of Inequality.* Englewood Cliffs, N.J.: Prentice-Hall.
Wegener, B. (1985). "Gibt es Sozialprestige?" *Zeitschr. f. Soziologie* 14: 209–235.
Wippler, R. (1987). "Kulturelle Ressourcen, gesellschaftlicher Erfolg und Lebensqualität." In *Soziologie der sozialen Ungleichheit*, ed. B. Giesen and H. Haferkamp. Opladen: Westdeutscher Verlag.

Wright, E.O. (1985). "Was bedeutet neo und was heißt marxistisch in der neomarxistischen Klassenanalyse." In *Die Analyse sozialer Ungleichheit*, ed. H. Strasser and J.H. Goldthorpe. Opladen: Westdeutscher Verlag.

4 Towards a Sociology of Postmodern Culture*

Mike Featherstone

4.1 Introduction: Postmodernism in Sociology

In *Social Theory and Modern Sociology*, Anthony Giddens outlines "Nine Theses on the Future of Sociology" in which the first thesis suggests that "Sociology will increasingly shed the residue of nineteenth- and early twentieth-century social thought" (1987a: 26). Here Giddens develops the currently popular argument that sociology is and will continue to be bound up with the "project of modernity." He does so to point away from the economic reductionism that he sees as a pervasive legacy of nineteenth-century thought, to focus on three other major parameters of modernity: the development of administrative power, the development of military power, and warfare. Finally, he states:

> There is the cultural dimension of modernity – something obviously highly complex in its own right. In some guises, the analysis of this dimension has long been a preoccupation of sociology. Sociologists have understood the emergence of their own discipline against the background of the rise of "rationalism" and the "disenchantment of the world" attendant upon secularization. But once more it would probably be true to say that the culture of modernity has been understood largely as the reflex of capitalism or industrialism. Even Max Weber's famous attempts to claim an independent role for "ideas" concentrated upon the conditions that initially gave rise to capitalism, rather than proposing a continuing role for a particular autonomous modern culture. Current controversies about what many have labelled "post-modernity" should perhaps rather be seen as the first real initiatives in the ambitious task of charting the cultural universe resulting from the ever-more complete disintegration of the traditional world. At a minimum they surely express the strong sense that pre-established models of cultural analysis were radically defective (Giddens, 1987a: 28–29).

Although there are many interesting issues in this quotation, only two brief points will be made here. First, Giddens highlights the potential of postmodernity, or perhaps we should say postmodernism, as a superior model for charting contemporary culture. Unfortunately, this point is not developed, and in Giddens' only previous reference to postmodernism in a paper entitled "Modernism and Post-Modernism," commenting on Habermas (1981), he does not, to my knowledge, refer to postmodernism in the text (Giddens, 1981). Giddens' emphasis on the potential of postmodern cultural analysis could perhaps be connected to his preference for a "middle strategy" that seeks to go beyond the duality of objectivism and relativism through the development of an "ontology of potentials" as part of his structuration theory (see Cohen, 1986,

* An earlier version of this chapter was given at a seminar at the University of Leeds. I would like to thank all who attended for their helpful comments.

1987). Second, the quotation is one of his few direct references to culture as a substantive dimension of modernity or of society. That Giddens (1987b) is now at last turning toward the development of a theory of a cultural production, which might underpin his discussion of the culture of modernity and postmodernity, is evident in his essay "Structuralism, Post-structuralism and the Production of Culture."

In more general terms, one cannot but be aware of the way in which the subject of this volume, *"Social Structure and Culture,"* bringing together representatives of various Sociological Theory Groups from a number of European nations, is merely another symptom of the general elevation of culture, to the center of theorizing within sociology in recent years. One could also point to the inclusion of a major symposium on culture with five sessions at the International Sociological Association Congress in New Delhi in 1986 and the recent formation of a Culture Section by the American Sociological Association which held its first sessions in 1987. It has been suggested by Donaldson Langer (1984: 9) that this recent upsurge of interest in broader cultural questions and perception of the sociology of culture as a legitimate field of inquiry represents a major shift within sociology. Up until the mid-1970s sociological interest in culture and the arts was often considered eccentric, dilettantish, and, at best, marginal. In this tradition the discipline boundaries between those sociologists, who had some interest in the arts, and literary critics and art historians, who saw sociology as irrelevant to understanding the sacred domain of culture, were relatively strong. One symptom of the breakdown of the barriers between the fields has been the emergence of a range of journals in the English-speaking world since the 1970s which have become open to theorizations of culture which draw their audiences from a wide range of disciplines. Some deal exclusively with culture. Here we can think of *Working Papers in Cultural Studies*; *Ideology and Consciousness*; *Oxford Literary Review*; *Block*; *Semiotext(e)*; *Tabloid*; *Substance*; *New German Critique*; *Diacritics*; *Theory and Society*; *Humanities in Society*; *Telos*; *Thesis Eleven*; *Praxis International*; *Canadian Journal of Political and Social Theory*; *Philosophy and Social Criticism*; *'Media, Culture and Society'*; *Politics, Culture and Society*; *Social Text*; *Theory, Culture & Society*, and the three new journals launched in 1987 by a British publisher: *New Formations*, *Cultural Studies*, and *Textual Practice*. The rise of interest in feminism, Marxism, structuralism, poststructuralism, semiology, critical theory, and psychoanalysis also helped to raise the profile of cultural questions. In addition, those interested in theorizations of culture – the relationship between culture and society and questions of ideology, language, knowledge, discourse, subjectivity, and agency, which have become intertwined with the explanations of changes in the arts and the cultural sphere – might well now expect to have to sift through a range of journals outside sociology and not only in cultural studies and the arts but also in politics, history, geography, art, architecture, philosophy, and planning. (For a brief discussion of these changes in relation to French social theory see Featherstone, 1986.)

These changes require careful documentation and explanation in terms of the dynamic of the academic and intellectual fields as well as their capacity to respond to and thematize sociocultural changes. They should not be taken just on the level of a paradigm shift or the victory of a superior set of methodologies, which is often how they have been presented to academic audiences, who could be forgiven a degree of bewilderment at the dazzling array of cultural theorists served up. The sociological theorist who had until recently some sense of a firm set of central issues and debates, which in their most ambitious form could aspire to provide a foundation for sociology to ground the other subjects in the social sciences, now had to take a step backward as deconstruction, post-structuralism, and postmodernism appeared on the agenda or even threatened to render the existing agendas obsolete. Foucault, Lyotard, Deleuze, Derrida, and Baudrillard have all recently been discussed in papers at the British Sociological Association's Theory Group meetings which now examines wider ranging topics with a cultural emphasis such as "Modernity and Postmodernity" and "the Body" as well as establishing stronger links with other European Sociological Theory Groups to accelerate the interchange of information.

For many sociologists the terms postmodernity and postmodernism may well have come first to the fore in the early 1980s with the "debate" between Habermas and Foucault. Both terms do, of course, have a much longer history in the first use of *postmodernism* was described as a minor reaction to modernism by Frederico de Onis in 1934; *postmodernity* was first coined to designate a new cycle in Western civilization by Toynbee in 1947 (see Hassan, 1985). The artistic use of the term, postmodernism, gained priority over the epochal use as the term became popular in the 1960s, when it was used in the United States by young artists such as Rauschenberg, Cage, Burroughs, and Barthelme and critics such as Fiedler, Hassan, and Sontag to refer to a movement beyond the "exhausted" high modernism which was regarded as having become institutionalized in the museum and in the academy. The term gained wider usage in architecture, the visual and performing arts, and music in the 1970s and then underwent a rapid series of mutations as it was exported to France in the late 1970s and adopted by critics such as Kristeva and Lyotard. It was then exported back to the United States largely in the form of Derrida's poststructuralist deconstructionism. The term was also exported to Germany in the late 1970s and assumed by Habermas (1981) in his 1980 Adorno prize essay in the context of a discussion of modernity as an uncompleted project in which he called Foucault and Derrida "young conservatives" (see Huyssen, 1984). The debates between Habermas and Foucault and Lyotard and Habermas and the formulations of it in terms of critical theory versus postmodernity have been largely conducted by third parties (see Bernstein, 1985; Hoy, 1986). There are many dimensions to the debate of which would like to make two salient points. First, Habermas' (1981) dissatisfaction with Foucault and Derrida (and by association with Deleuze and Lyotard) was for endorsing a decentered boundless subjectivity, content to experience expressive intensities that were effectively derived from the postmodernist avant-garde which had sought to break down the boundaries between art and everyday life and hence gave primacy to aesthetic experiences and gestures over morality and communicative modes of truth. Habermas, from earlier essays such as "Technology, Science and Ideology" (1971) onward, had sought to theorize and find ways to reverse the perceived invasion of the communicative structures of the sociocultural life-world by instrumental and strategic rationality. From this perspective to have to deal with a new threat to the sociocultural life-world's communicative potential arising from the aesthetic sphere presents a further unwelcomed complication. Second, Habermas' (1985: 203) own attempt to harness the critical potential of aesthetic experience to illuminate communicative truths should, one would expect, have only limited success given the difficulty of translating across two different cultural modalities.

The growth of interest in poststructuralism, deconstruction, and post-modernism, coupled with Habermas' (1984) work on the trajectory of and relationship between the different sectors of cultural modernity, science, morality, and art, therefore needs to be understood on a number of levels within the context of a more general emergence of interest in wider cultural questions. These point both to the metatheoretical foundations of modes of knowledge, as well as to the type of cultural complex that could best provide some version of the good, meaningful, or satisfactory life. Postmodernism effectively thrusts aesthetic questions toward the center of sociological theory: It offers aesthetic models and justifications for the reading and critique of texts (the pleasure of the text, intertextuality, writerly texts) and aesthetic models for life (the expressive aestheticization of life, art as the good of life).

This oversimplified narrative, then may help us to point toward the recent growth of interest in culture within sociology, one recent manifestation of which is Giddens' (1987a) acknowledgment of culture as a fourth dimension of modernity and his suggestion that postmodernism may potentially offer a superior mode of analysis with which to chart the modern cultural universe. Yet before we can unpack and try to assess the conceptual and anticonceptual apparatus within the postmodern arsenal – the emphasis upon discontinuities, writerly texts, paradoxes, ironies, its playful reflexivity, celebration of difference, and critique of universalizations and totalizations, including the end of meta-narratives and the end of history – we must return briefly to Giddens. His sixth thesis on the future of sociology states that "Sociologists will redevelop a concern with large-scale, long-term processes of social transformation" (Giddens, 1987a: 41). A claim that, on the face of it, seems to run directly counter to the assumption that postmodern modes of analysis are superior. It also, and Giddens is aware of this, runs counter to his previous endorsement in the first thesis of the need to break free from the tradition of nineteenth-century thought. Giddens argues that we need to focus on long-term processes to capture the large-scale social changes that are accelerating in the twentieth century.

Large-scale, long-term process sociology has undergone a revival in recent years. Here one thinks of the work of Wallerstein (1974, 1980), Habermas

(1984), Giddens (1985) himself, and, more recently, Mann (1986) and Hall (1985). Yet the major exponent who springs most immediately to mind is Elias with his theory of civilizing processes (Elias, 1978, 1982), the sociogenesis of sociology (Elias, 1984a), and the changing balance of power between the sexes (Elias, 1987a). Elias (1971) argues that sociologists should go beyond a common view of history held in sociology and history that tends to assume social changes are unstructured. Rather than see history as a ceaseless pilgrimage of groups that come and go, whose knowledge seems equally valid, we "have to investigate ... the structure of long-term changes in the intergenerational groupings of human producers and carriers of ... knowledge" (Elias, 1972: 125). We have to be aware that there are instances of knowledge produced by specialist groups gaining a momentum of its own, and that specialist groups of knowledge producers may gain a limited and relative autonomy in relation to other interdependent groups (Elias, 1971: 250). Hence according to Elias we can escape the quagmire of absolute relativism with its forced equalities and overstated polarities that occurs when we refuse to see the dynamics of knowledge. Rather we can investigate developments in particular funds of knowledge that bring about relative autonomy, in contrast to the emphasis upon breaks and discontinuities in the theories of knowledge of, for example, Kuhn and Bachelard (Elias, 1972)[1].

The discussion of long-term processes hence raises the question of whether we should aim to provide a sociology of postmodernism rather than advocating a postmodern sociology. If we seek to understand postmodernism should we forego sociological methodologies and use postmodern models of analysis to produce a postmodern account of postmodernism? This would effectively point to a sublation of sociology and a new postmodern sociology or antisociology. Let us speculatively examine some of the possibilities that might result. A postmodern account of postmodernism would resist the examination of developments in knowledge and the interrelation between specialists in symbolic production and other groups to provide a parasitical account – a parasite of a parasite – which would use postmodern strategies to play on the unities and differences within postmodernism, its paradoxes, ironies, incoherences, intertextuality, and multiphrenic qualities. Alternatively, it might follow the strategy of smuggling in a coherent meta-narrative, a tale telling a version of the fall, to announce the end of meta-narratives (Hutcheon, 1987 and others have accused Lyotard of this strategy). Yet a further possibility would be to assume that certain developments, long-term processes, have built up cumulatively to a final rupture that has rent the historical process to produce a new postsocietal configuration: postmodern culture. As this perspective argues that we are already within a postmodern culture any attempt to theorize postmodernism using the old techniques and methodologies would necessarily fail. The account of the postmodern simulational world developed by Baudrillard (1983a, 1983b) is of this type with its emphasis on the cultural overload produced by an overproduction of information via the media which leads to an implosion of meaning and a simulational world, a hyperspace in which we live beyond normativity and classification in an aesthetic hallucination of reality. Baudrillard is certainly one of the most extreme of the academic writers on postmodernism in pushing the logic of postmodernism as far as it will go, revelling in the postmodern linguistic tropes and images of a postsociety – the end of social – beyond the reach of sociological explanation (for a North American account of postmodern "excremental culture" that draws much from Baudrillard, see Kroker and Cook, 1986). For Baudrillard, any attempt to discuss the glutinous masses in terms of normativity, or class analysis in the manner of Bourdieu, is doomed to failure as it is a form of analysis belonging to the previous stage of the system now superseded.

A further implication of a postmodern sociology would be to emphasize not only the end of the social but also the end of history. The account of postmodernism presented by Vattimo (1985) emphasizes that postmodern is not just to be conceived as signifying a historical break that points to a move beyond modernity. Postmodernism involves the notions of a postmetaphysical and postmodern epoch, with the rejection of the modernist idea of historical development, or a unifying point of view that can be imposed upon history. In effect there has always already been the end of history; it is only now that we can recognize and accept it. Postmodernism's critique and rejection of the meta-narratives of modernity (science, religion, philosophy, humanism, socialism, feminism, etc.), all of which seek to impose some sense of coherence and cogency onto history, directs us away from universalizations toward the particularity of local knowledge. This is a shift that is advocated on a theoretical level via arguments that build on the work of Nietzsche, Heidegger, and Derrida; yet this advocated theoretical shift itself may well have come to the fore at a particular moment in time and therefore should be symbiotically related to what is regarded as a more general dehistoricization of experience that is taking place within contemporary consumer culture, which also undercuts universalizations and the sense of ordered narrativity on the everyday level through its accentuation of a multifaceted and ever-changing present.

The questions we face in trying to understand postmodern culture sociologically, therefore, revolve around understanding how these two aspects: The production and circulation of postmodern theories (many of which have a sense of end of history, albeit nontragic finality, about them) and the wider production and circulation of everyday postmodern cultural experiences and practices are related. Here we need not be for or against postmodernism, rather we have to explain sociologically how postmodernism is possible, and how an interest in the loose family of notions associated with it have come into being. This is despite the obvious accusation of advocates of postmodernism that this very enterprise is fatally flawed and represents an outmoded attachment to modernist meta-theory. In brief, then, we seek to understand and point toward the need for an explanation of these two aspects the theoretical, and everyday, of the claimed movement toward the postmodern, in which *postmodernism*, which is theorized and expressed in intellectual and artistic practices, can be seen as an index or harbinger of a broader *postmodern culture*, a wider set of changes in the production, consumption, and circulation of cultural goods and practices. Eventually it may be the case that these tendencies assume epochal proportions and hence signify a move toward *postmodernity*.

If we reject the notion of a postmodern sociology in favor of a sociological account of postmodernism and regard it as part of a large-scale long-term process we face a daunting task beyond the scope of this chapter. All that this chapter seeks to do is sketch the outlines such an approach might follow. *First*, we wish to contest some of the closures that occur if we follow postmodernism's claims (albeit often implicit) to be a superior methodology and to have detected a significant break in the historical process that puts us into or on the edge of a postmodern culture and eventual epoch or antiepoch of postmodernity. *Second*, the intention is to suggest tentatively that postmodernism should be understood in terms of processes taking place within the dynamic of intergroup relations[2]. More specifically, we need to ask who are the producers and carriers of postmodern symbolic goods. We need to examine the actual practices of postmodernism to discover the dynamics and processes that are at work within various fields – art, architecture, music, literature – and among intellectuals and academics, as well as examining ways in which new conditions emerge that increase the circulation and interchange between producers and disseminators in these fields. Here we can think of strategies of outsiders against the established, of monopolization and usurpation processes, the effects of inflation, etc. These changes themselves should be related to the long-term processes that have led to a general rise in the numbers of specialists in symbolic production, dissemination, and reproduction and changed their relationship to other groups in society and raised both their general valorization by society and their own capacity to argue for and demonstrate their social effectiveness. This is not to argue that the emergence, numerical rise, and increased powerpotential of these groups within the middle class and, more recently, what has been termed the new middle class, amounts to anything like the rise of a new class based on cultural capital that can challenge the old bourgeois class with its assumed increasingly obsolete power base in economic capital. The intellectuals and specialists in symbolic production are far from becoming the type of new hegemonic class that Gouldner (1979) argued. Yet having said this we should not underestimate the changes in the interdependencies and balance between economic specialists and symbolic specialists that have occurred. The emergence and expansion of sectors of the new middle class, or what has been termed the service class (Lash and Urry, 1987), creates not only specialists in symbolic production and dissemination but also a potential audience that may be more sensitive and attuned to the range of cultural and symbolic goods and experiences that have been labeled postmodern.

More specifically in relation to the emergence of postmodernism in the arts in the 1960s and in certain academic and intellectual fields in the 1970s we should focus attention on the emergence of a particularly large generational cohort "the 1960s generation" which entered higher education in larger numbers than ever before, and which developed orientations, tastes, and dispositions that are carried with them as they move through adult life. It can also be argued that artists and intellectuals detect, crystallize, and disseminate particular definitions of a generational consciousness to various publics and markets. In this sense the sensibilities of "the 1960s generation" that they articulated underrepresent the more stable and traditional orientations of members from business, industrial, scientific backgrounds of aspirations and play up the aestheticization of life, the emotional decontrol and informalization. It has often been observed that there are continuities between "the 1960s generation" and a whole range of countercultural movements going back as far as the Romantics (Abrams and McCulloch, 1975; Martin, 1981; Weiß, 1986; Sayre and Loewy, 1984).

What is of interest here is that this project of the aestheticization of life with its celebration of the artist as hero and the stylization of life into a work of art – both the expressivity of the artist's project and the life-style – found resonances in a larger audience beyond intellectual and artistic circles through the expansion of particular occupational groups specializing in symbolic goods who acted as both producers/disseminators and consumers/audiences for cultural goods. The expansion of the "new cultural intermediaries" as Bourdieu (1984) calls them, has involved a widening of the range of legitimate cultural goods and the breaking down of some of the old symbolic hierarchies. The new tastemakers, constantly on the look out for new cultural goods and experiences, are also engaged in the production of popular pedagogies and guides to living and life-style. They encourage an inflation in cultural goods, constantly draw upon artistic and intellectual trends for inspiration, and help to create new conditions of artistic and intellectual production by working alongside them. The new cultural intermediaries can be found in market-oriented consumer cultural occupations – the media, advertising, design, fashion, etc. – and in state-funded and private helping professions, counseling, educational and therapy occupations. To understand the receptivity to postmodern goods and practices we therefore need to investigate the processes within society that have brought into greater prominence specialists in symbolic production and, specifically, the changing relations between artists, intellectuals, academics, and cultural intermediaries and their shifting interdependencies in a wider figuration containing businessmen, politicians, and administrators. Of course the struggle between what has been called the new petite bourgeoisie (Bourdieu, 1984) and the old petite bourgeoisie, with Thatcherism in Britain mounting strong attacks on artists and intellectuals in the name of Victorian values, still continues. Yet it is interesting to note the resilience of the specialists in symbolic production and dissemination and their capacity to adopt new tactics in unfavorable situations. Rather perhaps we should see this process in the Eliasian metaphor of a balance, with swings toward the centers of symbolic production in the 1960s and 1970s and swings away toward the greater dominance of centers of economic production in the 1980s (Wouters, 1987). The notion of a struggle between symbolic and economic specialists should also not blind us to their basic interdependencies and ways in which excess finance capital in the 1980s may be used to finance postmodern architecture or inflate art markets, or the ways in which cities encourage symbolic specialists to move into renewal areas (e. g., SoHo in New York described by Zukin, 1982a, 1982b) to speed up gentrification and a general rise in the prestige and symbolic capital of the city. Hence there may be particular sites where what has been referred to as the process of "postmodernization" (Cooke, 1988) is taking place.

4.2 The Development of Postmodernism within the Cultural and Intellectual Fields

If we examine some of these changes in more detail it would be useful to first focus on the place of postmodernism within specific artistic, intellectual, and academic fields. First, there is not yet a unified view of postmodernism evident across the fields of architecture, literature, music, art, photography, the performing arts, philosophy, and criticism. Jameson (1984c: 62), for example, distinguishes between the promodernist postmodernism of Lyotard and the antimodernist postmodernism of Jencks. Recalling his first use of the concept in his book, *The Language of Postmodern Architecture*, Jencks (1984: 6) tells us that

> When I first wrote the book in 1975 and 1976 the word and concept of Post-Modernism had only been used, with any frequency in literary criticism. Most perturbing, as I later realized it had been used to mean "Ultra-Modern", referrring to the extremist novels of William Burroughs and a philosophy of nihilism and anti-convention. While I was aware of these writings of Ihab Hassan and others, I used the term to mean the opposite of all this: the end of avant-garde extremism, the partial return to tradition and the central role of communicating with the public – and architecture is *the* public art.

In the field of literary criticism the term postmodern had been used a few years earlier by Spanos, possibly ignorant of its previous use by other literary critics such as Hassan in the 1960s. Spanos (1987: 2), like Jencks, has recently recalled his first use of the term in setting up the journal *boundary 2*.

> In the fall of 1970 ... I persuaded my colleague the novelist Robert Kroetsch that the time or, as I would put it now, the occasion called for the inauguration of *boundary 2* the "journal of postmodern literature" we had corresponded about.... In subtitling *boundary 2* "a journal of postmodern literature" we were, it turns out, introducing a term that has become fundamental to the critical discourse of contemporary American literary history. At that time, however, I was not at all sure what we intended by the word *postmodern*. What prompted its use was my strong sense that literary modernism, especially as a critical discourse, had come to its end, that the differential space opened up by the boundary it had crossed in the late decades of the nineteenth century and early decades of the twentieth had been sealed off and thoroughly colonized by and within another boundary.

What the two examples seem to suggest is a preoccupation with the issues of their own particular field and the coining of a term that they wished to use to detect, indicate, establish, and legitimate a break and promote a new mode of analysis that was distanced from that of the established, especially the established modernism in their field: hence *postmodernism*. Since the mid-1970s there has been a greater circulation of information by commentators, artists, and academics who have latched onto and sought to explore the meanings of the term, which has furthered the possibility of a more generally accepted range of meaning for postmodernism.

The art of *naming* itself is an important strategy on the part of groups engaged in struggles with other groups. The use of a new term like postmodernism by outsiders or newcomers to the field may occur when their chances to move upward through the existing legitimate hierarchical structures are restricted. These avant-garde tactics are designed to create a space ahead of the established, which will ultimately lead to a reclassification of the field that redesignates the established as the outmoded.

It is tempting to see postmodernism as an avant-garde strategy, arising initially in the artistic field, and place it within a long history of avant-garde movements that go back to not only the 1850s and 1870s in Paris, but also to the Futurist, Dada, and Surrealist Movements and left avant-garde in Russia and Germany in the 1920s. The problem with this approach is that it tends to focus on the similarities of outsider strategies, the periodic break out of antagonism and conflict in the uneasy interdependence that the specialists in symbolic production find themselves engaged in with economic specialists, or the construction of an "eternal" cycle of activism, antagonism, militarism, and agonism which all such movements are meant to go through (Poggioli, 1973). It fails to sufficiently differentiate between the *general* conditions for the emergence of avant-gardes since the 1850s in metropolitan centers, with their access to publicity and communications, and the necessity of a professional and leisure class audience and the *particular* conditions of specific movements (Tagg, 1985/1986). In the case of postmodernism we can think of the need to examine the specific relationship between artists, critics, intellectuals, dealers, and the art institutions that occurred in the 1960s in New York when postmodern art emerged. We need to do this in the awareness that those active in the production and designation of postmodern texts/objects, antitexts/antiobjects may resist all attempts to draw similarities between their mode of work and previous avant-gardes, and indeed that circumstances may pertain that may make it unlikely for them to cohere into an avant-garde movement, despite efforts on the part of critics, dealers, and those active in art institutions to promote a distinct break and new avant-garde.

Indeed one of the characteristics of postmodern art in the 1960s was its attack on institutionalized art: on the museums and galleries, the critical academic hierarchies of taste, and the consecration of works of art as clearly demarcated objects of display. This attack on autonomous, institutionalized art was itself not new: As Peter Burger (1984) demonstrates it occurred with the historical avant-garde of the 1920s with its rejection of Aestheticism. In this context it is interesting to note that in the 1960s there was a revival of interest in the Dada and Surrealists Movements and in particular the work of Marcel Duchamp

(Huyssen, 1984). It has also been argued that postmodernism first occurred with the 1920s historical avant-garde who effectively practiced postmodernism *avant la lettre* (Lash and Urry, 1987). In the 1960s we have similar and perhaps more extreme attempts to break down the barriers between art and everyday life, to resist art becoming a museum commodity-object. Here we think of the "happenings" and landscape art devised by Christo, the Bulgarian-American artist, whose "events" included wrapping part of the Australian coast and draping an enormous curtain over a Colorado valley. Yet even this attempt at antiart, to deny a permanent art object by emphasizing a transitory experience that could not be objectified and commodified, soon found its way back into the art institutions via photographers, films, books, and exhibitions of Christo's work (Martin, 1981: 110).

One of the leading postmodern critics in the 1960s, Susan Sontag (1967), argued in this vein that the art object should not be a text, but another sensory object in the world. This new sensibility favored music, dance, painting, sculpture, and architecture over the novel. This emphasis upon sensation, on the primary immediacy of the figural as opposed to the discursive, has led the postmodern aesthetics to be characterized as an aesthetics of the body (Lash and Urry, 1987). Two brief examples can be given to illustrate this. The first is the body art of Oppenheim. A videotape entitled "I'm failing" shows Oppenheim trying to drown himself in a tank of water (a parody, perhaps, of Salvador Dali's earlier "Inverted Submarine" in which he nearly drowned himself; a description appears in his autobiography). Another video shows in slow motion rocks being dropped on Oppenheim's stomach. The videotape of his multimedia presentation, "Disturbational Art," is interesting in that it shows Oppenheim eating 10 gingerbread men and then microscopic color slides of the excreta of the gingerbread men, which are projected in galleries (open to misreading as merely abstract painting), alongside a running loop videotape of the whole ingestion and excremental process (Wall, 1987). The second example is that of the Australian body artist, Stelarc, who uses medical instruments to film the insides of his own body – blood flows, muscles, heartbeats –, his own interiority and "acoustical landscape" which shows the body as something both repulsive and fascinating (Kroker and Kroker, 1987: vi).

It is clearly difficult to conceive how such body art, happenings or art that plays on repetition and chance (in music we can think of Briers' "Sinking of the Titanic," which attempts to mimic music played under water and can be played in any number of ways to achieve a similar openness to some visual works or art, or Laurie Anderson's music in which all the instruments are synthesized bits of her own voice and the lyrics random chaining of cut-up vocal phrases) can be recuperated into established hierarchies of taste and aesthetic systems. This, of course, is the point: to collapse the old distinctions between high culture and mass culture, to challenge the notion of the autonomous creative artist and artisanal definition of art that modernism perpetuated, to show art is everywhere, not any in the body, but also in the degraded landscape of mass culture. Hence the rise of pop art in the 1960s and its characterization as a cultural break linked to the rise of the counterculture (see Hebdige, 1983; Huyssen, 1981; Martin, 1981).

There is an important sense in which the artists' own self-understanding of their project in producing postmodern works/antiworks of art only becomes articulated through their relationship to the critics and intellectuals. It is often remarked that in the case of postmodernism the critics have played a more powerful role than ever before, and that "Postmodernism has in some ways become a critics' term without ever quite becoming an artistic movement" (Bradbury, 1983: 325). While there has been a growth in the numbers of artists-theoreticians since the end of the 1960s (along with a general expansion of art institutions, publishing of books and journals dealing with art theory and culture criticism, and the various audiences that will be discussed later), we should not overlook the way in which this is related to a long-term process of expansion in the numbers and powerpotential of the specialists in symbolic production since the eighteenth century. From the eighteenth century onward we have had the growth of independent disciplines of aesthetics and art history, the growth of periodical literature, the emergence of the critic as an independent profession, and the growth of academies, exhibitions, and specific sites of artistic production and dissemination – studios, galleries, art schools, universities, museums, etc. (Burglin, 1985/1986). If the critic or philosopher is seen today as intervening more actively in not only articulating artistic practices but in promoting particular theories that the artist then tries to articulate, then it should be emphasized that this situation is by no means unique. Members of the Dada movement, which sprang up toward the end of World War I, as we have already mentioned, were concerned with the desecration of all art, with highlighting the absurdity of "art for art's sake" aestheticism, and with dismantling all codes, not least what they saw as the absurd war culture. The penchant for montage and the attack on the illusory unity of each text to reveal its polysemity shows the influence of Nietzsche's philosophy, and it is interesting to note that one of the founders of Dada, Hugo Ball, had previously written a thesis on Nietzsche (Kuenzli, 1987).

In the 1970s in the United States one detects a similar process with Derrida and deconstruction replacing Nietzsche to become appropriated as one of the central reference points for postmodern theory which was disseminated through a much denser network of secondary texts, journals, and journalistic commentaries. To take one example, in the field of photography deconstruction theory was promoted by New York critics such as Douglas Crimp to argue that photography could no longer aim to produce originality as photographs were always repetitions or "already-seen." Hence photographs should simulate and represent common images (Cindy Sherman), rephotograph unaltered images of recognized high art photographers (Levine) or rephotograph advertising images (Andre, 1984).

It can of course be argued that postmodernism does not so much represent a break or crisis in the larger social process but is a symptom of a more specific crisis within the intellectuals' own field. In effect postmodernism represents a loss of confidence on the part of the intellectuals in the universal potential of their project. A self-devaluation of the currency of intellectual goods that occurs at the same time is a more general social devaluation. Hence the emphasis in postmodern theory that Hassan (1985) detects and categorizes as tendencies toward *indetermanences*, the recognition of openness, pluralism, randomness, eclecticism, incoherence, paralogism, intertextuality, the primacy of the many over the one; and *immanences*, the acknowledgement of our innerworldliness, our own opaque symbolic self-constitution, our entrapment in a dissemination and diffusion of signs that derealize history and all the other meta-narratives. The emergence of antiphilosophical, antifoundational philosophy which is taken under the banner of postmodernism, it has been argued, reflects a loss of confidence on the part of Western intellectuals in the superiority of their project, in their authority and capacity to establish universal standards of truth, morality, and taste, toward which mankind will progress. Bauman (1988) links this acknowledgement of polyculturalism with a change in the societal role of the intellectuals linking this to the lack of use that today's state has for legitimation to reproduce the structure of domination. The intellectuals' status is further undermined by the massive expansion in the production of cultural goods which they can no longer control nor indeed are consulted about as "gallery owners, publishers, TV managers," and other "capitalists" or "bureaucrats," the "agents of the market" undermine things (Bauman, 1988: 224). We will say more later about the rise of what I would prefer to describe as "the new cultural intermediaries" or "new intellectuals" or "paraintellectuals" and the general conditions of inflation in the production of symbolic goods.

If we look at the intellectuals' field (bearing in mind the term intellectual is by no means an unproblematic concept that covers a range of specialists in symbolic production, the vast majority of which today have a base in academic institutions) we are struck by the parallels between their practice and artistic practices. As Bourdieu (1983: 4) remarks: "Resembling the artist ... the philosopher sets himself up as an uncreated creator, who owes nothing to the institution." The intellectuals' "intellectual centricism" prevents them thinking of their practice as practice, and while the antifoundationalism onto which postmodern theories have latched provides a necessary critique of philosophical universalism, there is often an inability to see this shift in other than dichotomous terms that cloud shades of differences between universalism and relativism and discount the possibility that the emergence of such concepts themselves need to be linked to the development of the fund of human knowledge. Hence the loss of universalism is seen necessarily as leading to pluralism and relativism in which the tendency for the intellectuals is still to see themselves as "uncreated creators" – if not now as creators of universal axioms, then in terms of selectivity, with the emphasis on the randomness and relativity of their choice between an assumed finite range of positions. The critique of universalism (often inflated into a straw man that it is hard to credit anyone believing) discounts the possibility of various blends and balances between universalism and pluralism, absolutism and relativism, involvement and detachment. There is also sometimes a back door importation of universalism in the assumption that the wheel of history has become fixed at this particular set of aporias, or that we have at last had the exhilarating courage to see through the deceptive representational signifying schemata into the eternal human condition of endless, yet ultimately meaningless and unsubstantiable, word-spinning. In effect all we can do is to join the game of signification, and art becomes the master paradigm for knowledge (Kauffmann, 1986), be it in the sciences, social sciences, or humanities. This may also be used as a justification for postmodern theorists to write "thin" or philosophical history to establish their points, as Arac (1986) argues is the case with writers like Lyotard and Rorty.

The focus on the apparent naiveté of the intellectuals of yesteryear, with their universalistic schemes, brings in a back door sense of our own progress in knowledge over theirs with which to castigate their own false belief in progress. It also neglects diversity within the intellectual field and the relation of postmodernism to the substantive antifoundational countercultural subcurrent that has been flourishing within Western intellectual life since at least the Romantics. This tradition sought to develop the relationship between artistic and intellectual modes of theorizing and to establish aesthetic taste as a criterion for knowledge, and the aestheticization of life as a guide for living: tradition in which one would have to place Nietzsche, who is revered by postmodern, poststructuralist, and deconstructivist theorists such as Derrida, Foucault, Deleuze, Baudrillard (see Megill, 1985; Rajchman, 1985).

For those intellectuals who, to work off Arac's (1986) metaphor, write "thicker" histories in that they draw on empirical materials to examine the rise of postmodernism – here Arac cites Anderson, Bell, and Jameson – there is at times a tendency to argue for the existence of a widespread postmodern culture by readingoff evidence from the intellectuals' experience. Here in particular we can think of the work of Jameson (1984 a, 1984 b) and Berman (1983). Jameson (1984 b), for example, identifies the two basic features of postmodernism as (1) the transformation of reality into images and (2) a schizophrenic fragmentation of time into a series of perpetual presents. In his description of the Bonaventure Hotel in Los Angeles, we are given a reading of the meaning of the hotel to Jameson that emphasizes the essentially postmodern experience this new "hyperspace" induces. The problem is that no evidence is presented as to how men and women engaged in everyday practices actually experience the building. One suspects that the experience only becomes a specifically postmodern one, after they have been told the building is postmodern. If this is the case then we need to build into our analysis the entrepreneurial role and strategies of intellectuals, architects, critics, and cultural intermediaries who have an interest in promoting the name and developing a pedagogy for postmodernism with which to educate various publics. In addition for all the emphasis upon intertextuality and multireadability of texts on the part of some postmodern critics, there are others who, in contrast to the assumed fragmentation and difference, presuppose a unity of experience prior to discourse that corresponds to the global process of capital logic or modernization and that gives rise to a range of expressions that can be read back by the critic as manifestations of the unity of the experience (Tagg, 1985/1986). This sense of totality leads to totalizations such as the "postmodern age," to subtotalizations like "postmodern culture," and to the "cultural sphere," which presuppose an integrated and unified culture, usually deduced from some master system imperative or process such as "capital logic," or "cultural logic" or "axial principle" (e.g. Jameson, 1984a; Bell, 1976). The actual practices of particular groups engaged in various struggles, power balances, and interdependencies are neatly avoided as a jump is made from experience to "higher" level integrating concept or vice versa.

Effectively a sociology of postmodernism would have to take into account the processes of competition, monopolization, demonopolization, and usurpation, the various strategies of outsiders and the established that take place between different groups of specialists in symbolic production, in which the term postmodernism becomes a stake in the struggle between groups. This would point us toward collecting evidence to enable us to answer the questions: Who is using the term postmodernism? In what specific practices is it used? Which groups resist its use? Where specifically is the term used? Are there particular sites of postmodernism? Part of the answer to those questions we have suggested should come from examining the emergence, development, and use of the term within specific intellectual, academic, and artistic fields and the changing nature of these practices which leads to greater interchanges between the fields. Yet we are also aware that these changes themselves may be dependent on and heightened by changes taking place that have brought into prominence increasing numbers of cultural intermediaries. The destabilization of existing symbolic hierarchies, then, may not occur merely in response to the usurpatory and avant-garde tactics of outsider artists and intellectuals, but in terms of an increase in both the demand for and capacity to supply symbolic and cultural goods of various types (including consumer cultural goods and not just artistic and intellectual goods). The growth of new cultural intermediaries and new audiences for symbolic goods within the middle class itself must also be understood in terms of changes in the wider interdependencies between the state, economic, and business specialists and the specialists in symbolic production which are part of a long-term process of the increasing valorization of art. A process that is likely to continue, despite the current round of cutbacks and the more negative evaluation of symbolic specialists as the balance of power shifts more strongly back toward economic specialists. We can now look at some of these changes.

4.3 The New Cultural Intermediaries and the Centers of Postmodernism

A good deal has been written about the new middle class in sociology. Indeed it has been argued that the rise of sociology itself can be linked to the hegemonic drive of this class in its attempt to increase the societal valorization of intellectual knowledge, symbolic goods, and cultural capital as against economic capital (Gouldner, 1979). While this view at times neglects the interdependencies between economic and symbol specialists and the important sense in which the growing autonomy of economic specialists and their theorists, who developed the autonomy of the science of economics that effectively become the first scientific analysis of society (see Elias, 1984a), it does direct us toward the development of the power potential of the specialists in symbolic production and dissemination within the middle class. There are long debates about the rise and composition of the new middle class and the problems of trying to explain their role within Marxist class theory, too complex to investigate here (see Bruce-Briggs, 1979; Burris, 1986; Carter, 1985; Barbalet, 1986). Some may dispute the terminology and prefer to refer to the "new petite bourgeoisie" (Bourdieu, 1984) or the "knowledge class" or the "new class" after Djilas, Galbraith, and others (Bruce-Briggs, 1979). Others (Lash and Urry, 1987) more recently have referred to the expansion of "the service class" (employers, managers, and professionals) which grew by practically 1/2 million jobs in Britain between 1971 and 1981 and in 1981 made up 13.2% of the labor force as against 11.0% in 1971 (see Cooke, 1988).

There has also been considerable debate (much of it unsympathetic speculations by journalists in the media) about the emergence of the "Yuppies" (young urban professionals), regarded as an elite segment of the United States baby boom generation, and it has been argued that this rapidly growing segment can be augmented by "psychographic" Yuppies who, while they cannot be counted as actual Yuppies, exhibit similar attitudes. The study states that while 14% of the baby boom generation (those born between 1946 and 1964) can be counted as Yuppies, nearly 50% of the baby boom cohort are "psychographic Yuppies," representing approximately 30 million people in the United States (see Burnett and Bush, 1986: 27). While a good deal of systematic research is needed on their life-styles and dispositions to see how far Yuppies are actually the selfish "perfect consumers" and the narcissistic, calculating hedonists they have been designated (for a useful start see Hammond, 1986), the very formulation of the concept Yuppie does direct attention to the large post-war cohort, many of whom had a childhood of relative prosperity, attained high educational levels, passed through the 1960s in their teens and twenties, and in the 1970s and 1980s have been entering an increasingly competitive occupational market in large numbers. It is possible that a distinct set of tastes and classificatory schemes have been formed in this cohort that may come to have an increasing social effect as some of them move into mid-life and attain positions of power within various organizations.

While definitions of the new middle class often include managers, employers, scientists, and technicians, the sector I would like to focus attention on is the expanding group of "new cultural intermediaries" (see Bourdieu, 1984). These are engaged in providing symbolic goods and services that were referred to earlier – the marketing, advertising, public relations, radio and television producers, presenters, magazine journalists, fashion writers, and the helping professions (social workers, marriage counselors, sex therapists, dieticians, play leaders, etc.). If we look at the habitus, the classificatory schemes, and dispositions of the group we should note that Bourdieu (1984: 370) has referred to them as "new intellectuals" who adopt a learning-mode toward life. They are fascinated by identity, presentation, appearance, life-style, and the endless quest for new experiences (see Featherstone, 1987a, 1987b). Indeed their awareness of the range of experiences open to them, the frequent lack of anchoring in terms of a specific locale or community, coupled with the self-consciousness of the autodidact, who always wishes to become more than he/she is, leads to a refusal to be classified, with the injunction to resist fixed codes as life is conceived as essentially open-ended. Bourdieu (1984: 371) remarks that their quest for distinction via the cultivation of life-style, a stylized, expressive life, "makes available to *almost* everyone the distinctive poses, the distinctive games and other signs of inner riches previously reserved for intellectuals." They actively promote and transmit the intellectuals' life-style to a larger audience and collude with the intellectuals to legitimate new fields such as sport, fashion, popular music, and popular culture as valid fields of intellectual analysis. Those cultural intermediaries working between the media and academic and intellectual life help to facilitate the transmission of popular intellectual program in the media such as the British Channel 4 series "Modernity and Its Discontents" and the BBC series on modern art "The Shock of the New" which helps to promote a new breed of celebrity intellectuals who have little distaste for, indeed who embrace, the popular. Effectively they help to collapse some of the old distinctions and symbolic hierarchies that revolve around the popular culture/higher culture axis. This general veneration for intellectual goods and the artistic and intellectual life-style thus helps to create an audience within the new middle class and potentially beyond, for new symbolic goods and experiences, for the intellectual and artistic way of life, which could be receptive to some of the sensibilities that are incorporated into and disseminated in postmodernism.

The origins of these sensibilities can, of course, be traced back a long way and should be regarded as a part of a long-term process in which specialists in symbolic production since the Romantics have engaged in a greater emotional exploration and informality (which can be contrasted to the specialists in economic production) that favors a loosening of restraints to facilitate artistic ends and the artistic-bohemian way of life. Clearly the 1960s was a period in which what became known as the "counterculture" developed an attack on emotional constraints and favored a relaxation of formal standards of dress, presentation, and demeanor. Contrary to popular perceptions at the time it has been argued by Wouters (1986), following the approach of Elias, that such manifestations of informality do not signal a lack or breakdown of controls, rather they depend upon greater self-control. The ability to confront dangerous and painful, previously repressed emotions effectively requires both a relaxation and a higher level of control: a "de-controlled control of the emotions." The less strict canons of behavior and relaxation of codes that accompanied the informalization process demanded that individuals show greater respect and consideration for each other as well as the ability to identify with and appreciate the other's point of view. It also favored changes in organizational structures toward management through negotiation as opposed to management by command and a higher degree of fluidity in hierarchical organizational structures and flexibility in performance of roles (de Swaan, 1981; Haferkamp, 1987). It can be argued that while the process of informalization has slackened in the late 1970s and 1980s (Wouters, 1986, 1987), the resultant "formalization of informalization" has not led to a complete erosion of the "gains" of the 1960s. It can be argued that sectors of the new middle class, the cultural intermediaries, and the helping professions (the latter are referred to as the "expressive professions" by Martin [1981]) will have the necessary dispositions and sensibilities that would make them more open to emotional exploration, aesthetic experience, and the aestheticization of life. Indeed the aestheticization of the body, which has been characterized as one element of postmodern art, necessarily requires an emotional decontrol both to produce and appreciate it. Likewise postmodern theories that detect or promote schizo- or multiphrenic intensities, or a "return" to a decoded preoedipal state of experiencing bodily intensities, are also asking for a greater emotional decontrol. It could also be argued that the style of management by negotiation has penetrated into academic institutions with outsider groups demanding and using more informal procedures and styles of presentation of works of art and selves. (In this context Pollock [1985/1986] provides an interesting discussion of challenges to the previous canons of aesthetic taste and modes of exhibiting works sustained by art college lecturers [largely men] by a new generation of young women students.)

The increasing sensitivity to aesthetics, style, life-style, the stylization of life, and emotional exploration within the new middle class has developed in parallel to a rise in the numbers of people working as artists and in intermediary art occupations and a more general societal rise in the level of respect that such occupations command. In effect there has been a "diminution of contrasts" with the artist's bohemian, outsider, difference rendered more intelligible and acceptable. In certain centers the rise in numbers of art occupations has been dramatic. Zukin (1982a, 1982b) in her study of the SoHo area of New York remarks that in the 1960s estimates of numbers of artists working in New York ranged from 1000 to 35,000, whereas census data at the start of the 1970s showed around 100,000. The increase in numbers of jobs was partly the result of increased state patronage of the arts (see DiMaggio and Useem, 1978) and the change in the attitude of some business leaders toward the arts. From 1965 onward in the United States the numbers of art jobs in state-supported educational and cultural institutions also increased rapidly. One of the effects was to close the distance between artistic and other occupations, and relatively secure career trajectories could be developed in the arts that brought the "artistic vision" closer to that of the ordinary middle class. Zukin (1982a: 436) writes that "far from 'shocking the bourgeoisie,' art became the aesthetic vision of the bourgeoisie." This emphasis gave rise to a generation of practitioners, instead of visionaries and innovators. Art became less elitist and more "professionalized" and "democratized." The SoHo area of lower Manhattan in New York became gentrified as part of this process and brought members of the new middle and upper class into a declining inner-city area to redevelop it as a center of cultural consumption: "the Disneyland for the aesthete" as one magazine referred to it (quoted in Jackson, 1985). Parallel processes have occurred in other major Western cities through a combination of state promotion of the arts resulting from the strategies of local and national politicians and the adoption of new strategies of capital investment by businessmen and financiers. Within such art centers there is an increasing manifest interdependency between figurations of artists, intellectuals, and various cultural intermediaries and various audiences and publics. While representatives of the business community and especially professional politicians who see themselves as guardians of the old petitbourgeois values, such as Margaret Thatcher, may express a strong distaste for many of these newer symbolic specialists and seek to cut government spending on the arts, the market inflated by the rise of a new generation of art investors continues unabated. Indeed under the pressure of new money, according to a spokesman at Sothebys in New York, "the art market has reached the point where it's almost another business" (*The Independent Newspaper*, 28 May 1987).

Hence the wider figuration, which has brought together professional politicians, government administrators, local politicians, businessmen, financiers, dealers, investors, artists, intellectuals, educators, cultural intermediaries, and publics, has resulted in new interdependencies and strategies that have changed power balances and produced alliances between groups that previously may have perceived their interests as opposed.

In more general terms in the 1980s the power balance may have swung away from centers in which acadamic, artistic, helping professionals, and cultural intermediaries are employed in large numbers toward the commercial and managerial centers who have long developed in a situation of tension and opposition toward their less powerful opponents (Wouters, 1987). Of course this type of tension balance and the peculiar strategies, interdependencies, rivalries, and conflicts it engenders occurs today in an extensive and far-reaching figuration of people which may make it harder to delineate. Nevertheless, it deserves more detailed and systematic sociological research, which could usefully draw on studies of similar processes. As Wouters (1987: 424) tells us, in some senses the tension balance between the academic, artistic or social care centres and the commercial or managerial centres resembles the tension balance Elias described between the nobility and the bourgeois intelligentsia in eighteenth-century Germany. At the time there was a similar distinction between the "depth (of feeling)", "true virtue" and "honesty" (of the bourgeois intelligentsia) and the "superficiality","falsity","ceremony" and "outward politeness" (of the nobility).

Of course, as we have argued, we are in a more extensive figuration and set of power balances with more groups involved today than was the case between the bourgeois intelligentsia (Bildungsbürgertum) and nobility in eighteenth-century Germany, yet the example may well be instructive in helping us develop a sociology of postmodernism.

4.4 Postmodernism and the Aestheticization of Life

In a recent and influential collection on postmodern culture (Foster, 1984) there is an article by Ulmer entitled "The Object of Post-Criticism" in which, in an argument that draws heavily on Derrida, he argues that the critic should not attempt to follow the old mode of trying to give a true or correct representation of the text or its meanings; rather the critic should be free to parasitically and playfully engage in nonlinear writing to subvert the text's central concepts and strategies. As Kauffmann (1986: 187) argues such a proposal and the demand for a "postmodern pedagogy" challenges "the distinction between art and criticism, arguing that critical writing must also be artistic." A similar valorization of art in which "artists are the heroes" who articulate the limits of our world by exploring the very "source" and limits of our language is detected in the work of Foucault (Rajchman, 1985; see also Wolin, 1986; Megill, 1985). One of the problems with this transgressive strategy is that it is targeted against the intolerant petitbourgeois consumer who is incapable of conceiving of "the other," who values speech above writing, etc. Yet it may be the case that if we examine the long-term changes that have brought into prominence specialists in symbolic production and dissemination, such a posture now strikes a resonance with a much larger audience – not that we have seen the end of the shockable traditional petit bourgeois, far from it. Effectively within the new middle class there may be increasing numbers who accept that the aesthetic life is the ethically good life, that there is no human nature or true self, that we are a collection of quasi-selves, and life is open to be shaped aesthetically (Shusterman, 1988). The desire to be continuously learning and enriching oneself, to pursue ever new values and vocabularies, the unending curiosity in which the artist and intellectual are heroes that some postmodernists advocate (Shusterman deals specifically with Rorty) has a long history that can be traced back to the Romantics. It also resonates with the concern for style, the stylization of life, "the no rules, only choices" slogan of the ever-renewable life-style, which is found within the new middle class and that, as cultural intermediaries, they attempt to disseminate to a wider population.

The emphasis on the aesthetic justification of life as a more widespread current within our culture has been met with a nostalgic lament and call for a religious revival by some (e.g., Bell, 1976) and an equally nostalgic lament to preserve the possibility of a Marxist utopia or truly "rational society" by others (e.g. Jameson, 1984a; see O'Neill, 1988 for a discussion of these positions). Jameson himself (1984c) has dealt with the tricky problem of sifting through postmodernism for progressive and retrogressive strains, yet he too cannot escape being instructed ironically by Hutcheon (1987: 23) that his former self-defined progressive modernist stance in (along with Eagleton) denigrating Lukács' realist position as passé is now compromised by the adoption of a reactionary hostility toward postmodernism. Such are the aporias of those who wish to assess and evaluate postmodernism. They arise from the difficulty of trying to understand the beginning of what may be a new movement in whose symptoms we are immersed and involved. They point to the need to understand the rise of postmodernism as part of a long-term process that has led to an increase in the powerpotential of specialists in symbolic production and dissemination: in effect to the need to work toward a sociology of postmodernism rather than a postmodern sociology.

Notes

[1] To follow the method Norbert Elias used in examining the long-term development of concepts like civilization and economics and focus on their derivation from everyday terms and subsequent alteration as a consequence of the changing structure of power balances between interdependent groups to their eventual theorization and canonization as universal or scientific notions, is in the case of the term postmodernity extremely difficult. Not least for the fact that we are looking at signs and traces of the very early stages of a process that may itself go off into a number of directions or even prematurely fizzle out. In effect while we may attempt to uncover traces of postmodernism *avant la lettre* (e.g., the 1920s avant-garde) we should be aware that the term itself may not yet be stabilized and may go the way of many recent academic fads and fashions. This would not of course imply that the process would cease, nor that the carriers of "postmodernism" may arrive at other descriptive terms. A further point is that the concepts of civilization and economics were linked to the rise of particular groups who enjoyed major power gains and a degree of success in monopolizing knowledge and means of orientation. In effect an ability to present their concerns as concerns that were somehow "in the nature of things" i.e., as foundational. If we try to conceive the trajectory of the concept postmodern there are numerous difficulties – not least that of being at the equivalence of a pre-Quesnay and Physiocrat stage in relation to the development of economics. We do not yet know what the power potential of the specialists in symbolic production and dissemination is. Knowledge specialists (i.e., priests) have attained a dominance in shifting power balances in the past; other knowledge specialists may yet do so again in the future. (For Elias' account of the relation between the various specialists of violence, knowledge, economic production, and means of orientation see Elias [1987b]). The current signs suggest however that in both the production of theories of postmodernism and postmodern cultural goods the tendency toward demonopolization. In short the hyperreflexivity, antifoundationalism, and polycultural "tolerance" found in postmodern theories and practices, tied as it is to the stylistic and fashion imperatives of the current markets in academic, intellectual, artistic, and consumer goods, may in its very dependence on publics educated in the quest for novelty, resist tendencies toward monopolization and the erection of a new stable symbolic hierarchy. In Elias' terms, then,

the capacity to develop relatively autonomous types of knowledge (e. g., science), on the one hand, or a relatively stable body of knowledge linked to the ability of a group to monopolize, on a societal level, a range of power resources, on the other, may not occur in this case. The further element of his approach to refer to (see Elias, 1987b) is his notion of "functional democratization" which points to a diffusion of the knowledge and the growing power potential of the masses. If continued this will further the tendency toward a certain openness and resistance to monopolization of knowledge. This is not to say that attempts at remonopolization will not occur and stable pedagogies be developed; however the lack of agreed unifying principles among cultural specialists in conditions of informational overproduction and the development of multiple competing centers of cultural taste may tend to reduce the possibility of a stable recentering and rehierarchization of knowledge and culture. Effectively we should consider those tendencies in terms of monopolization and demonopolization processes, and shifting power balances.

2 This is not to suggest that postmodern theory (and here I am thinking of Lyotard, Deleuze, Foucault, Derrida, Baudrillard, Vattimo, and Rorty and aware that some of them would object to be included in the category) is to be regarded as a troublesome, mischievously invented problem that merely represents a regression to earlier forms of irrationalism, and once explained away sociology can proceed much as before. On the contrary postmodern theory is reacting to changed circumstances in the organization of knowledge and culture in contemporary Western societies that have important meta-theoretical and methodological implications. The focus on the metaphysics of presence, the hidden meta-narrative legitimations of texts and the rhetorical structures, the recurrent figures and devices (metaphor, synecdoche, chiasmus, etc.) that can be identified within the schemes of historians at different times in history represents a definite gain in knowledge (see White, 1973; Bann, 1984). We have to be prepared to live with some of the problems that arise in not making a choice between objectivity and relativism – as Giddens does in his wish to retain the insights of postmodern modes of cultural analysis and champion the investigation of long-term, large-scale social processes. In effect we have to be careful not to be misrepresented and emphasize the antifoundational stance that can be built into theories of long-term, large-scale social processes as Elias' and Giddens' work both demonstrate, in their different ways.

References

Abrams, P. and McCulloch, A. (1975). *Communes, Sociology and Society*. Cambridge: Cambridge University Press.

Andre, L. (1984). "The Politics of Postmodern Photography." *Minnesota Review* 23: 17–35.

Arac, J. (Ed.) (1986). *Postmodernism and Politics*. Minneapolis: Minnesota University Press.

Bann, S. (1984). *The Clothing of Clio: A Study of Representations of History in Nineteenth Century Britain and France*. Cambridge: Cambridge University Press.

Barbalet, J.M. (1986). "Limitations of Class Theory and the Disappearance of Status: The Problem of the New Middle Class." *Sociology* 20 (4): 557–575.

Baudrillard, J. (1983a). *Simulations*. New York: Semiotext(e).

Baudrillard, J. (1983b). *In the Shadow of the Silent Majorities*. New York: Semiotext(e).

Bauman, Z. (1988). "Is There a Postmodern Sociology?" *Theory, Culture & Society*, 5 (2/3): 217–237.

Bell, D. (1976). *The Cultural Contradictions of Capitalism*. London: Heinemann.

Berman, M. (1983). *All That is Solid Melts into Air*. New York: Simon and Schuster.

Bernstein, R.J. (Ed.). (1985). *Habermas and Modernity*. Cambridge: Polity Press.
Bourdieu, P. (1983). "The Philosophical Institution." In *Philosophy in France Today*, ed. A. Montefiore. Cambridge: Cambridge University Press, pp. 1–8.
Bourdieu, P. (1984). *Distinction: A Social Critique of the Judgment of Taste*. London: R.K.P.
Bradbury, M. (1983). "Modernisms/Postmodernisms." In *Innovation/Renovation*, ed. I. Hassan and S. Hassan. Madison: Wisconsin University Press, pp. 311–328.
Bruce-Briggs, B. (Ed.). (1979). *The New Class*. New York: McGraw-Hill.
Burger, P. (1984). *Theory of the Avant-Garde*. Manchester: Manchester University Press.
Burglin, V. (1985/1986). "Some Thoughts on Outsiderism and Postmodernism." *Block* 11: 19–27.
Burnett, J. and Bush, A. (1986). "Profiling the Yuppies." *Journal of Advertising Research* 26 (2): 27–35.
Burris, V. (1986). "The Discovery of the New Middle Class." *Theory and Society* 15: 317–349.
Carter, R. (1985). *Capitalism, Class Conflict and the New Middle Class*. London: R.K.P.
Cohen, I. (1986). "The Status of Structuration Theory: A Reply to McLennan." *Theory, Culture & Society* 3 (1): 123–134.
Cohen, I. (1987). "Structuration Theory and Social *Praxis*." In *Social Theory Today*, ed. A. Giddens and J. Turner. Cambridge: Polity Press, pp. 273–308.
Cohen, I. (forthcoming). *Structuration Theory*. London: Macmillan.
Cooke, P. (1988). "Modernity, Postmodernity and the City." *Theory, Culture & Society* 5 (2/3): 475–492.
DiMaggio, P. and Useem, M. (1978). "Cultural Property and Public Policy." *Social Research* 45 (2): 356–389.
Donaldson Langer, B. (1984). "Studies in From the Cold." In *Sociology of Culture*, ed. C. Veliz et al. Department of Sociology: La Trobe University.
Elias, N. (1971). "Sociology of Knowledge: New Perspectives Part I." *Sociology* 5: 149–168.
Elias, N. (1972). "Theory of Science and History of Science." *Economy and Society* 1 (2): 117–133.
Elias, N. (1978). *The Civilizing Process, Volume I: The History of Manners*. Oxford: Blackwell.
Elias, N. (1982). *The Civilizing Process, Volume II: State Formation and Civilization*. Oxford: Blackwell.
Elias, N. (1984a). "On the Sociogenesis of Sociology." *Sociologish Tijdschrift* 11 (1): 14–51.
Elias, N. (1984b). "Knowledge and Power: An Interview by Peter Ludes." In *Society and Knowledge*, ed. N. Stehr and V. Meja. New Brunswick: Transaction Books, pp. 251–291.
Elias, N. (1987a). "The Changing Balance of Power between the Sexes." *Theory, Culture & Society* 4 (2/3): 287–316.
Elias, N. (1987b). "The Retreat of Sociologists into the Present." *Theory, Culture & Society* 4 (2/3): 223–247.
Elias, N. and Scotson, J. (1965). *The Established and the Outsiders*. London: Cass.
Featherstone, M. (1986). "French Social Theory: An Introduction." *Theory, Culture & Society* 3 (3): 1–6.

Featherstone, M. (1987a). "Lifestyle and Consumer Culture." *Theory, Culture & Society* 4 (1): 55–70.
Featherstone, M. (1987b). "Postmodernism and the New Middle Class." Paper delivered at the IALP Conference on Postmodernism, Kansas, 30 April–2 May 1987.
Foster, H. (Ed.). (1984). *Postmodern Culture*. London: Pluto Press.
Gershuny, J. and Miles, I. D. (1983). *The New Service Economy*. London: F. Pinter.
Giddens, A. (1981). "Modernism and Post-Modernism." *New German Critique* 22: 15–18.
Giddens, A. (1985). *The Nation State and Violence*. Cambridge: Polity Press.
Giddens, A. (1987a). "Nine Theses on the Future of Sociology." In idem *Social Theory and Modern Sociology*. Cambridge: Polity Press, pp. 22–51.
Giddens, A. (1987b). "Structuralism, Post-Structuralism and the Production of Culture." In idem *Social Theory and Modern Sociology*. Cambridge: Polity Press, pp. 73–108.
Gouldner, A. W. (1979). *The Future of the Intellectuals and the Rise of the New Class*. New York: Seabury Press.
Grana, C. (1964). *Bohemian versus Bourgeois*. New York: Basic Books.
Habermas, J. (1971). "Technology, Science and Ideology." In J. Habermas *Toward a Rational Society*. London: Heinemann, pp. 81–122.
Habermas, J. (1981). "Modernity versus Postmodernity." *New German Critique* 22: 3–14.
Habermas, J. (1984). *Theory of Communicative Action, Volume 1*. London: Heinemann.
Habermas, J. (1985). "Questions and Counterquestions." In *Habermas and Modernity*, ed. R. J. Bernstein. Cambridge: Polity Press, pp. 192–216, 228–231.
Haferkamp, H. (1987). "Beyond the Iron Cage of Modernity: Achievement, Negotiation and Changes in the Power Structure." *Theory, Culture & Society* 4 (1): 31–34.
Hall, J. (1985). *Powers and Liberties: the Causes and Consequences of the Rise of the West*. Oxford: Blackwell.
Hammond, J. L. (1986). "Yuppies." *Public Opinion Quarterly* 50: 487–501.
Hassan, I. (1985). "The Culture of Postmodernism." *Theory, Culture & Society* 2 (3): 119–131.
Hebdige, D. (1983). "In Poor Taste: Notes on Pop." *Block* 3: 54–68.
Hebdige, D. (1987). "The Impossible Object: Towards a Sociology of the Sublime." *New Formations* 1 (1): 47–76.
Hoy, D. C. (Ed.). (1986). *Foucault: A Critical Reader*. Oxford: Blackwell.
Hutcheon, L. (1987). "Beginning to Theorise Postmodernism." *Textual Practice* 1 (1): 10–31.
Huyssen, A. (1981). "The Search for Tradition: Avant-Garde and Postmodernism in the 1970s." *New German Critique* 22: 23–40.
Huyssen, A. (1984). "Mapping the Postmodern." *New German Critique* 33: 5–52.
The Independent (28 May 1987).
Jackson, P. (1985). "Neighbourhood Change in New York: The Loft Conversion Process." *Tijdschrift voor Economische en Sociale Geografie* 76 (3): 202–215.
Jameson, F. (1984a). "Postmodernism, or The Cultural Logic of Late Capitalism." *New Left Review* 146: 53–92.
Jameson, F. (1984b). "Postmodernism and the Consumer Society." In *Postmodern Culture*, ed. H. Foster. London: Pluto Press, pp. 111–125.

Jameson, F. (1984c). "The Politics of Theory." *New German Critique* 33: 53–65.
Jencks, C. (1984). *The Language of Postmodern Architecture*. London: Academy.
Kauffmann, R. L. (1986). "Post-Criticism, or the Limits of Avant-Garde Theory." *Telos* 67: 186–195.
Kolb, D. (1986). *The Critique of Pure Modernity*. Chicago: University of Chicago Press.
Kroker, A. and Cook, D. (1986). *The Postmodern Scene*. New York: St. Martins Press.
Kroker, A. and Kroker, M. (1987). "Body Digest." *Canadian Journal of Political and Social Theory* 11 (1/2): I–XVI.
Kuenzli, R. (1987). "Nietzschean Strategies: Dada and Postmodernism." Paper presented at the IALP Conference on Postmodernism, Kansas, 30 April–2 May 1987.
Lash, S. and Urry, J. (1987). *The End of Organized Capitalism*. Cambridge: Polity Press.
Lyotard, J.-F. (1984). *The Postmodern Condition*. Manchester: Manchester University Press.
Mann, M. (1986). *The Sources of Social Power*. Cambridge: Cambridge University Press.
Martin, B. (1981). *A Sociology of Contemporary Culture Change*. Oxford: Blackwell.
Megill, A. (1985). *Prophets of Yesterday*. Berkeley: University of California Press.
Newman, C. (1985). *The Postmodern Aura*. Evanston: Northwestern University Press.
O'Neill, J. (1987). "Religion and Postmodernism: the Durkheimian Bond in Bell and Jameson." *Theory, Culture & Society* 5 (2/3): 493–508.
Poggioli, R. (1973). "The Concept of the Avant-Garde." In *Sociology of Literature and Drama*, ed. E. Burns and T. Burns. Harmondsworth: Penguin, pp. 375–388.
Pollock, G. (1985/1986). "Art, Artschool, Culture: Individualism after the Death of the Artist." *Block* 11: 8–18.
Rajchman, J. (1985). "The Ends of Modernism." In idem *Michel Foucault: The Freedom of Philosophy*. New York: Columbia University Press, pp. 9–42.
Sayre, R. and Loewy, M. (1984). "Figures of Romantic Anti-Capitalism." *New German Critique* 32: 42–92.
Schuckling, L. L. (1966). *The Sociology of Literary Taste*. London: R. K. P.
Shusterman, R. (1988). "Postmodern Aestheticism: A New Moral Philosophy?" *Theory, Culture & Society* 5 (2/3): 337–355.
Sontag, S. (1967). *Against Interpretation*. London: Eyre & Spottiswoode.
Spanos, W. V. (1987). *Repetitions. The Postmodern Occasion in Literature and Culture*. Baton Rouge: Louisiana State University Press.
de Swaan, A. (1981). "The Politics of Agoraphobia." *Theory and Society* 10 (3): 359–385.
Tagg, J. (1985/1986). "Postmodernism and the Born Again Avant-Garde." *Block* 11: 3–7.
Ulmer, G. L. (1984). "The Object of Post-Criticism." In *Postmodern Culture*, ed. H. Foster. London: Pluto Press, pp. 83–110.
Vattimo, G. (1985). *La fine della modernita*. Milan: Aldo Garzanti Editore.
Wall, D. (1987). "Oppenheim Under the Sign of the Mirror." Paper presented at the IALP Conference on Postmodernism, Kansas, 30 April–2 May 1987.

Wallerstein, I. (1974). *The Modern World-System I.* London: Academic Press.
Wallerstein, I. (1980). *The Modern World-System II.* London: Academic Press.
Weiß, J. (1986). "Wiederverzauberung der Welt?" *Kölner Zeitschrift für Soziologie und Sozialpsychologie,* special issue 27: 286–301.
White, H. (1973). *Metahistory.* Baltimore: Johns Hopkins University Press.
Wolin, R. (1986). "Foucault's Aesthetic Decisionism." *Telos* 67: 71–86.
Wouters, C. (1986). "Formalization and Informalization: Changing Tension Balances in Civilizing Processes." *Theory, Culture & Society* 3 (2): 1–18.
Wouters, C. (1987). "Developments in the Behavioural Codes between the Sexes: The Formalization of Informalization in the Netherlands, 1930–85." *Theory, Culture & Society* 4 (2/3): 405–427.
Zukin, S. (1982a). "Art in the Arms of Power." *Theory and Society* 11: 423–451.
Zukin, S. (1982b). *Loft Living.* Baltimore: Johns Hopkins University Press.

Part III
Culture and Social Action

1 Choice and Culture: The Behavioral Basis of Cultural Impact on Transactions*

Siegwart Lindenberg

1.1 Introduction

In anthropology, there are two traditions that treat "culture" in opposing ways. The idealist tradition, of which Lévi-Strauss (1963) is a prominent modern exponent, is pitted against the materialist tradition which at present is represented in its purest form by the work of Harris (1979). Counterparts to these positions can be found in sociology, and here as in anthropology, most scholars see themselves as being somewhere in-between. The work of Max Weber is often quoted as proof that the traditions are not incompatible and that being "in-between" should therefore be interpreted as a theoretically argued rather than an eclectic position. Parsons (1961: 336) even maintains that modern sociology was born from a "marriage" of these two traditions. However, this kind of assurance is deceptive. In sociology and anthropology alike, the conflicting traditions do not mingle any better than water and oil, which implies that they tend to separate when not constantly stirred.

On the surface, integration seems easily accomplished. All that is needed for it to happen is reference to both material (e.g., economic) and symbolic (e.g., ideological) factors, and this can be done as easily in regression equations as in historical accounts. Yet, there is a powerful influence of heuristics in most analyses, creating a *de facto* separation of traditions, no matter how "mixed" the factors under consideration are. By and large, those who stress the importance of systems of meanings cannot or will not apply economic (i.e., scarcity related cost/benefit) analysis in any serious way, and those who stress the importance of economic analysis cannot or will not seriously analyze value-orientations, processes of legitimation, and the like[1].

My own position on this state of affairs is based on three informed convictions. First, the exponents of both traditions have no substantiated reason to believe that the other position will turn out to be unimportant. Second, progress within each tradition will become increasingly more difficult as the possibilities to advance without serious consideration of the other tradition become exhausted. Third, no serious integration of the traditions will be possible without first integrating the most prominent *behavioral insights* of both traditions: the insight (mainly from economics) that changes in relative

* I would like to thank Bruno Frey and Hartmut Kliemt for valuable discussions on this topic.

scarcities (i.e., in relative prices) will change behavior accordingly, and the insight (mainly from sociology) that the definition of the situation matters.

This chapter addresses this integration of behavioral insights. In order to do that, I will exploit the fact that most theories of action are theories of choice and most theories of choice implicitly or explicitly divide the choice process into three stages. In the first stage, the choice situation is cognized; in the second stage, the outcomes and alternatives are being evaluated; and in the third stage the choice is made according to some criterion. The crucial difference between the theories lies in what is assumed to happen in each stage. By comparing theories on these assumptions, it is possible to see where obstacles to the integration of behavioral insights are and what can be or is being done to overcome them.

The discussion will begin with a presentation of the theory of action proposed by Parsons and Shils (1951). It is one of the most serious representatives of the insight that the definition of the situation matters. After this, I will introduce subjectively expected utility (SEU) theory[2] as representative of the insight that relative prices matter.

My main thesis regarding the difference between these two is that each is based on a conception of choice so radically different from the other that they could not possibly by combined: One contrasts instinct versus choice, making learning the focus of constraint on choice; the other takes choice to be a consequence of the combination of goal-seeking and scarcity, making scarcity the main constraint on choice. If integration is to succeed then it matters a great deal which of the two is taken as a base. I will argue that aspects of learning (the definition of the situation) have to be brought into scarcity-based theories rather than the other way around.

This argument provides the structure for the rest of the chapter. Kahneman and Tversky's (1979) prospect theory is presented as the most prominent attempt to bring the definition of the situation (or "framing," as they call it) into scarcity-based action theory. Prospect theory, in turn, is criticized as rendering the definition of the situation so idiosyncratic that it is of limited use to social scientists.

A solution to this problem is sought in the discrimination model of stochastic choice, which is introduced in section 6. That model is scarcity-based, but it focuses on a central sociological aspect of the definition of the situation: the situational salience of goals. The relation between rational choice and culture is analyzed in the light of this model.

1.2 The Parsons-Shils Solution

In 1951, Parsons and Shils[3] stated that up to now the disciplines in the social sciences tended to "declare their theoretical independence from the other." In the exceptional cases in which interdependence among the disciplines was asserted, it happened in an ad hoc fashion and "without regard to the methodological and theoretical bases of such interdependence" (Parsons and Shils, 1951: 239). By contrast, they evaluate their own contribution as being to a substantial degree "permanently valid" and an "important advance toward the construction of a unified theory of social science[4]."

Parsons and Shils reject both the pure idealist and the pure materialist position. What disturbs them most about the idealist position is the view that action emanates directly from values, as if values had some independent existence and could "realize themselves" in personality and social structure without the intervention of motivation. What they find unacceptable in the materialist position is the view that society and culture are based on some given human nature, as if human nature had an existence independent of culture and society (Parsons and Shils, 1951: 240).

1.2.1 The Value Theory of Action

As we will see, values play a central role in Parsons and Shils' theory of action. Therefore, I will call it "a value theory of action." It begins with a list of relevant elements (Parsons and Shils, 1951: 56ff.): an actor ("ego") from whose point of view the analysis takes place; a situation of action, composed of social objects ("alter") and/or nonsocial (physical or cultural) objects; and ego's action orientation to the situation. The latter includes in any case ego's orientation to objects and to his own goals.

Every action involves an act of choice. That act is analyzed into three phases or stages. In the first stage, the action situation is being roughly structured; in the second stage, various courses of action are being evaluated and a definite set of alternatives is established; and in the third stage a course of action is being chosen from the set established in the second step (Parsons and Shils, 1951: 67ff.).

Let us look at these steps in more detail. The *first stage* consists of two kinds of "discriminations," the cognitive and the cathetic[5]. Here the actor distinguishes objects (or expected objects), establishes their significance for the gratification of her needs, and organizes these two kinds of information into a set of alternative courses of action[6].

At this point ego must decide either to choose a course of action (go directly to the third step) or to subject the choice situation to a more thorough evaluation[7].

In the *second stage*, the various alternatives are compared and evaluated. Sociologically, this is the most interesting step because it is here that value standards (i.e., rules) are being invoked in order to help the process of evaluation. *On the basis of learned rules, certain consequences of various alternatives are being amplified, and the range of open alternatives is being narrowed*[8].

In the *third stage* an alternative is chosen, either with short-term maximization of gratification (when stage two has been skipped) or with long-term maximization of gratification as choice criterion.

In this theory, values play a fundamental role. Parsons and Shils conceptualized values as solutions to certain choice dilemmas. The first such dilemma consists of the question whether or not to consider rules for making the choice (i. e., whether or not to skip to step two). Other such dilemmas consist of the choice between possibly conflicting sets of rules. Which set should have primacy? For example, should personal or impersonal standards be applied to alter? Values are answers to these kind of questions.

These values ultimately make society possible. Taken by themselves, values express "the desirable," and together they are part of what Parsons and Shils call "the cultural system." In more specific forms, values are expressed in expectations for action and attitudes for specific roles (the "social system"). Say, a judge is qua role expected to give primacy to impersonal ("universalistic") standards. At home, as mother, the same person will be expected to give primacy to personal ("particularistic") standards.

During the process of socialization, values become internalized, that is, they become directly constitutive of the "personality system." Thereby orderly interaction is made possible because the internalized values create reciprocal expectations among a variety of actors (i. e., they create a "social system"). The reciprocal expectations, in turn, are made possible by the fact that values govern the definition of the situation both in a normative ("cultural") and in a motivational sense. In other words, because the values are a constitutive part of the socialized personality, the person *wants* to define the situation the way she is *expected* to do. The judge is generally expected to let objective standards prevail in court vis-à-vis the accused, and in all likelihood she has been socialized in such a way that she wants objective standards to prevail.

To the degree that cultural, social, and personality systems are integrated, to that degree values are institutionalized and society runs smoothly.

1.2.2 Evaluation of the Parsons-Shils Solution: The Plasticity Paradigm of Choice

To my knowledge, there are no efforts to arrive at a sociological theory of action that are more ambitious than the one just presented. Yet, has it accomplished the task its authors set for themselves? Clearly, the theory is not materialist in the sense that it assumes that values influence the forming of personality, and it is not idealist because it allows a lack of integration between the three systems, that is, it allows that wants and social expectations differ. More importantly the theory specifies dimensions within which any situation is defined, and it explicitly introduces the possibility that the choice of a course of action is preceded by a choice of rules for the construction of the set of alternatives[9]. But have they thereby found the methodological and theoretical bases of the interdependence of the social sciences and moved toward a unified "theory of social science?"

One way to answer this question is to see what happened to their theoretical effort in practice. While it did bring sociology, anthropology, and psychology closer together for a while, it was never elaborated as a theory of choice, and it never managed to tempt behavioral sociologists and economists to join this venture. Parsons himself moved progressively more toward an idealist position[10]. Why this idealist turn?

While Parsons and Shils speak of "maximization" (and sometimes "optimization") in the third stage, they never deal with aspects of scarcity, and thus maximization is not subject to scarcity-related constraints. The reason for this neglect of scarcity has to be located in what I would like to call "the plasticity paradigm of choice," a paradigm that was used by Durkheim, Freud, and, to some degree, by Weber. All three, but especially the first two authors, had been crucial influences on Parsons and Shils.

This paradigm consists of three main guiding assumptions (Parsons and Shils, 1951: 63, 71, passim). First, organic energy (or effort or drive) is the dynamic element in action. Second, in instinctive action, energy is released by fixed object-action links of organic needs. There is no choice involved. Choice becomes possible through the fact that instinctive action makes way for "plasticity," which allows a variety of responses to given objects. Third, in some cases, action proceeds as if it were instinctive (i. e., skipping the evaluative step), but in most cases, effects of learning and culture govern action by creating and steering human choice.

Given this paradigmatic background, action is seen as being "oriented to the attainment of ends in situations, by means of the normatively regulated expenditure of energy" (Parsons and Shils, 1951: 53), and therefore the crucial question to be answered is: What learned (i. e., cultural) constraints are there on the release of energy? Against this background, needs are analyzed in terms of the combination of innate drives and learned wants into "need-dispositions" which prominently include the motivation to comply with situationally adequate rules. The rest of the behavioral dynamics is more or less devoted to the stabilization of this motivated compliance in situations in which conflicts have not been resolved through the application of rules in the evaluative stage. These are mechanisms of defense (such as rationalization and fixation) and mechanisms of adjustment (such as dominance and aggression).

It is important to notice that even without the heavy use of Freudian concepts, Parsons and Shils' solution could not accommodate aspects of scarcity due to their plasticity paradigm of choice. In this paradigm, changes in demand can only be modeled as changes in "need-disposition" (which, in turn, can be modeled as a result of learning). Given constant preferences (need-dispositions), the effect of changes in relative prices cannot be traced (see also Lindenberg, 1984a). Thus, as it stands, Parsons and Shils' effort forcefully reiterates the sociological insight that the definition of the situation matters but is does not offer a unified theory of action.

1.3 The Scarcity Paradigm of Choice and SEU Theory

Economic price theory has a long development of its own, but its successive versions have at least one thing in common: the scarcity paradigm of choice. In this view, choice is necessitated by the fact that one has to give up scarce resources in order to get something. These resources could have been used for getting something else. Thus, if the relative prices (i.e., relative amounts of resources) change for some goods, so will the pattern of choice[11].

There is a basic asymmetry between the two paradigms of choice. While scarcity effects cannot be brought into the plasticity paradigm, plasticity effects can be brought into the scarcity paradigm. For example, culture could be thought of affecting choice via an influence on costs and demand. Thus, client discrimination against a certain race will render employment of members of this race less efficient and thus possibly more costly. Scarcity-based theories of choice could also be expanded with assumptions about the cultural influence on preferences and expectations (i.e., these phenomena could be endogenized). Why then have economists been so unable or unwilling to incorporate cultural aspects into price theory?

The answers cannot be found in price theory per se but in the auxiliary assumptions that are used when it is applied. These assumptions have been traditionally chosen so as to allow strong simplifications in the analysis of supply and demand[12]. Preferences have been taken as given and the problem of expectations had been defined away by assuming that there are no situational uncertainties and conflicts of interpretation. To some extent, these uncertainties have been incorporated into price theory in a version called the "subjectively expected utility (SEU) theory" and therefore this version rather than price theory proper will be discussed.

Like the Parsons-Shils theory of action and like most other theories of choice, SEU theory is a three stage theory. In the first stage, the choice situation is cognized, in the second stage, the outcomes and alternatives are being evaluated, and in the third stage the choice is made. Thus the crucial difference between the Parsons-Shils and SEU theory and between various kinds of rational choice theory is not the number of stages, but what is assumed to happen in each stage. In all three stages the theory does not pretend to describe cognitive processes. Rather, the theory is an "as if" theory, meaning that all propositions should be read: "the individual behaves as if. ..."

In the *first stage*, the individual distinguishes alternative courses of action and various outcomes for each alternative, and she assigns a utility index number to each of the (projected) outcomes according to her ordered (and transitive) preferences.

In the *second stage*, the individual evaluates each outcome and the alternatives. She assigns subjective estimates of risk such that each outcome is weighted by a subjective probability of its occurrence, resulting in the expected value (or utility) of the respective outcome. By summing the expected values per alternative, the individual arrives at a subjectively expected value (or utility) for each alternative.

In the *third stage*, the individual chooses the alternative with the highest subjectively expected value (or net utility). This can be expressed in terms of the decision rule to choose the alternative with the highest weighted sum of utility index numbers ($\Sigma p_i u_i$).

As is the case with any other theory, SEU theory can only be applied with the help of auxiliary assumptions. Some of these assumptions are being made so frequently that they are generally taken to be part of SEU theory. Criticism of SEU theory is mostly directed at its auxiliary assumptions. There are many such auxiliary assumptions but for our purposes it suffices to mention only the most troublesome ones. One kind of assumption is strongly influenced by an implicit or explicit presupposition of *unbounded rationality* that renders strong simplifications in the application of SEU theory theoretically justifiable. Another kind of assumption deals with this minimal theoretical attention. Three important examples belonging to the first group are:

1. The kinds of goods that supposedly contribute to utility are specified in a utility function, that is the function that is being maximized in stage three subject to the given restrictions. Since attention is not limited by assumption, the kind and number of goods in a utility function are decided upon by the researcher so as to best suit her purposes at hand. In other words, there is notably no systematic theorizing about kind and number of goods in the utility function, nor is there any inherent push from SEU theory in this direction.
2. The assumption that subjective probability follows the principles of objective probability by adding to unity and by the former being a linear function of the latter; this assumption makes it possible to use objective probabilities in most cases as proxies for subjective probabilities.
3. Alternatives will be cognized and evaluated in such a way that they will coincide with the objective descriptions. Thus, if two alternatives are objectively equivalent they will also be subjectively equivalent (this is sometimes called the invariance assumption). Through this assumption, it is possible to disregard differences in wording and presentation, since the description of an alternative should not influence the decision.

The two most important assumptions in the second group are:

1. Subjective value (utility) is related to objective quantities of a good by a utility function. The general shape of this function is such that the subjective value of the next unit of the good (i.e., the marginal utility) decreases with increasing quantity (the *decreasing marginal utility assumption*). A utility function can, of course, also contain more than one good.
2. Subjective value is assigned on the basis of the total quantity of a good (or combination of goods) an individual has at her disposal. Thus the utility assigned to an outcome does not depend on comparisons of this outcome with a standard (unless, of course, the good itself, say status, consists of relative standing).

A few illustrations of these points will appear in the section on Kahneman and Tversky's prospect theory because these two authors have investigated many problems with auxiliary assumptions of SEU theory. Before that, the important question is: Is it possible to combine value theory and rational choice theory in such a way that the two most prominent *behavioral insights* of both traditions (i.e., the importance of relative prices and the importance of the definition of the situation) can be integrated into one action theory?

1.4 Reason and Rationality: Stinchcombe's Social Agency Theory

In a recent paper, Stinchcombe (1986) sharpened a Weberian argument by insisting that essential elements of value and rational choice theories are actually not combined by theoreticians but by society itself in a historical process of "rationalization". He distinguishes "reason" from "rationality." "Reason" refers to norms governing a body of thought recognized as authoritative in a culture, such as "legal reasoning" or the rules of accounting practice. "Rationality" refers to individual behavior that maximizes benefits or minimizes costs in achieving some goals.

To the degree that reason is institutionalized, to that degree rationality is likely to be affected by it. This is possible because reason contains an idealized utility function, and the individual practitioner is normatively held to maximize the institutional rather than his own utility function. In this way, faculties of rationality are applied "on behalf" of other people or values. For example, a judge is supposed to maximize "justice" and in the legal professions, there are authoritative criteria for what that means.

How does this solution differ from the value theory and the SEU theory? Clearly, Stinchcombe has combined both theories by interpreting the value standards (or at least the universalistic kind of standards) operative in the second stage of the Parsons-Shils theory as utility functions that are operative in the first stage of SEU theory. But what has he gained by doing this? Are people not simply socialized into institutional roles that are now called "institutional utility functions?"

The advantage of the Stinchcombe procedure issues from the recommended sequence: integrate a plasticity-based choice theory into a scarcity-based theory and not the other way around. He can now argue that (a) reason contains nested authoritative norms of rationality, but these norms are built on the human faculties to deal resourcefully with scarcity; (b) reason is the weak force compared to the strong force of personal passions and interests but that very fact is already discounted in the authoritative norms. For example, rules of legal practice anticipate interference of private rationality when there are strong conflicts of interest between the private and the institutional utility function. Thus the rules contain provisions for such cases and reason and rationality are interlaced. According to Stinchcombe, the standard example for this kind of theorizing is Max Weber's analysis of bureaucracy.

What then are the limitations of Stinchcombe's solution? One crucial limitation can be located precisely where the brunt of the criticism against Weber's theory of bureaucracy has been leveled (see, for example, Udy, 1959; Williamson, 1964; Tullock, 1965; Downs, 1967; Niskanen, 1971): One cannot assume that bureaucrats maximize an institutional utility function because much of their behavior must be explained on the basis of their private utility function given the constraints set by the institution. The other crucial limitation is the converse point: The behavior of bureaucrats and other practitioners cannot be adequately explained by assuming that they are entirely selfish, but then their unselfishness is precarious. For example, the phenomenon of loyalty does speak for the possibility of identifying with values, causes, and persons and thus for the possibility of substituting an institutional utility function for a private one. But loyalty is fickle, and its maintenance is precarious (cf. Schaar, 1957; Tumin, 1968; Hirschman, 1981; Akerlof, 1983). Thus, the very fact that "reason" is institutionalized does not guarantee that it supplants rationality. In some occasions it does, in others it does not. Unless we have an explanation of the possible interaction of the two, the idealist and the materialist traditions, reason and rationality, are likely to separate again even in Stinchcombe's solution. Yet, in order to learn more about the behavioral base of their possible integration, more has to happen to scarcity-based choice theory than the substitution of one utility function by another. Prospect theory, to be discussed in the next section, is meant to achieve just that[13].

1.5 Prospect Theory: Kahneman and Tversky's Alternative

Prospects are alternatives or "options" that may involve some risk, that is, they are the kind of alternatives to which expected utility theory applies. Kahneman and Tversky could show that, contrary to expected utility theory, the choices people make among various prospects also depend on the way the decision situation is formulated. Violation of this assumption can be illustrated by the following experiment (see Kahneman and Tversky, 1979): Subjects were asked to choose between winning a sure $ 500 and an even chance of winning $ 1000 or nothing. They were also told that they have just been given $ 1000. Of the subjects, 84 % chose the sure gain of $ 500. In a second experiment, subjects were asked to choose between a sure loss of $ 500 and an even chance of losing $ 1000 or nothing. They were also told that they have just been given $ 2000. The risky prospect was preferred by 69 %. In effect, the objective outcomes were identical in both experiments, but the choices differed due to the formulation of the prospects.

Maybe the most famous example of the violation of this invariance assumption is the following (with the percentage of subjects choosing a particular option in brackets).

Problem 1:

Imagine that the United States is preparing for the outbreak of an unusual Asian disease, which is expected to kill 600 people. Two alternative programs to combat the disease have been proposed. Assume that the exact scientific estimate of the consequences of the programs are as follows:

If Program A is adopted, 200 people will be saved. [72%]
If Program B is adopted, there is 1/3 probability
that 600 people will be saved, and 2/3 probability
that no people will be saved. [28%]
Which of the two programs would you favor?

In Problem 2, the same cover story is followed by a different description of the same prospects associated with the two programs:

Problem 2:

If Program C is adopted 400 people will die. [22%]
If Program D is adopted there is 1/3 probability that nobody will die, and 2/3 probability that 600 people will die. [78%]
Which of the two programs would you favor? (Tversky and Kahneman, 1981: 453).

Options A and C and B and D, respectively, are identical in terms of the effect the programs have on the number of people killed, yet subjects virtually reverse their choice due to the different formulation of the prospects. In Problem 1, their choice is risk averse; in Problem 2 their choice is risk seeking. Why is this so? Expected utility theory has no ready answer to this question. For Kahneman and Tversky, the formulation influenced the way subjects structured or *framed* the choice situation. Framing is a process whereby the situation is "defined," that is, whereby information is coded and evaluated in a certain way[14].

In Problem 1, the fact that 200 people can be saved by opting for A is judged against the fact that 600 people will die for sure if nothing is done and that they are still very likely to die if B is adopted. In Problem 2, the fact that there is at least a fighting chance of saving everybody is judged against the fact that otherwise 400 people will die for sure.

While the reversal in choice pattern can be made plausible by describing the situational interpretations in a certain way, prospect theory is supposed to explain *systematically* why the choice was risk averse in Problem 1 and risk seeking in Problem 2. What does this theory look like?

1.5.1 Prospect Theory

Like the Parsons-Shils and SEU theories, prospect theory is a three stage theory of choice. As a matter of fact, the big difference between the latter two theories lies in the auxiliary assumptions. Their kernel (presented previously) is virtually identical. The for us most important new auxiliary assumptions can be grouped by stage[15].

With regard to the first stage Kahneman and Tversky assume that the utility (or value) of some outcome is always subjectively measured in terms of gains and losses relative to some neutral reference point. While this assumption is not incompatible with the kernel of SEU theory, it does run counter the auxiliary assumption that outcomes are evaluated in terms of absolute states of wealth or welfare.

Next, they assume that utility (or disutility) decreases marginally with increasing gains (or losses). This implies an S-shaped utility function for gains and losses, with the neutral reference point being the point of inflection (see Figure 1.1).

Since it has been repeatedly observed that people weigh losses heavier than gains of the same amount, Kahneman and Tversky assume that the utility function is steeper for losses than for gains rather than symmetrical around the reference point. This is a very important assumption because it accounts for many effects previously not captured by expected utility theory, such as people's reluctance to accept fair bets.

Clearly, the reference point is very important because it determines what will be seen as gain and as loss. The authors state that it "is largely determined by the objective status quo, but it is also affected by expectations and social comparisons" (Kahneman and Tversky, 1984: 349) and they take it to be quite unstable (Tversky and Kahneman, 1981: 456).

With regard to an individual's selection of outcomes, they assume that an individual will by and large only consider the most direct consequences of an option, leaving out other aspects. These "minimal accounts" of a situation simplify evaluation in the second stage. Thus, in a gamble, people will generally concentrate on, say, the money to be won or lost, and they will leave out other assets or the outcomes of previous gambles. This concentration reflects people's intuition that consequences should be causally linked to acts, and it reflects the assumed fact that gains and losses (i.e., desirable and undesirable *changes*) are more important to people than steady states[16].

Regarding the second stage, the most important new assumption relates to subjective probabilities. Following SEU theory, Kahneman and Tversky state that the value of an outcome is multiplied by a decision weight before it is evaluated. For almost all values, this weight is a monotonic function of the stated or objective probability with which the outcome occurs, but, contrary to

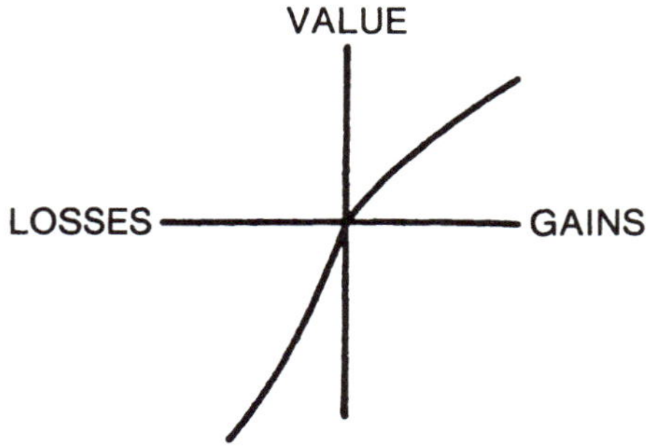

Figure 1.1 An S-Shaped Utility Function for Gains and Losses

SEU theory, it is not itself a probability. There is thus also no presumption that decision weights have to add to unity.

The assumptions Kahneman and Tversky make about decision weights can be summarized by depicting the weighting function in Figure 1.2. Small probabilities are overestimated while larger ones are underestimated[17].

Again, Kahneman and Tversky can show that with the help of this weighting function, choice phenomena can be explained that would be very puzzling to SEU utility theory.

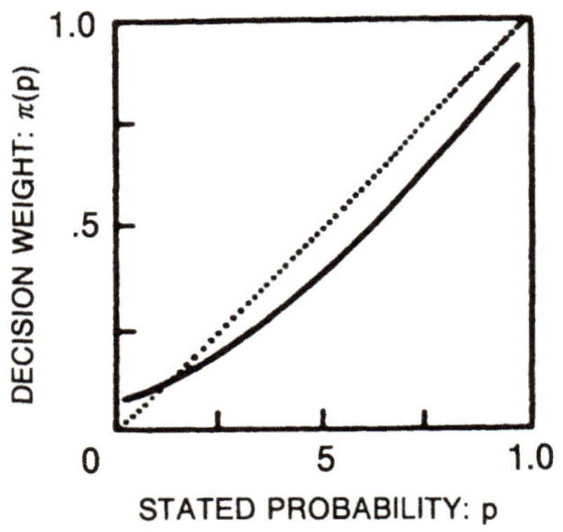

Figure 1.2 Weighting Function

1.5.2 Some Problems with Prospect Theory

Kahneman and Tversky had introduced minimal accounts as the most general way in which people select outcomes situationally. Yet, minimal accounts leave no room for the influence of other, less salient kinds of outcomes. The authors observe that *at times* inclusive accounts will prevail, but this makes their theory *ad hoc* on this point. For a theory of framing, this is rather damaging because by any reasonable understanding of what the authors mean by "account," it is central to people's definition of the situation.

This does not mean that it is really clear what exactly they do mean by "account." For example, they hint at the possibility that uncompensated losses (sunk costs) exert their influence through an inclusive account because, through them, a previous situation interferes with the present one. According to Thaler (1980) sunk costs do exert a considerable influence on behavior, contrary to neoclassical price theory. This would imply that inclusive accounts are much more general than Kahneman and Tversky make them out to be. Yet, it is not quite clear why one account is inclusive and the other is minimal. Supposedly, previous situations will always have some influence on later ones. The authors' theoretical elaboration is much too vague on this point.

Next, in prospect theory, reference points are crucial for the choice behavior because they govern what is gain and what is loss. But prospect theory contains no theoretical guidance as to what reference points people will have in a given situation. Sometimes it will be the status quo, sometimes it will be expectations, sometimes it will be social comparisons. When will it be what?

Third, when Kahneman and Tversky predict that, say, option A will be chosen, then they consider any choice percentage above 0.5 to be a confirmation of their prediction. The reduction of choice percentages from 55 to 45 is a "reversal" of choice, while the much larger difference between, say, 55% and 95% can be ignored because they both confirm the same hypothesis. Why do the choice percentages differ? The authors see no problem in this, and prospect theory offers no answer for it. Something important must have been left out of their theory.

Finally, they make framing out to be a very subjective process, but as Fischhoff (1983) found out, the frame people consciously prefer if given a choice is often not a good predictor of the frame they actually use. For sociological purposes this is a crucial point because in sociology changes in constraints rather than subjective states carry the major explanatory burden (see Lindenberg, 1984a)[18]. Of what I would take to be the five most important requirements for a useful behavioral theory in the social sciences (see Lindenberg, 1985: 108), prospect theory does not quite meet two: it requires much (too much) information about each individual to which it is applied, and it makes it difficult to formulate bridge-assumptions that link culture and social structure to the individual choice situation[19].

1.6 The Discrimination Model of Probabilistic Choice and Framing

An attempt to avoid the problems connected with prospect theory and yet to continue on the road of a framing theory of rational choice is the discrimination model of stochastic choice (Lindenberg, 1981). Like prospect theory, it has fared well in empirical tests, but unlike prospect theory, it is explicitly geared to sociological rather than psychological problems[20]. This will be made explicit in section 1.7.

The model is based on the assumption of bounded rationality and on the rejection of the (SEU theory) idea that an individual is able to discriminate as many aspects and objects in the choice situation as the researcher finds convenient to assume.

In the *first* stage (just as in the SEU theory), the individual distinguishes alternative courses of action and various outcomes for each alternative, and she assigns a utility index number to each of the (projected) outcomes according to her ordered (and transitive) preferences. However, unlike SEU theory, the discrimination model assumes that the cognitive limitations (including the limited span of attention) are so severe that human beings will be able to *focus only on one main maximand at a time*. This maximand is part of a "frame"[21] for the situation that steers the selection of alternatives and outcomes per alternative. A frame consists of a situational goal and of goal criteria, that is, of criteria for ordering situational outcomes in terms of degrees of goal realization. For example, in a particular buying situation, a person wants to be a smart consumer. That is her situational goal. For her, a "smart consumer" is somebody who gets the best bargains. Bargains, in turn, are ordered by buying price; the lower the price, the better the bargain. These are the goal criteria. Note that these criteria do not order the outcomes by the lowest overall costs incurred for getting the article. Thus, the cost of using the car to get from one store to the other, the trouble and time invested in finding the best buy, etc. play no important role in defining the choice situation. They will, however, affect the choice, as we will see in stages three and four.

In the *second* stage (like in SEU theory), the individual evaluates each outcome and the alternatives. She assigns subjective estimates of risk such that each outcome is weighted by a subjective probability of its occurrence, resulting in the expected value (or utility) of the respective outcome. By summing the expected values per alternative, the individual arrives at a subjectively expected value (or utility) for each alternative.

The *third* stage differs considerably from SEU theory. The individual is not assumed to choose the alternative with the highest subjectively expected value. Rather, she is expected to choose each alternative with a certain probability that, in turn, is a function of the degree to which the individual discriminates between the alternatives. Discrimination itself is defined against the background of nondiscrimination. If there are k alternatives and the individual does not detect a difference between the alternatives (i.e., each alternative has the same utility U_0) then each will be chosen with a probability of $1/k$. Discrimination of one alternative in relation to the other alternatives depends on two things: (1) the degree to which the utility of this alternative differs from U_0, and (2) the individual's sensitivity to this difference. Thus, discrimination is the weighted difference between the net utility of one alternative and the average utility of all alternatives. Assume now that there are two alternatives. If option 1 is seen as far superior to option 2, then the difference between the expected utility of option 1 and the average expected utility will be large, and option 1 will be chosen with a probability approaching unity. If the individual sees option 1 as only slightly better than the average, then the "better" option will be chosen with a probability close to 0.5.

The difference in expected utility between the alternatives is weighted by a factor that indicates the individual's sensitivity to the difference at a particular moment. This factor expresses the *situational salience* (a kind of marginal utility) of the goal[22]. For somebody rich, a small monetary difference may matter less than for somebody poor. What does this salience depend on? According to the theory, it is here that the "background" aspects of the situation play an important role. These aspects do not "define" the situation but influence positively or negatively the salience of the main goal. For instance, if the individual in our example receives much social approval from her friends for being a smart consumer, the motivating force for this situational goal increases and the chooser becomes more sensitive to small differences . If the gas price sharply increases, the costs incurred in getting from one store to the other also increase, and the motivating force of the situational goal decreases. As a consequence, the sensitivity to small differences in net reward decreases. In this way, situational aspects not belonging to the frame still influence choice by influencing the situational salience of the goal.

Expressed algebraically, the discrimination model looks as follows:

$$P_i = \beta(g_i - U_0) + 1/n \tag{1}$$

where β = situational salience of the maximand g; g_i = the sum of the utilities of outcomes of the ith alternative, each weighted by the appropriate event probability, $(i = 1, 2 \ldots n)$; $U_0 = (1/n)\sum g_i$, $(i = 1, 2 \ldots n)$; and, P_i = probability of choosing the ith alternative $(i = 1, 2 \ldots n)$

The situational salience is a function of situational background aspects (x_i):

$$\beta = f(x_i, x_2 \ldots x_n) \tag{2}$$

It is clear from equation (1) that as salience decreases, the choice probability moves toward nondiscrimination, and vice versa.

In contrast to the SEU theory, the discrimination model also distinguishes a *fourth* stage. Here the frame itself is evaluated and possibly replaced. A frame that does not allow the individual to discriminate between the alternatives (because its salience is too low for the given differences between alternatives and the average) is not useful for structuring the situation. What will happen? What other frame "comes to mind?" The "other" aspects available in the situation must be background aspects, and thus the individual will choose an alternative frame from these background aspects. Since β for the "old" frame has been small, no background aspect supporting the old frame will be very prominent. If there is any prominent aspect, it must be a negative one, that is, an aspect that had reduced β sufficiently to push choice toward nondiscrimination. The *frame switch* hypothesis is thus: *When the choice probability approximates nondiscrimination, the most prominent negative background aspect will become the new frame.*

Let me take an example. It is well known that friendships can suddenly turn "sour." How is this possible? Interaction between two friends may be steered by the frame "to be a good friend" with goal criteria that include the willingness "to help a friend in need." An increase in the cost of helping will be a negative influence on the situational salience of "being a good friend," and the probability of helping, though higher than 0.5, will decrease. If the friend keeps asking for help, the added costs keep reducing the situational salience of the frame. The probability for helping will thus approach 0.5, the frame "to be a good friend" ceases to provide a guide for choosing among the alternatives, and a new frame will appear, representing the most prominent of the background aspects, which, in this case, is likely to be "minimization of any further costs connected to this person."

So far the presentation of the discrimination model. How does it relate to the Parsons-Shils model and to prospect theory? How does it allow any insights into the relation between rational choice and culture not already apparent in the other models?

1.7 Culture and Rational Choice

1.7.1 Social Production Functions

The discrimination model neither confirms nor denies the two most prominent points of prospect theory: the importance of reference points due to the asymmetry of the gain and loss utility functions; and the possibility of a nonlinear subjective weight function. What is new in the discrimination model as compared to the prospect theory is first and foremost the situational salience of goals. Due to this feature, it is possible to show that framing effects are not so idiosyncratic as they appeared in prospect theory and that the definition of the situation (sociology) and rational choice (economics) are closely intertwined.

As I have frequently argued elsewhere (e.g., Lindenberg, 1984b, 1986b), there are good reasons to follow Adam Smith's lead in assuming that every human being wants to maximize at least two things: social approval and physical well-being. More recently (Lindenberg, 1986c), I have been persuaded to add one more to this list of general human goals: the *minimization of loss*, about which I will say a good deal more later[23]. Even if the reader is not quite prepared to agree to this list of general human goals, she may nonetheless join in the assumption that there are some such goals (cf. Stigler and Becker, 1977). Once this is granted, the emphasis shifts from man the consumer (microeconomics) or man the role player (sociology) to *man the producer*. All human goals below the highest level are now goals that are *instrumental* for achieving higher level goals. Where "tastes" in economics are assumed as given in any situation and where "values" are assumed as the product of socialization in the past, instrumental goals are *rationally* connected to higher level goals given the constraints of the situation. In technical terms: Utility functions turn into *social production functions* (cf. Lindenberg, 1986b) [24], and there is nothing idiosyncratic about production functions.

A culture can be interpreted as having characteristic social production functions for various social positions in various social situations. For example, in the *ancien régime*, aristocrats had privileges that confer status, such as tax exemptions, judicial privileges, and honorific rights; in addition, they had seignorial and other property rights that yielded income. Yet, by law or custom, direct business activity was not open to them. Other sources of prestige depended on action, such as pleasing people who dispense honors.

If action is required for the production of a social good, then situational goals will be part of the rational choice process, that is, they will be chosen as instruments for the production of that good. Social production functions specify what kind of actions that may be. The link with the discrimination model lies in the situational salience of goals. This salience must depend on the relation between the situational goal and the three general goals:

$$\beta = f(x_1, x_2, x_3) \tag{3}$$

where x_1 = social approval; x_2 = physical well-being; x_3 = loss avoidance.

In our society one would add a lower level goal, x_4 = income, in order to capture the special significance of a general medium of exchange. The weight for each element in the equation would largely be determined by a social production function. For example, "being a smart consumer" is connected with the production of social approval in some circles and will thus be a strong candidate for a situational goal in buying situations for members of these circles. Needless to say, the weight would also be influenced by other factors, such as the amount of the social good already commanded by the individual.

In this perspective, *socialization* is not something alien to rational choice but an integral part of linking culture and rational choice through learning effects. Many social production functions will be purposefully taught. Social etiquette is just one example. In addition, every frame also contains standards for judging the achievement of goods, and they will also be learned. In our example, the frame "to be a smart consumer" contained the standard of the lowest buying price.

Norms are situationally prescribed goals, and thus they operate via framing (cf. Lindenberg, 1983). The question why somebody conforms to norms is really only so difficult because norms are in effect prescribed framings. In this way problems can arise for both rational choice and for value theories. Consider what I call *the by-product paradox of social goods:*

> *Many norms have the effect that you only get what you really want by pursuing something else instead.*

For a theory of rational choice without framing, this is indeed paradoxical. For example, a judge who purposefully tries to maximize what she really wants, say social approval, will in all likelihood be seen as a judge who does just that, *thereby* reducing the likelihood of getting professional recognition (i.e., social approval) for what she does. Instead, a judge is expected to maximize justice, thereby defining each situation in which she acts as a judge *in terms of this situational goal,* applying standards for the approximation of justice and ordering the alternatives accordingly. Due to the complexity of the professional standards and the difference of opinion surrounding them, this ordering of alternatives would be different if the judge tried to maximize approval from colleagues at every one time. And this difference would be detected[25].

For value theories à la Parsons and Shils this may seem less paradoxical because value standards can be interpreted as framing norms. So how does framing differ from the application of value standards and from Stinchcombe's "reason?" Isn't the by-product paradox more or less a restatement of role theory? These questions can be succinctly answered. Practically speaking, there are many places in the book in which Parsons and Shils seem to assume something like the by-product paradox. In their language, physical well-being ("organically engendered need-dispositions") and social approval ("positive affective response") are the two most importat goods strived for by human beings (Parsons and Shils, 1951: 69), and social approval is often seen by them as a by-product of role-conformity[26]. Yet, theoretically, there is a problem. In their plasticity paradigm of choice, the major problem is the linking of psychic energies to social goals through appropriate learning episodes. Why social approval should continue to play a role once the individual is socialized into wanting to do what is expected cannot be answered by the value theory.

Stinchcombe, using the scarcity paradigm, also fails to come up with a theoretical accommodation of the by-product paradox. For him, the "weak force" (reason) only works if the "strong force" of personal interests is kept from interfering. There is no way to connect by-products theoretically with the weak force. For this very reason, Stinchcombe also does not have any theoretical guidance on the question under what conditions the weak force is more or less susceptible to the strong force. For example, why would professionals be more likely to keep to "reason" if they *thereby* receive professional recognition?

In the discrimination model, a frame is *always* connected to by-products through its situational salience. For this reason, the frame is vulnerable. If a judge were offered a large bribe for reaching a judgment that deviated from her professional standards, x_4 in equation (3) would greatly increase with a negative sign, reducing β. Unless the other elements are quite high, β will decrease so much that the choice probability will reach 0.5 and the frame is likely to switch to "maximizing one's income[27].

1.7.2 Culture, Social Norms, and the Avoidance of Loss

The discrimination model can also be used to specify conditions under which elements of culture will change. I would like to illustrate this with two examples: first with changes in the stability of framing in social interactions, and, second, with changes in the cultural production of meaning.

Although norms function via framing, they also stabilize framing because for most situations they prescribe a goal of action. Without norms, framing will be more dependent on moods and circumstances. Elsewhere, I have argued that the effort needed to socialize children in such a way that they routinely accept normative action frames increases at the same time that its rationale for the parents to do so decreases (Lindenberg, 1984b, 1986c). Briefly summarized, the reasoning is as follows.

Social norms arise when interacting individuals mutually exert positive externalities, so they would rather not split up, but they also mutually exert negative externalities that are thought to be reducible through the acceptance of behavioral rules. There are good reasons why negative externalities (potentially) exerted by children on parents have considerably decreased over time in our Western societies. First, when status is truly ascribed or truly achieved, children's behavior cannot influence the parents' status. It is in a mixed situation when ascription and achievement are both operative that children's behavior can matter a great deal for parents' status. With achievement on the rise in an ascriptive society, negative externalities should increase, and socialization should become a very important status activity in families (cf. Elias, 1939). With ascription on the decline, these negative status externalities should also decline. For parents, it should becomes less important to make sure they educate their children to do "all the right things" (choosing the "right" occupation, the "right" partner, etc.) when they grow up. Second, with increasing social insurance, it becomes less important for parents to educate their children in such a way that they will take care of them in later life. Third, with increasing income, it becomes increasingly cheaper to solve negative externalities in the home through the acquisition of goods rather than through the socialization of children. For example, if the living room has to be shared by many, people will get on each other's nerves unless they all follow some rules. If everybody has his or her own room, these negative externalities do not come up and do not have to be mitigated by social norms. Fourth, when training in social norms becomes generally less important, parents will receive less support from the outside world (visitors, teachers, neighbors, church members, etc.) for a strict socialization of their children. Also, when an economic solution to negative externalities is easily available, children will be less willing to accept rules they would not have to follow if the economic solution were chosen by the parents. In both cases, the cost of strict socialization increases as its importance decreases.

The fact that strict training in framing declines does not mean that "culture" ceases to influence choice. Rather, it means that culture will contain increasingly more variable elements, such as behavioral fashions and "open" norms, such as "put yourself into the shoes of the other and act accordingly." If the theory on social norms is slightly correct, then one can also predict a resurgence of "traditional" culture when negative externalities increase for a longer period, as during a longer economic recession. Thus, while the stability of framing may vary, framing effects and therefore "culture" will not go away.

The next example shows how framing effects are likely to be connected to the production of meaning. Remember that loss avoidance is supposedly one of the general human goals. This mean that the avoidance of uncompensated loss (i.e., the prevention of imminent loss and the reduction of recent loss) influences the salience of frames and, if it gets large enough, it will become the frame itself. This effect has been called "the loss hypothesis" (Lindenberg, 1986a) and formulated as follows:

a) the likelihood that avoidance of uncompensated loss dominates other possible frames in any given situation grows disproportionately with the size of the loss; and (b) the costs incurred in pursuing this goal may be higher than the value of the loss itself.

In price theory and SEU theory, sunk costs should not have any influence on behavior. Yet, it is well known that people find it very difficult to "cut their losses[29]." In novels, this theme has frequently been the central subject matter. The most famous example may be Kleist's "Michael Kohlhaas" and his contemporary counterpart "Coalhouse Walker" in Doctorov's "Ragtime." Both rather ruin their lives (and that of others) in the pursuit of getting their rights than cutting their losses and forgetting they have been wronged.

Seen as a framing effect, even the seemingly irrational sides of loss management can be incorporated into a rational choice theory, notably the idea that the cost incurred in loss management may be higher than the value of the loss. The reason for this is that once loss avoidance is the situational frame, costs will have only an indirect impact via the salience of "loss avoidance" until they are high enough to create a frame switch.

On the *collective level*, the possibility of loss avoidance as an action frame must influence culture. For example, a dispossessed people will in all likelihood incorporate the regaining of its rights into its culture even if that means continued isolation and other great sacrifices (cf. Wallace, 1956).

Weber's analysis of the historical importance of various forms of the theodicy of suffering for the fabrication of cosmic arrangements that make suffering meaningful and thus *compensated* (Weber, 1922) would be another example where loss is systematically related to cultural production. For the same reason that Weber assumed an important role for religion as provider of elaborate schemes for the meaning of life (not necessarily religion as a communal credo and activity), one would have to assume a decline of the cultural role of religion with a general decline in random shocks to valued assets. Weber himself observed that "the more privileged the position of the commercial class, the less it has evinced any inclination to develop an other-worldly religion" (1922: 91) while "the normal trend of thinking among all nonprivileged classes" is in terms of an *ethic of compensation* (1922: 96), that is, of loss management.

It is not argued that without the discrimination model these social phenomena would be neglected. Rather, it is argued that given such a model, the interplay of culture and rational choice can be systematically analyzed on the basis of one behavioral theory.

1.8 Summary and Conclusion

In this chapter the idealist and the materialist traditions are reconciled by showing that they can be integrated in one behavioral theory. The former tradition is linked to the important sociological insight that the definition of the situation matters; the latter tradition is linked to the important insight in economics that relative prices matter. Due to the different paradigms of choice underlying the two traditions (plasticity versus scarcity), it is of great consequence which of the two is taken as the basis. Integration, it is argued here, can only be achieved if scarcity is taken as the basis upon which (cultural) learning effects can be introduced as instruments and constraints of rationality.

The value theory of Parsons and Shils was presented as the most ambitious attempt at a theory of action in the idealist tradition. This was contrasted with subjectively expected utility theory as a prime representative of the materialist tradition. Stinchcombe's attempt to combine the two revealed many important aspects of the institutional context of rational action, but it did not integrate the two traditions at the behavioral base.

Such an integration has been explicitly attempted by Kahneman and Tversky in their prospect theory. However, their theory leaves much room for idiosyncratic definitions of the situation, which makes it less useful for the social sciences. As an alternative, the discrimination model of stochastic choice was presented. This model assumes that individuals can pursue only one goal in an action situation. A frame is a situationally specified goal together with the criteria for judging approximation of the goal. This goal acts like a special pair of glasses with which the situation is seen. The salience of the frame dictates the degree of discrimination of alternatives. Salience, in turn, can vary, and it is determined by other goals that are strong enough to exert some influence but, at least at the moment, too weak to displace the frame.

If it is assumed that there are goods generally aspired by all human beings (like social approval, physical well-being, and the avoidance of loss), then individuals must be primarily seen as producers of these goods, and culture provides to a large degree the instruments for doing so. In other words, culture prominently provides frames (situational goals and standards) systematically related to the production of the general goals. In this way, rational choice and culture are intimately intertwined at the behavioral level.

The model can also be used to shed some light on the changes in the production of cultural products. In this chapter, this is illustrated with the decline of social norms and of the importance of religion through changes in the material base of human interaction.

In sum, one may conclude that it is possible to integrate the idealist and the materialist traditions at the behavioral base. Whether this particular form of integration will withstand scrutiny and whether it inspires a novel and fruitful way of analyzing social phenomena remains to be seen.

Notes

1 See for example Eisenstadt (1986) and the literature discussed in his overview for the tenacity with which the heuristics of the idealist position will steer away from any serious economic analysis despite the expressed conviction that economic "factors" matter a great deal. See also Luke (1985) as an extreme example of this kind.
On the other side, the recent work of the economic historian North (1981) is instructive. North insists that economists have neglected the role of ideology. He states that "secular economic change has occurred not only because of the *changing relative prices* stressed in neoclassical models but also because of evolving *ideological perspectives* that have led individuals and groups to have contrasting views of the fairness of their situation and to act

upon those views" (North, 1981: 58, emphases added). Yet, despite this rhetoric, North offers no serious analysis of the development, maintenance, and impact of ideology.

2 In contrast to the pure neoclassical price theory, SEU theory allows at least for the explicit incorporation of uncertainty and thereby for the consideration of social and psychological influences on dealing with uncertainty. This is one step toward integration, and for this reason SEU rather than price theory is chosen here for discussion.

3 What I have called the "Parsons-Shils" solution is to a large degree already presaged by Parsons' work prior to 1951. However, nowhere before and nowhere after this collaboration with Shils did Parsons elaborate this theory of action so explicitly. Therefore it seems justified to talk about the Parsons-Shils solution. There is no space in this chapter to do justice to the elaborate detail of their work, but then it is also not necessary to do so for the purpose at hand.

4 This view is confirmed by neo-Parsonians, especially for Parsons' own development of the theory of action up to 1978 (see Alexander, 1978; Münch, 1981, 1982). Later in this chapter, I will take the view that Parsons developed consistently in an idealist direction after his collaboration with Shils, and I will blame this development on fact that relative prices never play any systematic role in Parsons' theory of action.

5 The authors use the Freudian term 'cathexis' to denote somebody's attachment to "gratifying" objects and rejection of "noxious" objects.

6 If confronted with one or more other individuals (social objects), the ego must decide during this phase (a) whether to focus on the categorial ("ascribed") or on the performance ("achieved") aspects of alter; (b) whether to focus on a broad ("diffuse") scope of possibly significant aspects or only on a narrow ("specific") scope. These and the initial choice for or against evaluation are three of the five "pattern variables" that structure any action situation (see note 8 for the other two).

7 In their own view, this choice is analogous to Freud's distinction between id and ego (Parsons and Shils, 1951: 85).

8 This process is governed by choices with regard to two alternative sets of rules: whether to apply moral ("collectivity oriented") or nonmoral ("ego oriented") standards; and whether to apply objective ("universalistic") or subjective ("particularistic") standards of evaluation.

9 Münch (1982) makes a great deal of Parsons' concept of "interpenetration." The interweaving of the choice of rules and the choice of a course of action can be taken as a way in which action systematically allows the "interpenetration of subsystems." However, as we will see, the choice of a course of action is not analyzed by Parsons and Shils as being anything else than the result of the application of rules. Here, again, the seeming integration of two important aspects vanishes upon closer inspection.

10 This can be nicely illustrated with his changing view on Durkheim's work. While he chastised Durkheim in 1937 for dropping action as a central theme in favor of an idealist position, he pronounced toward the end of his life that Durkheim had made progress precisely because he adopted this idealist position [see Parsons (1937: 445 f.) versus Parsons (1978: 213 ff.) see also note 6].

11 For a detailed discussion of the intricacies of conception of choice, see Buchanan (1969). However, he does not make the distinction between plasticity and scarcity theories of choice.

12 Why this strong simplification may not govern model building in economics to the same degree in the future is discussed in Lindenberg (1985).

13 Simon's theory of bounded rationality probably was the first major constructive revision of rational choice theory in economics and of expected utility theory, and his theory of "satisficing" may be the best known alternative theory. But Simon himself (1985: 295) observed that we have come a long way in the last thirty years, giving rise to numerous alternative formulations. Kahneman and Tversky's "prospect theory" is one such alternative and, in the opinion of experts like Einhorn and Hogarth, "the first *comprehensive*' attempt at an alternative formulation" (Einhorn and Hogarth, 1982: 34, emphasis added).

[14] The term "frame" refers to many different things such as construction and structure ("the frame of a house"), a mental or emotional disposition or state ("frame of mind"), borders and outlines of an object ("a picture frame"). In the psychological sense "frame" is used to refer to a way in which the experience of a situation is organized, to the "definition of the situation." In this usage, all three meanings of frame are combined. Related concepts are "conceptual scheme," "mind set," "frame of reference," "cognitive tuning," and "heuristics." Bateson (1955) may have been the first to use "frame" in a technical way for "the definition of the situation." Goffman (1974) has elaborated this concept and its use at great length.

[15] For a more complete list of assumptions and a more thorough critical evaluation of prospect theory see Lindenberg (1986a).

[16] At times, so Kahneman and Tversky assume, the minimal account may give way to some more inclusive account in which, say, the previous losses still play a role. The by now famous example of this is the following: You are asked to imagine that you decided to go to a play where admission is \$ 10 per ticket. As you enter the theater, you discover that you have lost a \$ 10 bill. Question: would you still buy the ticket? Of the subjects, 88 % said "yes." Contrast this to the following scenario. Same as before, but this time you have bought the ticket ahead of time and as you enter the theater, you discover that you have lost the ticket. Would you pay \$ 10 for another ticket? Now 54 % of the subjects answered "no." In the first case, the loss of \$ 10 is not specifically linked to the ticket purchase, while in the second case, the previous loss of the ticket still dictated the terms of the account in the decision to buy a new ticket. The value of the lost ticket was added to the price of the new ticket, and \$ 20 for the show was considered excessive for many subjects.

[17] At the extremes, the function is not well-behaved. Outcomes with very small weights can either be overrated or discarded as impossible. Close to the other end, the function can also make jumps: either increasing the weight to unity (certainty) or staying well below the true probability. In any case, going from "certainty" to "merely probable" can have large category effects.

[18] I do not mean to imply that as it is, it cannot be used in the social sciences. See for instance Thaler (1980) for imaginative applications of prospect theory to the theory of consumer choice. At the other end of the spectrum is a purely constraint-driven behavioral theory [see Frey and Foppa (1986) for an interesting suggestion in this direction].

[19] The other requirements for a behavioral theory in the social sciences are: (*a*) it must allow bridge-assumptions that link psychological (including physiological) theories to its parameters; (*b*) it must allow us to express our degree of ignorance explicitly (method of decreasing abstraction in model building); (*c*) it must be well corroborated as a theory of action (inclusive of human resourcefulness).

[20] For suggestions concerning some of the more psychological aspects of the comparison, such as the shape of the assumed utility function for gains and losses, see Lindenberg (1986a).

[21] The frame is like a *category* of things. For this reason, conceptual behavior will have an influence on choice.

[22] The difference of situational salience and marginal utility can be conceived as follows: Normally, marginal utility indicates the utility of the next unit of a good as a function of quantity of the good. Yet, there are considerations that increase or decrease the value of *any* unit of the good (and thus also the next unit) independent of quantity. For example, when doing business in a village that had recently been struck by a disaster, the value of money (relative to other things) may be less to me for every quantity of money. In order to distinguish between the two, I will refer to the latter as *salience*. Formally, if $U(g) = \beta g^{\alpha}$, then $\delta U(g)/\delta g = \beta\alpha(g^{\alpha-1})$, the salience parameter is β, while the "usual" related marginal utility parameter is α (of course, β can be split again into a salience and a simple scale parameter). As people own more of a good, their β for that good might decline while α may remain the same. This difference cannot be made in price theory and SEU theory because in both β is arbitrary.

[23] These three goals are meant to be summaries of clusters. For example, social approval is

likely to be composed of status (relative ranking), behavioral confirmation, and affect (cf. Lindenberg, 1984b, 1986b), and physical well-being is likely to contain physical pleasure and aesthetic pleasure (cf. Wippler, 1987).

24 Production functions specifiy the kind and amount of input needed for the production of a unit of a specific output. In economics, a typical production function specifies the amount of labor and capital needed for the production of a particular product. The reason I talk about "social" production functions is to indicate that their outputs (social approval, physical well-being, and absence of loss) are social products.

25 Akerlof (1983) argues in a similar vein that parents rationally teach their children to be honest even though the social rewards are only given for appearing to be honest. To make children appear honest, it is easiest to make them honest. There is of course a problem with the rational choice assumption here because by "being" honest you also refrain from being dishonest where there is no possibility of a penalty. Akerlof has no solution and points to sociological and psychological examples where acquired "traits" are difficult to lose even when they have become "dysfunctional."

26 In an article on the comparison of professionals with businessmen, Parsons (1939) comes quite close to an application of the by-product paradox, stating explicitly that the essential goals for the two are the same but the prescribed definition of the situation (i.e., the framing norms) is different.

27 This relationship between frame and salience can also shed some light on a problem with prospect theory: When are "accounts" exclusive and when are they inclusive (see section 1.5.2)? Because of framing, the situation is always defined in terms of *one* goal, making seemingly for exclusive accounts. But the salience of that goal depends on the weights of other factors which can even create a frame switch, thus making seemingly for an inclusive account when their influence is dramatic enough.

28 See Thaler (1980).

References

Akerlof, G.A. (1983). "Loyalty Filters." *American Economic Review* 73: 54–63.

Alexander, J.C. (1978). "Formal and Substantive Voluntarism in the Work of Talcott Parsons: A Theoretical and Ideological Reinterpretation." *American Sociological Review* 41: 177–198.

Bateson, G. (1955). "A Theory of Play and Phantasy." *Psychiatric Research Reports* 2, American Psychiatric Association, pp. 39–51. Reprinted in G. Bateson, *Steps to an Ecology of Mind.* New York: Ballantine Books, 1972.

Buchanan, J.M. (1969). *Cost and Choice.* Chicago: University of Chicago Press.

Downs, A. (1967). *Inside Bureaucracy.* Boston: Little, Brown & Co.

Einhorn, H.J. and Hogarth, R.M. (1982). "Behavioral Decision Theory: Processes of Judgment and Choice." In *Decision Making: An Interdisciplinary Inquiry,* ed. G.R. Ungson and D.N. Braunstein, Boston: Kent Publishing Co.

Einhorn, H.J. and Hogarth, R.M. (1985). "Ambiguity and Uncertainty in Probabilistic Inference." *Psychological Review* 92(4): 433–461.

Eisenstadt, S.N. (1986). *A Sociological Approach to Comparative Civilizations: The Development and Directions of a Research Program.* Jerusalem: Hebrew University.

Elias, N. (1939). *Über den Prozeß der Zivilisation.* Basel: Haus zum Falken.

Fischhoff, B. (1983). "Predicting Frames." *Journal of Experimental Psychology: Learning, Memory and Cognition* 9(1): 103–116.

Frey, B.S. and Foppa, K. (1986). "Human Behavior: Possibilities Explain Action." *Journal of Economic Psychology* 7: 137–160.

Goffman, E. (1974). *Frame Analysis: An Essay on the Organization of Experience*. Cambridge, Mass.: Harvard University Press.
Harris, M. (1979). *Cultural Materialism: The Struggle for a Science of Culture*. New York: Random House.
Hirschman, A.O. (1981). "Around 'Exit, Voice, and Loyality'." In *Essays in Trespassing*, ed. A.O. Hirschman. Cambridge: Cambridge University Press.
Kahneman, D. and Tversky, A. (1979). "Prospect Theory: An Analysis of Decision under Risk." *Econometrica* 47(2): 263–291.
Kahneman, D. and Tversky, A. (1984). "Choice, Values and Frames." *American Psychologist* 39 (4): 342–350.
Lévi-Strauss, C. (1963). *Structural Anthropology*. New York: Doubleday.
Lindenberg, S. (1981). "Rational Repetitive Choice: The Discrimination Model versus the Camilleri-Berger Model." *Social Psychology Quarterly* 44: 312–330.
Lindenberg, S. (1983). "Utility and Morality." *Kyklos* 36 (3): 450–468.
Lindenberg, S. (1984a). "Preference versus Constraints." *Journal of Institutional and Theoretical Economics* (ZgS) 140: 96–103.
Lindenberg, S. (1984b). "Normen und die Allokation sozialer Wertschätzung."In *Normgeleitetes Verhalten in den Sozialwissenschaften*, ed. H. Todt. Berlin: Duncker & Humblot.
Lindenberg, S. (1985). "An Assessment of the New Political Economy: Its Potential for the Social Sciences and for Sociology in Particular." *Sociological Theory* 3(1): 99–114.
Lindenberg, S. (1986a). "Rational Choice and Framing: The Situational Selection of Utility Arguments." Paper presented at the Rational Choice Group meeting, XI World Congress of Sociology. New Delhi, 22 August.
Lindenberg, S. (1986b). "The Paradox of Privatization in Consumption." In *Paradoxial Effects of Social Behavior. Essays in Honor of Anatol Rapoport*, ed. A. Diekmann and P. Mitter. Heidelberg/Wien: Physica-Verlag.
Lindenberg, S. (1986c). "Individual Economic Ignorance versus Social Production Functions and Precarious Enlightenment." *Journal of Institutional and Theoretical Economics* (ZfG) 142: 20–26.
Luke, T.W. (1985). *Ideology and Soviet Industrialization*. Westport, Conn.: Greenwood.
Münch, R. (1981). "Talcott Parsons and the Theory of Action. I. The Structure of the Kantian Core." *American Journal of Sociology* 86: 709–739.
Münch, R. (1982). "Talcott Parsons and the Theory of Action. II. The Continuity of the Development." *American Journal of Sociology* 87: 771–826.
Niskanen, W.A., Jr. (1971). *Bureaucracy and Representative Government*. Chicago: Aldine.
North, D. (1981). *Structure and Change in Economic History*. New York: Norton.
Parsons, T. (1937). *The Structure of Social Action*. New York: McGraw-Hill.
Parsons, T. (1939) (reprinted 1954). "The Professions and Social Structure." In *Essays in Sociological Theory*, ed. T. Parsons, revised edition. Glencoe: Free Press.
Parsons, T. (1961). "The Point of View of the Author." In *The Social Theories of Talcott Parsons*, ed. M. Black. Englewood Cliffs, N.J.: Prentice-Hall.
Parsons, T. (1978). "Durkheim on Religion Revisited: Another Look at The Elementary Form of Religious Life." In *Action Theory and the Human Condition*, ed. T. Parsons. New York: Free Press.

Parsons, T. and Shils, E. (1951). "Values, Motive, and Systems of Action." In *Toward a General Theory of Action*, ed. T. Parsons and E. Shils. Cambridge, Mass.: Harvard University Press.

Schaar, J.H. (1957). *Loyalty in America*. Berkeley: University of California Press.

Simon, H. (1985). "Human Nature in Politics: The Dialogue of Psychology with Political Science." *American Political Review* 79: 293–304.

Stigler, G. and Becker, G. (1977). "De gustibus non est disputandum." *American Economics Review* 67: 76–90.

Stinchcombe, A. (1986). "Reason and Rationality." *Sociological Theory* 4(2): 151–166.

Thaler, R. (1980). "Toward a Positive Theory of Consumer Choice." *Journal of Economic Behavior and Organization* 1: 39–60.

Toland, A. and O'Neill, P. (1983). "A Test of Prospect Theory." *Journal of Economic Behavior and Organization* 4: 43–56.

Tullock, G. (1965). *The Politics of Bureaucracy*. Washington, D.C.: Public Affairs Press.

Tumin, M. (1968). "In Dispraise of Loyalty." *Social Problems* 15 (3): 267–279.

Tversky, A., and Kahneman, D. (1981). "The Framing of Decisions and the Psychology of Choice." *Science* 211: 453–458. Also reprinted in G. Wright, *Behavioral Decision Making*. New York: Plenum Press.

Udy, S.J., Jr. (1959). "Bureaucracy and Rationality in Weber's Organization Theory." *American Sociological Review* 24: 791–795.

Ungson, G.R. and Braunstein, D.N. (1982). *Decision Making: An Interdisciplinary Inquiry*. Boston: Kent Publishing Co.

Wallace, A. (1956). "Revitalization Movements." *American Anthropologist* 58: 262–281.

Weber, M. (1922/1963). *The Sociology of Religion* (translated from *Wirtschaft und Gesellschaft*, 1922 by E. Fischoff). Boston: Beacon Press.

Williamson, O.E. (1964). *The Economics of Discretionary Behavior*. Englewood Cliffs, N.J.: Prentice Hall.

Wippler, R. (1987). "Kulturelle Ressourcen, gesellschaftlicher Erfolg und Lebensqualität." In *Soziologie der sozialen Ungleichheit*, ed. B. Giesen and H. Haferkamp. Opladen: Westdeutscher Verlag.

2 The Interplay of Culture and Social Structure in the Mind: The Social Actor as a Tangled Decision-Maker

Luciano Gallino

In much of the current social-scientific literature, culture and social structure sound as though they were able to speak to each other directly, without any entity doing something to, with, or between them. Culture builds symbols and norms, sometimes reflecting the structure, other times helping to shape it – depending on the school of thought; social structure gives rise to needs and interests, enforces norms, and distributes life chances; then behavior somehow follows. This way of proceeding is apparently grounded on the theoretical assumption that only what happens *between* human beings is of interest to social science. Some time ago this assumption was stated most clearly by Radcliffe-Brown:

> No amount of investigation can explain the characteristics of society by simple reference to the nature of human beings; but by an investigation of human beings *arranged in a certain order*, yes. The social scientist is studying the structural arrangement of the units *and takes the internal structure of the units for granted* (1957: 49).

We know, of course, that there have also been some branches of social science that did not really take for granted "the internal structure of the units." Prominent among these are the branches – virtually extinct nowadays – that were involved in a prolonged interaction with several schools of psychoanalytic thought. That happened mostly between the 1930s, when some major representatives of the Frankfurt Institute for Social Research emigrated to the United States, and the late 1960s, when the interest for the ways and means used by capitalism to manipulate the soul of men (that was the language of the *Zeitgeist*) reached its climax – just to drop sharply a few years later.

Today psychoanalysis is felt to be useless by most social scientists, or even dangerous, perhaps more because of its presuppositional binding with the politics of gender than for its obsession with sex. Unfortunately, this means also that as social scientists we have no longer, or not yet, any general model of "the internal structure of the units." And that notwithstanding a nagging suspicion that the explanation of behavior cannot be only reduced, or if you like inflated, to a kind of private dialogue between culture and social structure.

These are some of the considerations that have motivated the author to develop, starting several years ago, another model of a social actor, whose name Ego, though not its substance, is willingly a Parsonian reminiscence. In this model the social actor has a social mind, rooted somewhat loosely in a social brain. Both the brain and the mind are herewith social in a double sense – to begin with, because they are made up of several interacting units, thus composing a kind of federative system – the metaphor used by Gazzaniga. Second, because within each unit several social entities can be found "interned," that is represented by different kinds of mental models, some of them composed from images, some from propositional strings, or from subcognitive processes.

After an extensive screening of the literature of neurosciences, the submodel of the brain has here been taken almost wholly from MacLean (MacLean, 1973). As argued elsewhere (Gallino, 1987a, chapter 5), the model of the triune brain developed by MacLean does offer – as far as this writer can know – the best match available to date between a large set of neurological units, subsystems, and programs, established through the evolution of the human brain, and the functional and goal-oriented subsystems – themselves computational programs – working together in the mind of the social actors, as these subsystems are defined by the Ego model.

This would also explain why a social scientist carving his path toward a model of the social actor should ever worry about such arcane biological matters. Not only do the structures of the brain act as powerful regulators of behavior, mostly through the control of the emotion's flow. They contain program structures wherein cultural instructions find their proper locus; they even offer biological instructions to fill in the proper loci in behavioral programs whose structure is mostly cultural in origin. If social behavior, in a way, can best be understood as the biocultural evolutionary outcome of a program (Dawkins, 1976), the social behavioral scientist cannot avoid trying to understand both the program's structure and its ever-changing instructions. In the former as in the latter, biology and culture are intimately interlaced.

The model of the triune brain quoted previously can be correctly defined a social brain, for each of the brains built by evolution in the brain of modern man is cooperating – though quite often conflictually – with the other two. In such cooperation each brain enters with its own intelligence, memory, and plans of behavior. The label "social brain," however, must not be understood as implying an easy match between MacLean's and Gazzaniga's model (as exposed in Gazzaniga, 1985): if there is one, it is quite feeble.

But the brain and the mind of Ego are social in another, strongest sense – itself compounded. They are social, first of all, because of the crowd of representations of social entities, or objects, flowing through them: reference groups, biological and cultural kinfolks, all kinds of objects of identification and/or attachment. Most representations are cultural in origin; some are private constructions. Besides, they are social – the brain and the mind – as far as they currently use for their inner workings, such as representing situations, interpreting them by means of frames, dealing with emotional states, and generating behavior plans, a large set of cultural definitions. Among the latter, when needed, a contingent choice is made under the influence both of structural and contingent social rewards (positive and negative). Thus the interplay of culture and social structure looks much more intimate and intertwined, within the "internal structure of the units," than that is usually admitted by several paradigms having a "normal" status in social science.

Now, let us see how Ego becomes tangled in his/her own process of decision-making. According to this model, social action, even everyday social action – viewed externally at the level pertaining to social structure – pursues always one ultimate goal: to let its carrier, Ego, survive as long and as largely as possible, in time and space, in whatever form or combination of forms it is contingently feasible or convenient, be it physical or symbolic, hardware-like or software-like. One way is to survive as a physical body; another, as a symbolic structure in the memory of other people, or God's; still another, through biological kinfolks; one last way is to try to survive through cultural kinfolks or relatives.

In an ideal world, one could hope to live forever, as a body and a soul, in and through the largest number of biological and cultural relatives. But Ego is a mundane decision-maker, well conscious of the harsh limits within which action is hemmed by reality. So Ego tries constantly to reach a satisficing (in Simon's sense) joint optimization of the survival goal applied to all the referents, herefrom named formally as the body, the orientation system (again a Parsonian echo), the biological relatives, and the cultural relatives.

The main hypothesis supporting (i.e., extracted from) the model thus can be couched this way:

When confronted by an initial situation (the from-situation) and one or more end-situations (the to-situation(s)), in which he/she can transfer him- or herself, or stay, by choosing a given action or course of action, Ego will always choose the action, and thus the situation, which he or she expects to globally maximize – given the limits of his or her contingent resources – the sum of the survival time-space of all the referents.

Thus, comparable doses of positive contribution to survival of a given referent expected from his/her action can be exchanged with doses of negative contribution to (an) other referent(s). To die as a body, in order to live as a symbol – or vice versa; or, to have to choose between one's own health (physical or mental) and that of one's own kinfolk (biological or cultural): these are not only prescriptions for making martyrs. They are everyday dilemmas (though, fortunately, coming usually in lighter versions) confronting even the most common of social actions. As it has been noted by just a handful of authors (e.g., Margolis, 1982), it is somewhat surprising that such dilemmas take so little space in most current theories of action (but see Elster, 1986).

Should global survival, survival in the largest sense, as a body or as a symbol, through him- or herself or through others, be a monolithic goal, the decision-making process that Ego has to manage would already be arduous. There are more complications, however. For survival is, as a matter of fact, a bundle of several, though related, ultimate goals. There are, to begin with, two different kinds, or forms, of survival. One form is to live longer than a given entity of reference, be it a person, a group, an age cohort. As Canetti said so well, "Not only man wants always to be there; he wants to go on being there, when others are no longer there" (1981: 273). Another kind or form of survival is to succeed in escaping a threat, a potentially lethal challenge that has been successfully met by a physical or by a symbolic entity.

So, both forms of survival can be relevant to any of Ego's referents. Not only bodies want to survive, but even orientation systems, eventually at the cost of killing the body of which they are masters and guests. At the same goal do aim the actor's biological and cultural relatives, such as they are represented in Ego's mind as prolongations of his or her physical and symbolic or informational existence. Reconstructed in such representational form, they ask Ego to help them to survive. The evolutionary reason being, of course, that it is through them that Ego desires to survive.

Then there is the question of what really matters in survival. Most people would not be very happy should they survive, or seeing a relative of theirs surviving, in such an internal condition, or such an external shape, as to make impossible to say who is truly the survivor. In the movie, *The Fly*, the hero (how not to remember the Gregor Samsa of Kafka's *Metamorphosis?*) survives a risky scientific experiment, with his orientation system totally unscathed. Nevertheless, he is very much annoyed in discovering that his body has taken on the shape of a fly. So it seems that survival is not enough *per se*: we want, while surviving, to persist as we are.

But even the ultimate goal of persistence has to be split in two. Surely we want to survive, and seeing our referents surviving, provided that we and others looking at us or at them, can thereafter establish beyond any reasonable doubt that the survivor is the same entity as before. Therefore we feel that the maintenance of identity through time – psychical and/or physical – is a crucial goal.

We do not like, however, to find ourselves or our (biological or cultural) relatives surviving in such a shape as to make it impossible to distinguish us or them from other entities, though we know for sure that we, or they, are the same entities as before. Thus it may be said that beside identity, also individuality, the keeping of borders, the sense of uniqueness, is what matters in survival, under the more general goal labeled persistence. And depending on the problem faced by the actor in from- and to-situations, identity and/or individuality can be ultimate goals having, contingently, a higher order of priority than the forms of survival (in the stricter sense) themselves.

There is obviously one more way to survive in some form, which is again split in two levels, each of them embodying a different grain of evolutionary cleverness. Its name, rather unimaginatively, is reproduction. At the level of "cellular" components of a system, for an observer looking down from the system level i.e., its horizon as a model, reproduction can be seen as autopoiesis: the process through which a system sticks to its basic organization plan, making it the overall focus of its behaviors, in front of a continuous flow of change of its components. At the system level, things look different. Here, reproduction means producing identical replicas of the system referred to, thus becoming replication.

In this way, all in all, a set of three by two ultimate goals of behavior and action defines Ego's spatiotemporal area of biocultural reproductive success, or fitness: survival, split into comparative and absolute; persistence, under the cover of which one can glimpse individuality and identity; reproduction, with the two levels of autopoiesis and replication. All of these ultimate goals do apply to all kinds of Ego's referents, generating a foursome quadrant such as this:

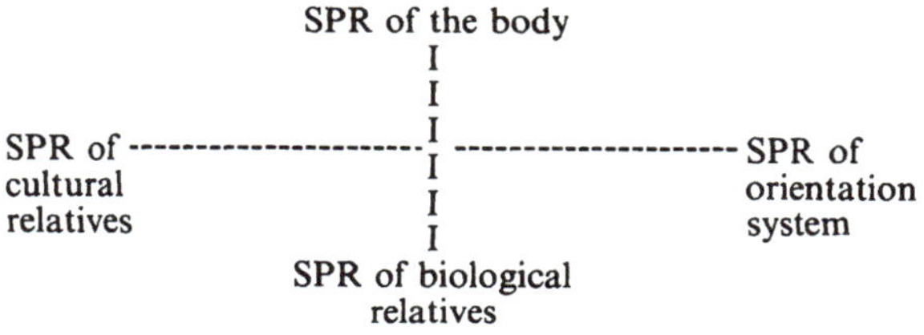

Figure 2.1 The Space of Bio-Cultural Fitness

Using this quadrant, any from-situation or to-situation can be represented by designing, with its proper size and shape, the corresponding area of biocultural reproductive success. Thereafter the Ego's model will foresee that the actor will choose the area that to him or her looks larger. From this comparison between two areas or more, the preferred situation, the possible actions, and the actual choice of an action, can be anticipated, too, with a fairly high degree of probability.

Such is the spatiotemporal area that Ego tries constantly to maximize, ever pushing the score on any and all the axes toward the farthest border; but also accepting losses on any given axis when Ego expects proportional or higher gains, in form of SPR probability, along any other axis.

In the decision process of the actor facing this space, as thereby modeled, culture is everywhere, and what the social structure does is orienting Ego in selecting its items according to his or her needs. First come the representations of Ego's referents, dealt with by a functional subsystem – a set of mental processes, or programs, serving a general function on behalf of the whole system, the mind. When planning an action allowing him to move around a set of from- and to-situations, Ego thinks – consciously or silently – of the referents, but Ego's thinking is preventively framed by cultural definitions.

Of Ego's body itself, an entity so obviously material, so close to the perception, he or she can think only through the mental models – images or else – offered by culture. Out of the total stock of body images available in the culture of his or her society, the one that is selected to fill in the quadrant of available action space at any given time will more likely be one belonging to the subset whose visibility is predefined by Ego's position in the social structure. This is what one means when speaking of the sociology of body images.

What is true of the body is even truer for the rest of Ego's referents. The biological relatedness to Ego of any biological relatives can actually be measured by means of blood tests, but only cultural representations – and social structure – are what tells him or her that a given person is, or is not, a biological kin, rather independently with respect to biological truth. It can here be remembered that discovering that a supposed biological relative is not of the same blood; or, conversely, that a supposed stranger is actually a biological relative, is a main theme of human tragedy.

By definition, all of Ego's cultural relatives are made up by positive reference groups, such as local, ethnic, religious, or political communities, including associations and primary groups inside them, which are defined and delimited by cultural representations. Each representation of these communities is being supported within Ego's mind by a different degree of identification and attachment. Finally, Ego cannot think of the orientation system, generated by the interaction of his or her evolutionary brains with culture and social structure, without making use of proper cultural representations – that is, without applying the orientation system to itself.

Representations wholly or largely cultural in origin are also filtering and shaping all mental processes dealing with situations, frames, emotions, and plans of behavior. Each of these (sets of) processes composes a semiindependent functional subsystem in the mind of the actor. Representations of situations have to do with cognition, the first (though already inferentially structured) imprint of experience; the business of frames is interpretation (Goffman, 1974), the organization of experience, including forebodings of what can follow from what has been cognitively ascertained.

Also, what kind of emotion one has to feel and to show when facing a given situation is notoriously, quite often, a matter of cultural representations, even though this cannot be taken to deny the universality of some emotions and the ways of expressing them. Nor must the actor, or can, conceive plans of behavior wholly original each time he or she wants to move from a situation to a different one. Culture keeps in store a large stock of prefabricated plans and components for self-made plans, among which Ego has only to choose.

Crossing transversally the functional subsystems dealing with representations of referents, representations of situations, frames, emotions, and plans of behavior, there are, in the overall plan of the model, several goal-oriented subsystems. Each of them is acting as a local decision-maker defending the interests, in form of survival, persistence, and reproduction probabilities, of each class of Ego's referents. It must be emphasized that the goal-oriented subsystems are composed of the same components as the functional subsystems dealing specifically with a single class of mental processes. There are no different or special functions in the local decision-makers that are not already observable in the functional subsystems.

But whereas any of the latter work out a single function involving all classes of referents, everyone of the former strings together in sequence all functions in order to affirm the ultimate goals of one referent (or more, provided they belong to the same class). One can think of the ensuing structure in this way (see below):

Local decision-makers for:	F U N C T I O N S				
	RR	RS	F	E	PB
Body	∧	∧	∧	∧	∧
Orientation system	∧	∧	∧	∧	∧
Biological relatives	∧	∧	∧	∧	∧
Cultural relatives	∧	∧	∧	∧	∧

Figure 2.2 The Internal Structure of the Model

Even a cursory examination can show that inside this structure uncounted possibilities of conflict are built in, at no less than four different levels. At the referents level, the interest of any one referent of a given class can be contrary to the interests of one or more referents belonging to a different class. That is, an action devised to improve the expected probability of survival, persistence, or reproduction of, say, the body, may at the same time carry with it a reduction of the probability of SPR of a biological or cultural relative (be it a person, a group, or a community), or of the orientation system.

The latter is actually the simplest case, as when Ego has to decide, for instance, between his or her own welfare and the welfare of a group or community to which Ego is tied by some form of identification or attachment. Internally, this is a conflict opposing different local decision-makers, each of them stubbornly defending the interests of its referent(s) against all others. This kind of conflict is apt to be resolved only through the intervention of a central decision-maker, a final subsystem by which the mind of the actor must come equipped – any resemblance to such instances as I, or consciousness, being unwelcome, but perhaps unavoidable.

Even a local decision-maker may be split internally, however, in different ways. What is good for survival of any one referent may carry with it no good for persistence, or reproduction, of the same referent. For instance, the struggle to keep intact – as one way to pursue symbolic persistence – the values built in one's own orientation system (or, more precisely, in its moral subsystem, according to the Parsonian map) may appear very unpromising for its chances of reproducing itself by way of replication. As much prone to such kind of conflicts is the body, that is its dedicated decision-maker; and so are the other referents.

But there are situations, too, if one looks at Ego's decision process from a different side, wherein the referents' own ultimate goals are not conflicting, and may even be synergic, but the referents themselves are in mutual conflict. When this happens, whenever Ego pursues the SPR of one referent he or she does simultaneously act, or can be judged externally to act, against the SPR of another.

The church and the state, or the party, to take an historical example, may be together and at the same time communities of reference for any one Ego, and as such sources of identifications and attachments equally strong. But, if they are conflicting, the local decision-maker in charge of cultural relatives' interests will be hard put for reaching a decision, that is, choosing a plan of behavior. In the same vein, also the subsystems of the orientation system may, on occasions, be harshly conflicting; and so the parts of the body, not to speak of the biological relatives.

Nor do the possibilities of conflicts inside the mind of the actor stop here. For there are referents who are, so to speak, double-sided. Take the case of a son. He is a biological relative, but at the same time he can be, or become, a cultural relative, or else a cultural Alter. Thus, an action carrying a benefit to the SPR in a given role can be noxious to the SPR in the other role; or the actor himself, Ego, may desire to benefit with his or her action his or her son in a given role, but not at all in the other.

One really wonders how human actors can make any choice after all; only even to choose every now and then, as they seem to do, among the options of loyalty, exit, or voice, in respect to the several social systems wherein they play their different parts or roles as actors. By way of summary:

a) Ego must deal with four different classes of referents, each of them (even those apparently unary, such as body and orientation system) composed possibly of a large number of entities.
b) Each class of referents is competing forcefully in/for the size and shape of his action space (i.e., the area of Ego's biocultural fitness or extended reproductive success); each one is playing its chances against those of any other class.
c) Any single, ultimate goal of any referent, be it an individual or a group, may be found conflicting with the rest of the goals accruing to the same referent.
d) Within each class, the referents themselves may be objectively involved in struggles against each other.
e) Finally, as we have just seen, the person-referents are only too often a sort of double agent.

In all this tangle, how go on to satisfactorily, and jointly, optimize one's own chances to survive in one or more different forms, physical or symbolic: that is the problem.

What usually helps Ego to unravel this decisional tangle are the selective mechanisms built into the situations, from- and to-. To them a number must be added of biosociocultural processes assigning differential weights, in form of expected values, both to referents and their goals. By itself a situation, a set of states in which Ego is unpleasingly located (from-situation), or wants more pleasingly (or less painfully) to locate him- or herself (to-situation), is a powerful selector of referents to be kept in account when planning an action. Say, a woman considering having a child notwithstanding an innate malfunction that put her life at risk (who is playing, that is, absolute survival against replication of body) is not usually bound to mobilize the representations of all cultural referents of hers, in her action space, before reaching a decision. So the whole gamut of referents that Ego has to face is drastically simplified by any given situation.

As for weights, that are so crucial in orienting a course of action, they reflect the fact that the desire for biocultural survival flows preferably through the channels of former biological, social, and cultural investments made by Ego. The current value of these investments is modified thereupon by the returns that Ego can still sensibly expect from them at the time when he or she must make a choice.

For that reason, the distribution by any one Ego of weights, or expected values, among goals, subgoals, and referents, comes down from several routes. To begin with, identifications and attachments form a stratified system in Ego's mind, with levels and circles having a different strength. The latter is not a determinant by itself, however. On the one side, a referent to which Ego is weakly attached, or identified with, can be a powerful factor influencing his or her choice of action in a situation that has preselected only referents comparatively weak, or weaker. On the other side, the stronger Ego's identification, or attachment, to a referent, the higher will be the relative importance of the latter in Ego's quadrant of joint optimization of the (global) survival chances.

Then comes Ego's position in the life cycle. For a young man or woman, physical replication is more important than that for an individual beyond normal reproductive age; but the lack of replication at the proper age may be, for the older individual, a factor increasing substantially the weight of referents different from body. A scholar getting old is likely to be increasingly worried more for what will happen in the close future to his or her symbolic self, and less for the current status of the scientific associations to which he or she belongs. A larger, and thus weightier, number of cultural relatives comes naturally along with a long and successful cultural career. Also, the existence of a large family of procreation, toward the end of an actor's reproductive life, push more easily biological relatives to the forefront of Ego's action space.

Thanks to these and many more processes, the biosociocultural clock of life modifies steadily the weights of goals and referents in the mind – the self-conscious as the silent one – of the actor. As a consequence, given that for some referents Ego's action will possibly increase, whereas for others will decrease, their probabilities of SPR, the actual set of those rewarded or penalized by Ego's action may be partially or totally subverted by the change in respective weights.

A major factor in assigning differential weights to ultimate goals and to referents must be seen, however, in the selective effects flowing naturally from Ego's position in the social structure. By "position" I mean here the point in a given social formation, and, within this, in a basic social system, where Ego happens to be located, predominantly because of his or her working status (that, of course, includes nonworking). As for basic social systems, a classification the author has found useful elsewhere is the one that splits social structure as a whole in four parts: the political system, the economic system, the system of sociocultural reproduction, and the system of biopsychic reproduction.

Within any system, states this model, the same basic activities can be organized according to different modes. Thus, inside the political system of any contemporary society one can observe the coexistence of different modes of political organization; within the economic system, different modes of production live side by side; inside the two reproductive systems, there are different modes of sociocultural and biopsychic reproduction.

Though belonging to different basic systems, some modes – of political organization, of production, and of reproduction – show a comparatively high coherence among themselves: Anyone of the resulting sets of modes is what is pointed to by the concept of "social formation" (Gallino, 1981, 1987b). Therefore Ego's social position is actually a specific point in a grid; that is, a point within a mode of organizing some necessary social function, which is itself placed – the point – at the unique crossing of a given basic system with a given social formation.

So conceptualized, Ego's social position looms as a major factor in selecting referents, assigning weights, and exposing the actor to specific sets of cultural representations. At the same time, it makes Ego blind to similar sets circulating in other points of the grid. To live embedded in any social formation is like living in a different society of its own: you see very little of what happens abroad, even just beyond the border.

The foursome quadrant of Ego's action space, as the actor looks at it through the dynamically reality-structuring filter of the functional subsystems working in his or her mind, is shaped globally, and locally furbished, even to details, by the selective activity related to Ego's position – as defined previously – in the social structure. It is true, as a result, that the tangle is always there; but only a small part of it is visible to the actors, so that, given sufficient time, they can learn to move efficiently through it.

We can aptly ask, therefore, what happens when much larger parts of the tangle rapidly acquire a new visibility for the actors, and contemporarily they have no time left to spend in learning. Several processes in contemporary societies cooperate to bring forth such conditions. I will comment briefly on three of these processes, the focal point of my discussion being the interplay of culture and social structure in the actors' mind, rather than the changes of the former or the latter *per se*.

Let us observe, for a while, an actor shuttling regularly and fast between two or more social formations in his or her own society – an extremely common condition in our times. Maybe the actor's family is quite traditional, still a piece of a peasant social formation, whereas the work is extremely modern, an expression of world-wide technetronic capitalism; or vice versa. Crossing repeatedly the border between different social formations carries with it several effects upon the shape both of Ego's action space and the quadrant of the referents; the contents of the latter; the representations through which he or she looks at it all.

One foremost effect is that the number of cultural relatives usually increases, while Ego is developing new identifications and attachments to actors belonging to the formation "other." But the latter are weaker, both because of their recency and because there is a factor of uncertainty in social identities acquired outside the formation where one was first socialized.

Also, the relative and absolute weight of goals, subgoals, and referents is perceived by the actor to be different in the other formation; but the quadrant whereupon the referents play their chances against each other is only one, in the actor's mind. In this way, Ego becomes uncertain about what stakes there are, and what are to be put, around the poles of the quadrant. New representations, frames, situations, patterns of emotion, become available to Ego; but most of them come without instructions for a proper use. The nature of entities that are important in survival becomes fuzzy.

To have a social identity means to be able to answer the question "Who am I?" with a firm reference to a group whose cultural traits are felt by Ego to be shared by his or her orientation system. Now, that is precisely the kind of answer that cannot be firmly offered when one is shuttling to and from between different social formations. The goal of surviving is always there, as strong as ever; but Ego is no longer sure about the entities to which it must be applied.

Then there are, to further complicate the already tangled decision process of the actor, the media-mediated representations, among which I shall consider especially the frames. Following Goffman (whose definition of frames came from Bateson), I define herewith "frames" as "definitions of a situation ... built up in accordance with principles of organization which govern events – at least social ones – and our subjective involvements in them" (1974: 10–11). In our model of the actor's mind, it will be remembered, there is a functional subsystem dealing specifically with frames: that is, retrieving, assembling, modifying, storing them. Most frames are basically external to the actor in origin; they are devised by culture, selected by social structure – that is, by Ego's position in it – and only within this predelimited and preselected stock Ego is allowed to choose according to his or her needs.

The communication society has brought in radical changes in the social production and circulation of frames among individual minds. It has revolutionized, to use a Batesonian code, the ecology of frames. In traditional society, most frames flowing through a representative actor's mind were partly popular constructs, coming down naturally from early socialization and enculturation, and partly institutional constructs, offered or enforced by the church and the local political power. All of them were communicated by human actors, and only a tiny fraction by written texts, inaccessible to most people.

In the communication society, most frames in the actor's mind are contrived and circulated by media supported by a specific technology, whatever their original source. The media technology – hereby including first and foremost the technology used to build the messages – has a double character. It is subservient to overall goals of the world economic system, without any individual or group having really invented them; also, it is strongly autotelic, that is, self-centered and self-reproducing. Thus, it cannot avoid building up, and spreading methodically around, standardized frames for the organization of experience.

Adopting Goffman's terminology, what happened is that even the primary frameworks, the frameworks "seen by those who apply it as not depending on or harking back to some prior or 'original' interpretation" (1974: 21), are subject to endless sorts of keys and keyings; a fair proportion of them have even been transformed in, or superimposed by, all kinds of designs and fabrications. Let us remember Goffman's definitions:

> Keying provides one basic way in which a strip of activity can be transformed, that is, serve as an item-by-item model for something else. Differently put, keyings represent a basic way in which activity is vulnerable. A second transformational vulnerability is now considered: fabrication. I refer to the intentional effort of one or more individuals to manage activity so that a party of one or more others will be included to have a false belief about what it is that is going on (1974: 83).

Planning to survive in a cultural universe wherein most frames once habitually used to interpret situations, though believed by the actor to be primary, are keyed or fabricated by means of a specific technology in order to fulfill ends unknown to the actor, is no longer what it used to be. As ever, the actor is bound to choose the action that will expectedly optimize his or her physical and/or symbolic spatiotemporal survival. The interpretation of situations, however, together with representations of referents, and the ways and means to reach the ultimate goals, are framed by meaning-giving items of culture artificially contrived to establish a symbolic order, cotextured with the economic order.

There is almost no escape from it. A body asking for replication, or renouncing it in order to improve its chances of persistence; a cultural relative asking – in the actor's mind – for a contribution to his or her persistence; an orientation system's evaluative subsystem pretending to survive even at the cost of endangering body, are actually representational entities wholly alien to what were formerly the natural principles of organization structuring Ego's action space.

This is due mainly to two reasons. First, because they were purposively fabricated, as representations, to pursue ultimate goals that are not simply some Alter's goals (that would not be an epochal novelty), but are produced and communicated by a technology meant to coldly and rationally substitute Ego's natural frameworks with artificial ones. Second, because they are fabricated at a very high degree of generality, in order to elicit analogous behaviors from the largest number of actors, without any intimacy with their specific situation patterns and rather intentionally overlapping them.

One last change in social structures I will consider. This is only to illustrate how Ego's initial parameters filling in proper instruction slots within the actor's behavioral programs, whatever the former can be, are being transformed both by objective changes in social reality and by subjective availability of representations adequate (or inadequate) to it. This change is the fading off of system boundaries. Especially evident in national economic systems, that is a condition affecting many kinds of organizations. It is a result of the externalization of all organizational functions, except those closest to the organization's mission; the spread of telecommunications and telework; the diffusion over very large spaces of an organization's sources of primary and secondary resources.

All this makes it very hard for everyone, placed outside or inside a given system, to tell what does belong to the inside of that system from what belongs to its outside. It makes one even wonder whether there is any boundary left between inside and outside – or, rather, whether the concept of a system's objective boundary maintains any meaning at all.

From this viewpoint, let us think now of an actor having to decide between loyalty, exit, and voice (just to simplify in rough Hirschmanian terms the much more complex and subtle phenomenology of association and dissociation) toward a social system he or she belongs to. The boundaries of this system are sort of invisible to the actor's eyes, and at any rate are not located at the assumed place. Several kinds of mistakes can follow from this. For instance, if the actor does opt for exit, he or she can find himself, even after exiting, still placed inside the same system – possibly without knowing it. Such mistakes, however, can be only the result of a decision. The trouble, in front of the fading of systems' boundaries, is how to reach it.

Any social action amounts to a distribution of SPR's expected values among referents preselected by the present situation. This implies a rational, round-the-quadrant calculation by the actor about possible consequences of the planned action i.e., loyalty, exit, or voice on (the probability of) the SPR of the referents. But how can this calculation be made if the system's boundaries are subjectively and objectively fuzzy? The contribution to survival, persistence, and reproduction (or to any other subgoal) of any referent may come out very differently, following the very same action, as a function of system boundaries' location and permeability.

Take the case of an action that Ego anticipates will bring some benefits (as ever in form of SPR's coins) to a given referent, provided that the system boundaries still are where they were supposed to be. Would Ego suspect that the system boundaries had moved elsewhere, or had just faded off, the identical anticipated action might then be seen by the same actor, placed in the same from-situation, as carrying only costs to the same referent. The contrary, of course, may also be true, whatever the combination of ultimate goals, subgoals, and referents, that makes up Ego's decisional tangle.

So, culture and social structure do not truly speak to each other directly, somewhere high above real actors' heads. Rather, they intermingle in unique ways in every social actor's mind, like warp and woof in a finely knitted fabric whose pattern is prodigiously being recast every time it is used.

In this perspective, we need to improve our understanding of the intricacies of inner microsystemic processes, working at different levels of mind, that link those ever-changing patterns to the decisions that, after all, are daily – or even, for that matter, exceptionally – made by social actors in all kinds of societies. For that purpose, we might need more models and theories that look more deeply into real actors' minds, rather than bent on explorating by preference, in a characteristically autoreferential way, the mind of the makers of social action theories.

References

Bateson, Gregory (1972). *Steps to an Ecology of Mind.* San Francisco: Chandler.

Bateson, Gregory (1979). *Mind and Nature: A Necessary Unity.* New York: Dutton.

Benn, S. I. and Mortimore, G. W. (Eds.) (1976). *Rationality and the Social Sciences.* London: Routledge and Kegan.

Bourricaud, François (1977). *L'individualisme institutionnel. Essai sur la sociologie de Talcott Parsons.* Paris: Presses Universitaires de France.

Brittan, Arthur (1973). *Meaning and Situations.* London: Routledge and Kegan.

Burke, Kenneth (1945). *A Grammar of Motives.* New York: Prentice-Hall.

Burridge, Kenelm (1979). *Someone, No One. An Essay on Individuality.* Princeton: Princeton University Press.

Canetti, Elias (1972). *Macht und Überleben.* München: Hanser.

Canetti, Elias (1981/1960). "Il sopravvissuto." In *Massa e potere.* Milano: Adelphi.

Dawkins, Richard (1976). "Hierarchical Organisation: A Candidate Principle for Ethology." In *Growing Points in Ethology*, ed. P. P. G. Bateson and R. A. Hinde. Cambridge: Cambridge University Press.

Elster, Jon (1979). *Ulysses and the Sirens. Studies in Rationality and Irrationality.* Cambridge: Cambridge University Press.

Elster, Jon (Ed.) (1986). *The Multiple Self.* Cambridge: Cambridge University Press.

Galimberti, Umberto (1984). *Il corpo. Antropologia, psicoanalisi, fenomenologia*, 2nd ed. Milano: Feltrinelli.

Gallino, Luciano (1981). *La societa'. Un' introduzione sistemica alla sociologia.* Torino: Paravia.

Gallino, Luciano (1987a). *L'attore sociale. Biologia, cultura e intelligenza artificiale.* Torino: Einaudi.

Gallino, Luciano (1987b). *Della ingovernabilità.* Milano: Comunità.

Gazzaniga, Michael S. (1985). *The Social Brain. Discovering the Networks of the Mind.* New York: Basic Books.

Giddens, Anthony (1984). *The Constitution of Society. Outline of the Theory of Structuration.* Cambridge: Polity Press.

Goffman, Erving (1974). *Frame Analysis: An Essay on the Organization of Experience.* Cambridge, Mass.: Harvard University Press.

Hampden-Turner, Charles (1981). *Maps of the Mind.* London: Mitchell Beazly.

Harsanyi, John C. (1977). *Rational Behavior and Bargaining Equilibrium in Games and Social Situations.* Cambridge: Cambridge University Press.

Hartfiel, Guenter (1968). *Wirtschaftliche und soziale Rationalität. Untersuchungen zum Menschenbild in Ökonomie und Soziologie.* Stuttgart: Enke.

Hernegger, Rudolf (1978). *Der Mensch auf der Suche nach Identität. Kulturanthropologische Studien über Totemismus – Mythos – Religion.* Bonn: Habelt.

Hirsch, Eli (1982). *The Concept of Identity.* New York: Oxford University Press.

Hirschman, Albert O. (1970). *Exit, Voice, and Loyalty. Responses to Decline in Firms, Organizations, and States.* Cambridge, Mass.: Harvard University Press.

Kirsch, Werner (1977). *Einführung in die Theorie der Entscheidungsprozesse,* 2nd ed., three vols. in one. Wiesbaden: Gabler.

Kurtz, Paul (1965). *Decision and the Condition of Man.* Seattle: University of Washington Press.

MacLean, Paul D. (1973). *A Triune Concept of the Brain and Behaviour.* Toronto: University of Toronto Press.

Margolis, Howard (1982). *Selfishness, Altruism, and Rationality. A Theory of Social Choice.* Cambridge: Cambridge University Press.

Oakley, David A. (Ed.) (1985). *Brain and Mind.* London: Methuen.

Oksenberg Rorty, Amelie (Ed.) (1976). *The Identities of Persons.* Berkeley: University of California Press.

Overbeck, Gerd and Overbeck, Annegret (Eds.) (1978). *Seelischer Konflikt – körperliches Leiden.* Reinbek bei Hamburg: Rowohlt.

Parsons, Talcott (1959). "An Approach to Psychological Theory in Terms of the Theory of Action." In *Psychology: A Study of a Science.* Study I: Conceptual and Systematic, Vol. 3: *Formulations of the Person and the Social Context,* ed. by Sigmund Koch. New York: McGraw-Hill.

Radcliffe-Brown, Alfred Reginald (1957). *A Natural Science of Society.* Glencoe: Free Press.

Schilder, Paul (1935). *The Image and Appearance of the Human Body: Studies in the Constructive Energies of the Psyche.* London: Paul, Trench, Trubner.

Shaver, Phillip (Ed.) (1985). *Self, Situations, and Social Behavior.* Beverly Hills: Sage.

Sorokin, Pitirim A. (1947). "Sociocultural Structure of Personality." In idem, *Society, Culture, and Personality: Their Structure and Dynamics. A System of General Sociology.* New York: Harper and Brothers.

Valabrega, Jean-Paul (1980). *Phantasme Mythe Corps et Sens: Une Théorie Psychanalytique de la Connaissance.* Paris: Payot.

3 The Role of the Game Between Culture and Social Action*

Carlo Mongardini

The history of sociology over the past century can be seen as that of its increasing conditioning by the concept of "society." While this concept was used with a great deal of caution up to the end of the last century, it subsequently came to predominate the field. In the early stages, conceptualization was limited to establishing the categories that allow us to think of society, but from the 1920s on, the image of "society" and "social systems" came to be the center of interest in sociological representation. After the 1950s, the concept of society symbolized the ideology by means of which the "enlightened" school of American thought was imposed upon Europe[1]. Finally, almost all totalitarian tendencies can be said today to come under the idea of "society."

When the history of this idea comes to be written, it will be seen to what extent its positing of a perception of the whole, and of unity, not altogether in line with experience[2], has hindered our knowledge of what society, properly speaking, really is; that is, of the processes whereby individuals associate with each other and dissociate from each other. The image is an image of unity, but the reality is one of change.

Strictly speaking, society is the process by which forms of human association change. What we are accustomed to call "society," on the contrary, is simply something we *perceive* to represent unity and stability, which for reasons of symmetry is in opposition to change. While society can be understood only through theories of social processes, in recent decades the tendency to accept as real that unity which is only a product of our minds has prevented research from proceeding along those lines. The concept of socialization, initially neutral[3], has come to be a synonym for integration. The effect of the dominant ideology has been such that even the work of those who, since the 1950s, have attempted to analyze processes like that of conflict, has been reduced to the study of the forms in which conflict is institutionalized.

In the 1920s, Georg Simmel (1968 b: 153) had already observed that the image of society was destined to represent our "vital reality," with respect to which the individual would come to be simply "a point where social lines cross, or even, like the atom, a fiction." This ideological condition has hindered the study of social processes. Process is change[4], and to understand change we need not a theory of action, but rather a *theory of the actor* that can evince not only

* This chapter is the first part of a longer essay on the subject which is not yet complete. These pages are dedicated to Friedrich H. Tenbruck, at whose home in Tübingen the main ideas of the study took shape, and to Arnold Zingerle, who discussed them with me in Bayreuth.

the individual's capacity to mediate between nature and culture, but also the possibilities open to him in accomplishing his desires as the expression of his freedom within the confines of the conditioning to which he is subject. A *humanistic sociology* cannot sacrifice a part of reality in order to obtain a more coherent image. The actor's will and his freedom are elements of reality that cannot be suppressed. A theory of the actor, and hence a theory of processes, can be built only on this terrain of will and of freedom, even if this creates a *zone of undetermination* within the boundaries of sociological theory that has to be taken into account.

The actor's margin of freedom, and the element of undetermination essential to understanding social processes, may perhaps be represented usefully by the *concept of the game*. This concept can play an important part in sociological theory, although obviously not in the sense of "game theory." In order to use this idea, it seems appropriate first to examine what we mean by games and the part they play in human behavior.

Insofar as he reacts to different and changing stimuli, the social actor shapes his action in a nonlinear pattern which in itself creates the premises for the condition of process. Certainly the image he seeks to project is one of continuity and coherence, but he obtains this result less by demonstration than by *justification* and by that whole set of elements that Pareto called "derivations." Moreover, the actor is subject to the pressures of a twofold reality. On the one hand, there are the drives originating in his inner world, which he recognizes, selects, diverts, or represses, and, in any case, attempts to control. On the other hand, there is the external world with its constrictive reality, partly objective and partly reproduced as image: the institutional framework, with its accepted significance, its imperatives, its prohibitions, its symbols. The social actor mediates between these two opposing forces – nature and culture – each of which attempts to prevail over the other.

But such mediation is not a purely passive operation. It is effected on the basis of an objectivated position of the self whereby the individual identifies with some of the various aspects of both realities, represses others, and attempts to incorporate still others. And not only is his mediation an active function, it is also one of *negotiation* based on the will he expresses and the ends he wishes to accomplish.

The social actor negotiates continually with the two realities and with the constrictions and limits they impose upon him. With respect to the social person who carries within him those drives that seek satisfaction through society, and with respect to the personage who is an expression of the exigencies of culture, the social actor expresses a third identity, that of the acting subject who not only mediates between the internal world and the external, but also has his own will, his own ends, and his own design for interaction that he seeks to affirm within the limits imposed by the two realities.

In his constant negotiation with the two realities, the social actor feels, on the one hand, a sense of belonging, of group ties, of collective values, and, on the other, a need to pursue the goals he himself has set, whatever the obstacles he may find in his path. This may be what Pareto meant by the two principle categories of residuals he called "the persistance of aggregates" and "the instinct for combinations," (Pareto, 1964). But the meaning of these categories is much more complex than Pareto could have supposed. The social actor's individuality and identity result from the mediation and negotiation he engages in, and cannot fail to include either the sense of belonging or the feeling of freedom asserted through his pursuit of his goals. The autonomy of the actor as the central figure in social processes originates in precisely this configuration, where he is partly a member of a community and partly an independent will expressing itself in the pursuit of self-set goals.

The social actor's mediation and negotiation bring about the action itself, which is thus the result of a process and produces sociality as process. Strictly speaking, society is actually this sequentiality of processes from which only subsequently we derive a unitary perception of real society and, almost consequentially, an idea of an ideal society and a social ideal.

This sequence of process which produce sociality, and hence society as a subsequent, abstract image of reality, is what Simmel described as "sociation" (*Vergesellschaftung*). The problem is that it has been virtually impossible to describe this condition of process in terms of the conceptual categories hitherto available. It cannot be described by a *theory of action*, which takes the inner drives as its sole point of departure for an understanding of how the actor operates, and it cannot be described by a *theory of structure*, which analyzes how the action is conditioned, nor, by some combination of the two, defined as a *theory of structuration*. All of these describe elements present in the social process, but not the process itself.

There is something more to the actor than simple mediation between the two realities – nature and culture – and something more than simply a way of acting that structures reality. There is a free definition of his ends and will that pursues them and negotiates on their behalf with the representations of the internal world and of the external. This reality cannot be represented as structuration, but rather must be seen as an ongoing process that our present-day concepts do not allow us to describe adequately.

Let us now see how we may approach this conceptualization. In social processes, that which is process in a strict sense – not the mechanical repetition of actions and reactions, but rather intense and lively interaction enhanced by unpredictable possibilities – is determined by what the individual sets value upon, be it person, thing, idea, or symbol. The value we attribute to a person or an object creates a tension in our personality that is then discharged in the intensity of the interactive relationship, where our will enters massively and impresses on the process an unpredictable pattern. The usual channels of negotiation with nature and with culture break down, and we reaffirm our freedom.

The more intensely a relationship involves a value, the more the resulting process will be dominated by the will and will elude nature's and culture's conditioning. Even time, one of culture's most highly resistant structures, may be almost obliterated by this tension of the personality and its will to achieve its end. If something interests us, and tension toward it is created in our personality, time "passes in a flash" without our even noticing it.

Among the things that surround us, we place a higher value on sociality than we do on the image of society, and there exist in sociality certain relationships that unleash processes in the strict sense of the term; that is, those that produce change. These more intense processes are the very ones that lend themselves least to theoretical definition and analysis. Moments and tendencies press hard one upon the other; they overlap and they contradict each other, and the very tension involved in the process makes it impossible to distinguish them. There is perhaps nothing so fluid and intensely interactive as love, precisely because it projects the personality's maximum tension into the interaction. But this is precisely why love is so difficult to delineate in conceptual schemes that represent social patterns. Many sociologists have attempted to do so[5], but the results have not been very satisfactory in terms of general theory. The forms of interaction involved in the process of falling in love, for example, are so complex that it is difficult to break the process down into distinct concepts susceptible of analysis.

Georg Simmel tried to reduce the complexity of these processes using the concept of "life," which he contrasted in its density, intensity, and contradiction to the idea of form, with its tendency to be fixed and repetitious. But the concept of life is a way of circumventing the complexity of processes, not of coming to grips with them and breaking them down into their components. First, the concept of life offers us a unitary representation of flux but is unable to represent forward and backward movement, convergence and contradiction among those tendencies present, for example, in the actor's negotiation, and which concur in determining sociality in the strict sense of the word. Second, even when the concept of life is referred to a single individual, it is an abstract representation that does not reproduce any moment in particular[6], while at the same time it constitutes a unity that does not exist in fact[7].

Everything whose nature is intensively one of process, and whose components, given the value and the tension of which it is a product, cannot be arranged in unilinear form, is commonly called a *game*. We speak of life as a game when we wish to define an area lying between chance and necessity (cf. Monod, 1970; Eigen and Winkler, 1985). We speak of the play of forces in describing situations produced by components that cannot be clearly established or defined. We speak of the game of love in representing moments, in themselves contradictory, which constitute – never in unilinear form[8] – mutual attraction. Finally, we speak of games in relation to people who wish, even on a symbolic or abstract level, to challenge fate, or other people, or when we want to represent a situation in which one engages all the tension of which his personality is capable, even in a context that may be constructed ritually or artificially.

Let us consider this concept of game, then, and try to apply it as a possible category in sociological analysis that may be useful for a theory of social processes. Its usefulness may be evinced above all when we realize that in order to describe social processes, our point of departure must be the actor's margin of freedom and not the conditioning to which the pressure of internal and external reality subject him. The concept of game seems the most appropriate to specify the ideas of process and interaction from within. These ideas, in fact, contain expectations, prefigurations, possibilities, alternatives, contradictions, and tensions that represent the evolving pattern of sociality, and that are typical of the player immersed in his game. We may therefore consider, on the one hand, the deepest meaning of games, or play, as an attitude and as a situation, and, on the other, the theoretical importance of the concept of the game for a theory of social processes[9].

Strictly speaking, the "game" element in games is not the set of rules that define a situation and are supposed to determine the actor's behavior, but rather the actor's ability to use those rules to achieve his goal. The rules of the game reproduce that constricted reality in which the actor must succeed in asserting himself. However, we have here a special type of reproduction, in that, as we shall see, *the rules do not change during the game; their duration is limited* to the time during which the game is played[10], and *the player identifies totally with the rules of the game* as a matter of principle. The game, properly speaking – what the Germans call "Spielraum" – is the *margin of freedom* enjoyed by the actor, who fulfills himself within the rules of the game just as he fulfills himself in life within the context of a personal condition and a cultural condition.

While in games the contextual data are fixed, defined, known, and accepted, in social processes the actor *begins by playing with himself.* Namely through choices and careful control, he must recognize, avoid, repress, and sublimate those drives that would otherwise lead to actions not compatible with external reality, or that would in the end not correspond to the "pleasure principle." The player's situation in the institutionalized game is therefore much simpler than that of the actor "playing" in society. First, the game situation is limited in time and space and acquires a meaning of easing the pressure of reality. Second, the player is subjected only to the conditions imposed by the game situation and does not need to mediate between two realities, of which one (culture) attempts to constrain the individual, while the other (nature) attempts to remove the obstacles to his attaining pleasure. In the game situation, moreover, the rules are the fully accepted premises of the situation. *The player plays not with the rules, but by the rules*: He does not question or revise them, since they are the conditions of a hypothetical, but definitively constructed, reality. The actor, on the contrary, begins to play with the rules that determine him, with which he identifies only in part, insofar as he identifies with the culture that surrounds him. Finally, in the game situation the rules and the player's conditioning do not change as they do in the course of social processes.

The first observation to which all these differences lead is that we must recognize the banality of trying to represent the conditions of real life and the processes of interaction by game theory. With respect to the evolution of sociality, game theory is actually a representation based on premises, such as the conditions of the game, which do not exist in real life. We have, then, no more than a "represented game" built solely on game conditions. Game theory, therefore, does not at all reproduce the behavior of the social actor; on the contrary, as we shall demonstrate here, *it is the actor who explains himself through games.*

The fundamental characteristic of the social actor must be seen, then, in his *predisposition to play*. By the same token, social processes having high rates of frequency cannot be interpreted without the category of games. In processes, the social actor is not simply a passive mediator among pressures brought to bear upon him from within and without. He is also the active individual trying to assert his own will, to obtain answers to his expectations, to realize the plan through which he prefigures the interactive relationship by *playing in the free areas* which the inner and the outer forces permit. Freedom is the game the actor succeeds in playing. His will is manifested with the conditioning and upon the conditioning imposed by reality.

The social actor's predisposition to play is manifested on three different levels. On the first level, which I would call *presocial*, in the logical sense, it may be referred to as the actor's *sociability* in building a given relationship and may be represented as the distance lying between the personality and the social relationship created. We build and evolve all of our social relationships, as Simmel (1968c: 27) says, holding back a part of ourselves that does not participate and is not without consequences for the development of the relationship. Thus every expression of sociality involves on the actor's part a certain degree of *sociability*, a datum that can be considered abstractly and represented in terms of the personality's proximity to and distance from the relationship created[11].

This state of being partly inside and partly outside the relationship – that is, this *play of individuality* with the practices the actor constitutes – varies as the relationship itself evolves and can indicate, on the one hand, greater distance, and, on the other, greater involvement and tension. It is precisely this ebb and flow, this playing with sociality, that determines the fact by which the developments of interaction lend themselves to structural and functionalistic modeling, or, on the contrary, become charged with tension, engaging the actor in a game within the social relationship. Sociability is thus an attitude that manifests itself only in the concrete forms of sociality, as an alternation of proximity and distance, and as such, determines the process according to which the relationship evolves.

A second level on which the social actor's predisposition to play manifests itself unfolds inside social situations. This means for the actor both a *playing with the rules*, in the sense that their validity is continually and implicitly reopened for discussion in the practices of everyday life[12], and a *playing among the rules*, utilizing or not utilizing the interstices available to the actor's will. The margin of play "among" the rules must be neither too broad nor too narrow. If it is too broad, the actor loses that *institutional security* that is the only thing onto which the "risk" of his game can be grafted. Also in social life *the game requires the rules and the rules stimulate the game.* If, on the contrary, that margin is too narrow, the actor senses that his area of freedom has disappeared, and with it the value of his participation. In this case he may be induced to seek countervalues outside the institutions or against them.

A situation of conflict comes into being, therefore, when there is no longer any margin for play; at least not any that the social actor perceives. With respect to explicit or to latent forms of conflict, therefore, the game appears to be their translation into cultural terms. Games thus appear to be the most complex and sophisticated form of conflict; they translate into cultural and then into abstract terms the aggressive tensions present in nature. Thus it is not conflict that is modeled on games, but games that can be seen as a sublimated form of conflict. It must be remembered that one of the essential functions of culture is to circumscribe and fix individuality, which, for its own part, is always lying in wait to break through culture's limitations and prohibitions through the operation of the "pleasure principle" (Freud). In social processes, therefore, alongside areas of compatibility between the two claimants, the actor must reckon with the inevitable areas of incompatibility, of breakdown, and of conflict manifested in different situations. Sometimes it is possible, through mediation and play, to reach a compromise or to sublimate conflictual situations. At other times the fragile veil of civilization is torn and conflicts break out again, often with the reappearance of painful primitive experiences. This is why the playful attitude has important functions not limited to the individual actor.

In addition to the presocial and the social levels, the social actor's predisposition for play is manifested on a third level, that of the *game as institution.* Here the game is a representation of life and of society that can, however, be built only within the limits in which our rationality is able to reproduce artificially the conditions of life and of society. *This possibility is as limited in games as it is in scientific representation,* and this is why game theory cannot bring us even one step closer to reality. The game as institution is based entirely on the fact that we understand it to be abstracted from life and limited in time and space, and it posits the absolute certainty and validity of the rules and the total socialization of the player, who in the society of the game realizes the model of the perfect society in which behavior and expectations are established with absolute certainty.

Such certainty is necessary if the luck or skill of the player are to be defined with the same degree of certainty. In the closed world of the game, limited in time and space and fixed by rules, each player throws down his gauntlet to destiny, to his opponent, to the image, to himself, as we can deduce from the four types of games identified by Caillois (1967): agon, alea, mimicry, and ilinx. As in the social world, however, the rule is not the game. The game, properly speaking, is, first, the type of challenge and the person or thing toward which it is directed and, second, the degree of tension with which the player's personality is involved in the process of using the rules to obtain the gratification sought.

Why do we enter the fictitious world of games so frequently? Not only, as some observers have noted, in order to lessen the pressure of reality, if not altogether to elude it. Often we enter games to measure our personality's capacity for tension in an institutional situation that is certain. In fact, the game situation alters the way our personality is present in social processes; we are at once further away from and closer to the interactive processes. Greater distance and greater relaxation are the products of our knowing we are acting in a fictitious world. Greater proximity is the product of our commitment in measuring ourselves in a situation in which the certainty of the institutional framework means that the result obtained *expresses only* our luck or skill.

There is another element, however, that induces people to engage in games, and that is the possibility they afford of creating a fictitious world in which the actor may be allowed to take possession of a reality otherwise adverse to or distant from him. This element is extremely important; its roots go deep, and it brings games closer to art or theater. To understand this mechanism better, let us look at children's games. Many observers have seen in children's play a reflection of the serenity and the security acquired in a calm, protected environment. Few, however, have considered that it might be seen as an attempt to *take possession of reality* gradually discovered as being something different from the child's inner world, hostile and oppressive to him in its imposition of the mechanisms of socialization and in its revelation through the predominance of the will of the adult. The child plays in order to construct a reality on his own scale, which he can take possession of and in which he can feel free to exorcize the burdens, hostilities, and pressures (even if motivated by affection) placed upon him by the adult[13]. The adult often reproduces this childhood condition in his own play; not only is he able to reduce in this way the pressure of reality, but he also discovers in play the possibility of taking possession, even if only symbolically, of a reality otherwise foreign or hostile to him. This aspect of the game as institution leads us back to its religious origins[14] as well as to the function played by magic in any type of society[15]. Like magic, play may become a *regressive activity* if the pressure of reality exceeds given limits.

The relationship between play and the pressure of reality leads us to consider from a specific point of view the fact that interest for games as institutions spreads and intensifies at certain moments in community life. Recently we have seen some types of games – from playing the stock market to games of fortune and "society games" – spread so widely in certain countries that observers have spoken of "game fever[16]." It is always difficult to give a simple explanation for complex phenomena, but certainly people's interest in the institutional game increases markedly when the margin of play within society becomes either too narrow or too broad for the social actor. A society that increasingly extends its regimentation to the innermost recesses of private life may certainly develop still further as a model or may temporarily reduce the damage wrought by an individuality that avoids participation in community life[17], but it certainly does decrease the social actor's margin of play. The consequent state of frustration and alienation is deflected toward the institutional game in an attempt to regain possession of an increasingly alien reality. At this point, not only those predispositions of the actor that find no outlet in community life, but also those ideals of the individual's that can find no means of expression in the mechanical repetitiousness of regimented life, are transfused into games. This may be why in certain abnormal situations, the power organization has often waged war on games, has suppressed games altogether, or has at the least taken over their administration. This has happened in modern society just as it did in ancient Rome. The purpose has perhaps been to impede that instinct for play that, finding expression in society games and containing projected ideals, may enter community life in the form of an "instinct for combinations."

We have seen how the actor's predisposition for play, in which he manifests his freedom, is fulfilled on the three different levels we have identified as the presocial, the social, and the institutional. The idea we wish to maintain is not only that the predisposition to play is the essential characteristic that distinguishes the figure of the social actor, but also that the actor's playful tendencies on these three levels must be given primary consideration if sociological theory is to be taken as a theory of social processes[18]. There are other tendencies in the actor, of course, that counterbalance and moderate the predisposition to play; the most important are the sense of belonging, of group ties, awareness of one's place in time, in space, and in social space. These are all tendencies that may be classified in that category of residuals that Pareto called the "persistence of aggregates[19]." But everything that in social life appears in the form of a process is the result of the actor's capacity for play. When we try to translate the complicated interdependence of human action into sociological theory, however, we often set aside the actor's capacity for play, perhaps because it might skew the symmetry of scientific representation. But then we realize that interdependent relationships cannot be systematized, not only because every relationship contains some reservations on the actor's part, but also because for the actor himself, every situation contains some potential for play that makes it impossible to pigeonhole in a defined scheme of repetition and uniformity.

Reaffirming his freedom through play, *the actor constructs his identity as actor*, separately from the identities and memberships that fix him in the dimensions of space and time. That which in the actor's behavior is, properly speaking, his margin of play, constitutes the sphere of *undetermination* which gives rise to processuality, especially in its more intense and more socially significant forms. The combination of our three levels of play might naturally lead us to suspect that all of sociality may be reduced to the dimension of play, and that sociology cannot succeed in defining anything but the pattern of processes. But this, too, would simply be an optical illusion, since the forces of culture are always present in strength to define, to circumscribe, and to fix individuality. What the dimension of play means is that on the level of action, especially in our modern world, rich as it is in formal freedoms, there is never just one possibility of choice for the actor, but rather a multiplicity of options. The use of the concept of the game to describe the dominant characteristic of the figure of the actor, and as a category to describe social processes, and the attribution of a *quality of undetermination* to the actor's intentionality and to interactive relationships, open broad perspectives for sociological analysis going beyond the contrast between action theory and structural theories.

If sociological analysis is understood not as *what must be*, but as a *set of possibilities* toward which the actor's will may be oriented, then only in a *theory of games* can we find the conceptual instruments we need to describe intentionality and processes. Nor does the actor have any reservations with respect to that pure processuality that can be described as play. In fact, while it is true that the actor is never willing to put the things he believes in "at stake," it is also true that it is just such values that activate those processes we cannot describe otherwise than by means of the category of play. If sociology can only be a "cognitive experiment" (Mongardini, 1985), the category of undetermination, introduced through play to represent both the actor's intentionality and the more intense processes, can be of notable importance in defending this type of knowledge from improvisation and from pure intuition, and in keeping it within the limits of a humanistic conception of the social sciences.

Notes

[1] On the ideological use of the concept of "society," cf. Tenbruck (1984).

[2] Pareto had already noted the uncertainty and the possible ideological use of the concept of society along these lines. Cf. V. Pareto (1973: 193 *et. seq.*).

[3] This was what Simmel meant, in 1894, by "Vergesellschaftung." Cf. G. Simmel (1968 a).

[4] Even if change does not exclude the reoccurrence of similar experiences.

[5] Among others, Simmel (1957) and, recently, Alberoni (1979) and Luhmann (1982).

[6] Simmel notes that we are "fragments not only of mankind in general, but also of ourselves" (1968 c: 25).

[7] In fact, an individual never apprehends identical experiences or identical feelings in the same way. Furthermore, how can it be possible to identify "a" life when at least three vital processes coexist interdependently?

[8] It is the nature of the human mind, writes Simmel (1968 c: 191), "not to let itself be tied to another individual by one thread alone, even though scientific analysis ends only with the elementary units in their specific cohesive force."

[9] Our task here is made easier by the fact that the tendencies to play games have multiplied in contemporary society, considering games both as institutional activities and as a manifestation of freedom within institutions.

[10] This is the basis upon which a distinction has been made between "finite games" and "infinite games" (cf. Carse, 1986).

[11] The relationship may be similar in some respects to the one between a given culture and a foreigner. Many of the aspects that characterize the figure of the "foreigner" may be likened to the state of distance/proximity of the personality with respect to many relationships characteristic of modern culture. On the figure of the foreigner, cf. Tabboni (1986).

[12] For this interpretation see Popitz (1980: 1 *et seq.*).

[13] On this subject see Freud (1927).

[14] Cf. the entry "Spiel" in Galling (1962: VI, 244).

[15] See on this subject Mongardini (1983 b).

[16] For a discussion of this phenomenon, see the German weekly *Die Zeit*, 27 February, 1987. On playing the stock market in particular, see the Italian daily *La Stampa*, 28 October, 1986.

[17] See on this subject Mongardini (1983 a).

[18] It is not easy, writes Norbert Elias (1977) to transform sociological theories in which human society, or even all mankind, is seen as a usually unalterable structure, into a theory in which society is recognized as an ongoing set of processes. But only when we are able to do so, will we be able to give full and proper meaning to the problem of those long-range tendencies that have not been planned by social development and that are not accounted for in theoretical returns to apparently unmodifiable social systems or in empirical research oriented exclusively toward the present.

[19] We can thus rediscover the presence and the heuristic value of that pair of residuals Pareto identified as "instinct for combinations" and "persistence of aggregates."

References

Alberoni, F. (1979). *Innamoramento e amore*. Milano: Garzanti.

Caillois, R. (1967). *Les jeux et les hommes: La masque et la vertige*. Paris: Gallimard.

Carse, J.P. (1986). *Finite and Infinite Games*. New York: The Free Press.

Eigen, M. and Winkler, R. (1985). *Das Spiel: Naturgesetze steuern den Zufall*, 2nd ed. München: Piper.

Elias, N. (1977). "Zur Grundlegung einer Theorie sozialer Prozesse." *Zeitschrift für Soziologie* 6: 127–149.

Freud, S. (1927). *Jenseits des Lustprinzips*, 3rd ed. Leipzig: Internationale Psychoanalytische Vereinigung.

Galling, K. (Ed.) (1962). "Spiel." *Die Religion in Geschichte und Gegenwart: Handwörterbuch für Theologie und Religionswissenschaft*, 3rd ed. Tübingen: Mohr.

La Stampa. 28 October 1986.

Luhmann, N. (1982). *Liebe als Passion: Zur Codierung von Intimität*. Frankfurt/a.M.: Suhrkamp.

Mongardini, C. (1983 a). "Legittimazione e consenso in una società in transformazione." In *La società liberal-democratica e le sue prospettive per il futuro*. Roma: Bulzoni.

Mongardini, C. (1983 b). "Sul significato sociologico del pensiero magico." In *Il magico e il moderno*, ed. C. Mongardini. Milano: F. Angeli.

Mongardini, C. (1985). *Epistemologia e sociologia*. Milano: F. Angeli.

Monod, J. (1970). *Le hasard et la nécessité: Essai sur la philosophie naturelle de la biologie moderne*. Paris: Edition du Seuil.

Pareto, V. (1964). *Trattato di sociologia generale*, 3rd ed. Milano: Comunità.

Pareto, V. (1973). "L'individuale e il sociale." Reprinted in *Vilfredo Pareto dall' economia alla sociologia*, ed. C. Mongardini. Roma: Bulzoni.

Popitz, H. (1980). *Die normative Konstruktion von Gesellschaft*. Tübingen: Mohr.

Simmel, G. (1957). "Fragment über die Liebe." Reprinted in G. Simmel, *Brücke und Tür*. Stuttgart: Koehler.

Simmel, G. (1968 a). "Das Problem der Soziologie." Reprinted in G. Simmel, *Das Individuelle Gesetz: Philosophische Exkurse*, ed. Michael Landmann. Frankfurt/a.M.: Suhrkamp.

Simmel, G. (1968 b). "Der Konflikt der modernen Kultur." Reprinted in G. Simmel, *Das individuelle Gesetz: Philosophische Exkurse*, ed. Michael Landmann. Frankfurt/a. M.: Suhrkamp.

Simmel, G. (1968 c). *Soziologie: Untersuchungen über die Formen der Vergesellschaftung*, 5th ed. Berlin: Duncker & Humblot.

Tabboni, S. (Ed.) (1986). *Vicinanza e lontananza: Modelli e figure dello straniero come categoria sociologica*. Milano: F. Angeli.

Tenbruck, F. H. (1984). *Die unbewältigten Sozialwissenschaften oder Die Abschaffung des Menschen*. Graz/Wien/Köln: Styria Verlag.

Die Zeit. 27 February 1987.

4 The Cultural Construction of Social Identity: The Case of Scotland

Josef Bleicher

4.1 Introduction: Social Identity and Nationalism

The relationship of culture and social structure considered in this chapter revolves around the structural conditions in which social identity becomes an issue.

The aspect of "construction" referred to in the title then points to the fact that a group's self-understanding, once it is brought from the prereflexive attitude of everyday life into the sphere of conscious formulation and dissemination, requires the mediatory or interpretive efforts of interested sections which, with Bourdieu (1984), I want to refer to as "cultural producers."

In the case considered here, that is, the construction of *Scottishness*, social identity has had "the nation" as its reference point and can therefore be defined as *cultural nationalism*. The analytical differentiation between *cultural* and *political* forms of nationalism derives its justification from the realization that some degree of commonality, of cultural integration, forms the prerequisite for any political or politicized articulation of perceived "national" concerns.

4.2 Culture, Nation, and the Absence of Political Nationalism

Here I shall in the main be concerned with cultural nationalism, the articulation of Scottishness as a separate cultural identity within the British state and its relationship to political nationalism. The issue involved here can be considered usefully in relation to the question: "Why is there not more nationalism?" posed by an eminent author in the area of Scottish culture and politics (Nairn, 1981).

This question is initially surprising in that "being Scottish" forms a pervasive dimension in members' perception of themselves and their relationship to outsiders; it has permeated social life and is firmly anchored in its social institutions (Church of Scotland, the legal system, the education system)[1]. Scottish identity has been shaped by centuries of experience of forming a "terminal community of fate," in Geertz' (1975) telling definition of the "nation," with the "boundary problem"[2] resolved long ago.

Political demands in Scotland have been, and still are, largely output-oriented. They concern the provision of resources as well as the quality of the decision-making process within the British state, or "Westminster government" as it is often, and tellingly, referred to. They are framed in terms of some perceived Scottish interest and tend to portray England and English interests as the source of current social and economic problems in Scotland. This perspective is grounded in the general attitude, shared to some extent even by nonnationalist members, toward England and the widespread perception of Scots and Scotland as the victim of the scheming, uncaring, domineering, and exploitative conduct of its southerly neighbor.

All that is absent is a distinct will to translate this cultural identity into political practice, to move from cultural to political nationalism, and for Scotland to regain the right to govern itself.

We are therefore faced with a paradox: "Scotland has a clearly defined territory and a strong sense of national identity, but a traditionally weak sense of political identity" (Mac Iver, 1982).

In this light, the question posed assumes that real nationalism is about political power and economic benefits – just as its "real" causes would be looked for in the political disintegration of the British state and uneven capitalist development; any other manifestation of social identity constituting, at best, a kind of "sub-nationalism," in Nairn's phrase.

It can, however, be argued that Scottishness, as a social identity, is "underpoliticized" for good, structural reasons – rather than indicating a paradox or a lack of some kind. It should be possible to identify the conditions that gave rise to cultural nationalism without stimulating an upsurge in the kind of political radicalism that would qualify it in the eyes of some observers as "real" nationalism.

To arrive at some understanding of nationalism it would be of help to consider it as a particular manifestation of a general process, that of the creation and articulation of social identity, and ask the following questions:

1. What were the structural conditions for the emergence of cultural nationalism and the construction of an ethnic identity, Scottishness?
2. Why has there not been a transition from it toward a sustained, vigorous "political ethnicity," as Geertz (1975) defines (political) nationalism?

Once these questions have been considered in relation to the Scottish situation, it may be possible to draw more general conclusions as to the relationship of culture and social structure in the formation of social identity and nationalism.

4.3 Culture, Modernity, and Social Identity

The task of clarifying the relationship between culture and social structure in the formation of social identity is greatly facilitated by a recent important statement on these issues, Gellner's *Nations and Nationalism* (1983).

The concept of "culture" is directly interwoven with the central macro-structural change, the rise of modernity. If by "culture" we mean a "way of life," then this perspective leads us to consider that

The general emergence of modernity hinged on the erosion of the multiple petty binding local organizations and their replacement by mobile, anonymous, literature, identity-conferring cultures (Gellner, 1983: 86).

This process, then, forms the subject of this chapter in which I consider the *cultural construction* of social identity in a historical context marked by the transition from "structure-oriented tribalism" to "culture-mediated nationalism" (Gellner, 1983). In the case considered here, this takes the form of the articulation of a "shared literate culture," as Gellner defines "nationality," in Scotland after the Union of Parliaments, the political fusion of Scotland and England, in 1707.

In contrast to the nationalism of the nineteenth century, which can be seen as modernizing ideologies, the cultural nationalism arising in Scotland after 1707 is perhaps better seen as an anti-modernizing movement. For this reason it also appears to be similar, more to the current resurgence of quests for ethnic identity than to classic nationalism[3] which sought to bring about the congruence of culture and power, ethnicity and state.

In considering the cultural construction of social identity, here Scottishness, I shall follow Gellner's general view of nationality as an identity-conferring idea; the hold it has "over modern man springs from the erosion of the old structures, which had once provided each man with his identity, dignity and material security..." (1983: 85).

In the case of Scotland, it is possible to provide fairly plausible arguments why this quest for identity should have had "the nation" as its point of reference. Scotland had been an independent, if internally fragmented, political unit since about the ninth century. She finally surrendered her independence in the eighteenth century, but could still draw on this memory or, maybe more correctly, mythified versions of the past[4] when her identity and/or territorial integrity came under threat.

For this reason, Scottish nationalism did not have to create its object, " the nation[5]," but could use this, often invoked, memory as a readily available resource. This point accounts to some extent for the fact that rather than being a modernizing ideology in the wider sense, the nationalism espoused by the middle and upper classes at the turn of the nineteenth century was generally backward-looking and romanticizing; it could serve its political purpose after Union with England by remaining cultural.

4.4 The Construction of Scottishness

It is possible to pinpoint two major waves in the construction of a Scottish identity with their own particular "mix" of cultural and political aspects. The first of these two waves can be associated with the social and cultural activities surrounding the Scottish Enlightenment, and the second phase as the Scottish (Literary) Renaissance at the beginning of this century. The sociopolitical contexts of these movements are very different. It is hoped that an account of these throws light on the formative dynamics underlying and shaping nationalism in Scotland, in particular, and the interplay of culture and social structure, in general.

Scotland is apparently the only nation-state that freely relinquished its sovereignty. The Union of Crowns in 1603 and the Union of Parliaments in 1707 left Scotland a nation without a full state, a "decapitated nation," within the new state of Great Britain.

Discontent with the Union soon arose as hoped-for benefits failed to materialize, some voices even clamoring for its termination. But generally, any discontent remained within the confines of the structure that had been established: Scotland as the junior partner in Great Britain Ltd. – or unlimited as it was about to become with the incipient establishment of the Empire in which the Scots played an important role.

Being a part of a now prospering state while worrying about the dominant influence of her more powerful neighbor/partner, accepting the economic advantages of Union while resenting cultural incursion, gave rise to that slightly schizophrenic position characteristic of Scottish identity[6]. This ambivalence can be detected even today with social, economic, and political interests joining in a common lament over the damage English self-interest (or neglect) has inflicted upon Scotland, and still the Scottish people shy away from taking any radical political steps.

During the period (1750–1850) under consideration here, the ambivalence referred to was heightened by the ever encroaching cultural and administrative hegemony of England – most often a product of thoughtlessness rather than design. After the initial disappointment with the lack of immediate benefit from the Union had passed, most of the dominant sections in Scotland found a way of furthering their interests while maintaining a psychological distance from England. It is this mix of interest and identity, of wanting to derive the benefits of association with a more powerful and prosperous neighbor – while having to establish the limits to which they would allow this power to intrude on their lives – that provides the setting for the social identity that came to emerge in Scotland.

As far as aspiring Scottish elites were concerned, developments placed them in a position where they had to solve the tension between affirming their Scottishness yet at the same time use the opportunities and openings offered by the Union to their full advantage. They had to do so in the face of both the ongoing cultural assimilation – anglicization –, that proceeded at a rapid pace and the administrative encroachment on a range of spheres that had been guaranteed independence by the Treaty of Union: from the legal system to local government, the banking system, to matters affecting the Established Church[7].

All of these issues involved both material and prestige interests of privileged sections of Scottish society; interests that could more effectively and legitimately be pursued once framed in terms of their national, Scottish, dimension.

As any other articulated, constructed, "national" identity, "Scottishness" is necessarily a cultivated product, nurtured and implanted in the space once occupied by "wild cultures" (Gellner, 1983). As the systems of kinship and community came to be eroded, so a high culture fostered by intellectuals took their place. In this context, the cultural creation of social identity and the myths it often propounds "invert reality: it claims to protect an old folk society while in fact helping to build up an anonymous mass society" (Gellner, 1983: 124).

Gellner here arrives at the core of the articulation of Scottishness in the hands of the *literati* of Edinburgh, and above all, Sir Walter Scott.

The sense of Scottishness that came to be established in this period not only reflects the structural imbalance within the Union between England and Scotland but also articulates the worries and legitimatory attempts by dominant sections. While the structural location of the construction of Scottishness centered largely on newly emerging social elites (in particular, lawyers and merchants), the articulation of a social identity appropriate to changed circumstances was the mission of the stratum of cultural producers referred to in the Scottish context as the *literati.*

Identity formation rests on similarity and difference, on the "boundary problem" indicated earlier. In Scotland's case, the outsiders have always been clearly marked: To be Scottish is to be non-English, if not anti-English. Latent fear or animosity toward a more powerful neighbor is nothing unusual, and it always helps members to establish that demarcation. But while being non-English forms an important element of Scottishness, more than merely negative definitions are required to establish a viable social identity.

Walter Scott, The Wizard of the North, accomplished that task almost single handedly. He created, in his novels, a conception of Scotland revolving around aspects of Highland culture that had only recently been legalized after the last Jacobite rising in 1745. This act of constructing Scottishness culminated in his stage-managing the visit of George IV to Edinburgh in 1822.

The Scottishness that emerges here revolves around the "cult of the Highlander," forming the predominant image both internally and abroad. Aided to respectability later on by Queen Victoria[8], it entered popular culture – from the *Kailyard* in literature to the music hall.

Scott's evocation of past, and often invented, aspects of Scottishness was not intended to galvanize his nation into political action or even to reassert its political independence. The symbolism of Jacobite or Highland culture would 50 years ago, have represented a challenge to the Hanoverian monarchy and the Union with England. But by the time Scott's first novel, *Waverley*, which revolves around the Jacobite Rising was anonymously published in 1814, Highland virtues and vices evoked no more than a nostalgic afterglow of a tamed and already fading part of the national memory.

In the hands of Scott, himself a lawyer, member of the landed gentry, and, very importantly, a committed Tory, Highland culture could come to embody the values of loyalty, paternalism, unquestioned hierarchy, and aristocratic leadership that modernizing and reforming trends had already undermined. Not surprisingly, therefore, the Scottish identity Scott helped to shape in the first half of the nineteenth century was conservative (1) culturally and (2) politically: (1) to conserve, if only as a memory, what was already disappearing as a lived culture, and (2) to secure Scotland's full and unchallenged integration into the British state.

In this light, the essence of Scott's endeavor appears as the fostering of a social identity that could act as a substitute for political self-determination; national honor, having found a source and focal point, was secure; ruling and middling sections could devote themselves to the real business of getting on in life with their self-esteem intact.

4.5 From Cultural to Political Nationalism

The Unionist-Conservative romanticization of aspects of Highland culture with the purpose of integrating Scotland internally as well as confirming its cultural independence within the British state represents only one way of constructing and using Scottishness. But it is one that proved resilient to the point of being dominant in Scottish culture. At the same time, it came to be resented as a sentimental, second-rate sham by nationalist and radical sections.

Concern with a viable Scottish identity emerged again with vigor at the beginning of this century, largely in the shape of the Scottish Renaissance movement. The role of its central figure, Hugh Mac Diarmid, the major Scottish poet after Burns, has been described such: "His work for a Scottish Renaissance was not simply a literary endeavor: it was bound up with questions of Scottish identity...[9]."

Political nationalism requires cultural roots, it was suggested earlier, but it should not be assumed that the struggle for power and the quest for meaning and identity interlink smoothly at all times.

It is possible to identify a particular person as the "father" of political nationalism: John Mac Cormick who left the Labour Party and became the first leader of the Scottish National Party (S.N.P.) in 1934. There are numbers of instructive aspects surrounding the early years of the nationalist movement.

1. The S.N.P. arose from the fusion of differing groupings who were either politically or culturally oriented. It came about in 1934 when the Scottish Party, an experienced political elite with Conservative and Liberal leanings, and the National Party of Scotland, dominated by ex-Labour radicals, decided to merge. This move toward a serious political challenge was preceded by a purge, led by MacCormick the year before, of the romantic literary movements concerned with the revival of Scottish culture within his NPS.

2. That party itself has its origin, in 1928, in the euphoria created by the rectorial election at Glasgow University which initially led to the formation of the Glasgow University Scottish Nationalist Association, led by MacCormick, then a law student. As Hanham indicates quite rightly, "it soon became clear that the students alone had the enthusiasm, the dynamism and the capacity for hard lobbying which a nationalist movement needed" (Hanham, 1969: 151).

The S.N.P. understands itself as spearheading a political movement. Its manifesto and its activities are no longer concerned with social identity[10]. Linked to this development, the "purge" of the culturalist elements in the nationalist movement referred to earlier may carry a twofold lesson: One, once a sense of Scottishness had become pervasive, the activities of professional and amateur producers of culture, with their interminable petty squabbles (whether, for example, Scots or Gaelic should be the national language) were a positive hindrance in the attempt to acquire respectability in the eyes of a public preoccupied with the mundane matter of making a living. Two, the transition toward the political framing of demands signifies to some sections a maturing of the movement, a clearheadedness and purposiveness formerly absent. The current appeal by the S.N.P. to voters is based on purely material-instrumental "output" terms[11] containing not a single reference to Scottish culture or identity.

The division within the nationalist movement was consequently one between culturally oriented fundamentalists and politically oriented pragmatists. It was straddled by one person, the enigmatic MacDiarmid, who managed both to combine within himself a concern with cultural restoration that drew not only on the Scots language but extended to the Gaelic and Pictish roots of his country and political radicalism, and to find himself in and out of the Scottish nationalist and communist parties. The proximity of nationalist and socialist ideologies may, at first sight, seem perplexing. But in Scotland, recent attempts to politicize Scottishness have originated largely from center or left-of-center positions[12].

It should also be noted, however, that before the recent conversion of most left-wing sections to devolution, support for nationalist demands had created divisions within the Left. The British Labour Party and the Communist Party of Great Britain were, as their titles suggest, prepared or committed to work within the framework of the Union. They, furthermore, on the whole held to the received wisdom that nationalism – which in the British case implies a greater or lesser amount of separatism – is inherently divisive. Existing inequalities have to be fought by solidarity in the class struggle across cultural boundaries. Even so, there have long existed significant strands in both parties that advocated the pursuit of nationalist and socialist goals in tandem. Most interesting might be the case of John Maclean, who is something of a folk hero in the Scottish left-wing movement. A friend of Lenin – he was the Soviet Consul in Scotland – he strove for a Scottish Communist Republic. While his follower, William Gallacher, accepted Lenin's policy of a united Marxist movement in Great Britain, Maclean argued the Scottish case in reference to the pragmatic viewpoint that "the social revolution is possible sooner in Scotland than in England. ... Scottish separation is part of the process of England's Imperial disintegration" (Hanham, 1969: 139).

Some groupings on the Left still argue in basically similar ways, only now, with the end of Empire already behind us, the task is to remove the last vestiges of this past and end the colonial status of the Scottish and Welsh nations within the United Kingdom. Such a "break-up of Britain," the final act in the disintegration of the Empire, would provide the space for the creation of a socialist republic of Scotland.

Reformist perspectives that have espoused nationalist appeals focus on more immediate, traditional issues – where they have to share the field with the S.N.P.[13]. How can one, then, interpret that fairly recent "nationalist turn" amongst socialist intellectuals and politicians?

Apart from a certain "bandwaggon effect," one structural reason may be the decrease in the relevance of class among voters as a whole, which leads politicians and intellectuals in search of causes to represent the Scottish dimension in British politics. Nationalist orientations carry the further benefit of constituting an area largely vacated by Conservative opinion while at the same time having been well rehearsed and given respectability in years of debate concerning British membership of the European Economic Community[14].

It is worth noting that the argumentation employed tends to follow traditional class-based politics and transposes established analyses onto a different plane: It is now Scotland that is regarded as suffering from a lack of power, resources, general neglect, etc. The economism characterizing these viewpoints becomes even more apparent when hopes are pinned on some economic event that will galvanize Scottishness into political action – be it the discovery of North Sea oil in the 1970s or the impending demise of manufacturing industry in Scotland. What is presupposed in this argumentation is the possibility of a nation-*in*-itself being transformed into a "nation-*for*-itself" on the basis of some material interest. Appeals to, and representations of, a shared Scottish interest are, however, in danger of misconstruing both the nature of the motivations underlying social identifications and the use of existing cultural identity for political – and that must here mean sectional – interests.

Have we come any closer to giving an answer to the question posed earlier: "Why is there not more nationalism in Scotland?" The answer may lie in the possibility that the question itself is misdirected.

An underlying assumption in this question links nationalism to the articulation of class interests, seeing "the Scottish nation" as "the working class" writ lage. Following on from this an identity is ascribed to a group, a common interest is imputed, one which is economic in nature and which overrides all other dimensions in the existence of its members.

As was stated at the outset, Scotland is thoroughly infused with a national(ist) spirit; what some observers see as an absence here may therefore be only a lack of the "right kind" of nationalism – as defined by the observer/theorist, of course. The approved expression of social identity appears to be conceived within the paradigm of class politics – and shares its frequently objectivistic bias.

Ultimately and primarily, Scottishness is an issue of identity, and that is to stand here for a sense of belonging, self-respect, and a range of similar motivations arising from within a set of definite structural conditions.

On the level of conceptualization, it appears important to distinguish between cultural and political nationalism. Political nationalism requires the prior cultural integration, or the desire of such, of the group, in its pursuit of systemic resources of power and economic goods. This use of social identity involves aspects of social honor or prestige, but it is not primarily directed at their furtherance. Cultural nationalism, by contrast, is located in the sphere of the life-world and revolves around issues of identity, of belonging, and tends toward the conservative-restorative cultivation of mores that have either already passed or are on the verge of disappearing. It is for this reason that it tends to romanticize or invent its own history. It appears, further, that cultural identity can not only be constructed differently but, once it has been articulated as a generalized, diffuse body of ideas and sentiments, can be used as a resource by interested groups for quite different purposes[15].

4.6 Some Implications

One implication has already become apparent, that is, the recognition that any account of the relationship of ideas (or meaning) and interest – if it is permissible to rephrase the relationship of culture and social structure in this crude way – has to involve an analysis of interested groups: cultural producers, intellectuals in the wider sense, but also of politicians and other (self-) appointed spokespersons. "Structure" can then stand for the objective context, the figuration, for the play of cultural processes; a context that will also shape their content. Whether and how "objective interests," however conceived, are actualized depends on the mediation by groups with their own interests to pursue in the social struggle for ideal and material rewards. The more or less subtle ways in which this is carried out is hinted at by Weber when he attributes to carriers of culture "partially materialistic and partially idealistic interests" as they transpose the "naked prestige of 'power' ... into the idea of a 'nation'" (Weber, 1980: 528).

Social groups, whether they focus their attention on cultural or political issues, have a direct stake in the creation of a social identity. This view is supported by one of the most perceptive accounts of Scottish nationalism. Hanham states, first, that: "The Scottish literary renaissance had stood for the principle that the Scottish nation needed a Scottish literary class to give meaning and depth to its culture. ..." Second, the separatist S.N.P. "must be regarded as a much more conservative body than its critics on the left and right are inclined to make out. ... Independence simply meant a transfer of power to a new group of politicians, while the structure of the state and of society was but little changed" (Hanham, 1969: 162, 212).

Since we began with a reference to Gellner's work on nationalism, it may be appropriate to conclude with a reference to it. First, Gellner states that: "It is not the case that nationalism imposes homogeneity out of a wilful cultural Machtbeduerfnis; it is the objective need for homogeneity which is reflected in nationalism" (Gellner, 1983:46). "Nationalism" as one manifestation of the quest for identity, has earlier been described more in terms of the satisfaction of a *Sinn*beduerfnis in conditions of social dislocation. Furthermore, if the case of Scotland is anything to go by, then some forms of nationalism do not reflect a need for homogeneity but rather the opposite, that is, the wish to remain culturally different, to preserve valued social institutions that are seen as embodying the essence of Scottishness.

Gellner seems given to objectivistic language; more of a stylistic shorthand than anything else, one assumes, but it does connect with an objectivistic conception of social identity, where there is an assumption operative that national consciousness or identity can be regarded as a social fact that is somehow shared across social space.

However, if it is a cultural construct then we have to assume that it will be appropriated differently in different contexts. Scottishness could evoke glorious episodes in the military history of Scotland or it could conjure up romantic landscapes (the "ben and glen" view of Scotland); to others it suggests astuteness in business transaction; others, yet again, find in Scotland a radical and democratic tradition lacking in England, and so on[16].

It would therefore be useful to follow the practice of some cultural anthropologists and regard Scottishness as a symbol (see Cohen, 1985). One could then argue that rather than being the expression of an objective need, a sense of being Scottish is integrative not because it embodies socially shared ideas and ideals but because it functions as a symbol, as a sign that can be interpreted differently, be imbued with differing, even opposing meaning content, while preserving amongst members a *sense* of identity – and awareness of difference in relation to outsiders. Cultural "homogeneity" then, is a supposed one, a convenient myth propounded by interested groups[17], and there is no reason for theorists to accept it as anything more.

It is worth asking whether this point can be extended to the sphere of cultural production as a whole: Culture, as a universe of symbols, binds people not because they agree on their meaning but because they think they do. Only in this way does it become possible for cultural ideals that transcend the person or the group to paper over existing divisions and conflicts[18].

Second, when Gellner refers to an "objective need" for nationalism, or that "the economy needs both the new type of central culture and the central state" (Gellner, 1983: 140) he does so in preference to voluntaristic interpretations of nationalism. Consequently, he is led to discount the role of cultural producers in the articulation and use of social identity and to reject the ideological dimension in nationalism. Gellner refers to "intellectuals, the driving force of initial nationalism" (1983: 118), but in his polemic against Elie Kedourie he appears to regard them as the blind pawns of some historical necessity[19].

If looked at from a less great theoretical height, what appears as the "objective need" for nationalism, or any cultural construction of social identity, decomposes into the pursuit of material and ideal interest by carriers of culture – intellectuals and politicians – in specifiable historical conditions.

Culture and social structure are mediated neither by voluntarism, which Gellner rejects, nor by the objectivism he espouses. Culture has to be produced by interested sections acting for discernible reasons and becomes socially effective in structured conditions.

In Scottish nationalism, these interests are mainly cultural, even where they appear as politically or economically motivated. The latter act as acceptable and convenient ciphers for concerns that cannot easily be articulated in their own terms. MacDiarmid, who played a central part in the reaffirmation of Scotland's national virtù, can serve as an example of this view because "Nationalism for him is only superficially a political programme. At bottom, its object is to provide a means of responding properly to experience[20]."

I would argue that this concern pervades Scottish nationalism in general: It is about identity, it is cultural in essence. Where it manifests itself in the political arena, it does so as a cleverly packaged claim for resources – or as a safety-valve for frustrations experienced in everyday life. As Phillipson (1969: 170) has so aptly stated in the context of the age of assimilation and Walter Scott's creation of Scottishness, the "ideology that develops is not one of action but of inaction. We shall find Scotsmen learning how to grumble about the Union safe in the knowledge that they were doing nothing to harm it."

Notes

1 For example, hardly a day passes without letters to newspapers making references to "the Scottish nation," "one of the oldest nations in Europe," etc.

2 This anthropological term describes the dialectic of identity and difference; see Barth (1969).

3 A weakness in some discussions of nationalism in general, including Gellner's, and of Scottish nationalism in particular, relates to the paradigmatic use of classic nationalism, with the result that the specificity of particular cases is overlooked and they are judged as note quite "the real thing."
The relationship of current nationalism with social identity, the loss of identity in uniformist and rootless modern industrial society is the topic of Mayo (1974).
The kind of nationalism referred to here, which will be referred to as cultural nationalism, is also different from, what Nairn calls, neonationalism, see Nairn (1981: 128), which is too strongly oriented on economic causes.

4 I shall return to the issue of homogeneity within Scotland later on. The idea of the construction of "the past" has been treated in a variety of ways. Among the most interesting are Lowenthal (1985), Hobsbawm and Ranger (1983), and Wright (1985).

5 It is one of Gellner's central theses that "It is nationalism which engenders nations" (1983: 55). The Scottish experience is distinctly different in this respect.

6 See on this point, for example, Nairn (1981: 172).

7 Phillipson (1969: 167–188) provides an excellent account of these events.

8 See Brand (1978: 93) for an interesting depiction of this.

9 Professor David Daiches, as quoted by MacDiarmid himself in his autobiographical work; see MacDiarmid (1966: 28).

10 The only reference to social identity to be found in the "Statement of Aim and Policy of the S.N.P." adopted on 7 December 1946 appears as the opening clause of Article 2, headed "Local Government" (!) and reads: "Scottish Nationalism is based primarily on spiritual values, on the recognition of the needs of the individual and the right to express himself

fully and freely within the framework of a community knit together by ties of an enduring tradition" (from the manifesto printed in Hanham [1969: 213–214] and reprinted from *Scots Independent*, January 1947).

11 "Play the Scottish Card. Together we can win Scotland a better deal," *SNP News*, Election 1987 issue.

12 The main exception being the proposals by the Conservatives in the early 1970s for Scottish devolution. Previously, that program had its staunch support in the Liberal Party – and still has.

13 The S.N.P., in some respects, carries more conviction because the problem areas both parties identify require a radical cure that the Labour Party, according to the S.N.P., can not deliver because (a) it is tied to the British framework and (b) Conservative majorities derived from the prosperous South-East are being imposed on Scotland.

14 See Nairn's (1981) brilliant analysis.

15 Max Weber differentiates between political and culture-oriented claims to power, relating the former to the idea of the "state" and the latter to the "nation" (see Weber, 1980: 530).

16 The different interpretations and "memory" of the national hero, Robert Burns, could instructively be analyzed in this context.

17 The "over-simple view of the homogeneous nature of British culture [is] a caricature much exploited by politicians and the mass media, although thoroughly misleading and reviled by the members of localities, who see in it a gross misrepresentation of their special circumstances and of their distinctive cultures" (Cohen, 1982: 1).

18 I would surmise that the differences concealed by the shared sense of being "Scottish" would emerge in ways that may be quite disconcerting for some if Scotland achieved independence.

19 Gellner states that "It would be genuinely wrong to try to reduce [the] sentiments [of nationalist intellectuals] to calculations of material advantage or of social mobility" (Gellner, 1983: 61). I hope to have shown that the Scottish case does not wholly support this view.
It is not necessary to impute conscious motives to agents following a course of action that "pays" – even if only in the long run. Bourdieu's concept of the habitus would go a long way to help resolve the subjective/objective dichotomy: "The habitus is necessity internalized and converted into a disposition that generates meaningful practices and meaning-giving perceptions ...; [its schemes] ... owe their specific efficacy to the fact that they function below the level of consciousness and language, beyond the introspective scrutiny or control by the will" (Bourdieu, 1984: 170, 466).

20 David Daiches on MacDiarmid, as quoted in MacDiarmid (1966: 29).

References

Anderson, B. (1983). *Imagined Communities*. London: Verso.

Barth, F. (1969). *Ethnic Groups and Boundaries*. London: Allen & Unwin.

Bourdieu, P. (1984). *Distinctions. A Social Critique of the Judgement of Taste*. London: Routledge & Kegan Paul.

Brand, J. (1978). *The National Movement in Scotland*. London: Routledge & Kegan Paul.

Cohen, A.P. (1982). *Belonging. Identity and Social Organization in British Rural Cultures*. Manchester: Manchester University Press.

Cohen, A.P. (1985). *The Symbolic Construction of Community*. London: Tavistock.

Coupland, R. (1954). *Welsh and Scottish Nationalism. A Study*. London: Collins.

Geertz, C. (1975). *The Interpretation of Cultures*. London: Hutchinson.

Gellner, E. (1983). *Nations and Nationalism*. Oxford: Blackwell.

Habermas, J. and Henrich, D. (1974). *Zwei Reden*. Frankfurt: Suhrkamp.

Hanham, H.J. (1969). *Scottish Nationalism*. London: Faber & Faber.
Hobsbawm, E.J. and Ranger, T. (Eds.). (1983). *The Invention of Tradition*. Cambridge: Cambridge University Press.
Kedourie, E. (1966). *Nationalism*. London: Hutchinson.
Lenman, B. (1981). *Integration, Enlightenment and Industrialization*. London: Edward Arnold.
Lowenthal, D. (1985). *The Past Is a Foreign Country*. Cambridge: Cambridge University Press.
MacDiarmid, H. (1966). *The Company I've Kept*. London: Hutchinson.
Maclver, D.N. (1982). "The Paradox of Nationalism in Scotland." In *National Separatism*, ed. C.H. Williams. Cardiff: University of Wales Press.
Mayo, E.P. (1974). *The Roots of Identity. Three National Movements in Contemporary European Politics*. London: Allen Lane.
Nairn, T. (1981). *The Break-up of Britain*, 2nd expanded ed. London: New Left Books.
Phillipson, N.T. (1969). "Nationalism and Ideology." In *Government and Nationalism in Scotland*, ed. N.J. Wolfe. Edinburgh: University of Edinburgh Press.
Sillars, J. (1986). *Scotland. The Case for Optimism*. Edinburgh: Polygon.
Smith, A. (1979). *Nationalism in the Twentieth Century*. Oxford: Martin Robertson.
Smout, T.C. (1969). *A History of the Scottish People*. London: Fontana.
Smout, T.C. (1986). *A Century of the Scottish People*. London: Fontana.
Weber, M. (1980). *Wirtschaft und Gesellschaft*. Tübingen: J.C.B. Mohr.
Williams, C.H. (Ed.). (1982). *National Separatism*. Cardiff: University of Wales Press.
Wolfe, N.J. (Ed.). (1969). *Government and Nationalism in Scotland*. Edinburgh: University of Edinburgh Press.
Wright, P. (1985). *On Living in an Old Country*. London: Verso.

Part IV
Culture, Ideology, and Science

1 The (Re)Colonization of Science by the Life-World: Problems and Prospects

Ullica Segerstråle

1.1 The Problematic Relationship between Science, Culture, and the Life-World

In his recent book *The Theory of Communicative Action*, Jürgen Habermas (1981, 1984, 1987) discusses the threat that the "systems world" provides for the "life-world." According to him, there is a danger that the type of means-end rationality typical of and legitimate in the sphere of the state or the economy will spread to other spheres where a different type of rationality ought to prevail: the rationality of communicative action. This, then, is roughly what he means by "colonization" of the life-world by the subsystems of state and economy.

In his overall scheme, Habermas has relegated science to the life-world, not the systems world. This may appear surprising at first, considering his earlier writings on science and technology as ideology (Habermas, 1968a, 1970), or his three "knowledge interests," where natural science represented an instrumental interest (Habermas, 1968b, 1971). The reason why science is placed in the life-world in this book is now because Habermas is looking at the structure of scientific discourse as one type of communicative action. Scientific discourse for him represents, namely, such conditions as ought to prevail in general if communicative action is to be made possible: symmetrical access to the discussion, "bracketing" of interests of other kinds, such as power and money ones, and the possibility to reach rational consensus through argumentation.

In the present book, the concept of communicative action has been further developed and differentiated. Science represents now only one specific type of communicative action, namely action oriented toward knowledge about the objective world. In this book, Habermas has subdivided the types of communicative action in three: theoretical discourse, practical discourse, and expressive discourse. These represent, respectively, the objective, social, and subjective sphere. Furthermore, these discourses are handled by "cultural experts" of different kinds: scientific, legal or ethical, and aesthetic ones. Habermas, then, regards science as part of culture (and the life-world) in the sense that it represents one of the stocks of knowledge on which the social actors can draw. In "the rationalization process of the life-world," not only have the subsystems of state and economy become differentiated out from the life-world (and regulated by a different type of rationality), but within the life-world itself, also culture has become differentiated and taken over by various types of experts[1].

What could one then mean with "the colonization of science by the life-world"? Such a conception would have to base itself on a different view from the one put forth by Habermas regarding the relationship between science, culture and the life-world, and/or a different view of the meaning of these terms. (I will deal with the idea of (re)colonization later.)

In the following, while I am willing to regard science as part of culture, I am not going to use Habermas' notion of science as equaling an idealized structure of discourse. Neither am I going to view science as merely a stock of knowledge produced by scientific experts to be drawn upon by the social actors. Instead, I will look at science as a *real activity* of the cultural experts called scientists. First, I am going to allow scientific communication also to deal with things other than theoretical knowledge and argumentation about facts. Particularly, I will consider specific *intrascientific* power considerations neglected by Habermas. Second, I am going to examine the conditions under which scientific discourse, despite its ostensive emphasis on cognitive aspects, does – or could in principle – represent a forum for *practical discourse* (i.e., discussion about norms and values).

In a sense, I am following Habermas' original "undifferentiated" notion of communicative action as typically oriented to practical discourse (e.g., Habermas, 1968b, 1971)[2]. Habermas' present "translation" of communicative action to universal pragmatics and his assumption that all kinds of language utterances are a priori normative enable him to regard scientific discourse as communicative action, even though (or just because) it is limited to dealing exclusively with truth claims about the objective world. At the same time, this precludes the *theoretical* possibility of an explicit normative discourse within science[3].

Thus, I am going to examine the possibility of practical discourse within the framework of scientific communication. How does now the life-world enter this scheme? Here I will employ a notion of the life-world that is slightly different from Habermas'. I will provisionally accept his limitation of the life-world to encompass the realm of communicative action, that is, general knowledge about the physical and social world, and social know-how (this is, excluding instrumental action and technical know-how, even though I doubt the solidity of this, considering the "craft-nature" of science pointed out among others by Ravetz, 1971). But contrary to Habermas, I will take the view that the life-world is much less differentiated than he maintains. I will accept that science for practical purposes can be seen as a differentiated realm of general culture and conducted by experts, but I regard this differentiation as at the very least incomplete[4].

I am particularly interested in the relationship between scientific expertise and taken-for-granted conceptions in society at large. This means I am concerned with the ways in which the scientists' own anchoring in the life-world affects their work as "experts" and how, in turn, these "experts" affect the conceptions in the lay community. I want to show how, on the one hand, the scientists as cultural experts are dependent on the conceptions and cognitive processes that they bring to science from the general life-world, while learning new cognitive repertoires during their training as scientists in specific fields. On the other hand, I want to demonstrate how these experts, through their very activity, may be either challenging or sustaining the social status quo in a society heavily dependent on the authority of science.

A discussion about the (re)colonization of science by the life-world might then in a primitive sense simply amount to admitting the existence of other than purely cognitive concerns in science, or to demonstrating how "common sense" reasoning processes routinely enter scientific discourse[5]. In a more important sense, however, it would mean an investigation of the role of science as a forum for practical discourse, that is, an arena where concerns of the life-world at large are being examined and evaluated. The concrete question here deals with the actual possibilities and problems as regards science's playing such a role in today's society.

But there is a third sense in which one could talk about the (re)colonization of science by the life-world. This would involve a historical dimension. I am here referring to the social conditions of the very institutionalization of science as a differentiated realm of culture, pursuing the specific type of activity that one often ascribes to an inherent scientific rationality. Taking into consideration the Charter of the Royal Society in seventeenth-century England, explicitly guaranteeing that the scientists would refrain from "Meddling with Divinity, Metaphysics, Moralls, Politicks," it appears that science as we know it got its specific tasks defined for it through a political compromise. Before, cognitive and moral/political discussion were in practice inseparable (Mendelsohn, 1977; van der Daele, 1977; Shapin and Schaffer, 1985)[6]. The (re)colonization of science would then mean a reconsideration of this historical contract and the explicit reintroduction of practical discourse as part of scientific discourse.

1.2 Possibilities and Problems of Practical Discourse in Natural Science

In this chapter, then, I will not consider an obviously important problem facing the scientific enterprise today from the "outside," namely the increased steering of science by systems considerations. Instead, I will deal with problems within science itself, as part of culture. I will limit my examination to natural science, because this branch of science, on the face of it, appears to be the most unexpected candidate for "colonization by the life-world."

I think we may have been too easily persuaded by Habermas (1968b, 1971) and the prevailing "story-book image" of science to believe that only an instrumental interest is prevalent in natural science. In fact, it is quite possible to demonstrate that all of Habermas' famous three cognitive interests can be found within different realms of natural science and in the very make-up of the interests guiding individual scientists. I would argue that an important reason why the natural sciences *appear* to be predominantly guided by an instrumental interest is that the hermeneutic and critical interests in this realm have been prevented from emerging by problems originating within science *itself*, above all the present make-up of the scientific reward system. Furthermore, natural science is made up of a number of different fields with different criteria for "good science," depending on such things as the argumentative structure of the field, which in turn is linked to methodological possibilities and subject matter.

Evolutionary biology is an example of a science that traditionally has been guided by an interest in understanding and communication. At the same time, this field has since its conception had the potential for a critical interest as well, to the extent its findings have been seen as relevant for human beings' conception of themselves, for social policy decisions, etc. At the present time, with society's increased reliance on science as a guide in social matters of different kinds – whether we like this or not – it is noteworthy that some critical movements have come about within the biological community itself. These have had among their ostensive goals the enlightenment of the lay public, the criticism of ideological conceptions in science, and warnings of social abuse of scientific knowledge. But, as I will argue, these ambitions have been short-circuited by the prevalence of another important interest of scientists: *the competitive struggle for scientific authority.*

This becomes clear in recent "nature-nurture" controversies in science, such as the sociobiology and IQ ones. At the same time, I want to demonstrate that in the present situation in science, these controversies in an indirect way may serve as a *needed forum for meta-scientific discussion* within the scientific community, that is, a discussion about epistemological and ethical issues and the relationship of the scientific expert to the lay community. I will later discuss in what sense this discourse can be regarded as a forum for discussion of social norms and values as well i.e., a forum for practical discourse.

In any case, "normal" scientific discourse does not provide the scientists with a forum for the discussion of such meta-scientific issues. Papers are most often tied to former research within a relatively narrow area of science, and discussion of epistemological and ethical issues is traditionally left to philosophers. Furthermore, in the prevailing model of science, scientists' own contributions to a critical discussion of the nature of science at a meta-scientific level are likely to be considered extrascientific or illegitimate. In any case, such criticism is not going to be specially encouraged or rewarded. This is because the reward system is based on mutual recognition of "useful" information. Those scientists who are most "useful" to others are therefore those who provide others with ideas for workable puzzles within established science.

Thus, science has itself instituted such a communication system that makes discussion of its own foundations difficult. This goes back to the sociopolitical and epistemological conditions for the institutionalization of science in the seventeenth century, resulting in a deliberate break with its earlier nature as a simultaneously epistemological and moral enterprise.

I now wish to demonstrate that this break has never really been total. The differentiation of science as a realm of culture is not once and for all completed.

In fact, scientific experts are constantly engaged in a battle to retain their expert status against new knowledge claims (cf. Berger and Luckmann, 1967; Gieryn, 1985). Thus, one could say that at the most abstract level, this chapter now deals with the ways in which the scientific community regulates its relationship to society over time, that is, the process through which the social legitimacy of science is sustained over time while science is responding to changing social demands. In the scientific community, one can see this process as *an ongoing negotiation of the boundaries of science*, in which the nature of science and the moral/social role of the scientist are under constant tacit discussion.

As I will argue, these concerns now surface in scientific controversy, particularly in scientific controversy of the "nature-nurture" kind i.e., with implications for human beings' view of themselves. However, as we shall see, this happens in a very transformed way. In these controversies, general concerns are formulated as attacks of individual scientists on one another.

At the same time, common-sense conceptions and concerns creep into scientific discourse particularly through the *plausibility arguments* routinely employed in scientific argumentation. In science, one is always dealing with knowledge that is more or less incomplete. In "nature-nurture" controversies, the plausibility arguments now have to do not only with scientific knowledge claims as such, but also with the perceived implications of these for society at any specific time.

1.3 Disagreement among Scientific Experts: A Case Study

In the following I will discuss a case of disagreement among scientific experts. In the course of this I hope to show how various "life-world" aspects are evident in the argumentation, and particularly how these are being unproblematically and routinely coupled to assessments of scientific knowledge claims. Furthermore, I will show how an interaction between cognitive and strategical concerns of opponents in a scientific controversy comes to transform *inherent problems of contemporary science* into *scientific and moral "errors" of individual scientists*. Finally, I discuss the role of "nature-nurture" controversies for the scientific community and for the general public.

When it comes to interpretation of the meaning of scientific knowledge claims and their social relevance, there now exist different subuniverses within the life-world, and within the world of science as well. As I will show, there are two opposed but coexisting interpretations of reality, which draw on *different* "stocks of knowledge," or at least interpret the same "facts" differently. Members of these subcommunities of meaning also tend to process information in different ways, because of different "logics-in-use." At the same time, both subcommunities share an overall common life-world, which is at the same time the condition for their strong disagreement with each other as to the moral/social implications of certain knowledge claims.

My focus here is especially on a recent controversy – the sociobiology debate

– which started at Harvard about a decade ago around the publication of Edward O. Wilson's *Sociobiology: The New Synthesis* (1975a). However, my analysis is relevant also to the earlier IQ controversy, from which sociobiology inherited much of its criticism and many of its critics. (That debate started as a reaction to psychologist Arthur Jensen's 1969 article, where he suggested a possible genetical explanation to the 15 point difference in IQ test scores between white and black Americans.) Both these debates have been generally construed as typically politically motivated "nature-nurture" controversies between conservative hereditarians and progressive environmentalists. Here, I want to show that this is in fact a misconstrual of which the participants themselves are largely guilty, at the same time that the issues under dispute are really of a broader meta-scientific nature, dealing with both epistemological and ethical concerns of contemporary science. Furthermore, I will show that "nature-nurture" controversies of the sociobiology and IQ kind, far from being abnormalities, in reality illustrate various aspects of standard practice in science. My conclusions are based on my own empirical studies, especially on extensive interviews with participants, observers, and "arbiters" in this debate (Segerstråle, 1983, 1986).

Let me first briefly sketch what happened in the sociobiology controversy. Wilson's book came out in the summer of 1975. The first reviews, chiefly by biologists, were very appreciative. After all, Wilson had spent about 5 years trying to put together the latest theories and empirical studies about animal social behavior. The idea of sociobiology as a new discipline is to treat animal social behavior as a trait evolving through natural selection, the same way as one has earlier treated various morphological traits. The thing that biologists find especially thrilling about sociobiology is the possibility it offers to deal with altruistic behavior in animals. Animal altruism was, namely, one of Darwin's great unsolved problems when he tried to account for animal behavior on the basis of individual selection and "the survival of the fittest." The newer sociobiological models, developed in England during the last few decades, now look at animal behavior from the point of view of the "interest" of a *gene*, not the whole individual organism. Because animals share genes with their relatives, it is possible to calculate, through quasi-economic analysis, in what kinds of situations it would be advantageous from the "gene's point of view" to have the gene-carrying individual struggle for its own survival, and under what circumstances it would make evolutionary sense for this animal to sacrifice its own life or reproductive capacity for close relatives (in the latter case, by being sterile, like some bees). The new concepts introduced here are "kin selection" (instead of individual selection) and "inclusive fitness" (instead of individual fitness).

Unfortunately, what Wilson did in his book was not only to present and synthesize these new models and empirical studies, but to add some thoughts of his own on the applicability of sociobiology to *human beings*. Thus, he had a first and last chapter in his book that explicitly discussed human sociobiology. In the last chapter he speculated about a possible genetic basis for such things as sex role behavior, xenophobia, and even basic ethical values. The main group he wanted to provoke were the social scientists, who he thought were being "unscientific" in their refusal to consider biological dimensions in their explanations. At the same time, he suggested that sociobiology combined with neurobiology would soon make such progress that mankind would be able to get hold of its true evolutionary nature. This would partially make us understand ourselves better, partially perhaps enable us to "pick and choose" those traits that we really wanted to keep, and thus plan our own future.

It is clear that such a biologistic approach soon came to irritate those among the American intelligentsia (including many biologists), who were convinced of man as a predominantly cultural being. In the fall of 1975, a group of Wilson's own colleagues from Harvard and others in the Boston area launched a very hostile attack on him in the form of a letter in the left-wing liberal magazine *The New York Review of Books* (Allen et al., 1975). They labeled Wilson's extension of sociobiology to humans as an example of an old trend of "biological determinism" which they connected to Social Darwinism, Nazism, and racism. They said that his aim was to prevent social reform by claiming evidence for a fixed human nature, suspiciously similar to status quo in present American society, and that Wilson's whole sociobiological theorizing was tailored to make this point. The thing that caught the general public's fancy was that among the co-signers of this letter were a couple of Wilson's closest biology colleagues from Harvard (for a collection of the polemics, see Caplan, 1978).

The critical campaign initially launched by the letter-writers, called The Sociobiology Study Group, has continued to this day, despite protests from Wilson as regards his real motives. One change is that the criticism against Wilson's sociobiology has gradually come to focus more on the scientific difficulties and less on the political message of sociobiology. But the initial positions remain locked. The critics, in different ways (and different books) call Wilson a "biological determinist," while Wilson, in turn, persists in labeling the critics "*tabula rasa* environmentalists," which he identifies with Marxism[7]. This name-calling has continued, despite both sides' attempts to rebut the accusations. At the same time, the academic community has got polarized in pro- and anti-Wilson positions, and "Wilson" and "sociobiology" soon became ugly words for many.

How are we now to understand this controversy? In the following, I will first offer a cognitive explanation, showing the permeability of scientific discourse to life-world conceptions. Thereafter I will demonstrate how these cognitive differences are interacting with strategical concerns of the scientists involved.

1.4 Cognitive Differences among Scientists and the Permeability of Scientific Discourse to Life-World Thinking

A cognitive explanation would now be the following. Different fields in science have their own standards for tolerable plausibility arguments, what is to be regarded as a reasonable assumption, etc. Socialization to a field at the same time means training in how to read a scientific text in the "right spirit" (cf. Bazerman, 1981). Now, in a situation where scientists from *different* fields enter the *same* scientific discourse – which is exactly what happened in the sociobiology and IQ controversies – these scientists will have widely different conceptions of standard argumentation and writing style, and they will want an explanation for any deviance. In turn, as Mulkay and Gilbert (1982) have shown, beliefs and practices at variance with a scientist's own conception of "good science" are routinely explained away as other scientists' "extrascientifically" motivated "errors[8]."

This cognitive mechanism now surfaces in the polemics of the current debates. Because claims about the biological basis of human behavior are perceived as sociopolitically relevant, claims in such debates will now be routinely subjected both to scientific and moral/political scrutiny, leading to different "obvious" conclusions depending on what one takes for granted as a scientist and as a member of the larger society.

In both the IQ and the sociobiology controversy in their American setting one can now perceive a clustering of views, leading to a polarization of conceptions within the scientific community. On the one hand, there is a "meaning universe" characterized by a prediction-oriented, "operational" or model-building approach, combined with a positivist belief in the inherent morality of science and a "communicative interest" in sharing the present knowledge for the benefit of society. On the other hand, there is a totally different "meaning universe" whose typical features are the search for an "underlying reality," a belief in the "hardest" possible data as representing the best science, a critical attitude to scientific epistemology, and a critical attitude to scientific statements, which are searched for "hidden agendas[9]."

These two general subcommunities of meaning within science simultaneously appear to reflect the larger interests of two groups and their respective scientific and moral/political socialization: traditional "positivist" scientists and the 1960s radical generation. Specifically, the two camps tend to have different conceptions of their own duty as scientists: They are either "weeders" or "planters" in regard to tentative knowledge in fields with potential sociopolitical implications. This, in turn, is related to their different taken-for-granted views of the state of society and the potential for social change[10].

In both cases, however, the groups are operating with views that are experienced as unproblematic, both by themselves and within the lay community.

But there is an additional cognitive process operating in both cases: an unproblematic *coupling of scientific and moral interests*. For the first community of scientists, scientific knowledge is objective and thus unconnected to its social origin or social use. For the second community, "bad science" is ideologically motivated and therefore lends itself to social abuse, while "good science" is/does not. The logic here is that if *dangerous consequences* can be inferred from a theory, then it "must" be *ideologically motivated* as well as *scientifically bad* or old-fashioned. This is why in the sociobiology controversy, E.O. Wilson's attempts to derive lessons for human behavior from new findings about animal social behavior meant that his basic biological reasoning, tentative data on humans, model-building attempts, etc. "had" to be both scientifically wrong and ideologically traceable[11].

We can now start understanding why the sociobiologists' scientific work was subjected to a severe "moral reading" by the critics. It was not only Wilson that was attacked, but also others, for example, Richard Dawkins, author of *The Selfish Gene* (1976), who in his last chapter explicitly exempted humans because of their cultural heritage. The plausibility arguments presented by sociobiologists as a matter of course "could not," from a critical "hard data" point of view, be intended as "serious science" and were therefore instead analyzed for social implications. Political motives were then inferred as causes for these "moral errors" committed by the targets of criticism. However, some extreme cases of misinterpretation and the persistence of the miscommunication indicate that an "active misreading" is involved. This means that we have to introduce a *strategical* dimension in the analysis in addition to the cognitive processes taking place within the scientific and the moral realm.

1.5 Strategical Action in Scientific Discourse

When it comes to strategical interests in science, there is no help to be gained from Habermas. In his characterization of scientific discourse, he employs an idealized model where power interests are "bracketed." For a "real" situation, we have to turn to someone who acknowledges such interests. Here, Pierre Bourdieu's (1975) notion of a struggle for scientific recognition as "symbolic capital" seems the most useful one. Expanding on Bourdieu I now wish to introduce the concept of *moral capital* as another form of symbolic capital worth accumulating in the context of scientific discourse.

The struggle for moral recognition can explain some puzzling features in the recent "nature-nurture" controversies. From the point of view of capital accumulation, it seems that the more "immoral" someone can be construed as being, the more symbolic capital can accrue to the "revealer" of this fact. This is why association of someone's research with Nazism or racism gives obvious chance for moral capital gain. No wonder then that maximum moral capital has been extracted from especially Jensen's 1969 paper by "radicalization" of his conclusions, or by stating that he "asserted" that there are genetic racial differences in IQ. Similarly, it explains why there have been laborious attempts to "prove" that Wilson is "really" a racist[12] and an IQ meritocrate[13].

However, the very fact that moral recognition is granted and that the critics' interpretations and active misconstruals are not challenged on a broader basis shows two things. One is that there is a place in contemporary science for moral authority in addition to scientific authority. The other is that moral criticism of scientific texts is evidently taken at face value, without detailed and critical examination of the foundation of the claims. This is not particularly surprising if we accept the fact that behavior in controversy illustrates general scientific behavior. Because in this case, if a criticism of a text is not compared with the original text, this could be seen as simply an example of normal scientific practice in regard to a primary source – a secondary source is trusted to represent its content "for all practical purposes."

Because of the coexistence of different views of the relationship between morality and science, different subcommunities within science are now willing to grant moral recognition for different contributions. This means that moral capital can be obtained *both* for revelation of the (undesirable) moral/political beliefs that lie behind (erroneous) scientific standpoints *and* for actively upholding the traditional banner of scientific objectivity against any suggestions of "extrascientific" influences of an ideological or other kind. Examples abound[14].

In this way, the coupling of scientific and moral "error" is not only a cognitive process, but it is done in the strategical interest of a participant in a controversy. If scientific and moral error is perceived as going together, then any convincing demonstration of the error of the opponent will bring victory in two realms at the same time. It is thus not only the "positive" contributions in science that bring reward: Efficient criticism can bring in ample symbolic capital (more than the possibly meagre scientific reward) if the target is carefully chosen.

The striving to increase their moral capital now explains why the opposing camps in the recent "nature-nurture" controversies have persisted in attributing scientific and political views to one another that both parties insist they do not have. Another avenue to moral recognition by other scientists are the popular media which give controversial scientists special visibility[15]. In a sense, the scientific debate about "value relevant" issues has partially moved out of the trade journals and has come to involve the moral recognition of different groups in the *lay community* as well[16]. Due to a convertibility factor through which moral capital may be redeemable in scientific currency (and vice versa), time and effort spent in activity in the moral realm is not "wasted" from the point of view of capital accumulation in science[17].

Another consequence of the struggle for moral authority in addition to the scientific struggle is that there has to exist a basis for the continuous accumulation of moral capital and for the protection of earlier investments in this realm. In practice, this means that new opportunities for capital gain have to be found, and this, in turn, implies that there has to be a supply of new targets to "reveal." At the same time, the line of criticism has to be continuous, that is the targets have to be shown to commit the "same moral error." This explains some features in the recent "nature-nurture" controversies that have been difficult to understand for many observers[18]: the acrimoniousness of the criticism, the "quoting out of context" and "blatant misunderstanding" of sociobiological texts, and the scientifically surprising equation of research in human behavior genetics with "racist" research, etc.[19]. It also explains the intriguing fact that many of the critics of IQ testing and sociobiology in their contributions either lecture on *commonly* known genetic principles or espouse *commonly* shared liberal meritocratic views. However, in order for such "common-sense" remarks to get moral acknowledgement, it is imperative first to subject the intended target to a thorough "moral reading," which extracts the "true meaning" of his text (see, e.g., Lewontin, 1970; Allen et al., 1975; Alper, 1978; Chorover, 1979).

In distinction from scientific capital, moral capital is both an individual and a collective good. Thus, there are larger moral subcommunities in science who accumulate a collective stock of scientific facts and arguments to be drawn upon by members[20]. These facts and arguments are then quoted as unproblematic truths by members from other academic fields and the lay community, and they may even become the subject of export abroad[21].

But the accumulation of moral symbolic capital does not only take place through criticism of suitable targets for their scientific-cum-moral "errors." The coupling of scientific and moral interests has also a "positive" side. This is expressed by the fact that the scientists with such a coupling tendency in their own research also routinely combine their scientific and moral concerns, which means that the issues they choose reflect a conjunction of what is professionally and morally relevant for them. Of course, this is most easily done if "value relevant" scientific issues demonstrably lie within the professional expertise of the scientist.

The coupling of scientific and moral interests is thus not only a cognitive process, but also a strategical one. At the same time, however, I believe it simply illustrates a normally occurring process in science: the *optimization strategy* typical for most successful scientists. Successful scientists tend to choose the area and line of research that promise the greatest symbolic capital gain at any given time. Optimizers with moral interests in addition to their scientific ones now tend to choose such research topics that will give not only scientific but also moral credit. Put more simply, they focus on "value relevant" issues, or, conversely, they make their own scientific research "value relevant." One of the foremost optimization strategies is now a combination of a scientific-cum-moral criticism of another scientist which simultaneously serves to boost one's own demonstrably "value relevant" scientific theory[22]. But it is not always possible to optimize, not even for "couplers." The recourse is then to accumulate symbolic capital in separate realms and hope for a possible "convertibility factor" to operate[23].

1.6 "Coupled Reasoning" and the Prevention of True Communicative Action

The operation of these optimization strategies is not without consequences for the scientific community as a whole and for the prestige of science. First, it is in the interest of morally concerned scientists to discuss a "value relevant" topic as a concern of *science*, not of, for example, religion or moral philosophy. This tends to reinforce the belief that scientific facts ought to be important for social policy decisions. Second, socially and morally relevant issues are not debated within the scientific community on basically *moral* grounds but tend to deal with *technicalities* of different kinds. Despite critical concerns, the scientific community, then, has not become the new forum for moral philosophical discussion. Instead, the scientists are going about their business, and it is only on the basis of a demonstrable error in science that a moral point is raised.

In the light of the tendency to strong coupling of scientific and moral interests in "nature-nurture" controversies, what is the chance for the issues involved to be criticized on purely scientific or meta-scientific grounds? It turns out that "nature-nurture" controversies, at the same time as they present an opportunity for many scientists, are a deterrent for others. Thus, in the case of sociobiology, serious scientific critics refrained from publishing their criticisms after the all-out attack on Wilson in the *New York Review of Books* letter, not wanting to be morally or politically stigmatized[24]. At the same time, there are a few scientists who are profoundly interested in "good science" in general, and who feel obliged to criticize any scientific effort that they perceive as methodologically questionable, independently of the moral or political position such an effort ostensibly supports. (The function of these "uncouplers" is rather to clarify the situation for the rest of the scientific community, since the participants in the controversy themselves tend to perceive such neutral attempts as partial[25].)

Another subcategory of scientists are those who belong to two "meaning universes" at the same time, a critical and a traditional one, both in an epistemological and an ethical sense, and are trusted by members of both. These "mediators" feel as their calling to actively try to increase communication between both sides in a controversy, clear up semantic misunderstandings, distinguish scientific problems from their perceived moral/political implications, explain the "true intentions" of one side to the other, and clarify any scientific confusions[26].

At least at the beginning of a controversy, however, the effect of "uncouplers" and "mediators" tends to be minimal. Instead, the cognitive and strategical processes operating result in one party presenting its own view as scientifically "correct" and the opponent's view as scientifically "erroneous" – independently of the fact that both sides may be operating entirely with plausibility arguments. "Correct" and "wrong," in turn, has to do with perceived conformity or deviance from "normal" scientific practice. Thus, there is a genuine difference in conception of the nature of scientific practice involved, and this may entail both epistemological, methodological, ontological, and "procedural" aspects, while being probably partially out of awareness for the scientists themselves.

Because of the identification of *scientific correctness* with *moral virtue*, those scientists who share the same moral "meaning universe" tend to take one another's scientific work as beyond need for closer scrutiny. This means that scientists who share the same moral/political concerns will be regarded as "experts" while those who do not may be labeled "incompetent." One could see this as merely a reflection of a "normal" process in scientific practice: the tendency to trust "secondary sources" (here: moral credibility) instead of going to the original source and finding out for oneself. At the same time, the critics who eagerly turn general problems of scientific standard practice into moral errors of individuals sometimes seem to commit the very similar kinds of errors themselves[27]. On the basis of this, is there any guarantee that the scientific discourse in "soft" fields in science may not get totally out of hand and that research in these fields may not meet the most elementary scientific standards? Does this mean that we here have the danger of a new "treason of the intellectuals" (cf. Benda, 1927)?

1.7 The Role of Moral Argumentation for the Cognitive Content of Science and the Short-Circuit of Practical Discourse

The answer is that in "soft" fields in science this could well be the case if the aforementioned coupling tendency did *not* operate. It is exactly because of the identification of scientific with moral error (and the opportunities for accumulation of a double dose of symbolic capital if scientific errors can be found), that growth of knowledge in "soft" data fields can be achieved. The enhanced interest in controversies to scrutinize the opponent closely for any possible weak points (as well as the interest in finding a target in the first place) now leads to a much more thorough search than usual of ways to refute his claims. Not only are the primary references and sources looked into, but more general scientific points are made in order to make the criticism more forceful. (Still, any "error" found is attributed to the opponent's moral "error.") Thus, it is only because of an intense *moral* interest that time and effort will be spent on needed scientific criticism of another scientist's work. The standard processes of "normal" scientific practice and the known psychological bias of scientists to be less critical than desired of their own work would most probably not have led to fundamental checks on assumptions, methodology, etc.[28].

Thus, it is in fields where the data are not yet in that a tacit or overt meta-scientific discussion can be kept alive and that the growing points are for modification of scientific practice as a whole. This is because arguments always refer to prevailing (divergent) views about the nature of "good science." At the same time, because there is the interest in winning the argument in a "soft" field, more research is stimulated, this time with better methodology; this research will again be closely scrutinized by critics, and so on, until relatively "hard" data have been obtained. There is evidence that both sides in a controversy would agree on really reductionist data, were such only available; the dispute is not about "hard" data but about the scientific and moral/political acceptability of available tentative evidence[29].

The optimization strategies of scientists, then, play a crucial role for the accumulation of scientific "knowledge." In "hard" fields this takes place through field-specific procedures, and in "soft" fields through two other processes: (1) the "pooling" of arguments and evidence from a large number of scientific fields (through the establishment of a moral network of trust and loyalty); and (2) the close scrutiny of the scientific details of those who for moral reasons are classified as adversaries. In this way a *moral* interest can have *epistemological* consequences. On the other hand, as discussed earlier, it is not obvious that a moral interest as expressed within science can have social consequences in the larger society, at least not in the short run.

In fact, the situation analyzed so far rather supports Bourdieu's notion that the existing social structure is reproduced at the symbolic level through the cultural experts' pursuit of their own professional interests in different realms of "symbolic power" (Bourdieu, 1977).

There is, however, a fundamental difference between Bourdieu's conception and the one advanced here. According to Bourdieu, academics as cultural experts reproduce social structure through the structural isomorphism between the organization of society and the basic rules for the structure of an acceptable academic argument by which they abide (Bourdieu, 1977). These rules, among others, posit that in an academic paper there ought to be a thesis and an antithesis and an adjudication between these. For Bourdieu, this "forced neutrality" represents nothing else than an argumentation structure that satisfies the aims of an increasingly bureaucratized society.

The view of the present chapter, on the other hand, is that there is a profound moral/political *disagreement* among academics about what the correct rules are for academic practice. Some believe in "objective language," "fair criticism," etc.; others do not. However, because of the fact that the scientific competition has spread to the moral realm as well, *the critical ambitions to change the game rules for science in practice get morally short-circuited*, in effect reinforcing the traditional authority of science in society.

However, whether there is, in fact, a possibility to obtain moral recognition within a specific scientific community has to do with the make-up of that community at the point in time. For instance, it is primarily in the United States that moral benefits can be reaped from "revelations" of, for example, "racist" or "sexist" bias, because of the general subjectivist orientation and easily triggered social guilt in this country. In a country like England, for instance, with a stronger political tradition and with less of a tendency to personalize matters, scientific and moral issues tend to be viewed separately (except by some moral philosophers)[30].

The critics of recent research in human behavior genetics and sociobiology have missed an opportunity to make a direct contribution to epistemological change because of their preoccupation with moral guilt. Especially, it has not been in their immediate interest to examine in a more detached way the "objective" ways in which scientific theories may have sociopolitical consequences *independently* of the intentions of their creator and the "correctness" of the research procedure and data. Interest in symbolic capital gain has prevented the critics from a more abstract level of analysis. The critics have for example not addressed the possibility that theories in sensitive fields could work as self-fulfilling prophecies, and thus be *technically "correct" while sociopolitically and morally undesirable*[31]. Assumptions about human nature and society have been unproblematically seen as "correct" or "incorrect" and attributed to moral and political bias.

There may exist another professional/strategical reason for the critics of sociobiology, both within science and among the laymen, to fiercely combat even *balanced* views of humans as cultural-cum-biological beings. Zygmunt Bauman, in his contribution to this volume, suggests that today's intellectuals have lost any real social influence. According to him, they have already fulfilled their "enlightenment mission." It therefore becomes important for the intellectuals to safeguard a social space for themselves where they can protect their professional interests and legitimately continue with their fading project. The realm of culture now serves exactly this purpose. Bauman points out that, as such, "culture" is an artificial construct and only sustainable as an opposition to the realm of "nature." For the intellectuals, it therefore becomes an absolute necessity to maintain the realm of culture as a separate sphere. In turn this means that any contamination of this realm with "nature" will have to be strongly counteracted.

To the extent, then, that the critics of sociobiology see themselves as "Enlightenment" intellectuals and scientists at the same time, they would simply have to crack down on even moderate admissions of biological factors in human behavior.

In an indirect way, however, the IQ and sociobiology controversies, exactly because of their moral undertone, have come to create the foundation for possible new epistemologies for research on human beings. The protagonists of these controversies have become *crystallization points* for various scientific concerns in their symbolic roles as articulators of these, independently of their actual scientific or moral/political beliefs[32]. In this way scientists from diverse fields are brought in contact with one another, and the possibilities are increased for the necessary groundwork to be laid for a fundamentally new paradigm for human behavior that would take into account the most pertinent philosophical, methodological, etc. problems so far raised. This is, then, the way in which scientific controversies can create an infrastructure for practical discourse. At the same time, this again points to the interlinkedness between cognitive and moral/political interests in the very production of the body of scientific knowledge.

On the other hand, for the laborious work to be done, a change in the *scientific reward system* is required, whereby "quick and dirty" research is not given its present prominence. However, there is no indication of any negotiation for a change in the reward system in the context of the recent "nature-nurture" controversies. Instead, the reward system has been extended to include the moral realm as well. Thus, there is a basic contradiction between the critics' wish for better science and their own demonstration of the difficulty of changing the conditions for scientific recognition.

At the same time, however, scientific controversies can be seen as attempts to change the "game rules" of science in order to insure retroactive credit to the side who has been playing according to the "correct" rules. The pieces used by the players in science are the *plausibility arguments* routinely used by both sides. However, these pieces are invisible, both to the players themselves and to the onlookers. For scientists in "soft" areas it is important to stress the values of positivist science in order to lend more credibility to basically tentative statements and to attempt to sound as quantitive as possible. Meanwhile, critically oriented scientists are suspicious of quantitative arguments in "soft" fields and stress methodological and logical difficulties in the research. In either case the scientists act as if their own and their opponents' claims were based on "hard" data, and this is the view that the general public gets of science. The choice of the "innocent layman" and public policymakers then becomes one of which experts to trust. No one is telling them of the basic reliance in science on plausibility arguments and the very incomplete knowledge that we have, for example, about the biological bases of human behavior.

Thus, there is a reinforcement of the prevailing view of scientific knowledge as reliable. The "precipitation" of plausibility arguments by the "moral short-circuit" effect discussed in this study can therefore be regarded as nothing else than a concerted effort by both sides in a controversy to further their common professional interest, that is, *to sustain the authority of science in relation to the lay community*. Science deserves the respect it has; it is only that it needs weeding out of "bad" science. The public can rest assured, however, because there are some very alert gardeners around taking care of the weeding. In a way, one could say that the targets of moral outrage, like Jensen and Wilson, are sacrifices of the scientific priesthood in order to guarantee to the lay community the continuous reliability of scientific expertise.

To the extent society is dependent on scientific guidance for social decisions, this would tend to have a conservative effect on the social status quo. On the other hand, to the extent there is legislation to regulate the possible abuse of scientific findings, such an effect may be counteracted (cf. Engelhardt and Caplan, 1987; Segerstråle, 1987b).

But at the same time, one could claim that just because of the aforementioned cognitive and strategical processes operating in science, scientific controversy of the recent "nature-nurture" kind is a way for the scientific community to conduct a meta-scientific discussion about the nature of "good science" and the moral/social role of the scientist. Because of the interest of the participants in a controversy in scientific and moral symbolic capital, a controversy can really be seen as *a negotiation about the basic rules of science*, both at the epistemological and ethical level. The basic reason is that the side who eventually wins will be able to claim retroactive credit for its achievements. "Nature-nurture" controversies could be regarded, therefore, as important forums for scientific boundary negotiation.

Therefore, what seems to be especially under (tacit) negotiation right now is really the question whether *a new norm of science* ought to be introduced: Scientists would be required to reflect on the potential for social abuse of scientific results. In fact, it was this norm that got lost in the institutionalization of science in the seventeenth century.

Maybe we are now in for a new era in science, one that reintroduces the ethical aspects as legitimate for scientific discussion? Could one turn Weber and Habermas on their heads and, in the case of natural science, postulate a (re)colonization of science by the life-world, representing among others a reintegration of two of the "differentiated" areas of culture, namely science and ethics or law. Perhaps it is not law, as Habermas suggests in his 1984 book, but science that holds the key to practical discourse in today's society, just because of its strongly established social position? (At the same time, science will have to resolve its position in regard to the increased colonization from the systems world, or the subsystems of state and economy.)

Such a suggestion would have to be based on certain assumptions. One would have to start by granting natural scientists all of Habermas' interests as guides for their action and except them to be able to be reflective about their moral and social role as scientists in an increasingly complex interrelationship between science and the state and economy. That such a reflectiveness is at least possible is shown in the previously discussed controversy. Furthermore, one would need a different type of socialization process for scientists, sensitizing them to the social context of their research. That such a thing is regarded as possible and desirable is shown by the growing programs in Science, Technology, and Society at leading technical institutes in the United States, with M.I.T. as a forerunner.

Finally, one would have to believe in the possibility of change in the reward system of science, so that abstract and time-consuming reflective efforts by scientists would be rewarded in some way, without getting "precipitated" into short-sighted winning-or-losing considerations and cheap shots at colleagues who have a different conception of the scientific enterprise. But this, again, may admittedly be difficult, exactly because of the relative permeability of science to life-world conceptions and concerns.

As I have demonstrated in this chapter, the reason that the critical effort of the critics of science got frustrated in this round was primarily due to inherent contradictions in the scientific enterprise itself. I especially emphasized the precarious nature of the scientific reward system, which suppresses the hermeneutic interest in understanding the world and causes an *internal power short-circuit* of critical ambitions. It is an unexamined question what the exact relationship is between the scientific reward system as we now know it and the social structure of Western society. For instance, is scientific competition of the present kind structurally or organically connected to the capitalist market economy, and if so, is this a necessary relationship? There may exist no discoverable "truth" in this matter, but we are instead getting to one more meta-level of discourse: What is or ought to be the nature and function of science in society today? Do we expect science to chiefly produce "useful" knowledge in an immediately applicable way, or do we want it to be "useful" in the long run, for example, to produce alternative solutions or even function as a think-tank for more general problems facing mankind[33]?

Notes

1 In his book, Habermas distinguishes between three components or structures of the life-world: (1) *culture*, which is a stock of knowledge upon which the social actors draw; (2) *society*, or social institutions, based on norms; and (3) *personality*, which is a set of competences required for social interaction.

2 Throughout his books, Habermas has operated with a chief distinction between the cognitive categories of "labor" and "communication."

3 In the present book, Habermas regards such discourse as taking place within "society," the second structure of the life-world.

4 It is often unclear whether Habermas is working with ideal-typical constructs or believes he is describing an empirical reality. It is not hard to demonstrate empirically that such a differentiation is at the very least incomplete; a different question is whether one could "prove" in some way that such a differentiation will always necessarily remain an abstraction.

5 On the basis of more recent studies in sociology and social psychology of science, this is getting more and more obvious. I think about such studies as Ian Mitroff's *The Subjective Side of Science* (1975), Michael Mahoney's *The Scientist as Subject* (1976), Bruno Latour and Steven Woolgar's *Laboratory Life* (1979), Karin Knorr's *The Manufacture of Knowledge* (1981), Nigel Gilbert and Michael Mulkay's *Opening Pandora's Box* (1984).

6 At that time, ethical and political concerns were undistinguishable from epistemological ones. For example, as Shapin and Schaffer (1985) have recently shown, the opposition between the experimentalists and the deductivists as to the nature of natural science ("natural philosophy") can partly be connected to concerns with the perceived social consequences of different epistemologies in Restoration England (cf. Segerstråle, 1987a).

7 Some of the leading critics in fact represent a brand of Marxism that regards human beings as creators of their own destiny. Other Marxist views, however, stress the political importance of the assumption of a basic human "species being." Interestingly, Noam Chomsky, a prominent left-wing academic who takes the latter view, kept out of the sociobiology debate mainly for this reason (cf. Segerstråle, 1986).

8 Mulkay and Gilbert interviewed different biochemists about the scientific merits of competing current theories in their field. Even though there was at least a tacit controversy, in this case there was not an overt conflict like the sociobiology controversy.

9 See Segerstråle (1986) for how this search is typically conducted. The foremost example in this respect is Wilson's chief opponent, Richard Lewontin, who already in 1970 developed, and was quite explicit about, this general strategy. His target then was Arthur Jensen.

10 While the critics of sociobiology generally are guided by a "ruling class" or "power elite" theory, Wilson and the "traditionalists" are firm believers in the democratic process (Segerstråle, 1983). For a detailed analysis of the conceptions of the New Left in the 60s – which reflect the current beliefs of most of the radical critics of sociobiology – see Jacoby (1973).

11 This belongs to the accumulated "knowledge" of the Left. It is disappointing to discover that part of this "knowledge" consists of reified "facts" that have been reiterated over and over again, without a check in respective primary references (Segerstråle, 1983: chapter 7). Stephen J. Gould appears to be one of the perpetuators of the "fact" that Jensen "asserted" a genetic difference between racial groups (e.g., Gould, 1977), while Lewontin (to his credit) in his initial criticism of Jensen (1970) thought that Jensen's formulations were *too*

"judicious" and "cautious," and they therefore had to be reformulated and "radicalized" to bring forth their real meaning. This was exactly the task he undertook in his criticism. (For more details about Lewontin's strategy as a critic, see Segerstråle [1986].)

12 For a more "academic" attempt, see, for example, Joseph Alper (1978). On the occasions of Wilson's public lectures at Harvard, the CAR (Committee Against Racism) was distributing more untempered pamphlets.

13 Stephen Chorover attempts this in his book *From Genesis to Genocide* (1979). In my opinion he does a rather clumsy job. This is no wonder, considering the problem Chorover is up against: In his infamous last chapter, Wilson, in fact, devotes some space to playing *down* the importance of IQ! This means that the case against Wilson has to be constructed on the basis of indirect "evidence." Chorover resorts to a couple of obvious misrepresentations to make Wilson say what he "ought to" (cf. Segerstråle, 1983).

14 Representative writings of the first group are, among others, Lewontin (1970, 1981), Allen et al. (1975), Alper (1978), Chorover (1979), and Gould (1981). The arguments in the other group are best represented by Jensen (1982), Davis (1985), and Wilson (1978b). Bernard Davis is the most ardent spokesman for the group of scientific traditionalists and has invented the term "Neo-Lysenkoist" to describe the stand of the critics of "biological determinism" (cf. Segerstråle, 1987a).

15 See Goodell (1977, 1987) for an analysis of "visible scientists."

16 A significant point is that much of recent "nature-nurture" controversy is conducted in the form of book reviews in the *New York Review of Books*.

17 Both Salvador Luria, left-wing activist and molecular biologist at M.I.T., and Wilson commented on the fact that valuable time from research goes into the critical activity. (As a matter of fact, Luria was not involved in the sociobiology controversy himself, because he thought it was not a "good" political issue.) While Wilson did not think any scientific reward could be obtained for criticism in science, Luria speculated that Lewontin and others would "have to get something out of" all the time and energy devoted to examining Wilson's texts. He did not come up with any suggestion, however, as to what the reward might be. The thesis advanced here is that the reward consists in both scientific *and* moral "symbolic capital" (Segerstråle, 1983).

18 The Harvard biologist, Ernst Mayr, when asked whether acrimonious controversies are not common fare in the history of science, replied that from his experience as a historian of science as well as an evolutionary biologist, the behavior of the critics in this case belongs to the exceptions in "dishonesty." He wondered why the critics had to use political arguments when they had such "good" scientific ones. In the light of my study, the explanation to this is, that in order to ensure the accumulation of critical moral *as well as* scientific capital, a "moral reading" first had to be made of Wilson (Segerstråle, 1983).

19 See Segerstråle (1986) for a detailed examination of the "logic-in-use."

20 See notes 12, 13, and 28.

21 It was in this form that the sociobiology controversy was imported to at least Finland and Sweden, to judge from the polemics in the newspapers and the general approach of a Swedish book dealing with the dangers of sociobiology (von Heijne and Israel, 1985).

22 The prime example here is perhaps Stephen J. Gould, who is indirectly promoting his own "punctuated equilibria" theory by attacking "the adaptationist program" in evolutionary biology, and especially the applicability of the latter to humans. In turn, Gould's wish to kill two (or more) birds with one stone can explain why he persists in attributing a "gradualist" stand to people he disagrees with (including Jensen – see Gould's 1980 review and 1981 book). This has puzzled other biologists (e.g., Levinton, 1982; Maynard Smith, 1981), who wonder why so much controversy is suggested between "punctuativists" and "gradualists" when no such conflict really exists.

23 Bourdieu (1975) believes in the ready convertibility of symbolic capital to academic positions and prestige, which in turn are convertible to material assets. I here discuss the possible convertibility between moral and scientific capital. For instance: If someone "reveals a racist," this good deed might be credited to him in some way that would increase his scientific reputation.

24 According to Mayr, the critics' letter in the *New York Review of Books* was a deterrent to other, highly critical scientific reviews that were in the making. He suggested that the reviewers did not want to be associated with the Nazi ideology and Social Darwinism conjured up by the critics as necessary correlates of any defense of sociobiology (cf. Segerstråle, 1983, 1986). This tendency may have continued throughout the controversy, because in 1981, Lewontin suggested (personal communication), that he knew about at least two well-qualified scientists, highly critical of Lumsden and Wilson's *Genes, Mind, and Culture* (1981), who had not voiced their views in public. Also Lewin (1981) reports the same phenomenon from his preliminary survey of reactions to this book. In a way, then, the "moral precipitation" of the criticism of sociobiology, in fact, may have allowed the sociobiological program to proceed relatively intact. This means that it was able to fortify itself against future *scientific* attacks – perhaps an example of a fortuitously created quasi-Feyerabendian situation? (I refer to Feyerabend's [1975] idea that one should leave scientific theories or research programs alone until they can be put to serious tests by appropriate scientific methodology.)

25 The most ironic example of this is perhaps the reception of my own attempt at analysis of the sociobiology controversy (in particular, Segerstråle, 1986). Some of my friends on the left feel that I have "betrayed the cause," while some scientific traditionalists think I have been too lenient on the left-wing critics. From the point of view of the first group, any attempt to "exonerate" Wilson automatically puts one on his side. The other group, again, dismisses any suggestion that the critics may have legitimate fundamental disagreements with Wilson's approach to science. The reactions of Wilson and Lewontin themselves to the article in question are quoted in Campbell (1986). As an interested party, I wish to suggest that one explanation for Lewontin's reaction can perhaps be found by comparing that article to Maynard Smith (1986).

26 Two biologists who have systematically attempted to "mediate" between the left-wing critics and their sociobiological targets (particularly Wilson and Dawkins), are John Maynard Smith (e. g., 1978, 1982; Maynard Smith and Warren, 1982) and Patrick Bateson (e. g., 1981, 1982).

27 Much has been made of sloppy referencing (see, e. g., Hirsch, 1975 on Jensen; Lewontin, 1981 on Lumsden and Wilson). The most amusing example of the fact that the record on the left is not snow-white either, is perhaps the following. Leon Kamin, in his 1974 book, heavily critical of Jensen, refers himself to the "wrong" article by Henry Goddard when quoting the latter's notorious early IQ test results for American immigrants. This example is instructive especially because *other* left-wing academics have routinely quoted Kamin's (erroneous) reference i. e., not checked Kamin's sources (e. g., Chorover, 1979). (This was pointed out to me by Richard Herrnstein.)

28 See Kamin (1974) on his discovery of Sir Cyril Burt's "twin fraud." Kamin and others felt that Cyril Burt, the undisputed "father" of IQ testing for school placements in Britain, had arrived at a suspiciously consistent (and high) heritability of IQ. It later turned out that Burt in his studies has used fraudulent data on twins (see Hearnshaw, [1981] and Thoday, [1981], for assessments of this fraud and its consequences).

29 However, the critics never explicitly discuss what we are to do if/when we have the desired "hard data." Their cognitive and strategical concerns lead them instead to dismiss the tentative evidence as "bad science." (Segerstråle, 1983).

30 I refer particularly to the polemics between the philosopher Mary Midgley (1980) and the biologist Richard Dawkins (1981) because of the ethicist John Mackie's application of some of Dawkins' ideas to ethical theory.

31 For a development of this idea, see Joachim Israel (1972).

32 Cf. David Hull (1978), who makes this point in regard to the (changing) scientific content of sociobiological theory.

33 Nicholas Maxwell (1984), in his book *From Knowledge to Wisdom*, suggests that if science wants to be really useful, it ought to abandon its present "philosophy of knowledge" approach. According to that philosophy, the social benefits of science are seen as merely happy by-products of the main business of the scientific community: the pursuit of

knowledge. But if science's main task is to be socially useful, why should it not turn directly to the "philosophy of wisdom?" This would mean that science would recognize the urgent need to solve the problems of mankind, and thus concentrate scientific creativity and resources *directly* on this intellectually challenging task, instead of proceeding in a roundabout way.

References

Allen, E. et al. (1975). "Letter." *The New York Review of Books*, October.
Albury, W. R. (1980). "Politics and Rhetoric in the Sociobiology Debate." *Social Studies of Science* 10: 519–536.
Alper, J. (1978). "Ethical and Social Implications of Sociobiology." In *Sociobiology and Human Nature*, ed. M. S. Gregory, A. Silvers, and D. Sutch. San Francisco: Jossey Bass.
Bateson, P. P. G. (1981). "Sociobiology and Genetic Determinism." *Theoria to Theory* 14: 291–300.
Bateson, P. P. G. (1982). "Synthesizing Views about the Origins of Behaviour." In *Toward a Liberatory Biology*, ed. S. Rose. Allison/Busby: Schocken.
Bazerman, C. (1981). "What Written Knowledge Does." *Philosophy of the Social Sciences* 11: 361–387.
Beckwith, J. (1981–1982). "The Political Use of Sociobiology in the United States and Europe." *The Philosophical Forum* (2/3): 311–321.
Benda, J. (1927). *La trahison des clercs*. Paris: Grasset.
Berger, P. and Luckmann, T. (1967). *The Social Construction of Reality*. New York: Doubleday/Anchor Books.
Bouchier, D. (1977). "Radical Ideologies and the Sociology of Knowledge." *Sociology* 11: 29–46.
Bourdieu, P. (1975). "The Specificity of the Scientific Field and the Social Conditions of the Progress of Reason." *International Social Science Information* 14 (5/6): 19–47.
Bourdieu, P. (1977): "Symbolic Power." *Critical Anthropology* 13.
Campbell, C. (1986). "Anatomy of a Fierce Academic Feud." *The New York Times*, 9 November, Section 12.
Caplan, A. L. (1978). *The Sociobiology Debate*. New York: Harper & Row.
Chorover, S. (1979). *From Genesis to Genocide*. Cambridge, Mass./London: MIT Press.
Daele, W. van der (1977). "The Social Construction of Science." In *The Social Production of Scientific Knowledge*, ed. E. Mendelsohn, P. Weingart, and R. Whitley. Dordrecht: Reidel.
Davis, B. D. (1985). *Storm over Biology: Essays on Science, Sentiment, and Public Policy*. Buffalo, N. Y.: Prometheus Books.
Dawkins, R. (1976). *The Selfish Gene*. New York: Oxford University Press.
Dawkins, R. (1981). "In Defence of Selfish Genes." *Philosophy* 56, October: 562–579.
Engelhardt, H. T. and Caplan, A. (Eds.) (1987). *Scientific Controversies. Case Studies in the Resolution and Closure of Disputes in Science and Technology*. New York: Cambridge University Press.
Feyerabend, P. K. (1975). *Against Method*. London: New Left Books.

Gieryn, T. (1985). "Boundary Work and the Demarcation of Science from Non-Science." *American Sociological Review* 48: 781–795.
Gilbert, G.N. and Mulkay, M. (1984). *Opening Pandora's Box: A Sociological Analysis of Scientists' Discourse.* Cambridge/New York: Cambridge University Press.
Goodell, R. (1977). *The Visible Scientists.* Boston: Little, Brown & Co.
Goodell, R. (1987). "The Role of Mass Media in Scientific Controversy." In *Scientific Controversies,* ed. H.T. Engelhardt and A.L. Caplan. New York: Cambridge University Press.
Gould, S.J. (1977). *Ever Since Darwin.* New York: W.W. Norton & Co.
Gould, S.J. (1980). "Jensen's Last Stand." *The New York Review of Books,* 1 May.
Gould, S.J. (1981). *The Mismeasure of Man.* New York: W.W. Norton.
Gould, S.J. and Lewontin, R.D. (1979). "The Spandrels of San Marco and the Panglossian Paradigm: A Critique of the Adaptationist Programme." *Proceedings of the Royal Society of London* B, 205: 581–598.
Habermas, J. (1968a). *Technik und Wissenschaft als Ideologie.* Frankfurt: Suhrkamp.
Habermas, J. (1968b). *Erkenntnis und Interesse.* Frankfurt: Suhrkamp.
Habermas, J. (1970). *Toward a Rational Society.* Boston: Beacon Press.
Habermas, J. (1971). *Knowledge and Human Interests.* Boston: Beacon Press.
Habermas, J. (1981). *Theorie des kommunikativen Handelns,* Vols. 1, 2. Frankfurt: Suhrkamp.
Habermas, J. (1984). *The Theory of Communicative Action. Volume I: Reason and the Rationalization of Society.* Boston: Beacon Press.
Habermas, J. (1987). *The Theory of Communicative Action. Volume II: Lifeworld and System: A Critique of Functionalist Reason.* Boston: Beacon Press.
Hearnshaw, L.S. (1981). *Cyril Burt: Psychologist.* New York: Vintage Books.
Heijne, G. von and Israel, J. (1985). *Skapelsens herre eller genernas slav? En kritisk granskning av sociobiologin.* Stockholm: Ordfronts forlag.
Hirsch, J. (1975). "The Bankruptcy of 'Science Without Scholarship." *Educational Theory* 25: 3–27.
Hull, D.L. (1978). "Sociobiology: Scientific Bandwagon or a Traveling Medicine Show?" In *Sociobiology and Human Nature,* ed. M.S. Gregory, A. Silvers, and D. Sutch. San Francisco: Jossey-Bass.
Israel, J. (1972). "Stipulations and Construction in the Social Sciences." In *The Context of Social Psychology: A Critical Assessment,* ed. J. Israel and H. Tajfel. London/New York: Academic Press.
Jacoby, R. (1973). "The Politics of Subjectivity: Slogans of the American New Left." *New Left Review* 79: 37–49.
Jensen, A.R. (1969). "How Much Can We Boost IQ and Scholastic Achievement?" *Harvard Educational Review* 39: 1–123.
Jensen, A.R. (1982). "The Debunking of Scientific Fossils and Straw Persons." *Contemporary Education Reviews* 1: 121–135.
Kamin, L.J. (1974). *The Science and Politic of IQ.* New York: Halsted Press.
Knorr, K. (1981). *The Manufacture of Knowledge.* Oxford: Pergamon Press.
Latour, B. and Woolgan, S. (1979). *Laboratory Life: The Social Construction of Scientific Facts.* Beverly Hills/London: Sage Publications.
Levins, R. and Lewontin, R.C. (1985). *The Dialectical Biologist.* Cambridge, Mass.: Harvard University Press.

Levinton, J.S. (1982). "Charles Darwin and Darwinism." *BioScience* 32: 495–500.
Lewin, R. (1981). "Cultural Diversity Tied to Genetic Differences." *Science* 212: 908–909.
Lewontin, R.C. (1970). "Race and Intelligence." *Bulletin of the Atomic Scientists*, March: 2–8.
Lewontin, R.C. (1976). "Sociobiology – A Caricature of Darwinism." *Proceedings of the Philosophy of Science Association 1976*, Vol. 2, ed. F. Suppe and P. Asquith. East Lansing, Mich.: Philosophy of Science Association.
Lewontin, R.C. (1979). "Sociobiology as an Adaptationist Program." *Behavioral Science* 24: 5–14.
Lewontin, R.C. (1981). "Sleight of Hand." *The Sciences*, 23 July–26 August.
Lumsden, C.L. and Wilson, E.O. (1981). *Genes, Mind and Culture: The Coevolutionary Process*. Cambridge, Mass.: Harvard University Press.
Mackie, J.L. (1978). "The Law of the Jungle." *Philosophy* 53: 455–465.
Mahoney, M.J. (1976). *The Scientist as Subject*. Cambridge, Mass.: Ballinger.
Maynard Smith, J. (1978). "Constraints on Human Behavior." *Nature* 276: 120–121.
Maynard Smith, J. (1981). "Did Darwin Get it Right?" *London Review of Books*, June.
Maynard Smith J. (1982). "Genes and Memes." *London Review of Books*, February: 4–17.
Maynard Smith, J. (1986). "Molecules Are not Enough." *London Review of Books*, February: 8–9.
Maynard Smith, J. and Warren, N. (1982). "Models of Cultural and Genetic Change." *Evolution* 36: 620–627.
Maxwell, N. (1984). *From Knowledge to Wisdom*. Oxford: Blackwell.
Mendelsohn, E. (1977). "The Social Construction of Scientific Knowledge." In *The Social Production of Scientific Knowledge*, ed. E. Mendelsohn, P. Weingart, and R. Whitley. Dordrecht: Reidel.
Midgley, M. (1980). "Gene-Juggling." In *Sociobiology Examined*, ed. A. Montagu. Oxford/New York: Oxford University Press.
Mitroff, I. (1975). *The Subjective Side of Science*. Amsterdam: Elsevier.
Mulkay, M. and Gilbert, G.N. (1982). "Accounting for Error." *Sociology* 16: 165–183.
Popper, K.R. (1945). *The Open Society and Its Enemies. Vol. II.* London: Routledge and Kegan Paul.
Ravetz, J. (1971). *Scientific Knowledge and Its Social Problems*. Oxford: Oxford University Press.
Segerstråle, U. (1983). "Whose Truth Shall Prevail? Moral and Scientific Interests in the Sociobiology Controversy." Ph.D. Thesis in Sociology. Harvard University (unpublished).
Segerstråle, U. (1986). "Colleagues in Conflict: An 'In Vivo' Analysis of the Sociobiology Controversy." *Biology and Philosophy* 1: 53–87.
Segerstråle, U. (1987a). "Scientific Controversy as Moral/Political Discourse." *Contemporary Sociology* 16 (3): 544–547.
Segerstråle, U. (1987b). "Debates Involving Science." *Science* 238: 1296–1297.
Shapin, S. and Schaffer, S. (1985). *Leviathan and the Air-Pump: Hobbes, Boyle and the Experimental Life*. Princeton, N.J.: Princeton University Press.
Thoday, J.M. (1981). "Probity in Science: The Case of Cryil Burt." *Nature* 291: 517–518.

Wilson, E.O. (1975a). *Sociobiology: The New Synthesis*. Cambridge, Mass.: Harvard University Press.
Wilson, E.O. (1975b). "For Sociobiology." *New York Review of Books*, 11 December.
Wilson, E.O. (1975c). "Human Decency Is Animal." *New York Magazine*, October.
Wilson, E.O. (1978a). *On Human Nature*. New York: Bantam Books.
Wilson, E.O. (1978b). "The Attempt to Suppress Human Behavioral Genetics." *Journal of General Education* 29: 277–287.

2 Subjective Rationality and the Theory of Ideology

Raymond Boudon

The chapter of sociology dealing with ideology is probably both one of the most extended and also one of the least unified. The definition of the concept of ideology appears as variable from one sociologist to the next. And there is little agreement among sociologists as to the nature of the basic mechanisms responsible for the ideological phenomenon.

Beyond the confusion around the definition of the concept, it seems possible, however, to identify a simple cleavage line. Some sociologists use a definition of ideology in which the categories of truth and falsehood play a central role. Others, as Professor C. Geertz (1964: 47–76) for instance, contend that this logical criterion should not be considered.

In the first case, ideology is viewed as a caricature of science. Ideological statements, ideological theories are defined as statements that appear or are interpreted as scientific, but that are not scientific. Such a definition can be found, for instance, in Marx' work. According to Marx, ideologies are pseudoscientific theories that are inspired to the social actor by his class interests, and that become influential because they serve class interests. But the same type of definition can as well be found in the work of modern writers owing little to Marx' thought. Thus, Talcott Parsons (1959: 25–49) defines ideological theories as theories that appear as scientific although they are not. And Professor Popper holds a similar view, in his book on *The Poverty of Historicism* for instance. To him, historicism is the common denominator of ideological theories of social change. The theories that can be classified under this label are presented and often perceived as scientific, but, according to Popper, they use methods of reasoning generally considered as inadequate by scientists.

According to the second category of writers, ideology should not be defined by reference to the truth/falsehood criterion. Karl Mannheim, for instance, belongs to this category. His theory of ideology starts from the observation that many ideas appear to social actors as having a meaning to them although they can be considered neither true nor false. Thus, he explains, in the early Middle Ages, the taboo against charging an interest on loans had a meaning for most social actors (Mannheim, 1954). For it was well adapted to the economic system of that time, a system in which reciprocity played a dominant role. Such a belief is neither true nor false. But it made sense to the social actors, since in a system where economic exchanges are limited and take place essentially among actors knowing each other, *A* can easily expect that if he, say, lends money to *B* today, *B* will reciprocate tomorrow in one way or another: more easily, at any rate, than in a system dominated by impersonal economic relationships.

Mannheim's view of ideology has been endorsed by modern writers, notably by Geertz. To Geertz, ideologies have to be considered as systems of positive and normative ideas that guide the social actors in a complex social world. They are useful. They are even indispensable to social life. But they can be considered neither true nor false. Thus, from Mannheim to Geertz, an almost uninterrupted line of writers contend that the first point to note when dealing with ideology is that it should not be defined with reference to science.

What type of definition is better? Obviously, Mannheim and Geertz are correct when they say that many ideas have a meaning for the social actors, although they can be considered neither true nor false. But the question is whether ideology is the right label for this type of ideas.

Obviously there is always some part of arbitrariness in any decision about definitions. But as far as I am concerned, I would tend to prefer the traditional definition, that is, the definition retained by Marx, Popper, or Parsons, for instance, to the modern definition, that is, the definition proposed by Mannheim or Geertz, for the following reasons, listed below.

First, for historical reasons, I do not want to spend time on the history of the word *ideology*. But it is useful for our discussion to recall that this term appears and becomes progressively institutionalized in the nineteenth century, because it is perceived as describing an entirely new phenomenon, – I mean the effort inaugurated by Locke and later by Montesquieu and the thinkers of the Enlightenment to ground the social and political order on a scientific basis. In a famous page, J. Locke (1823/1963: 186) expressed his hope that a Newton would appear and discover the laws of the social world. Repeatedly, Adam Smith refers to the "natural order" of the human world. And in the first page of *L'Esprit des Lois*, Montesquieu describes his endeavor: to discover the laws to which men and social systems are subjected.

Thus, historically, the term ideology describes this new ambition that appears in the eighteenth century and becomes confirmed in the nineteenth century: grounding in science a social order that during centuries had been conceived as grounded in tradition. At the same time, the negative and derogatory connotation that very soon become attached to this new word indicated possibly that this ambition was perceived as being to a large extent excessive and illusory.

Thus, a first argument in favor of what I have called the *traditional* definition of ideology i.e., the definition of Marx, Popper, or Parsons would be that it is congruent with the historical meaning of the word.

A second argument is that it is also congruent with the current meaning of this word. Still today, when we talk of an ideological theory, we currently mean a theory that deals with social questions, looks or presents itself as scientific, but is not scientific.

A third argument is that the alternative definition, the *modern* definition used, for instance, by Mannheim or Geertz, has failed to become widely accepted, probably because it creates a category, the extension of which is so wide, that one can easily wonder whether it is at all useful. Actually, it is hard to see how the notion of ideology in Mannheim's or Geertz' sense can at all be distinguished from another familiar notion, the notion of culture. Another flaw of their definition is obviously that it pays no attention to the historical meaning of the word, ideology, and that it fails to see that this concept – as the concepts of capitalism or absolutism, for instance – has the logical status of an idealtype, as we say after Max Weber i.e., of a concept describing a historical singularity.

My fourth argument in favor of the traditional definition is that all ideologies to which we can refer – liberalism as well as Marxism, or, to take more modest modern ideologies, developmentalism for instance, or the ideology according to which the exchanges between the developed world and the Third World should always be detrimental to the latter, – all these ideologies present themselves as leaning upon arguments of the scientific type. Whence it follows that they fall under the jurisdiction of the truth/falsehood criterion.

So, we have good reasons, it seems to me, to follow the tradition exemplified by Marx, Popper, or Parsons and to define ideology as the set of ideas, statements, and theories dealing with social questions that (*a*) can be considered uncertain, doubtful, or false (*b*) although they present themselves as resting upon scientific arguments.

Beside its intrinsic merits, this definition has the advantage of raising a question of utmost sociological interest: How and why are such false or uncertain ideas and theories so easily considered as true? Why are they so easily held as credible?

This question was, of course, raised by all the writers who had adopted the traditional definition of ideology. Marx' general answer to it is well known: The social actors belonging to the dominating classes are blinded by their class interests, and the dominated classes are under the influence of the former. Parsons', Popper's, or Raymond Aron's (1968) answers to the same question are of course different. Actually, they are directly inspired by the classical philosophical considerations on the causes of human errors: The social actors believe in ideologies because they are blinded by their passions, by their fanatism, by their feelings, or because they judge with precipitation. So, despite the obvious differences, the answers given by all these writers have something in common: For all of them, the social actors endorse easily false beliefs – ideologies – because they are *irrational*.

As I said, I incline to agree with these classical writers as far as the definition of the concept of ideology is concerned. But I strongly disagree with their explanation of the ideological phenomenon. In other words, I do not believe that it is indispensable to consider the social actor as irrational in order to explain why ideologies appear as so easily credible and influential. On the contrary, I think it is possible to show that the social actor very often has *good reasons* to believe in these false or uncertain ideas that build up ideologies in the traditional sense of the word. I would like to suggest, in other words, that, while the dominant theory of ideology is irrational, it is possible to develop a rational theory that, it seems to me, is more acceptable and fruitful. This theory was already suggested by some classical sociologists, notably by Max Weber (1922) and Vilfredo Pareto (1917).

Obviously, the *good reasons* that lead a social actor to believe *X* as true can be objectively good, or they can be subjectively good without being objectively good. But even when they are not objectively good, we may still accept in many occasions the reasons of the actor. To describe this type of cases I will use the notion of "subjective rationality."

I disagree also with the dominant theory of ideology, as illustrated by Marx, Popper, Aron, or Parsons, on a second important point: It is true, as they all contend, that false and/or doubtful beliefs can lean upon theories using ways of reasoning generally considered as illegitimate from a scientific point of view. But this should be considered, it seems to me, rather as a particular than a general case. For, as I shall try to show, these doubtful or false beliefs can also rest on theories belonging to what, after Kuhn, is generally called the "normal science."

In order to show that the *homo sociologicus*, the anonymous social actor considered in sociological thinking, can very normally and very currently have *good reasons* to believe in false, doubtful, or uncertain ideas, it is useful to identify and consider three types of effects. When combined with one another, they can, in my opinion, explain ideological beliefs to a large extent. To a large extent, I repeat, since, obviously, ideological beliefs cannot always be explained by good reasons. Sometimes, they are also produced by irrational factors.

I shall call these effects, respectively: *position* and *disposition* effects, *communication* effects, and *epistemological* effects.

Let us deal, first, with position effects. By this expression I want to convey the idea that sometimes, because of his social position, a social actor can have good reasons to perceive his environment in a certain way, and in a way which can be possibly different from the way another actor, in a different position, would perceive it.

I shall take some examples to illustrate this idea. The first one is the following (Katona, 1951: 45ff.): Some decades ago, the Keynesian theory was the object of much consideration and agreement. On one subject, the relationship between taxation and inflation, the theory insists upon the deflationary effects of taxes: increasing taxes will likely reduce the demand for goods and services and consequently the prices of the latter.

In the late 1940s, the social psychologist Cantril conducted a survey among American businessmen in which he explored their beliefs on a number of economic questions. To the question as to whether increasing taxes have inflationary or deflationary effects, a large majority of them expressed an opinion contrary to the Keynesian dogma. To them, taxes were more likely inflationary than deflationary.

Why is this so? At his own level, a business leader will likely observe an inflationary effect. If the taxes weighing upon his business grow, he will normally, if he has the impression he can do so without risks, transfer at least a part of their increase to the consumer, in the form of a price increase of his products. Thus, because of his social position, he will have good reasons to believe that an increase in taxes has normally inflationary effects. And even if he is aware of opposite views, he may have some difficulty in accepting them without resistance.

This example illustrates what I call here position effects. Because of his position, the businessman has good reasons to perceive the causal relation between taxation and inflation in one way, while, at the same time, the Keynesian economist has good reasons to perceive it in the opposite way. Obviously, I am not interested here in who is right, but only in the fact that social actors can have good reasons for seeing the world in different manners when they perceive it from different viewpoints.

I shall consider a second example, very different from the first in its nature, but leading to the same moral – the example of the Luddite movement in eighteenth century Britain.

Many historians have interpreted the Luddite movement in an irrational manner: They saw the behavior of the Luddite workers as expressive rather than instrumental. By damaging the machines, the workers would not have followed any definite end; they would rather have expressed a protest against a novelty that disturbed their traditional environment. This traditional interpretation may contain some part of truth. But it has often been criticized in recent years. Particularly well-known among sociologists is Lewis Coser's work (1964), in which he proposed a purely strategic interpretation of the Luddite movement: The British workers would have destroyed the machines with the objective of threatening the employers, of displaying their nuisance power in the hope of drawing material advantages from this threat. As the former, this interpretation may contain some part of truth.

But it can also be noted that, because of their position, the workers had good reasons for perceiving the introduction of new machines as a major cause of unemployment, since they could effectively observe, at the local level, that because of the machines, many workers were fired while others failed to be hired.

Therefore, they had good reasons to have a view on this subject of the causal relationship between mechanization and employment contrary to the view of other social actors, for whom it was evident for many reasons that more machines generate more work, notably because workers are needed to conceive, build, and maintain the new machines. Incidentally, it may be added that the main reason why many historians gave an irrational interpretation of the Luddite movement probably lies in the fact that, to them, the positive effect of mechanization on employment was obvious, since the correlation between the two variables appeared beyond doubt as positive on the long term. This was so for many decades, at least until the recent years. Thus they failed for good reasons to see that, from another point of view, the correlation could not only be perceived as but be negative. Consequently, they could have difficulty in understanding the reasons of the Luddite workers.

As in the previous case, I do not want to discuss the causal relationship between the two variables for itself, but only to stress the point that, because of their position, different social actors may have good reasons for having opposite views as to the sign of the correlation. And I may add that this is true not only of British history at the time of the Luddite movement, but also, for instance, of French modern history. This can be seen in the fact that, book after book, during several decades, the French demographer and economist, Alfred Sauvy (1963) tried to convince an audience, that obviously had to be convinced on this point, that in the long run the correlation between the two variables is positive. Plausibly, the resistance to Sauvy's view was due to the fact that at the local level many people could observe empirically a negative relation.

Many other examples of position effects, of course, could be evoked; some of them are well known. Thus, it is sociologically trivial that according to his social role or to his social position, in the stratification sense of this expression, an actor can develop not only distinct preferences, but also distinct cognitive views on such and such questions. In the same fashion, it is well known that as a function of his social and cultural distance with a social object, an observer can develop distinct views of this object with good reasons. To take a simple example, a sociologist who tries to give an interpretation of the behavior of a category of people close to him will not only have to be more careful; he will at the same time be more protected against projective interpretations than if he interprets the behavior of socially distant people.

This latter remark leads me to what I called earlier disposition effects – another ingredient of a rational theory of ideology. I take here the word disposition, a venerable word in the philosophical tradition, in a simple sense: in the sense in which the Austrian philosopher Wittgenstein proposes to use it. To Wittgenstein (1930) a disposition is simply something that I know, because I have experienced or learned it, that is not currently present to my consciousness, but that will be mobilized possibly in a half-conscious fashion in appropriate circumstances. Thus if somebody tells me that $2 + 2 = 6$, I will immediately mobilize implicitly all kinds of statements present in my head ($2 + 2 = 4$, "everybody knows it," etc.) and, on the basis of these statements, draw such and such plausible interpretation of his behavior.

Why is the notion of disposition, in this simple cognitive sense, important in the analysis of false beliefs? Simply because, while these cognitive dispositions are often essential to a correct interpretation and perception of the world, they can also lead the social actor to false views and inaccurate interpretations.

To come back to one of my earlier examples, let us take the case of the nineteenth century historian who undertakes to write the history of the Luddite movement. He is convinced that the machines have been of major source of social progress and considers as obvious the fact that they have contributed to increase, multiply, and diversify human activities. That they tend to increase the number of available jobs is to him an evident statement. But this disposition has the effect that, with good reasons, he interprets the behavior of the Luddite worker as emotional, doomed to fail, and on the whole as absurd and irrational.

As we saw earlier, other interpretations are possible that are more plausible and also more congruent with historical data. But, because of their cognitive dispositions, these early historians could hardly envisage the idea of interpreting the Luddite movement in a rational fashion.

In its simplicity, this example shows that, if knowledge can in many cases make our understanding of the world easier, it can also create in the mind of the social actor and of the observer dispositions that will occasionally inhibit rather than facilitate their understanding of the world. Not only prejudices, i.e., false knowledge can have this inhibiting effect, but also true knowledge.

Without calling them by this name, a sociologist has very well seen the importance of what I call here disposition effects, Max Weber's theory of magic illustrates brilliantly, it seems to me, their importance.

Magic is a phenomenon that has always been considered by Western observers as deeply puzzling. For this reason, a tremendous number of works have been written on the subject, in which two main interpretations with many variations can possibly be distinguished.

According to the first interpretation, which can be found for instance in Frazer's work or in Levy-Bruhl's early work, magic would indicate that the mind of the primitives would operate with logical rules different from the ones we are following (obviously, I simplify greatly here, but this assumption is the core idea of these theories).

The second interpretation, represented, for instance, by Pareto (1917) and later by Wittgenstein (1930) or by Beattie (1964) is a proposal to the effect of exorcizing magic, so to speak: This second theory starts from the idea that primitive people do not really believe in the efficiency of their magical rituals. They would not believe for instance that their ritual gesticulations have the effect of bringing rain. By these rituals, they would rather express a wish: the wish that rains falls on their crops. So, magical rituals should be interpreted as expressive rather than as instrumental. They should be explained, using Schütz's vocabulary, by *weil-Motive* rather than by *wozu-Motive*.

These theories of magic are interesting for our purpose for a primary reason: clearly, they reflect the presence in the mind of their authors of dispositions, but of dispositions of the normative type. Wittgenstein's or Beattie's aversion toward Frazer is obviously due at least in part to the fact that Frazer's or Levy-Bruhl's theories can be easily perceived as treating primitives in a derogatory fashion. By interpreting magical rituals in an expressive fashion, Wittgenstein, Beattie, and their like gave a picture of the so-called primitives that was more congruent with their values, and also with the *Zeitgeist*. In the same fashion, as Horton has rightly suggested, Frazer's or Levy-Bruhl's theories were congruent with values and feelings widespread in their own time.

But I would like to insist rather on cognitive than on normative dispositions, since the effects of the latter on beliefs are more easily recognized. To this effect, I will now turn to a third theory of magic, Weber's theory (1922). Its importance is, in my opinion, not sufficiently recognized, probably because it is exposed in very short and allusive texts. The core of Weber's theory is made of what I call here disposition effects. The impression of puzzlement that we experience when we are confronted with magical rituals does not derive from the fact, suggests Weber, that these rituals would be actually puzzling, but from the fact that, when we observe them, we cannot easily help mobilizing a number of dispositions that we owe to our own culture. Because of the education to which he is normally exposed, any Westerner has a rough idea of the laws of the transformation of energy. A long philosophical tradition has made the notion of cause familiar to him. He is aware of the relationship between the notions of cause and of frequency, etc. All these dispositions explain easily that he feels puzzled by the fact that the primitive believes, or at least seems to believe, that the magical rituals of the rainmaker are as efficient as the gestures of the firemaker. Without these dispositions, the concept of magic would even not have been created, since it designates precisely all these acts that seem to rest upon nonvalid causal relations.

Suppose now that, instead of mobilizing them passively as we ordinarily do, we pay attention to this bundle of dispositions of ours, and that we take seriously the evidence that the primitive has no reason whatsoever of conceiving as natural notions and principles that, like the principle of the conservation of energy, the notion of cause, the relationship between cause and frequency, Western thought has identified and clarified after centuries. As soon as we do so, magical rituals appear immediately as less puzzling. The primitive has dispositions different from ours. For this reason, suggests Weber, to him, but obviously not to us, the acts of the rainmaker are exactly as rational as the acts of the firemaker.

Weber's theory is simple. Moreover, it is credible. Although I cannot insist upon this point here (Nisbett and Ross, 1980), many findings of modern cognitive psychology tend to corroborate it strongly. These findings show, namely, that when educated people from Western countries are confronted with problem-solving situations, they can very easily produce, despite their diffuse familiarity with experimental procedures and with statistical concepts, inferences as puzzling and objectively ill-grounded as those that seem to inspire the magical practice of the primitives.

Thus, in one experiment (Nisbett and Ross, 1980), a majority of subjects detects a causal relation between two variables on the basis of an incomplete contingency table. Now, the table not only fails to show any correlation between the two variables, it forbids it to draw from the available data any conclusion as to whether the two variables are correlated or not.

This experiment and many others that could be quoted suggest that causal inference and inference shortly can easily be affected by subjective factors, even in the case of educated Westerners. It suggests *a fortiori* that it would be not only unfair but absurd to expect more objectivity from primitives. Given *their* dispositions, it is not unwarranted, as Weber rightly suggests, that they believe in the efficiency of the rainmaker as well as in the efficiency of the firemaker. Given *our* dispositions, it is not unthinkable that we see magical rituals as puzzling.

These examples illustrate sufficiently, I think, what I call here position and disposition effects. They may be also sufficient to show that, because of these effects, we can in many circumstances believe for good reasons in false ideas. As the examples of the theories of magic and of the Luddite movement suggest, these effects can even inspire false ideas to those, the scientists, for whom objectivity is a central value. But one need not suppose the scientists irrational to understand why they endorse such ideas: They have good reasons for doing so.

I turn now to what I called communication effects. They can be illustrated by a very simple case. Let us suppose an economist, a sociologist, a physicist, or a chemist proposes some theory and that, for some reason, it attracts the attention of many people who are not themselves economists, sociologists, etc. because the theory proposes a way to solve a problem of general interest. These people will have an interest in the theory, but most of them will not be able to judge its validity by themselves. If I can use this metaphor, they will treat the theory as a black box. So, they will accept it on the basis of what may be called the authority principle. Take the case of an economic theory. If its author is perceived as highly respected by the economic profession, and if the theory is of interest to a decision-maker, the decision-maker can endorse it and treat it as valid, less because he will have, tested it by himself, than because of the scientific status of its author.

In the hard sciences, these black box effects are of limited importance for two reasons, related to one another. The first is that, as Simmel (1922) has rightly noted, the natural sciences are esoteric in the sense that the general public shows in general little interest for their explanations and is rather interested in their applications. The second is that, say, a physical theory will only be brought to the attention of a broader public once it has been carefully tested by the competent scientific community.

By contrast, the social sciences tend to be exoteric – not only their applications, but their explanations are often of interest to a large public. Take the case of Weber's Protestant ethic or of Lenin's theory of imperialism. The ideas contained in such works have clearly interested a broad public beyond the limited circles of the social scientists. As Simmel has suggested, the general public has little interest in the physical theories about the structure of matter, while many people, and not only the social scientists, are interested in the causes of crime, of inequality, of suicide, or in the causes of the rise of capitalism.

This natural interest, so to speak, of many social actors for the theories produced by the social sciences, combined with the fact that, because of their dispositions, these actors will have to treat these theories as black boxes, explain that on many occasions a theory will become influential, even in the case where its validity is weak. Suppose, for instance, a theory arouses a strong interest in the public and that the scientific community takes some time before being able to say whether the theory is valid or not. In that case, the theory will likely be accepted by many people who will not wait for the verdict of the scientific community before endorsing it.

A famous example can illustrate this first type of communication effect, namely, the example of the reception of Weber's Protestant ethic.

First, it should be noted that the theory developed by Weber in his Protestant ethic – a theory that I need not summarize – is beyound doubt a genuine scientific theory. Weber starts from a number of well-established facts: that, since the sixteenth century, the puritans are overrepresented in the European economic elites; that the countries with a strong puritan tradition appear as more dynamic economically, etc. In order to explain these phenomena, he introduces – as any scientist would – a hypothesis: that the Protestant ethic induces a positive attitude toward economic achievement. And he tries to show that his hypothesis is well supported by the available data.

This theory very soon was widely received in many places and circles. This probably occurred for two reasons. The first one is that Weber's theory immediately aroused a deep interest. First because of what I would call its philosophical dimension: it suggests – against materialism – that ideas and values can have the logical status of independent rather than of dependent variables. Second, because of its wide scope: Weber's theory proposes an explanation of the most important mutation in modern history, the rise of capitalism. Moreover, to use Piaget's vocabulary, because of sociocentric reasons, his theory was naturally perceived as appealing by many of those who had been educated in the puritan tradition. The interest of the theory, combined with the fact that the theory not only can be perceived as but is beyond doubt a genuine scientific theory, made it an easily received idea. While Weber's *Ethic* is probably not his most solid work, it is by far the most popular.

But this transformation of a scientific hypothesis into a received belief can only be explained if another factor is taken into account: for a long time, its validity remained indeterminate. Leaving the details aside, I would say that Weber's *Ethic* has stimulated an interminable discussion in the scientific community and that the conclusions of this discussion did not become clear before the 1950s. As a result of this discussion, the correlations between puritanism and capitalism, which Weber's theory tried to explain, can to a large extent be accounted for by factors that Weber did not consider. Thus, the British historian Trevor-Roper (1967) has shown that, because of its hostility toward the bourgeois, the Catholic church had pushed the businessmen into the arms of Erasmus, and then of Calvin. On the other hand, with the rise of the Counter-Reformation, many businessmen chose to emigrate toward warmer waters and moved from the areas under Catholic control to the Lutheran or Calvinist states, partly because they were exposed to the risk of being prosecuted for their sympathy toward Calvinism, but also because business was much easier in the Protestant countries. In short, the discussion concludes an inversion of the causal relation proposed by Weber. The businessmen of the sixteenth and seventeenth centuries were attracted by Calvinism and moved toward the Protestant countries because they were businessmen. They did not become businessmen because they were Calvinists.

Thus, it is clear today that Weber's theory, although it is a scientific theory and contains some truth, cannot be taken at its face value any more. But, as the conclusions of the scientific community came very late and remained confined to narrow scientific circles, the received idea to which it had given birth remained alive.

To complete the vocaculary I used earlier, I would say that this belief was produced by the combination of a black box effect and of what I would call a short-circuit effect: Many people had good reasons to be interested by the hypothesis proposed by Weber, and they had also good reasons to treat it as a black box, that is not to try to determine themselves whether or not it was valid, since, as the subsequent discussion of the theory has shown, this was not an easy task. Moreover, as the scientific community considered the theory as scientifically serious and did not raise important objections against if for many decades, those who were interested in the theory had no reasons for doubting its validity and waiting for a final scientific verdict before believing in its truth.

This example illustrates the fact that doubtful beliefs can sometimes be generated by genuinely scientific theories. It also demonstrates that communication effects play an important role in the generation of false or doubtful beliefs.

Obviously, Weber's hypothesis in the Protestant ethic is an idea and not an ideology. But the influence of the communication effects that I have illustrated by this example can be traced also in the case of ideologies.

To exemplify it, I shall consider the example of an ideology of our time, Developmentalism, which enjoyed a strong influence, in the 1950s. The core idea of this ideology, if it is acceptable to summarize it in a crude fashion, is that the injection of foreign capital and foreign aid are the most efficient ways and may be the only ways of drawing a poor country from its underdevelopment. The word Developmentalism was, of course, created by those who had doubts about this idea: These doubts are well expressed by the ism ending of the word. Today, this theory counts fewer believers than in the past. But in the 1950s and still in the 1960s it was perceived in many circles as a kind of dogma, mainly because of the influence of communication effects.

As in the previous case, the doubtful beliefs gathered under the label Developmentalism were originally generated by a genuinely scientific theory, more exactly by a set of convergent scientific theories.

I shall consider briefly one of these theories, maybe one of the most popular: the theory of the vicious circle of poverty (Nurkse, 1953). It can be roughly summarized by the following statements:

1. If a country is poor, this country has a low saving capacity.
2. When the saving capacity of a country is low, its investment capacity is low.
3. As its investment capacity is low, its productivity will not likely increase.
4. If its productivity does not increase, its standard of living will remain stagnant.
5. Whence: in the absence of foreign aid and of foreign capital, a poor country will remain poor.

This theory, as have many other theories of the same type, has immediately aroused a strong interest in many circles. Why? Because in the 1950s and 1960s, the underdevelopment of the Third World is perceived as an essential political problem. Because a number of people, not only in the Third World but also in the developed countries were directly or felt directly concerned by this problem. In other words, there was a strong public demand for development theories. A theory such as the theory of the vicious circle of poverty had the interest of identifying the causes of underdevelopment and of providing a guideline to development policy. Moreover, these theories were proposed by scientists who were generally highly considered.

As in the previous case, the influence of these theories is the effect of a number of communication effects: black box effects, authority effects, and also short-circuit effects. Theories such as the theory of the vicious circle of poverty were not only considered interesting, they were also considered by many people directly concerned with the problem of development as true and valid. And few of those who had an interest in them cared much about the limits of their validity.

This theory is far from general, however; on the contrary, it is true only under very restrictive conditions. For this reason, its conclusion that foreign aid is a necessary and sufficient condition of development can be considered ideological. Ideology rests here upon a misrepresentation of the true range of validity of a scientific theory.

Let us go back for a while to the first statement. It looks analytical: Saying that a country is poor and that it has no saving capacity is saying the same thing twice? But it is rather quasi-analytical. For, the notion of poverty can mean either that everybody is poor, or that most people are poor with the exception of the elites. In other words, poverty means low median or average income. But this notion says nothing as to the standard deviation of income. A country may be poor and be characterized either by a low or by a high standard deviation of its income distribution. Now, the theory of the vicious circle supposes implicitly that this standard deviation is low, and by so doing, introduces a first assumption that reduces its generality. This raises the question as to whether this assumption is realistic. Obviously, the answer is no, since most underdeveloped countries are characterized by a strong income inequality.

Let us now consider the third statement: Costly investments are the condition of any significant increase in productivity. It is true that, in our societies at least, productivity increases are generally costly. But is that a general case? The answer is again no, since considerable gains in productivity can be produced and are actually often produced at no or little cost, especially in societies with a low level of development.

The theory introduces many other implicit assumptions that I cannot review in detail. Thus, it assumes also that the ideal-typical society it considers has no exchanges with its environment. Otherwise it could, for instance, benefit from gains of productivity produced in the environment.

On the whole, this theory is valid only under a very restrictive set of assumptions. In other words, it does not show at all that foreign aid is a necessary and sufficient condition of development. In fact, a short moment of reflection shows that if it were true in general, Britain in the eighteenth century and Japan in the twentieth century should never have developed.

These two examples, the Protestant ethic example and the example of the theory of the vicious circle of poverty show that ideological beliefs do not necessarily rest, as Marx and Popper believed, on sophistical pseudo-scientific theories. They can also rest upon genuinely scientific theories. Weber's theory in his *Ethic*, the theories of development, such as the one I have considered, are beyound doubt scientific. They belong to what Kuhn has called the normal science. But because of the influence of communication effects, they have generated false, doubtful or ideological beliefs. For many people had good reasons for being interested in these theories and no reasons for becoming aware of their narrow validity.

It is probably useless to insist upon the fact that these two examples illustrate a typical process. For, it occurs very frequently that a theory proposed for instance by a sociologist or by an economist (*a*) arouses in such and such group a deep interest, and that (*b*) the individuals in the group have to treat the theory as a black box. If I am not an economist myself, I can very well be interested by the fact that the theory proposes, say, an easy remedy against unemployment, and recognize at the same time that I am not able to judge its validity. Now, if the theory is fragile or false, two conditions will be needed to stop its influence: (*a*) Its evaluation by the scientific community will have to be rapid and if possible fair: (*b*) it will have to be visible. Needless to say, it happens very often that the two conditions are not satisfied.

Possibly, these remarks are sufficient to show why I disagree with the principles of what I called earlier the dominant theory of ideology. Beyond their differences, the theories of ideology developed by Marx, Popper, or Aron have two principles in common: They assume that ideological beliefs are generated by theories that are not scientific, and that the social actor endorses false beliefs because he is irrational.

By contrast, I have tried to show that false beliefs can be generated by scientific theories. On the other hand, there is often no need to see the social actor as irrational, to explain why he endorses false beliefs: In the 1950s, the political man in charge of elaborating a development policy had good reasons to believe that the theory of the vicious circle of poverty represented a valid theory and a useful guideline. More generally, the communication effects I have described occur, not although but because social actors are rational: Our political man believed in the conclusions of the theory of the vicious circle because: (*a*) it looked respectable; and (*b*) he saw well that he had not the resources to judge of its validity by himself.

By so saying, I do not mean that these two principles of the dominant theory of ideology are false, but only that they describe a particular rather than a general case. For, obviously, false beliefs can also be generated by sophistical theories. But even in this case, one need not always suppose the social actor irrational to understand why he endorses such theories.

To illustrate this case, I will take the example of the influence of Foucault's theory in *Supervise and Punish*.

The theory rests beyond doubt upon a sophism. Foucault starts from the well-known idea that prison can generate labeling effects, that a man or a woman who has spent some time in jail can have, because of this fact, a harder time finding a job and thus can relapse into crime. From this idea, he draws the false conclusion that, since prison increases the rates of recidivism, it increases the rate of crime. At no point in the book does he raise the question as to whether prison would not have also a dissuasive effect. Going one step farther, he raises then the following question: Since prison increases the rate of crime, while its function would be to reduce them, why do we keep it? And he dramatizes the question by quoting, in very erudite pages, a number of texts showing that, from the eighteenth century to our own time, all the experts have been aware of the effects of prison on the probability of recidiving. His own answer to his strange question is drawn from vulgar Marxism: Prison serves, for various reasons, the interests of the dominant classes.

One of my students reviewed the articles that were published in the French press on Foucault's book. He found that the book was, in general, positively received: The erudition of the book from the historiographical viewpoint was generally stressed. The theory was presented as serious, since it started from the well-known idea that, because of the labeling effects, prison tended to increase recidivism. Nobody mentioned the fact that prison can increase the rates of recidivism and still, on the whole, contribute to the decrease in the rate of crime.

How can such a benignity be explained? By the combination of cognitive and of communication effects, I think. First, the erudition of the book permitted it to be easily perceived by reviewers as serious, as scientific. Second, it appeared at a time when the works of the labeling theorists had become well-known, not only among sociologists and the professionals directly or indirectly concerned with criminal policy, but also among a broader audience. Now, while the labeling theorists have spent much effort trying to show by more or less sophisticated statistical methods that, other things equal, prison increases recidivism, they never mention the fact that prison can also have dissuasive effects, maybe partly for ideological reasons, but also because these effects have nothing to do with the labeling theory that they wish to test and advertise. As to the works that attempt to measure these dissuasive effects, they had attracted little interest and were little known. To these circumstances, it should be added that, objectively, the dissuasive effects are not only more difficult to measure than the labeling effects, they are also, more abstract, since they refer to potential events that do not occur.

On the whole, the reviewers had good reasons for perceiving Foucault's book as scientific – its erudition was striking. It was also congruent with what they knew of modern criminology, essentially the works inspired by labeling theory. Thus, its validity could be taken for granted, and their attention was not caught by the sophism upon which Foucault's theory rests, since nobody seemed concerned with the dissuasive effects of prison.

Finally, I will turn very briefly to the third type of effects I mentioned earlier: the epistemological effects. They derive from the well-known fact that any scientific theory necessarily rests upon principles and beliefs that, not only the author of the theory, but his public as well, will likely take for granted. Kuhn has made this idea popular again in the recent past, but the idea is an old philosophical one. Aristotle (1968: I, 4) had already stressed the fact that any theory starts from principles that – as the word principle suffices to indicate – cannot be deduced from a theory and thus have to be taken for granted. Actually, I would say *cum grano salis* that I do not see much difference between the Aristotelian notion of principle and the Kuhnian notion of paradigm.

Why is this idea important in the explanation of ideology? Because, when a paradigm appears as scientifically fruitful, it frequently tends to be not only taken for granted but also considered as true. This circumstance can generate an attitude of intolerance toward alternative paradigms, or simply make the limits of validity of the paradigm, as well as the interest and validity of alternative paradigms, not able to be perceived. For these reasons, because of its scientific fruitfulness, a paradigm can contribute to the generation of false beliefs and one-sided views of the world.

I will consider first a very simple example. An economist specializing in the problems of development will normally take for granted the framework designated by the expression development economics, and he will frequently fail to see that this very expression includes a number of beliefs. First, the expression implies that the notion of development is clear and distinct. Second, the notion of development itself includes an evolutionary view as well as implicit normative statements (development is normal, underdevelopment is not). Moreover, since development is a singular word, the expression easily suggests that all development processes have something in common, and that the main task of a theory of development is to discover the general mechanisms of development and the general causes of underdevelopment. Finally, the framework described by the expression development economics suggests that the causes of development and of underdevelopment have mainly to be searched for on the side of economic variables.

Needless to say, all these principles are debatable and actually have been questioned. Partly because of the failure of the development policies that were precisely founded on the belief that simple and general mechanisms of development could be easily identified, we have become more aware today of the fact that development depends to a large extent on singular and often on contingent factors. Consequently, we are now incited to pay more attention to the importance of what I would call the historical paradigm or the historical approach in the study of development. We tend to believe more in case studies than in general theories.

But 20 and still 10 years ago, the intellectual climate was entirely different. The implicit paradigm contained in the expression development economics had produced all kinds of interesting new ideas. The theories built up within this framework had succeeded in identifying a number of factors responsible for development and underdevelopment in many actual cases. So that, during one or two decades, the main principle on which they rested was taken for granted. Not only the economics of development, but many people outside the circle of the professional economists believed that it was possible to identify the simple general mechanisms responsible for development and underdevelopment and to design a development policy founded on this knowledge. At the same time, little attention was paid to those who had worked within the framework of what I called earlier the historical paradigm and who had insisted on the singular aspects of development processes. On the whole, the fruitfulness of the development economics paradigm induced and legitimated not only debatable beliefs, but a philosophical view after all not far away from the view Marx had expressed in his famous *de te fabula narratur*. Like Marx, many people believed again that history followed simple laws.

So, even simple words such as development economics carry a number of beliefs that are easily taken for granted. They designate not only a field, but a framework or a bundle of principles, that are useful and fruitful, but that can also generate false beliefs as soon as their logical status of principles is forgotten.

Many examples of the same type could be developed. I shall consider, for instance, the case of functionalism, a popular paradigm in the social sciences. Incidentally, it can be noted that, as ideologies, paradigms often wear names with an ism ending.

The core idea of functionalism represents beyound doubt an extremely important scientific innovation. Briefly summarized, the idea behind it is that social institutions can be explained not only as historians use to explain them, by making intelligible the way they are born, but also by identifying their functions. To take a simple example: Democratic societies very frequently solve the problem of the aggregation of individual preferences into a collective decision by using the majority rule. Now, this institution can be explained in two ways. First, the historical one would consist in analyzing when and how the institution was born and how it was diffused. This type of analysis is brilliantly exemplified in the work of the Belgian historian Léo Moulin for instance, who has shown that most of the procedures that we use to solve this aggregation problem, and notably the majority rule, have been devised and have become institutionalized in the Benedictine cloisters and then spread toward other parts of the Middle Ages society.

The second explanation, the functional one, is exemplified, for instance, by Buchanan's and Tullock's book, *The Calculus of Consent*, which shows that under general conditions, the majority rule is the best solution to the aggregation problem, since it minimizes the sum of two costs that inevitably appear in any situation of collective decision: decision costs and external costs. Thus, if the future citizens of a society were asked which kind of rule they want to adopt to solve the aggregation problem, they would likely choose unanimously to use in many circumstances the majority rule. This mental experiment has the advantage of providing an answer to the question as to why the majority rule is currently accepted and perceived as legitimate.

Evidently, the functional method, as exemplified by the Buchanan-Tullock example is of utmost importance. It can contribute to making social institutions intelligible even in the case where we have no informations about their origin. When we know their origins, it can explain why they are perceived as legitimate and why they have become routinized. As Durkheim has very well seen, in order to explain an institution, one should always try, ideally at least, to explain its genesis and its function, that is, explain why people tend to find them useful and acceptable.

It can be noted, incidentally, that the importance of the idea of function, in this sense of the word, for the analysis of social institutions was recognized, not only by modern sociologists, but also, long ago, by philosophers, since the core idea of contractualism is the same as the core idea of functionalism.

But the intrinsic importance and interest of the idea of function contributed also to legitimating false beliefs about societies. So, a number of writers forgot that the word function as used in an expression such as functional theory is a mere metaphor, and they developed pictures of society where social institutions were analyzed as having a function exactly in the sense where the eye or the stomach have a function. Sometimes, they started from the assumption that all institutions should be considered as having a function. On the whole, the powerful and acceptable methodological idea summarized in the word function turned into a debatable world view according to which social systems should be seen as analogous to living systems. And, for a while, as these views seemed legitimated by the authority of science, they became received ideas.

The same analysis could be made of many other paradigms, of utilitarianism, for instance. When Bentham proposed to analyze human behavior in cost-benefit terms, as we would say in our modern language, he proposed an important idea and a scientifically fruitful one. But as soon as the idea is perceived, not as a principle, but as a true and realistic picture of the human being, it can generate and has, in fact, generated questionable beliefs and world views. Adam Smith knew very well that moral sentiments could not be understood in cost-benefit terms. Today, one has sometimes the feeling that this important idea is forgotten. Thus, probably because of the authority of the utilitarian paradigm, the feelings of indignation that people normally experience when they learn that a crime has not been paid at its fair value are currently interpreted as feelings of fear, while, as Durkheim has rightly suggested, they are not feelings of fear, but of moral indignation.

So, the words as well as the paradigms used by the social sciences can legitimate false beliefs as soon as they are taken for granted, as realistic pictures of the world, the validity of which would be scientifically grounded. And the same could be said of models.

I need only recall here the model of the vicious circle of poverty. It is a genuinely scientific model. As any model, it is valid only under a restrictive set of assumptions. But these restrictive assumptions are often forgotten. In the case of the theory of the vicious circle of poverty, they were disregarded, especially by the consumers of the theory: for instance by those who had an interest in the theory, because it provided them with a political guideline. For, in most cases, these consumers took this theory and the other similar theories for granted and for obvious reasons, this was easier than examining the theory for its truth or falsehood.

Incidentally, it might be noted that the great German sociologist, Georg Simmel (1922), has analyzed the ideological influence of Marx along the same lines. If Marx' theories had been sophistical, suggests Simmel, they would not have had a lasting influence. In fact, Marx developed a number of models (this is not Simmel's vocabulary but his idea). And Simmel makes clear that, to him, there is no reason not to consider many of these models as scientific. But at the same time, Marx had the genious of insisting on his so-called materialism and, by so doing, of convincing his readers that his idealized models should be taken as a realistic picture of the world.

I recognize easily, with the classical theory of ideology, that ideological beliefs can be the effects of fanatism, blindness, or passion. I recognize also that false beliefs can be inspired by false theories, by sophistical theories, by pseudo-scientific theories, and also, of course, by theories that, like religious or philosophical theories, do not claim to be scientific.

What I have shown is that in many cases, doubtful, false, ideological beliefs are also produced by the so-called normal science. On the other hand, one need not necessarily describe the *homo sociologicus* as irrational in order to explain why he often easily endorses false beliefs. On the contrary, he has often good reasons for doing so.

The anthropologist who observes magical rituals may forget, with good reasons, that what seems to him natural is the product of his socialization, and that the primitives have not the same cognitive dispositions as himself. The economist who builds up a theory of development may forget, with good reasons, that he works within a particular framework. The worker who has been fired because he has been replaced by a machine has good reasons for believing that mechanization is a major cause of unemployment. The businessman has good reasons for believing that taxation has always inflationary effects. The political man who uses a theory as a guideline for his action has good reasons for endorsing it in consideration of the professional status of his author. And all kinds of people in all kinds of circumstances have good reasons for believing in the truth of ideas, of theories, which they cannot or are not willing to evaluate by themselves. As the British philosopher, Price, once put it, without what he calls natural credulity, no social life would be possible, since we cannot hope to check by ourselves more than a very small part of the huge bunch of ideas that we have to take for granted if we wish to survive in a complex world.

I conclude by a remark of a general nature: I have shown that on the subject of ideology as on the other main sociological subjects, it can be fruitful to follow the two basic principles of methodological individualism: Consider any collective phenomenon as the product of individual actions, behaviors, or beliefs; and try, as far as possible, to interpret these actions or beliefs as rational, that is, as inspired by good reasons. By so doing, we can eliminate, it seems to me, the main difficulties raised by the classical theory of ideology. Let us consider, for instance, the interpretation proposed by Simmel of Marx' influence: Many people have good reasons for being interested in his ideas and no reasons for seeing that his models, far from representing a realistic picture of the world, rest upon highly idealized and restrictive assumptions. It seems to me that such a theory is much more credible than, say, Popper's or Aron's interpretation, according to which Marx' theories, unscientific as they were, were easily endorsed because many people are irrational.

As I mentioned earlier, the weaknesses of this classical theory of ideology were well seen by Geertz. Following Mannheim's lead, he stressed rightly the fact that social actors have often good reasons for believing in ideas that can be considered neither true nor false (as when people in the Middle Ages believe in the taboo of charging an interest on loans). But he went too far, it seems to me, when he proposed, in the name of axiological neutrality, to define ideology without any reference to the truth/falsehood criterion.

I have tried here to follow a third lead, Max Weber's, who, in his theory of magic, for instance, showed that people can have good reasons for believing not only in all kinds of ideas that are neither true nor false, but also in false ideas. Moreover, as I have suggested, it has to be recognized that in many circumstances these false ideas can very well be inspired by the most normal science.

References

Aristotle (1968). *The Nicomachean Ethics.* London: Heinemann/Cambridge, Mass.: Harvard University Press.

Aron, R. (1968). *L'opium des intellectuels.* Paris: Gallimard.

Beattie, J. (1964). *Other Cultures.* London: Cohen & West.

Coser, L. (1964). *The Functions of Social Conflict.* New York: The Free Press/ London: Collier Macmillan.

Geertz, C. (1964). "Ideology as a Cultural System." In *Ideology and Discontent,* Glencoe: The Free Press.

Katona, G. (1951). *Psychological Analysis of Economic Behavior.* New York: MacGraw-Hill.

Locke, J. (1823/1963). *Some Thoughts Concerning Education. Works.* Reprint Aalen: Scientia.

Mannheim, K. (1954). *Ideology and Utopia.* New York: Harcourt Brace/London: Routledge & Kegan Paul.

Nisbett, R. and Ross, L. (1980). *Human Inference.* Englewood Cliffs, N.J.: Prentice-Hall.

Nurkse, R. (1953). *Problems of Capital Formation in Underdeveloped Countries.* Oxford: Blackwell.

Pareto, V. (1917). *Traité de sociologie générale.* Lausanne/Paris: Payot.

Parsons, T. (1959). "An Approach to the Sociology of Knowledge." *Transactions of the Fourth Congress of Sociology*. Milano, pp. 25–49.
Sauvy, A. (1963). *Théorie générale de la population*. Paris: Presses Universitaires de France.
Simmel, G. (1922). *Die Probleme der Geschichtsphilosophie*, 5th ed. München: Duncker & Humblot.
Trevor-Roper, H. R. (1967). *Religion, the Reformation and Social Change, and Other Essays*. London: Macmillan.
Weber, M. (1922). *Wirtschaft und Gesellschaft*. Tübingen: Mohr.
Wittgenstein, L. (1930/1980). *Philosophical Remarks*, ed. Rush Rhees et al. Chicago: University of Chicago Press.

3 Sociology and the Professional Culture of Philosophers

Richard Kilminster*

3.1 Introduction

This chapter explores the balance of power between two contemporary culture groups – sociologists and philosophers – through a close scrutiny of the culture of one of them – that of the philosophers. Here I am using the concept of culture to inquire into a particular problem in a preliminary way. My usage is the conventional and uncontroversial one of culture as an ordered pattern of symbols, knowledge, beliefs, and ways of thinking and acting characteristic of a definite social group. This definition follows the long-established tradition of Edward Tylor (see Schneider, 1973: 120) and Talcott Parsons (1951: 327ff.)[1], but I provide the inquiry with a sociologist's stress on demonstrating the involvement of culture with group structure and power. I thus treat the academic establishment of philosophers sociologically as a structured professional group with a characteristic culture of its own and standing, for the most part, higher than sociologists in the hierarchy of status and prestige of groups of scientific and other specialists.

My examples draw mainly on the British experience, though my argument involves, as we will see, situating this case in the wider and longer term development of sociology in European societies over the last two centuries. In my view, the rise of sociology has had profound and irreversible repercussions on the subject matter of philosophy and hence on the fate of its practitioners as a group. Readers will need to make their own corrections for differing patterns in the development of other national sociologies and philosophies, where the relationship between the two groups may have played itself out in different ways from that in Britain.

However, the more controversial aspect of this chapter derives from the extent to which the investigation in the sociology of culture inevitably spills over into what is usually called the sociology of knowledge, radically conceived. I am compelled again and again by the nature of my inquiry to begin to make comparative judgments about the cognitive value of the statements of

* *Acknowledgments*
I am very grateful to Roy Boyne, Norbert Elias, Ian Varcoe, and Terry Wassall for many stimulating discussions of the themes of this chapter and to Hans Haferkamp, Jerry Ravetz, and Alan Scott for their detailed comments on an earlier draft. Numerous discussants at the Bremen Symposium in June 1987 helped me to clarify the argument, and I valued, in particular, further conversations with Bernhard Giesen, Richard Münch, and Richard Pieper.

philosophers. The study of the culture of philosophers and the historical relationship between them and sociologists cannot be understood without taking into account the plausible hypothesis that, over a long period, philosophers have become defunctionalized as a group as the result of a number of interwoven social processes, one of which is the rise of the social sciences and sociology in particular. It is in the light of this finding (substantiated only in a preliminary way in this chapter) that I am able to evaluate the credibility and plausibility of philosophers' changing claims to disciplinary autonomy that I find embedded in their culture. This procedure, then, inevitably has implications for how we conceive of the proper and desirable involvement of sociologists with philosophy at the present time.

3.2 The Culture of Philosophers

The subject matter of philosophy is notoriously difficult to pin down, partly because of its purely discursive character. It is much more straightforward to grasp the nature of the relationship between sociology and other social sciences such as economics, politics, or social-psychology than it is to understand the relationship between sociology and philosophy. In the former cases, we can refer to the different, but related, levels of the total social process upon which each focuses, but sociology and philosophy cannot be related in this way because philosophy does not have an "object" of inquiry in that sense. And the problem is compounded by the considerable vagueness and disagreement within philosophy itself about the nature of its task and aims. As the historian of science, Ernan McMullin (1970: 23), recently commented:

> In attempting to define what is meant by "philosophy" of science, the first problem one encounters is the notorious vagueness of the term "philosophy".... Philosophy can in practice be anything from a cloudy speculative fancy to a piece of formal logic. The term has become almost hopelessly equivocal in modern usage.

Philosophers have indeed described the nature of their inquiries in a bewildering number of ways: as logic, as conceptual clarification, as method, as semantics, as thought-about-thought, or even simply as an activity[2]. But most of its practitioners seem to agree that pure reasoning forms the basis of philosophy or, put another way, that their discipline possesses a nonempirical or perhaps "transcendental" subject matter[3]. Philosophers' deliberations are, then, of a purely discursive nature, their culture placing a high premium on rigorous reasoning and logical argumentation. Now, all scientific specialists rely *partly* on their professional standing to provide the source of authority for their knowledge and expertise. But the nonempirical character of philosophy has an important consequence in this regard. It means that philosophical statements (they cannot accurately be described as findings) are not subject for their plausibility or justification to the direct control of evidence about the structure of social or natural processes in the same way as the scientific statements of sociologists or other scientists[4]. Without this external control from publicly verifiable empirical data, however, the authority and credibility of philosophers' statements must ultimately reside *entirely* in their standing as philosophers, in the social weight of their status as a professional group.

There are, of course, other groups of specialists whose disciplines also do not possess an "object" of inquiry in the way that sciences do. But the important difference between, say, literary criticism or the history of ideas and philosophy, is that unlike philosophy those practitioners do not set themselves up as the authoritative epistemological and conceptual arbiters of the sciences, including sociology. This alone is a good reason for subjecting the professional warrant for the pronouncements of philosophers to systematic scrutiny. It was probably both the vagueness and lack of consensus within philosophy as well as this latent arbitrariness that Fustel de Coulanges had in mind when he said that "to philosophize is to think what one wants[5]." Later, in the 1930s, Paul Nizan (1971) said much the same thing in his epic polemic *Les Chiens de garde*, which was a savage political attack on the philosophers in the Sorbonne at the time. But beneath the surface of Nizan's scathing hyperbole and *parti pris* is, however, an accurate perception of the dubieties and indefiniteness of the philosophy that we encounter in modern educational institutions. He wrote:

> Philosophy can say whatever it wants: it has no eternal vocation, it is not (and has never been) univocal; indeed, it may well be the ultimate form of equivocation. Philosophy-in-general is what is left of the different philosophies when these have been emptied of all substance and nothing remains but a kind of family atmosphere, an indefinable effluvium of traditions, private understandings and secret meanings. It is an entity composed solely of words (1971: 8).

It will be objected that whilst there may be equivocality and lack of consensus in philosophy, a similar lack of unity also exists within the fragmented discipline of sociology, which suggests that my comments so far are a paradigm case of the pot calling the kettle black. I am aware that sociology today is not in a unified phase of its development. It contains a good deal of interparadigm conflict such that many sociologists would disagree with my whole approach and basic thesis presented here. But two points must be made immediately: (1) The extent of the disarray within sociology has been exaggerated, there being much more common ground among sociologists than appears to the outsider; and (2) there is a longer term tradition of sociology stretching back more than 200 years in various national contexts that provides a core of theoretical and empirical findings and problems, within which the current variegated state of sociology is probably only a momentary phase, explicable partly by the cultural and structural dynamics outlined here. In other words, some of the disunity in sociology arises precisely from sociology's inability to emancipate itself sufficiently from philosophy, which engenders doubt and failure of nerve on the part of sociologists. Many of the competing schools in sociology are philosophically inspired (e.g., phenomenological sociology or ethnomethodology) or undergirded by philosophical abstractions of a Kantian kind (e.g., structuralism or Althusserianism)[6]. This chapter is partly intended as a contribution toward correcting for this tendency by re-posing the question of the relationship between sociology and philosophy from the less accustomed sociological point of view.

Returning to the culture of philosophers, two more features stand out as important for understanding their relative advantage in the pecking order of academic establishments.

1. Philosophy possesses enormous prestige. This often has the effect of concealing its vagueness and equivocation. We tend to give philosophers the benefit of the doubt just *because* they are philosophers. The prestige of philosophy also partly accounts for why so many sociologists, representing the lower ranking discipline, have been attracted to philosophy and for their general deference toward the tradition. The aura of philosophy must not be underestimated. Philosophy has developed, and actively cultivates, an image of profundity. It seems to offer involvement with the deeper truths of the human condition – basic questions about the nature of knowledge, reality, and moral choice. The discipline is presented by philosophers as an ancient one, the repository for questions about the nature and meaning of existence itself. The appeal of being associated with, and conversant in, work of this level of grandeur and ambition is obvious.

2. By its very nature, philosophy is a highly verbal activity. Indeed, the standing and reputation of philosophers depends a great deal upon their ability to reason logically with rigor and skill, in order to be able verbally to convince others, apparently by force of argument alone. This skill is central to the *raison d'être* of philosophers. Not surprisingly, they are very good at it. Public disputation with philosophers of high intelligence and verbal dexterity – particularly those trained in the analytical school – can be an intimidating experience for people not trained to perform in this way. One consequence is further to increase the professional invulnerability of philosophers because few outsiders are willing or able to challenge them on their own verbal terrain. When applied to sociological theory and research, the philosophical style of analysis (either verbally or in writing) often takes the form of making a number of fine distinctions, the evaluation of fetishised "claims," "theses," and "positions" and the location of puzzles or paradoxes in sociologists' works[7]. The danger is that this activity can become an end in itself, blinding us to consideration of substantive matters. A disillusioned philosopher, Jerry M. Cohen (1972: 8) sardonically described some of these negative consequences. The professional philosopher is one who is:

> Always on the scent of the slight mistake in what someone has said, abstracting from the idea or general conception it contains, who picks up the minute, carping put-down. ... It is characteristic of this type that they come to think they can dismiss a complex theoretical system such as Marxism or psychoanalysis in a few deft "moves" or with a few clever points, and to distrust whatever is not put in the professional patois of "claims," unpacking, entailment, and which does not have the sleek professionalism and glibness that usually passes for brilliance and rigour.

The massive institutional expansion of the social sciences and of sociology in particular in the advanced societies in the 1960s and 1970s provided rich pickings for the philosophers (see Abrams et al., 1981). They were able to bring their logical and conceptual skills to bear on the theory and research of the burgeoning discipline of sociology. And the sociologists automatically looked to the prestigious philosophers for guidance and clarification. But these reactions and attitudes were nothing new. In the French Third Republic at the turn of the century there was a comparable interest by philosophers in the activities of the fashionable and budding science of sociology. They sought to circumscribe the field of the discipline and to curb the forays of its more ambitious practitioners into the fields of ethics and the solution of social problems. Unlike the situation today, however, at that time many more sociologists *did not welcome* the attentions of philosophers. Gabriel Tarde, for example, shunned the philosophers with some sarcasm:

In the stories of our ancestors, when a child was born, all the fairies assembled around its cradle and each gave it a talisman with which it could perform miracles. At present when a science is born or even begins to announce its arrival, a certain number of philosophers encircle it, each bringing his own method for it to follow with the assurance of the greatest success if its rules are applied promptly and with perseverance, as if it were a method or program of discoveries of which nascent science is most in need[8].

However much the nominalist Tarde disagreed with the realist Durkheim about the nature of the object of sociology, they shared the belief in the tactical need for sociology to distance itself from philosophy. As Durkheim declared:

If sociology wants to live, then it will have to reject the philosophical character that it owes to its origin and approach the concrete realities via special research. It is desirable for the public to know that sociology is not purely philosophical and that it requires precision and objectivity[9].

The point is that the expansion of sociology in the contemporary period continues in a new phase a much longer term sociological tradition going back to the classical *fin-de-siècle* age and earlier to the pioneers of the early nineteenth century, all of whom, as today, had to settle their accounts with philosophy in one way or another. In order to illuminate the current phase of this dialogue, it will be helpful to take a brief excursion into the origins of sociology in order to show how – right from the beginning – sociology took on board and transformed to a new level questions about man and society that were previously the province of philosophers. Then, armed with this information, I will return to the role of philosophical culture today.

3.3 The Sociological Revolution

The emergence of both the two first social sciences – political economy and sociology – in the late eighteenth and early nineteenth centuries was part of fundamental changes taking place in the structure of European societies[10]. Under the *ancien régime*, prior to what is usually regarded as the period of the onset of "modernity," political economists such as the Physiocrats and Adam Smith were showing, using evidence, that self-regulating laws operated in society independent of kings and ministers. They realized that there was a range of social phenomena, such as the circulation of income between classes and its annual distribution, which had a measure of autonomy in relation to individual people's actions, no matter how powerful they were. Later, into the nineteenth century, the power of the industrial bourgeoisie and the working classes, with whom they were closely interdependent, increased considerably in relation to that of the aristocrats. This process made possible the extension of the science of political economy to embrace the autonomous social regularities of "the economy" as such. This concept referred to the impersonal regularities of national and international markets and business cycles set in motion by free competition and independent of the actions of governments. It was the political economists who were first to establish, in Gabriel Tarde's words, the superiority of scientific observation in the social field over "juridical, artistic, moral, theological and metaphysical points of view[11]."

The pioneers of sociology such as de Bonald, de Maistre, Saint-Simon, Comte, Marx, and Spencer were largely a product of post-Revolutionary Europe, though only Comte and Spencer, of course, would have welcomed the label sociologist. The others saw themselves as having very different political and scholarly aims. But they all shared a common belief that there was a broader field of self-regulating social forces wider than (though including) the autonomous regularities of the market located by the political economists. Marx is the most equivocal of the writers in this respect. Occasionally, as in the *Grundrisse*, he hints in an almost Durkheimian fashion at the "general bond and all-round interdependence"[12] between people; but for the most part he only sees the spontaneous, objective bonds between interdependent people in their economic form, or otherwise as derivative of economic bonding[13]. All the writers we now see as pioneers of sociology were all symptomatic of a growing realization in this period of the enigma of "society." People had become aware (and were often disoriented or afraid as a result) that in complicated ways individuals' planned actions had unplanned outcomes that they could not have foreseen and that could not be explained by the plans and intentions of people *who could be named*. These outcomes stemmed from the far-flung chains of interdependencies in which people were becoming intertwined to a greater and greater extent. The growing realization of the complex "moral density" (Durkheim) of society in which people were living had important repercussions for the way in which philosophers of the time and later tried to understand the questions of individual freedom and moral responsibility. Now there was a vortex of social changes that had an unplanned order that often, though not always, operated to thwart the wishes of individuals, for whom both the extent of their freedom of action and its limits were constrained by their interdependence with persons they did not even know.

In the seventeenth and eighteenth centuries one could say that people did not experience their social interconnectedness as "society," but rather the experience of society resulted from the actions of leading persons such as kings and ministers. The upheaval of the French Revolution of 1789, the revolutionary wars, the Restoration in France, the reaction, the competing social movements, and unrest of the period all contributed to this realization. In order to try to capture the sum total of objective social relations that were self-regulating and unintended in these complex and ill-understood ways, the meaning of the word "society" was spontaneously recast. It became from the late eighteenth century onward the general word used to describe these impersonal forces, changing its meaning from the more specific sixteenth and seventeenth centuries meaning of active companionship (Williams, 1976: 246).

The sociologists, and the increasingly professionalizing economists, though both focusing on the emergent social reality *sui generis*, had different emphases. The economists sought to elucidate the static regularities of markets, prices, income, and profit, while the sociologists had in mind the broader and grander questions about the longer term development of humankind and its future fate. They were able to build on the ground and credibility already prepared and established by the political economists. Their stock-in-trade included the concepts of development, progress, tendency, and other similar ones, with which they tried to grasp the driving forces of history that seemed to have torn apart the traditional society. All of them saw humankind as passing through a critical phase. They looked for the longer run significance of the social processes the momentous leading edge of which they felt they were living through and tried to discern the shape of the future from the overall development. Though not a sociologist in any recognized sense of the term, François Chateaubriand showed an eloquent awareness of the profundity of the changes through which a generation of European peoples, including many of the sociological pioneers, lived. Writing in 1834 he expressed his forebodings:

> What the new society will be I know not; I no more understand it than the ancients could understand the slaveless society born of Christianity. How fortunes will be levelled, how wages will be equalized with labour, how womanhood will attain complete emancipation, I do not know. Presumably the *human species* will grow in stature, but it is to be feared that the individual man may decline, certain eminent faculties of genius be lost, and imagination, poetry and the arts perish in the cells of a hive-society in which each individual will be nothing more than a bee, a cog in a machine, an atom in organized matter.... Modern society has taken ten centuries to establish, and now is in process of decomposition.... This declining world will recover its energies only when that process has reached its final stage, whereafter society will begin to ascend to a new level of life[14].

From its inception, sociology took on board the range of broader questions rhetorically expressed here by Chateaubriand, which we today would call "moral," "political," "evaluative," or "existential" matters. My contention is that these issues – transformed to be sure – became *embedded in the conceptual structure* of the emerging science of sociology. At the time they were regarded as the province of philosophers and theologians, or they were locked up and obscured within one or other of the great nineteenth century ideologies of liberalism, conservatism, and socialism, where they could only be addressed in a highly one-sided manner. This historically "philosophical" character of sociology is not always obvious to us in the present period when both sociology and philosophy have become very specialized, fragmented, and methodologically technical as part of their increasing professionalization. To put the same point another way, in the nineteenth century the pioneering sociologists directed their energies toward accumulating social-scientific evidence that would help them to make sense of the bewildering and far-reaching social changes that were enveloping everyone, including themselves. But they did so in order also to contribute to an understanding of the feasibility of the plans and goals offered by the various political doctrines and parties of the time to solve the consequent social problems. The sometimes explicit but often implicit intention was to delineate the social conditions for and limits of reform programs and revolutionary manifestos that were phrased in the dominant philosophical-political language of the time: "freedom," "democracy," "equality," "tradition," "socialism," "emancipation," "individualism," and so on. A more comprehensive, inclusive and realistic assessment of these plans and hopes was only possible via sociology.

The case of Auguste Comte is instructive because here the serious, world-changing, evaluative, and, in a wider sense, "political" intent is made explicit. As is very well known, Comte believed that if sociology could be encouraged to achieve the positive stage of development of human knowledge, then it would embrace a form of nontheological, nonmetaphysical knowledge more appropriate to the emerging secular, industrial order in which the power of the church was diminishing. He conceived of positivism (a term that did not then possess the negative connotations it does now) as the fusion of two impulses, one deriving from philosophy and the other from science. On the one hand, there was Condorcet's emancipatory theory of progress that, however, blinded people to the achievements of the Middle Ages, which were dismissed out of hand as archaic. The writings of de Maistre, on the other hand, although inspired by a reactionary philosophy, provided the important and affirmative corrective about the earlier centuries that had been lost from view in the revolutionary ardor of the post-1789 period. Ambitiously, Comte saw sociology as providing a reconcilation between these two antagonistic influences:

> The reconciliation could only be accomplished in a region of speculation lying above both revolutionists and reactionists. Here it is that the philosophic root of positivism joins its scientific root, which alone could furnish inspiration capable of becoming universal[15].

It would be easy to dismiss Comte's formulation as naive. But the point is that we can see Comte here struggling with an important issue, but still having to do so in a cumbersome philosophical language: "speculation," "reconciliation," "becoming universal." With hindsight we can see his problem: it is how to put on to the sociological agenda social processes the effects of which exceed the scope and intentions of specific interest groups within the total social mesh. This may then imply a human unity beyond those perspectives – perhaps the emerging unity of humankind in general across the globe. He represents an early phase in the development of a *nonpartisan* (but not value-free) sociology that has as its heirs a whole tradition of inquiry cutting across national boundaries until the present day.

Many of the early pioneers as well as the sociologists of the "classical" age of sociology at the turn-of-the-century encountered problems connected with constructing a science of society in the works of influential and prestigious philosophers or learned them within the culture of philosophers. Many of them were trained in philosophy, and all of them were either inspired by, rebelled against, or, at the very least, were influenced by their teachers. And then, as now, they felt *compelled* to engage with the works of a group who constituted a higher ranking group of intellectuals than the one they aspired to join – the sociologists. This partly accounts for the energy and passion that they invested in settling their accounts with the philosophical tradition. To take, briefly, three examples, it can be seen that Hegel, Rickert, and Renouvier stood behind Marx, Weber, and Durkheim, providing the social scientists with certain problems – posed in a philosophical manner – which they then tried to solve in different ways and with varying degrees of success, *sociologically*. I will single out three from a whole range of issues involved in the work of these pairs of writers, in order to make the point: (*a*) the relationship between "being" and "consciousness" (Hegel/Marx); (*b*) the prescriptive force of subjective values in science (Rickert/Weber); and (*c*) the moral significance of the individual's sense of dependence on others (Renouvier/Durkheim)[16]. The sociologists' responses centered on (*a*) Marx' attempt at a sociological theory of knowledge in his base and superstructure model; (*b*) Weber's concepts of rationalization and the ethic of responsibility in political matters; and (*c*) Durkheim's analysis of individualism under conditions of organic solidarity. I cannot go into these questions in detail here. But the point to stress is that in all three cases, and in different ways, each of the three sociologists concluded that the problems were potentially more easily soluble if they made a *break* with philosophy. It was not a sharp break, and they were all burdened in various ways with traces of what they were trying to transcend, as we saw in the case of Comte. Their projects involved more of a transposing of the philosophically posed questions on to a higher level, consonant with the historical trend of sociology of which they were a part. The contemporary encounter between sociologists and philosophers in part recapitulates the substance and structure of the earlier interchanges but does so in a new guise, on new questions, reflecting among other things the changing nature of philosophy over this period. This change has been a shift toward technical problems, which reflects a change in the power ratio[17] of professional philosophers *vis-à-vis* scientific specialists, including sociologists, slightly more in favor of the latter groups.

In the light of the interpretation of the historical development of sociology outlined here, I will return in the next two sections to the impact of philosophical culture upon sociologists in the present period. In the course of these remarks some of the points established here will be expanded further.

3.4 Sociology and Philosophy Today

Returning to contemporary sociology, however, we find that, with few exceptions, sociologists are much less ambitious than their forbears and much more deferential toward philosophy. During the recent expansion of sociology, it was the sociologists, not the British philosophers, who mainly brought into intellectual debate in Britain the work of Continental philosophers such as Hegel, Nietzsche, Heidegger, Husserl, Merleau-Ponty, and Western Marxists, including the Frankfurt School. Many of the recognized authorities on the work of these philosophers are sociologists or teach on sociology courses. British sociological theory has become permeated with philosophical terminology and assumptions about the range of properly philosophical matters *vis-à-vis* sociological ones, derived from these traditions. These assumptions (as we will see in Figure 3.1) reinforced the already influential picture of the province of philosophy as "second-order" analysis claimed by the indigenous Oxford analytic tradition.

The result of this philosophical deluge has been that sociologists have come to accept as a matter of course a number of principles: (*a*) that sociology raises or presupposes philosophical problems; (*b*) that sociology makes truth claims and hence needs philosophy to sort them out; (*c*) that sociological controversies (particularly conceptual ones) are partly philosophical and therefore cannot be settled in any other way than philosophically; and (*d*) that sociologists must separately settle the philosophical foundations of their research prior to empirical enquiries commencing or continuing. Anthony Giddens goes so far as to create (or rather to resurrect from the 1930s) a distinction between sociological theory and "social theory," partly in order to leave the door open to philosophical issues, tacitly assumed, without any argument, *to be autonomous*. He writes:

> I use the term "social theory" to encompass issues that I hold to be the concern of all the social sciences. These issues are to do with the nature of human action and the acting self; with how interaction should be conceptualized and its relation to institutions; and with grasping the practical connotations of social analysis. ... "Social theory" involves the analysis of issues which spill over into philosophy, but it is not primarily a philosophical endeavour. The social sciences are lost if they are not directly related to philosophical problems by those who practise them (1984: xvii).

Many sociological works also contain the common disclaimer that there are irreducible philosophical questions that will perennially remain beyond the reach of sociology and apparently remaining unaffected by its findings. For example, Berger and Luckmann (1967: 13) write:

> The philosopher, of course, will raise questions about the ultimate status of both this "reality" and this "knowledge." *What is real? How is one to know?* These are among the most ancient questions not only of philosophical enquiry proper, but of human thought as such. ... We immediately disclaim any pretension to the effect that sociology has an answer to these ancient philosophical preoccupations.

In modestly excluding those "philosophical" questions from the purview of sociology, these authors are following a conventional division of labor between sociology and philosophy. This is one that, broadly speaking, allocates empirical inquiries to sociologists and a range of abstract reflections arising from that work to the philosophers. But notice that the respective responsibilities have been *defined by the philosophers*. Sociologists have acquiesced in this allocation in a taken-for-granted way, mostly out of deference toward the tradition of philosophy, when in fact the whole tenor of the sociological revolution in knowledge in the modern period (as we saw in the last section) points in the opposite direction – towards the supersession of philosophy as such and the reformulation for the problems once generated there on to a higher level by sociology.

Much contemporary discussion within sociology (and its parasociological satellites such as social theory and social philosophy) implicitly embodies the conventional division of labor in the assumptions made and categories employed. Below Figure 3.1 depicts the dichotomies that have been created by philosophers (from various traditions found within the culture of philosophers) in order to delineate, and thus *to legitimate*, the areas of competence of the two disciplines. As is characteristic of many philosophical distinctions, the oppositions are formalistic:

For the most part the accuracy and legitimacy of these oppositions has been unquestioned and unchallenged[22]. But a few remarks are in order in this direction, within the limited scope of this chapter.

	Sociology		*Philosophy*	
1. Neo-Kantians	historical inquiry empirical study facts	↔ ↔ ↔	systematic inquiry transcendental (nonempirical) reflection values	[18]
2. Logical empiricists	context of discovery empirical matters genesis	↔ ↔ ↔	context of justification cognitive issues validity	[19]
3. Analytic school	"first-order" questions descriptive (Is) factual	↔ ↔ ↔	"second-order" questions normative (Ought) conceptual	[20]
4. Phenomenologists and existentialists	concrete historical expressions historical-causal hypotheses ontical inquiry (entities)	↔ ↔ ↔	universal subjective structures *apriori* presuppositions ontological inquiry (being)	[21]

Figure 3.1 Philosophers' Stipulations of Disciplinary Fields

1. One can see how these pairings represent a typically philosophical viewpoint on the nature of sociology and human societies. Common to each grouping of oppositions is that the focus of philosophy is always to be on what is regarded as timeless, static, unchanging, transcendental, perhaps eternal. This is true even in the apparently purely technical conception of philosophy in the analytic school as reflection upon a range of mainly conceptual questions arising from the work of the sciences, including sociology. As Becker (1977) points out, conceptual (i.e., nonempirical questions) exist in mathematics, but what distinguishes these from philosophical ones is that the latter are essentially "open," and thus not usually capable of resolution. In other words, this range of questions is bound, therefore, to be *continuously* available for scrutiny, thus providing philosophers with a perennial rationale. He writes:

> The fact that a question is not finally resolvable does not mean that attempts to answer it are pointless. Progress on such questions amounts to increased sophistication rather than the achievement of solutions. Solutions are approached as limits (1977: 250).

I think that this location of a unity of outlook within the segments of philosophical culture entitles us to say that philosophy constitutes a "style of thought" in the sense developed by Karl Mannheim (1929/1968: 276; 1969: 76–77).

2. Within the terms of the oppositions, if it is possible to show that in societies (considered dynamically, developmentally, and in the longer term) and/or in ongoing research practice that there exists considerable interpenetration of the respective sides of these pairings, then some interesting consequences follow. Significant interplay between them would suggest that their mutually exclusive status as definitive of autonomous areas of disciplinary competence is not so much based in reality as in the analytical fiat of the profession of philosophers. This evidence could shed new light on the issue of the autonomy of "philosophical" questions in relation to sociology.

Much more research needs to be done on the applicability and usefulness of these oppositions, and I cannot take the matter very far here. But two examples might be interesting and indicate how different the problem looks from the sociological point of view. (*a*) The empirically based procedures of sociology can redefine the scope and limits of philosophers' statements (say about the centrality of the individual knowing subject for epistemology) with reference to historical evidence about the origins of the concept in the self-experience of people (particularly aristocratic and bourgeois intellectuals) during specific phases of the development of Western societies (see Elias, 1978, 1982). This wider relocation of the problem affects the nature of the epistemological problem as originally posed by the philosophers. In this way we can demonstrate how "genesis" affects "validity," provided we proceed with a wider and more differentiated picture of the nature of human knowledge to include a range of knowing beyond the simpler, formal, logical types that made the "genetic fallacy" argument plausible. (*b*) I think it is also possible to transcribe what are usually called ethical issues or ought questions into sociological terms. Here, too, one makes an empirical, sociological detour in order to redefine, for example, an assertion about the open possibilities of human "freedom" as perhaps implying an untenable romantic suggestion that people can live without any degree of social constraint and self-restraint when all the evidence from a range of societies points to the contrary. Having located the partiality of the contention and its presuppositions, one is able to return to the problem as posed, but in a new form[23].

3.5 Conclusion: Philosophy As a Culture of Defense

Let us draw together the strands of the preceding sections. I have been arguing that the tendency of the sociological revolution in knowledge in the modern period has been toward the supersession (transcendence) of philosophy by sociology. With the rise of the social sciences, particularly sociology, philosophy was no longer the discipline competent to study and explain the social processes that became known as "society." Step by step, over a long period of time, the epistemological and ethical deliberations of philosophy became taken over on a new level by sociology[24]. The epistemological issues became the province of the *sociology of knowledge* and the questions raised by philosophy under the heading of wisdom, that is, matters concerning the good life, human happiness and fulfillment, democracy, freedom, morality, and so on, were transformed into the wider enterprise of *social diagnosis* from a sociological point of view. It is only our experience of the highly technical disciplines of sociology and philosophy in contemporary times that blinds us to the broader and more profound character that sociology historically possesses. The trend of philosophy has been that it has become more and more technical, concentrating on questions of method increasingly, and less and less preoccupied with the grander questions about human happiness and fulfillment. The philosophers have become historically gradually further and further defunctionalized, retreating into conceptual work, clarification, logic, and such technicalities as the hallmark of the profession in the age of the social sciences. Instead of viewing their relationship to philosophy from a historical and, above all, sociological point of view, the sociologists in contemporary times, through deference to the profession of philosophers to whose prestige they aspire, have acquiesced in the philosophers' definitions, as I showed earlier (Figure 3.1).

It is only through acceptance of the philosophers' stipulations as to the respective areas of competence of the two disciplines that sociologists have come to accept as a matter of course that there are "philosophical" problems in the social sciences and in sociology in particular. Whereas, the historical tendency of sociological inquiry points in the opposite direction: It suggests – to invert the customary formulation – that there are sociological problems in philosophy. It also suggests that there are sociological problems *for* philosophy, because once the radical nature of the sociological revolution is understood, the philosophers' claims to disciplinary autonomy emerge as questionable, if not perilous.

One must not imagine that the break with philosophy to which I have referred was a sharp, clean, or sudden one. I am rather talking about a long-term process – yet to be fully consummated – through which sociology has taken on board and transformed the concerns of philosophy, which are preserved within it in a reformulated state, both on the level of epistemology and ethics. Underlying this synthetic trend are extratheoretical processes of group conflict through which sociological and philosophical specialists have struggled for the autonomy of interpretation and diagnosis of the structure and tendency of the overall social process. The work of sociologists – as we saw with Comte earlier – often bears the marks of the philosophical forms of expression that they are struggling to transcend. This is clear, for example, in the writings of Marx[25]. He tries to utilize the category of practice in order to transcend the traditional dualistic epistemology of the rationalists and empiricists who preceded him. For Marx, in the *Theses on Feuerbach*, there is no point in reducing cognition to either of its material or ideal poles because both sides are, and always have been, in an active relation in human practical activity. But Marx is unable to sustain this drive away from ontological reductionism, since the older dualisms of traditional metaphysics reemerge in his attempt at a sociological theory of knowledge. The theory of base and superstructure or the determination of social consciousness by "social being" Marx (1859/1973: 181) falls back into the old static dualism, implicitly assuming that the reified economic base and the superstructure of ideology are two separate entities[26].

Comparable tensions and ambiguities can be detected in the work of Durkheim. As is well-known, Durkheim attempted, in *The Elementary Forms of the Religious Life*, among other things, to develop a sociological theory of knowledge that related collective representations to the structure of group life. His ambition (described as "vaunting ambition" by the philosopher Steven Lukes [1974: 446]) was to resolve the old philosophical debate between *apriorism* and empiricism in a sociological manner. He was able to account for the origins of the collective and constraining Kantian categories that he felt the philosophers had left vague. At the same time he satisfied the scientific aspirations of sociology by proceeding empirically, but without the individualistic implications of traditional empiricism (Durkheim 1915/1969: 19). But the new theory is in effect a static sociological version of the two equally static philosophical doctrines that he was trying to transcend. He has begun to make the sociological transition but his thinking still possesses a fundamentally philosophical cast from which he has been unable to free himself. He therefore laid himself wide open to the subsequent Kantian objection made by Charles E. Gehlke and later Lukes (1974: 447–448)[27] that he had confused the social causation of the specific categories with the *faculty or capacity* to think spatially, temporally, or whatever, which was already presupposed and *apriori*.

If my general assessment of the historical supersession of philosophy by sociology is correct, then how are we to explain the continued existence of the discipline and the continued acceptance within sociology of the autonomy of philosophical questions? The answer to this question is *not* that there are academic Departments of Eternal Verities in universities *because* there are eternal verities in the human condition perennially available for reflection (*philosophical* version). Rather, the answer lies in the dynamics of the status- and power-differentials between the sociological and philosophical academic establishments (*sociological* version). Viewed in the longer term, philosophy has been the higher ranking and relatively more powerful discipline. (Though the power ratio has been subject to fluctuations either way, relative to other scientific and political establishments across society as a whole.) It has tended, therefore, to impose its categories and models of thinking on to the lower ranking disciplines, for example, sociology[28]. As I showed earlier, sociologists have come to accept what emerges under scrutiny as a dubious set of oppositions created by philosophers that demarcate the subject matter of the two disciplines, but that merge and blur on examination. (For reasons of space I was only briefly able to mention two – genesis/validity and descriptive/normative – and point out the similar structure of thinking underlying them all. But a more detailed case could be made out for interplay between each of the other dualisms.)

These dichotomies legitimize a division of labor between the two disciplines and form part of a culture of professional closure to protect the peculiarity and specificity of the area of expertise claimed by the philosophical establishment, which has been increasingly under threat by the rise of the social sciences and sociology in particular. Philosophy is, however, by no means a monolithic discipline, and there is little consensus within it as to its aims and scope. Its purely verbal character makes it vulnerable to the charge that its statements in general are uncheckable and arbitrary, depending for their plausibility only on the social prestige, and hence credibility, of philosophers as a profession. As outsiders, we are also reliant solely upon this status for accepting the proposition that there are autonomous philosophical questions at all. As will be obvious from my remarks so far, I do not think that this can be taken for granted. Though I have no doubt at all of the integrity and sincerity of philosophers in pursuing their inquiries, which for them have the highest value and most profound import.

In addition to Figure 3.1 of disciplinary responsibilities that I assembled earlier, the philosophers' culture has also generated a range of specific self-definitions of the scope of philosophy that are closely related to the right-hand side of the figure and that, to some extent, overlap with it. In briefly discussing some of these self-definitions, my strategy will be the same as before: to undermine the plausibility of these justifications of the philosophical enterprise in such a way as to reveal the anatomy of the academic philosophical establishment underlying them, for which they provide a culture of defense. (My exposition will have to be a brief one for reasons of space, so I cannot do full justice to all the ramifications of the definitions and arguments presented nor to the fullness of the traditions from which they derive.)

1. There is a cluster of conceptions of the subject matter of philosophy that centers on the hallmark of *technique*. These regard the central subject matter of philosophy to be either logic, method (sometimes referred to merely as an activity), or conceptual clarification. These ideas derive from the influential analytic and linguistic schools of philosophy associated with Bertrand Russell, G. E. Moore, and Ludwig Wittgenstein and their later followers. The conception of philosophy as "second-order" theorizing is also associated with this tendency[29]. Logic is the study of inference and its rules and is a discipline dealing with pure relations between symbols. It is closely related to mathematics and some of its component parts are widely regarded as being part of mathematics (e. g., set theory). It is not, therefore, a very strong argument to equate philosophy with logic since it is an independent discipline. Such a move simply cedes the autonomy of philosophy rather than establishing it. Nor is regarding philosophy as a method or an activity to provide the discipline with an indubitably irreducible subject matter, except in a trivial or circular sense. Philosophers sometimes say, following this view, that philosophy is a way of looking at things or perhaps a "puzzle-solving" activity. The problem here, though, is that puzzles come in many guises and occur in many fields and human activities and are solved, concretely, in given cases. Astronomical puzzles are solved by astronomers, chemical ones by chemists, sociological ones by sociologists, and so on. In many cases, philosophers would be unqualified to solve some puzzles, though they might be able to solve others. It is not a strong claim to disciplinary autonomy to say that philosophy is a generalized sense of puzzlement about anything puzzling within the competence of the philosopher. This view is perilously close to the empty circularity that philosophy is what philosophers do, so what they do must be philosophy.

The self-definition of philosophy as conceptual analysis presents an image of philosophers as conceptual trouble-shooters, arriving on the doorstep of the sciences, including sociology, with a conceptual tool-kit ready to tune up their theories. Parasitic upon sociology, philosophers provide a rigorous, conceptual expertise in the interest of clarification. As one sociologist sympathetic with this conception recently expressed it:

> Philosophy of science can help us here. It cannot do the job for us; it isn't the philosopher's stone so long sought by sociologists. But it can help us to clarify quite what is involved in empirical inquiry, and what limits must be imposed upon the claims that we make. In offering us a kind of map, a framework within which to conceptualize our activities, it can guide us, though no more than that, to the places at which we must forge new connections (Tudor, 1982: 182).

The thrust of this chapter is to argue against the viewpoint expressed here. Sociology is an empirical discipline and as such has both a theoretical and an empirical level that are interrelated. The theoretical side is composed of concepts and of course in this area sociologists have to be rigorous, systematic, concise, and clear in their formulations. But there is no reason why sociologists cannot learn these skills and, indeed, many already possess them. The philosophers might also be so skilled and, indeed, this is their *raison d'être* in many cases, but as far as sociology is concerned, conceptual clarity is part of sociological theory. A separate profession of conceptual clarifiers is redundant[30]. Moreover, one deleterious consequence of the kind of philosophers' advice mentioned in the previous quotation is that it could lead to the surreptitious imposition on to sociological research of rigid, static philosophical categories and modes of thinking that could block the development of new insights. Furthermore, the schools of philosophy I have been invoking here have been famous, in opposition to all forms of metaphysics, for advocating that philosophy should tackle small, modest, and manageable topics in a piecemeal fashion. This circumspect attitude has probably already percolated into sociology, producing a constraining effect on the ambitions of sociologists, deflecting them into a cautious choice of narrower questions and problem areas.

2. Many philosophers have described their field as inquiries of a *transcendental* (nonempirical) kind. This program derives mainly from influential Kantian tradition, though variations of the same idea are found in phenomenology and in inquiries into "fundamental ontology." (The oppositions listed under group four in Figure 3.1 exemplify the distinction between empirical and transcendental inquiry applied to cognition and ontology[31].) In Kant, what was transcendental was the logical apparatus of concepts and principles common to all rational minds (the categories of the Understanding). In the "new *apriorism*" of recent philosophers such as Karl-Otto Apel and Jürgen Habermas, the scope of transcendental inquiry has shifted away from "consciousness as such" toward the transcendental importance of language and language communities[32]. But the structure of this mode of thinking remains the same: Transcendental inquiry is said to be an autonomous level of reflection that seeks out the "conditions of existence" (variously also referred to as "presuppositions," "preconditions," or "that which makes possible ... X or Y") of society, the sciences, particularly the human sciences, and human speech acts as part of communication. It is in this area of investigation that many philosophers have staked their claim to autonomy.

The most well-known contemporary product of transcendental inquiry that has been taken up by sociologists is the notion of the "ideal speech situation" postulated by Habermas. Built into all individual speech acts, he says, is the assumption that one can be understood by potential interlocutors who are equal partners in the discourse. This is a transcendental presupposition for all communication (Habermas, 1970). In a similar fashion, Apel (1980: 280) claims that the *real* communication community that has developed socially and historically presupposes an *ideal* communication community in which people are capable of adequately understanding each other's arguments and judging their truth. For Apel, an ideal "unlimited community of interpretation" (1980: 123) is a transcendental presupposition of all discussion. Apel then makes dependent upon the plausibility of "regulative principles" derived from these assertions a whole range of moral and political principles and commitments (1980: 282)[33].

But my feeling is that if one sows these intellectual seeds one has planted a very low yield crop. What does the inquiry produce, when boiled down to its essentials? It produces highly abstract transcendental generalizations that are of little cognitive value. It would be tempting to dismiss Habermas' and Apel's work on the ideal speech community as a high-flown way of expressing the banality that when people speak to each other they expect they will be understood. But, taking transcendental inquiry of this type seriously, it is surely legitimate to ask what is the significance and cognitive pay-off of the abstract propositions about the conditions of existence of speech acts. Does not this kind of inquiry produce only empty abstractions?

3. Philosophers often absolutize their activity by claiming that what they are doing – philosophy – is just the contemporary continuation of what is a *permanent feature* of the relationship between man and the world. This condition continually reproduces human wonderment and hence the characteristic philosophical problems of the ages: to do with knowledge, reality, and the good[34]. (The insistence on the *permanence* of philosophical problems and hence the perennial renewal of the subject is itself a defensive posture, a reaction in the modern period to the rise of sociology and the challenge of historicism.) Accepting a phenomenological version of this conception of philosophy, Maurice Merleau-Ponty was able to make sociology and philosophy compatible by regarding them as different modes of knowing both fundamentally based in intersubjective lived experience:

> Philosophy is thus not defined by a particular domain of its own: all it speaks of, just like sociology, is the world, men and the mind. What distinguishes it rather is a certain *mode* of the awareness that we have of others, nature or ourselves: ... We not only have to say that philosophy is compatible with sociology, we have also to say that it is necessary for it, as a constant recall to its tasks, and that each time that the sociologist comes back to the living sources of his science, to what it is that operates in him as the means of understanding even the most distant cultural formations, then he is spontaneously already engaged in philosophy. ... Philosophy is not a particular science, it is the vigilance that does not let us forget the source of all science (1960/1978: 157).

It follows for Merleau-Ponty (1960/1978: 146) that: "The sociologist begins to do philosophy to the extent that he takes it on himself no simply to note down facts, but rather to understand them." This is because in "understanding" he or she must automatically exemplify the fundamental intersubjective commonality of all human beings: and this is a universal presupposition of all inquiry that philosophy as a discipline merely expresses.

All the self-definitions discussed in this subsection are variants on the theme of philosophy as autonomous because it expresses an ineliminable human level of experience of nature and other people. It produces the peculiar circularity that when people are wondering or understanding they are doing philosophy and doing philosophy is to wonder and to understand. It is also a viewpoint that enables the philosophers to take their place alongside the sciences, even though their object of inquiry (this is true also of the ideal communication community mentioned earlier) is entirely of their own creation. Finally, this conception of philosophy also inspires a common philosophical rejoinder to venturesome sociologists and others who have proclaimed "the end of philosophy[35];" and it is one that will also be levelled at this chapter. It is that the sociologist or critic has produced a philosophical refutation of philosophy. That, in the very act of trying to eliminate philosophy one has exemplified precisely what one is attempting to move beyond. (This is a species of transcendental argument.) But on examination one can see that this rejoinder carries little weight. It is an ingenious artifice of reasoning that depends for its effect on a cleverly expressed paradox. Moreover, it does not prove anything at all, relying as it does on an irrefutable assertion of the immanence of philosophizing in the human condition as such. The function of the argument, however, is clear: It provides a weapon of the last resort with which the philosophical establishment can defend itself against any attack whatsoever.

Notes

[1] It has been pointed out that Parsons' four primary subdivisions of the cultural system (cognitive, moral-evaluative, expressive, symbolic) follow the actual order of listing of items contained in Edward Tylor's often-cited anthropologist's definition of culture of 1891, though rephrased (see Schneider, 1973: 120). Parsons was also alert to the nature of modern philosophy. For him it is a belief-system combining "nonempirical" reference and "existential" significance or relevance to the system of action. For belief-systems of this kind that are below a certain level of explicitness and logical articulation Parsons reserved the term "proto-philosophy" (Parsons, 1951: 331, 359ff.).

[2] Lawrence C. Becker (1977: 251) defends a definition of philosophy that contains this idea that philosophy is an activity: "The nature of philosophy as an ongoing enterprise – as a way of life rather than a set of doctrines – is also suggested by the definition. Its ultimate allegiances appear clearly as discursive truth reached by reasoned argument, and its character as a way of life (it follows) must be disciplined, intellectual, and comprised of conduct consistent with what is known by reason." This conception of philosophy is satirized by Hankinson (1985).

[3] The transcendental character of much European philosophy in modern times is perceptively discussed by Hartmann (1966).

[4] This straightforward fact is expressed with characteristic philosophical obscurity by Roy Bhaskar (1979: 64): "The syncategorematic (or, as it were, only proxy-referential) character of the nevertheless irreducible discourse of philosophy ... has to be contrasted with the directly referential character of social scientific discourse." I am aware of the "constructivist" tendency in the sociology of scientific knowledge in recent years, which has swung the explanatory emphasis on to the artefactual or constructed nature of scientific objects as decisive in the development of scientific knowledge. This move virtually eliminates the controlling effect of the structure of the object itself upon scientific concepts upon which my argument about sociology's autonomy in the text relies. A few remarks on this approach are therefore necessary.

The program has been inspired by phenomenology, ethnomethodology, Kantianism, and by the philosophical thesis of the underdetermination of theory by evidence derived from Willard Quine, Pièrre Duhem, and Jules Poincaré. For the constructivist school, the objects of science are "cultural objects" constantly created and recreated by scientists discursively in their ongoing activity, providing a means by which objects in the world can be recognized as such. Consistent with its latent Kantianism, this conception of science tacitly assumes that the structured levels of the real world are structure*less*. The conceptual constructions of science are simply part of discourses that are constitutive of social life and that enable us to orient ourselves. Karin D. Knorr-Cetina (1983: 136) says that her constructivist epistemology "conceives of *the order generated by science* as a (material) process of embodiment and incorporation of objects in our language and practices" (my emphasis). In the short run, and particularly in regard to the institutional complexity of modern scientific specialisms and the highly technical character of many branches of physics and biology, the apparently entirely esoteric, self-referential, and constructed character of scientific objects in general can seem self-evident. This view will be reinforced if one restricts one's field of enquiry, as do many exponents of this approach, to the here-and-now situation of one laboratory or one short episode in the history of a particular science. As relatively autonomous human knowledge, scientific knowledge indeed has a cultural character in relation to its original producers, but its nature is not arbitrary, being determined to no inconsiderable degree by the structure of its object to which, in the longer run, it may tend to become more adequate. It is this dimension that helps us to distinguish scientific from other forms of discourse. Moreover, had scientific knowledge not become highly adequate to the nature of its object, in many fields, it would be difficult to explain how it has been possible to control natural events and processes for human purposes through its utilization.

[5] Quoted by Steven Lukes (1974: 61).

[6] I have explored the issue of Kantianism in sociology at length in Kilminster (1983).

[7] I have shown the deleterious results of the philosophical style of analysis in more detail when reviewing a collection of philosophical papers (Ball and Farr, 1984) about Marx' contribution to sociology (Kilminster, 1985: 628–630).

[8] From "La sociologie" (1898), in Clark (1969: 73–74).

[9] From a debate between Tarde and Durkheim in 1904, in Clark (1969: 137).

[10] The sociological account of the origins of sociology in the text follows a number of standard accounts but draws especially on research by Elias (1962: 51–53). A longer version appears as "On the sociogenesis of Sociology," *Sociologisch Tijdschrift*, 1984, 11 (1).

[11] From "La sociologie," in Clark (1969: 75).

[12] Marx (1857–1858/1973: 161). The compatibility of the views of Marx and Durkheim about the inherent sociality of individuals, against the assumption of isolated individuals made by contract theories of society, is noted also by Frisby and Sayer (1986: 92ff.)

[13] Note for example the following statement by Marx (1845/1968: 41): "By social we understand the co-operation of several individuals, no matter under what conditions, in what manner and to what end. It follows from this that a certain mode of production, or industrial stage, is always combined with a certain mode of co-operation, or social stage, and this mode of co-operation is itself a productive force."

[14] Quoted in Evans (1951: 9).

[15] From Comte's *Système de politique positive* (1848–1854), quoted in Thompson (1976: 11–12).

[16] I realize that the social scientists were simultaneously fighting battles on other fronts, both theoretical and political, and that, unlike Marx, Durkheim, and Weber worked in university institutions in conditions very different from those of the exiled Marx living in London and supporting himself through journalism. Clearly too the development of Marx' ideas into forms of Marxism was presupposed as a critical point of departure for Weber and Durkheim. But for the sake of argument in the text I have pulled out the philosophical strand from this complex development for scrutiny.

[17] This concept is taken from Elias' (1987:117)"The Fishermen in the Maelstrom."

[18] These pairs of Kantian concepts underlie, for example, the critiques of Karl Mannheim's sociology of knowledge in the early 1930s by the philosophers Ernst Grünwald and Alexander von Schelting: see Grünwald's papers (1970) and von Schelting's (1936) review of *Ideology and Utopia.*

[19] The influence of the Logical Empiricists on the sociology of science is explained by Dolby (1972).

[20] See the "Introduction" to Benton (1977) and Becker (1977).

[21] These oppositions have been developed by transcendental philosophers of various schools. See, for example, Schutz and Luckmann (1974: 262, 289, 304, 311, 326); Luckmann (1983: 22ff.); and Heidegger (1927/1973: 31ff.).

[22] Some exceptions are: Benton (1977: 4ff.) on the factual/conceptual and "first-"/"second-"order distinctions; Mannheim (1929/1968: 262ff.) on genesis/validity; and Elias (1982: 32) on the historical/systematic distinction.

[23] While a new and more inclusive sociological framework is still in the course of development, one is inevitably constrained to some extent by the language of the older ways of posing the epistemological, ethical, and existential questions. (As were Marx, Comte, and others of the nineteenth century pioneers, to an even greater degree, as we saw in the text.) So at this stage, in attempting to move beyond the conventional division of labor between sociology and philosophy and its attendant assumptions and terminology, one is therefore operating at the edge of both intelligibility and credibility. The inquiry courts the common accusation of failing to engage with the philosophical questions in the manner in which they have actually been posed. This objection, however, comes from the more dominant philosophers' standpoint, and its cognitive power cannot be taken for granted. In fact, after a sociological reframing of the problem one returns to the issue better armed for seeing the partiality of the philosophical formulation as it is absorbed into a wider explanatory framework. The exclusively philosophical mode of elaboration then becomes simply untenable. However, this provokes anxiety in those for whom an important part of their identity is dependent upon the security of a philosophical way of thinking and acting that they sense is threatened by these sociological moves. The issue of the "nonengagement of the question" is just as much an emotional as a conceptual one.

[24] I have given – for reasons of compression – less attention in this chapter to the fate of the philosophies of existence and "fundamental ontology" of the twentieth century in the light of the rise of sociology within the processes outlined. Briefly, however, I think that fundamental ontology in the field of society (e.g., in the works of Heidegger) constitutes a blurred way of talking about the routine subject matter of the sociological tradition: the "social" as a structured range of impersonal social regularities *sui generis*. The furthest point possible within fundamental ontology is the vaguest statement that the "mode of being" of humankind is always being-with-others, or a similar hyphenated formulation, that tries to capture social realities in a nonindividualistic manner (Kilminster, 1988).

[25] I have explored the tensions in Marx' thought at much greater length in Kilminster (1979: part one; 1982a).

[26] The dualistic nature of Marx' theory of base and superstructure was pointed out long ago by Karl Mannheim (1972: 142–144, 162–163); and more recently by Heideggerians – see Axelos (1976: 145ff.).

[27] Gehlke's critique was in his book (1915).

[28] There have been some periods in the development of advanced societies when an institutionally strong discipline of sociology in a particular country has achieved a sufficiently high prestige ranking, relative to others, to enable certain philosophers to shelter under *its* wing. Julien Freund (1978: 184) cites – with disapproval – the case of the Frankfurt School in exile in the United States in the 1940s as an example: "Even if this school contributed to the progress of sociological research, especially during its American period (that is, in exile), it still misled scientific sociology into an impasse. Its members took advantage of sociology's prestige to put across a primarily philosophical message." It has been asked of the argument, at this point, what would happen if sociology were to become more powerful than philosophy – would it not then defend itself with instruments of power? Perhaps against its better judgment? I think that this objection looks forward to a hypothetical situation, the advent of which is not in any case in the hands of the sociologists alone, no matter how hard they may fight their battle for autonomy from philosophy. The fate of sociology depends in specific cases upon the outcome of a whole network of competing power groups – scientific, political, philosophical, both national and international. Moreover, nowhere is power ineliminable in the relations between groups,

including that between sociologists and philosophers. The sociologists cannot choose whether or not to exercise it, as the objection implies. The issue now becomes what will be their power chances, and will they be able to take good advantage of them?

29 The distinction between "first-" and "second-order" questions is also found, in a slightly different form, in the work of Alfred Schutz.

30 On the tendency of imperialism by 'tool-providing' fields in the sciences, see Ravetz (1973: 88ff.).

31 As Klaus Hartmann (1966:224) points out, on the European continent a large number of philosophers and schools from Fichte, Hegel, Husserl, to Heidegger, Sartre and hermeneutic philosophy, come under the scope of "transcendental" philosophy, broadly conceived.

32 The work of Roy Bhaskar (1979: 6) on the realist theory of science also exemplifies this transcendental tendency. He writes: "If philosophy is to be possible ... then it must follow the Kantian road."

33 There is an extended critique of the contradictory consequences of Apel's transcendental philosophizing when embodied in speculations about the conditions for the realization of utopian societies in Kilminster (1982b).

34 This common picture of philosophy as immanent in the human condition has been painted by many philosophers. A typical account can be found in Nathan Rotenstreich (1972: 183–185).

35 The philosopher A.R. Manser (1973: 13) is fascinated by this issue. He finds parallels between Marx and Wittgenstein who both, in their different ways, declared the dissolution of philosophy. But instead of moving in the beckoning sociological direction from this comparison, he falls back on the stock philosophers' device: "The two programmes for the end of philosophy thus themselves give rise to a further philosophical problem, that of deciding between them."

References

Abrams, Philip et al. (Eds.) (1981). *Practice and Progress: British Sociology 1950–1980*. London: George Allen & Unwin.

Apel, Karl-Otto (1980). *Towards a Transformation of Philosophy*. London: Routledge & Kegan Paul.

Axelos, Kostas (1976). *Alienation, Praxis and Techne in the Thought of Karl Marx*. Austin/London: University of Texas Press.

Ball, Terence and Farr, James (Eds.) (1984). *After Marx*. Cambridge: Cambridge University Press.

Becker, Lawrence C. (1977). "A Definition of Philosophy." *Metaphilosophy* 8 (2/3): 249–252.

Benton, Ted (1977). *Philosophical Foundations of the Three Sociologies*. London: Routledge & Kegan Paul.

Berger, Peter L. and Luckmann, Thomas (1967). *The Social Construction of Reality*. London: Allen Lane.

Bhaskar, Roy (1979). *The Possibility of Naturalism: A Philosophical Critique of the Contemporary Human Sciences*. Brighton: The Harvester Press.

Clark, Terry N. (Ed.) (1969). *Gabriel Tarde: On Communication and Social Influence: Selected Papers*. Chicago and London: The University of Chicago Press.

Cohen, Jerry M. (1972). "Philosophy in the Academy." *Radical Philosophy*, Summer: 7–9.

Dolby, R.G.A. (1972). "The Sociology of Knowledge in Natural Science." In *Sociology of Science*, ed. Barry Barnes. London: Penguin Books.
Durkheim, Émile (1915/1969). *Elementary Forms of the Religious Life*. London: George Allen & Unwin.
Elias, Norbert (1962). "The Break with Traditionalism and the Origins of Sociology." *Transactions of the Fifth World Congress of Sociology*. Washington, D.C., Vol. III, Louvain: International Sociological Association.
Elias, Norbert (1978/1982). *The Civilizing Process*, 2 Vols. Oxford: Basil Blackwell.
Elias, Norbert (1982). "Scientific Establishments." In *Scientific Establishments and Hierarchies*, ed. Nobert Elias, Herminio Martins, and Richard Whitley. Dordrecht: D. Reidel.
Elias, Norbert (1987). "The Fishermen in the Maelstrom." In ders. *Involvement and Detachment*. Oxford: Basil Blackwell.
Evans, David (1951). *Social Romanticism in France 1830–48*. Oxford: Oxford University Press.
Freund, Julien (1978). "German Sociology in the Time of Max Weber." In *A History of Sociological Analysis*, ed. Tom Bottomore and Robert Nisbet. London: Heinemann.
Frisby, David and Sayer, Derek (1986). *Society*. London: Tavistock Publications.
Gehlke, Charles E. (1915). *Émile Durkheim's Contributions to Sociological Theory*. New York: Columbia University Press.
Giddens, Anthony (1984). *The Constitution of Society*. Cambridge: Polity Press.
Grünewald, Ernst (1970). "The Sociology of Knowledge and Epistemology" and "Systematic Analyses." In *The Sociology of Knowledge: A Reader*, ed. James E. Curtis and John W. Petras. London: Duckworth.
Habermas, Jürgen (1970). "On Systematically Distorted Communication." *Inquiry* 13: 205–218.
Hankinson, Jim (1985). *Bluff Your Way in Philosophy*. London: The Bluffers Guides.
Hartmann, Klaus (1966). "On Taking the Transcendental Turn." *Review of Metaphysics* 20 (2): 223–249.
Heidegger, Martin (1927/1973). *Being and Time*. Oxford: Basil Blackwell.
Kilminster, Richard (1979). *Praxis and Method*. London: Routledge & Kegan Paul.
Kilminster, Richard (1982a). "Theory and Practice in Marx and Marxism." In *Marx and Marxisms*, ed. G.H.R. Parkinson. Cambridge: Cambridge University Press.
Kilminster, Richard (1982b). "Zur Utopiediskussion aus soziologischer Sicht." In *Utopieforschung: Interdisziplinäre Studien zur neuzeitlichen Utopie*, Vol. 1, ed. Wilhelm Vosskamp. Stuttgart: J.B. Metzler.
Kilminster, Richard (1983). "From the Standpoint of Eternity." *Theory, Culture & Society* 2 (1): 118–133.
Kilminster, Richard (1985). "Review of Ball and Farr." *Sociology* 19 (4): 628–630.
Kilminster, Richard (1988). "The Sociology of Philosophy: Extended Review of Susan Hekman, *Hermeneutics and the Sociology of Knowledge*." *Contemporary Sociology 17 (3): 377–380.*
Knorr-Cetina, Karin D. (1983). "Towards a Constructivist Interpretation of Science." In *Science Observed: Perspectives on the Social Study of Science*, ed. Karin D. Knorr-Cetina and Michael Mulkay. London: Sage Publications.
Luckmann, Thomas (1983). *Life World and Social Realities*. London: Heinemann.

Lukes, Steven (1974). *Émile Durkheim: His Life and Work*. Harmondsworth: Penguin Books.
McMullin, Ernan (1970). "The History and Philosophy of Science." *Minnesota Studies in the Philosophy of Science*, Vol. V. Minneapolis: Minnesota University Press.
Mannheim, Karl (1929/1968). *Ideology and Utopia*. London: Routledge & Kegan Paul.
Mannheim, Karl (1969). *Essays on Sociology and Social Psychology*. London: Routledge & Kegan Paul.
Mannheim, Karl (1972). *Essays on the Sociology of Knowledge*. London: Routledge & Kegan Paul.
Manser, A. R. (1973). "The End of Philosophy: Marx and Wittgenstein." Inaugural Lecture. University of Southampton.
Marx, Karl (1845/1968). *The German Ideology*. London: Lawrence & Wishart.
Marx, Karl (1857–1858/1973). *Grundrisse: Foundations of the Critique of Political Economy*. Harmondsworth: Penguin Books.
Marx, Karl (1859/1973). "Preface to a Contribution to the Critique of Political Economy." In *Karl Marx and Friedrich Engels, Selected Works in One Volume*. London: Lawrence & Wishart.
Merleau-Ponty, Maurice (1960/1978). "The Philosopher and Sociology." In *Phenomenology and Sociology*, ed. Thomas Luckmann. Harmondsworth: Penguin Books.
Nizan, Paul (1971). *The Watchdogs: Philosophers and the Established Order*. New York/London: Monthly Review Press.
Parsons, Talcott (1951). *The Social System*. New York: The Free Press of Glencoe.
Ravetz, Jerome (1973). *Scientific Knowledge and Its Social Problems*. Harmondsworth: Penguin Books.
Rotenstreich, Nathan (1972). *Philosophy: The Concept and Its Manifestations*. Dordrecht: D. Reidel.
von Schelting, Alexander (1936). "Review of *Ideology and Utopia*." *American Sociological Review* 1 (4): 664–674.
Schneider, Louis (1973). "The Idea of Culture in the Social Sciences: Critical and Supplementary Observations." In *The Idea of Culture in the Social Sciences*, ed. Louis Schneider and Charles M. Bonjean. Cambridge: Cambridge University Press.
Schutz, Alfred and Luckmann, Thomas (1974). *The Structures of the Life World*. London: Heinemann.
Thompson, Kenneth (1976). *Auguste Comte: The Foundation of Sociology*. London: Thomas Nelson.
Tudor, Andrew (1982). *Beyond Empiricism: Philosophy of Science in Sociology*. London: Routledge & Kegan Paul.
Williams, Raymond (1976). *Keywords: A Vocabulary of Culture and Society*. London: Fontana/Croom Helm.

4 Legislators and Interpreters: Culture as Ideology of Intellectuals

Zygmunt Bauman

Antonio Gramsci (1957) reserved the marker, "organic," for those intellectuals who articulated the world view, interests, intentions, and historically determined potential of a particular class; who elaborated the values needed to be promoted for such a potential fo be fully developed; and who legitimized the historical role of a given class, its claim to power, and to the management of social process in terms of those values.

Ideologies were the product of such articulation, elaboration, and legitimation. Their production, discursive defense, and dissemination were the work of organic intellectuals: the activity that simultaneously defined the specifically intellectual praxis and the function played by the intellectuals in the reproduction of the social system.

As "organic," intellectuals remained invisible as the authors of ideological narratives. The pictures of society or history they painted seldom contained their own representation. As a rule, the organic intellectuals hid behind the broad shoulders of their ostensible heroes. In class-related ideologies, the role of historical actors was normally assigned to classes defined by activities different from those that distinguished their intellectual authors.

A closer scrutiny would, however, pierce the camouflage. It would reveal the uncanny resemblance the stage actors of ideological scenarios bore to the intellectual scriptwriters. Whoever happened to be named as the sitter in a given portrait-painting session, the product was invariably a thinly disguised likeness of the painter. In organic ideologies, the intellectuals painted their self-portraits, though only rarely did they admit this to be the case.

Like other authors of narratives, organic intellectuals could hardly eradicate or dissolve their presence in the products of their work; this much has been readily admitted of virtually all kinds of authorship, though paradoxically the pretensions of objectivity in the field of ideological narratives tend to be defended with more zeal than elsewhere. Yet in organic ideologies the intellectual authorship leaves a particularly heavy imprint – and this in two respects above all.

First, the intellectuals' own mode of praxis serves as the natural base line against which the features of the ostensible sitter of the portrait are plotted. The sitter's own characteristics tend to be trimmed, underplayed, or domesticated, while the painter's experience is projected onto the finished work. Thus the portraits invariably represent heroes accredited with acute interest in knowledge, disinterested pursuit of truth, moral proselytism, and other traits inextricably associated with the self-interpretation of the intellectual mode of life.

Second, the ostensible heroes of organic ideologies are assigned the role of "historical agents" inasfar as they are believed to promote a kind of society in which the continuation of the intellectual mode of life is guaranteed to be untrammelled and is assigned a considerable, if not the central, importance in the work of the social system. In other words, the "good society" of which the heroes are believed to be agents, is a projection of the intellectual mode upon the society as a whole; alternatively, it is a model trusted to provide optimal conditions for the proliferation of such a mode.

There is, however, one ideology in which the intellectual authors of the narrative appear virtually undisguised; in which they constitute, so to speak, part of the plot. To use Gramsci's terms again, in this ideology the intellectuals appear as the "organic intellectuals of themselves." This unique ideology is one of culture: that narrative representing the world as man-made, guided by man-made values and norms, and reproduced through the ongoing process of learning and teaching.

The notorious diversity of definitions of culture given currency in sociological, anthropological, and nonacademic literature – even of discursive contexts in which the concept of culture is situated and given meaning – should not conceal the common basis from which all such definitions and approaches derive. However the phenomenon of culture is defined, the possibility of the definition, of the very articulation of culture as a phenomenon of the world, is rooted in a particular vision of the world that articulates the potential, elaborates the values, and legitimizes the role of the intellectuals.

The vision in question is directed by three tacitly, yet axiomatically accepted premises.

First, human beings are essentially incomplete and not self-sufficient. Their humanization is a process taking place after birth, in the company of other human beings. The distinction between the inherited insufficiency and acquired completeness is conceptualized as the opposition between "biological" and "social" aspects of the "homo duplex," or between "nature" and "nurture."

Second, humanization is essentially a learning process, split into the acquisition of knowledge and the taming, or repressing, of animal (and almost invariably antisocial) predispositions. The distinction between knowledge to be put in place of the natural predispositions, and the predispositions it is to replace, is often conceptualized as the opposition between "reason" and "passions," or between "social norms" and "instincts" or "drives."

Third, learning is just one side of the relation of which the other side is teaching. The completion of the humanization process, therefore, requires teachers and a system of – formal or informal – education. The educators hold the key to the continuous reproduction of cohabitation as a human society.

Thanks to the profuse historical studies (originated by Lucien Febvre, Febvre et al., [1930]) we can locate the birth of this thoroughly modern vision of the world fairly precisely. It took place in the later part of the seventeenth and the first half of the eighteenth centuries and coincided with the birth and the institutionalization of the modern intellectuals.

The ideology of culture represents the world as consisting of human beings who are what they are taught. It therefore brings into relief the induced diversity of human ways of life; it makes possible the articulation of plurality of "ways to be human." This feature of the ideology of culture lends plausibility to a supposition that the birth of the "cultural vision" of the world was linked primarily to the newly acquired modern sensitivity to cultural differences. The story often found in the sociological and anthropological texts is that of Europe suddenly opening its eyes to the diversity of cultural modes of life previously unnoticed or considered uninteresting. This story, however, misses the point crucial for the birth of cultural ideology: the perception of diversity *as* culturally induced, of differences *as* cultural differences, of variety *as* man-made and brought about by the teaching/learning process. It was a particular articulation of diversity, and not newly aroused sensitivity to differences, that was the constitutive act of the ideology of culture.

Europeans were avid travellers; pilgrims to the Holy Land, late medieval sailors could not help noticing strange ways of life alongside unfamiliar shapes of shelters or unusual physiques of people they met on their way. They recorded what they saw in a similar "alongside" manner; all perceived differences appeared as if on the same plane, variety of skin colors being a part of the order of things in the same way as the variety of customs and revered idols. Fashionable travelogue literature revelled in reporting genuine and fantastic findings as so many curiosities in the same fashion the early-modern *Kunstkamera* collected them – mixing double-headed calves with strange man-made implements of unknown destination. The founder of modern taxonomy, Linnaeus, considered the differences between straight and curly hair equally symptomatic for the differentiation of human species as the variety of the forms of government.

The contemplative mood in which European travellers viewed the richness of human forms they found in the foreign lands was an attitude trained at home. The premodern society was split into self-enclosed ranks; each rank carried a life deemed uniquely suited to it and to no else, and advised to "stick to its own kind" or admonished for peeping beyond the confines of its own station. Ranks were part of the "great chain of being," a testimony to the preordained order of things; they lived together, equally ancient and immutable, guarded against contaminating each other; emulation across the boundaries was frowned upon and considered morally morbid – a tinkering with the divine order. Not that the idea of self-improvement was totally unheard of; individual members of the ranks were indeed encouraged to strive for perfection. But the ideals of perfection were as numerous as the ranks themselves; and as impenetrable, separate, and – in theory – immune to change. "Self-perfection" meant becoming more like the model assigned to the rank and avoiding confusion with other models.

Such a coexistence of forms of life, with none considering itself as a universal model for imitation and none bent on submerging or eradicating the others – provided no room for the "nature-culture" or "nature-nurture" distinction. Only once it had broken, could the "culture vision" as a peculiar modern intellectual ideology emerge.

The cultural ideology became possible when the ostensibly peaceful coexistence between forms of life turned untenable; either through the malfunctioning of its reproductive mechanism, or because of its unsuitability for the novel form of social domination, or for both reasons. The reality cultural ideology reflected at its birth was one of the abruptly changing relations between rank-ascribed forms of life: with some forms of life becoming *problems* for some others, problems calling for being acted upon. Forms of life (or their selected aspects) came to be seen as "culturally produced" after they had turned into objects of practice, became things one "had to do something about" in order to contain them, change, or replace. It was the intention to terminate their existence, and the underlying practice of enforced uniformization, that cast the diversity of the forms of life as an artificial, contingent, "merely man-made" phenomenon. A "historical origin" of forms of life was postulated once their "historical end" had been envisaged as a practical and desirable possibility.

It was the extent of ambitions to interfere with forms of life, and of resources available to support such ambitions, that determined the newly discovered boundary between "nature" and "culture" and its subsequent shifts. In the previously uniformly preordained world, an enclave had been cut out that invited human designs (and had been theorized, therefore, as humanly designed). Its growth, at the expense of shrinking "nature," followed closely the expansion of proselytizing ambitions, systemic needs that made such ambitions necessary, and the mobilization of social power that rendered them realistic.

The appearance of proselytizing practices and ambitions was in the early-modern Europe linked to a number of far-reaching structural dislocations; among the latter, the breakdown of the traditional mechanisms of social control and societal reproduction and the gestation of the modern state must be offered pride of place.

Surveillance-based, disciplinary power was the major tool of social control throughout the history of premodern Europe (a fact glossed over in the otherwise seminal Foucault's analysis, [1980]). This particular tool was not, however, employed by the state, confined as it were to the "sovereign" power of the prince, focused almost solely on securing the princely and the aristocratic share in economic surplus. Instead, disciplinary power was deployed within communities and corporations small enough to make surveillance reciprocal, ubiquitous, and comprehensive. Social order at the level of daily life was reproduced through the pernickety and oppressive surveillance exercised matter-of-factly, thanks to the permanent physical proximity of its, simultaneously, subjects and objects.

It was the breakdown of self-enclosed communities and the ensuing appearance of the "masterless men" – vagabonds, vagrants, shifting population nowhere at home, belonging to no specific community or corporation, at no locality subject to continuous and all-embracing surveillance – that rendered the issue of social control, and of the reproduction of social order, problematic. The heretofore invisible, "natural" flow of things had been brought abruptly into relief as a "mechanism" – something to be designed, administered, and monitored, something not functioning, or not functioning properly, unless attended to and operated skilfully. The timeless, yet never before problematized, control-through-surveillance, reproduction of order through disciplining bodily drill, had turned into an object of systematic inquiry, specialized skills, and a function of experts. The diffuse activity of community had been transformed into an asymmetrical relationship between the subjects and the objects of the supervision. As such, it called for a support in a supracommunal authority. It needed resources no community could provide. It required deployment by the state; it rendered the state a systemic prerequisite of the reproduction of social order, the mainstay of the perpetuity of social domination. By the same token, the crisis of traditional vehicles of social control ushered in the modern state.

The latter meant first and foremost the centralization of social powers previously localized. This, however, was not simply a matter of transferring power from one setting to another; the very character of power changed considerably in the process. The destruction of *les pouvoirs intermédiaires*, which the entrenchment of the modern absolutist state was about, was tantamount to the annihilation of the only institutional setting in which control could be exercised in a "traditional" way (i.e., unreflectively) without the purpose of the exercise having been clearly articulated and the exercise itself transformed into a specialized function. The advent of the absolutist state was hence tantamount to the transformation of control into a consciously administered, purposeful activity conducted by specially trained experts. The state had now to take care of creating conditions in which surveillance and bodily drill could be effectively operated.

If the community-based social control resulted in the perpetuating and reinforcing local differentiations of the forms of life, the state-based control could only promote supracommunal uniformity. Universality as an ideal and an measure of social improvement was born of this need of the modern state; and of its practical ability to act on such a need.

Bent on uniformity, the unprecedented practice of the early-modern state was bound to clash with the still well-entrenched reproductive mechanisms that constituted the substance of communal autonomy. Concentration of power could never be complete without that autonomy being shattered – weakened or preferably uprooted. An indispensable part of the absolutist state bid for comprehensive power was therefore the notorious culture crusade that took off in the seventeenth century and continued well into the nineteenth. The crusade redefined the relations between diverse forms of life; mere superiority turned into hegemony.

Ranks were "lower" or "higher" well before the advent of modernity. So were their ways of life. Yet they were seen as separate entities, to be prevented rather than encouraged to come into direct contact with each other – each being viable in its own right and dependent but on itself for its own reproduction. "Superiority" of one rank over another (and of corresponding ways of life) was hence a category of comparison, and not a concept standing for a specific task the "superior" rank bore in relation to other ways of life. Such a task, on the other hand, is the essence of the thoroughly modern idea of "hegemony": the role of the "superior" way of life and its carriers as the moral mentor, missionary, and pattern to be followed by all the others.

The universalistic ambitions of the modern state led inevitably to further weakening of the localized mechanisms of reproduction of previously autonomous ways of life; such mechanisms appeared to central power as so many obstacles on the way to the kind of society it projected, given its tendency to uniform administrative principles. Differences between ways of life were correspondingly redefined as relations of active mutual engagement. Popular, locally administered ways of life were now constituted, from the perspective of universalistic ambitions, as retrograde and backward-looking, a residue of a different social order to be left behind; as imperfect, immature stages in an overall line of development toward a "true" and universal way of life, exemplified by the hegemonic elite; as grounded in superstition or error, passion-ridden, infested with animal drives, and otherwise resisting the ennobling influence of the truly human – shortly to be dubbed "enlightened" – order. Such a redefinition placed the elite, for the first time, in a position of a collective teacher on the top of its traditional role of the collective ruler. Diversity of ways of life has become now a temporary phenomenon, a transient phase to be left behind in the effort aimed toward the universal humanity.

The new character of relations between forms of life inside the society, now claimed by the absolutist state, served as a pattern for consideration of the relations between ways of life in general. The same active, proselytizing stance – once extended beyond the confines of own society – constituted alien forms of life as ossified relics of the past, or otherwise artificially arrested stages of human development. Such aspects of human life as the emerging absolute power was bent on reshaping, or bound to reshape, had been selected as the bearers of a special status: men were about to reform them, hence they had to be conceived of as man-made in the first place. Those aspects were now seen as distinguished by their plasticity, temporariness, transitoriness – and, above all, amenability to purposeful regulation. The relative inferiority of the strange forms of life was interpreted, therefore, as the outcome of wrong regulation, and the local equivalents of the judging powers were charged with responsibility for the evil. On the whole, the inferiority of other forms of life, and the range of those of their aspects to which the judgment of inferiority was applied, were a function of the judging power's ambitions – their scope and administrative skills to back it.

The aspects of human life now picked up for conscious regulation came to be known as "culture." Historians agree that for almost a century, up to the last quarter of the eighteenth century, "culture" (its French form of "civilisation,"

German of "Bildung," English of "refinement") was used in the public discourse as a name of activity, of something some people were doing, or exhorted to do, to others – much as a farmer cultivated his plants to ennoble the seeds and enrich the crop. The immediate interest that led to the coining of the idea of "culture" as such aspects of human life as can be consciously regulated and given deliberatedly selected shape (unlike the other aspects that human powers were still unable or unwilling to reach) was one in the practice of changing the ways of life viewed as a symptom, and a source, of the morbid resilience of local autonomy pitted against the universalistic ambitions of the modern state. Culture, civilizing, refining were so many names given to the crusade proclaimed against the "vulgar," "beastly," "superstitious" habits and customs and the forces allegedly presiding over their perpetuation.

The givers of names were the first modern intellectuals – the members of *la république des lettres*, of *les sociétés de pensée*, men free of all institutional dependencies and loyalties, united solely by their voluntary participation in a discussion of issues that, thanks to the public nature of the discussion, came to be defined as "public." It was the action of that new brand of educated elite (brilliantly analyzed by François Furet [1978], in reference to the rich ideas contained in the literary legacy of Alexis de Tocqueville, and to heretofore little known studies of Augustin Cochin [1978]) that provided an experience from which the new vision of the social world, as constituted by the learning/teaching activity, was to be extrapolated. I have described the process at length in Bauman (1987).

In response to the demand potentially present in the expanding ambitions of the absolutist state, *la république des lettres* offered the ideal design of the polity toward which the lawgivers should strive, the method of its attainment (the process of enlightenment through the diffusion of right ideas), and their own skills as the guarantee that the method would be applied effectively. The overall effect of the triple offer was the constitution of knowledge as power; the establishment of a privileged, foolproof access to right knowledge as the legitimation of the right to tell the others, deprived of such an access, what to do, how to behave, what ends to pursue, and by what means.

The cognitive perspective grounded in the practice of *la république des lettres* rearranged the vision of the diversity of forms of life, now seen as first and foremost a cultural diversity. Other forms of life were now seen as products of a wrong kind of teaching, of malice or error, of ignorance at best. Behind the teaching, teachers were surmised in the image of the conscious educators of the day. *Les philosophes* named the clergy, old wives, and folk proverbs as the teachers responsible for the lamentable state of popular habits. In the new vision of the social world, nature did not tolerate void – for every way of life there had to be a teacher responsible for its shape. The choice was not any more between a guided and regimented education and the autonomous self-constitution of forms of life – but between good and bad education. Not only knowledge was power; all power was knowledge. All efficient power had to rely on good knowledge for its efficiency.

The power/knowledge syndrome was, from the very start, a double-edged phenomenon, and hence prone to internal contradiction. On the one hand, it contained what came later to be called the "rational government" – a global administration of the society as a whole aimed at creating and maintaining conditions eliciting "good" behavior and eliminating or preventing the "bad" one. On the other, it entailed a direct manipulation of cognitive maps, values, and motives of the individual members of the society in order to prompt what came later to be called "rational behavior." In the cultural ideology of the Enlightenment, rational society and rational individuals were presumed to harmoniously reinforce each other, though their articulation as separate phenomena, subject to relatively autonomous sets of determinants, took some time (and a certain amount of frustration) to set up.

The idea of rational government constituted a true novelty. It was concerned not merely with a substitution of a better policy for an inferior one, good laws for bad. It entailed a wholly new concept of government, its scope, and responsibilities. The government was now seen as the force that – knowingly or by default – shapes the external framework of human life; the idea that society is "man-made" represented the unprecedented ambition of the modern state to actually *make* the society; and an unheard-of mobilization of resources that rendered such making a viable proposition. The concept of state laws was also new; the idea of their postulated "rationality" represented a new intention to use legislation for moulding social reality according to the precepts of reason. All in all, rational government meant the newly perceived malleability of social life, its need for being shaped, its amenability to being remade according to designs embodied in the action of external agencies – power being tantamount to the effectivity of such action.

The idea of rational individual was also novel in a revolutionary way. The gist of the idea was not a mere substitution of something for something else; reasonable and reliable thinking for an erroneous or superstitious one – but a wholly new concept of the human being whose conduct is shaped by his/her knowledge, and whose knowledge is shaped by knowledge givers, those who are, truly or ostensibly, "in the know." Again, the true novelty consists in the vision of the individual, his thoughts and his behavior, as flexible and malleable entities, as objects of practice, of purposeful redirection. The vision of the individual who determines his conduct by writing the motives he selects into his cognitive map of the world was something that could have been achieved only from the perspective of the new active stance toward the aspect of the world defined as "culture," that is, as man-made (as men were bent on remaking it). The latter could pursue their intention through supplying the individuals with the determinants of their conduct, and thus indirectly determining that conduct for them.

Metaphorically, the kind of authority in which such a vision of the world established men of knowledge could be described as "legislative." The authority involved the right to command the rules the social world was to obey; and it was legitimized in terms of a better judgment, a superior knowledge guaranteed by the proper method of its production. With both society and its members found wanting (i.e., shapeable yet heretofore shaped in the wrong way), the new legislative authority of men of knowledge established its own necessity and entitlements.

It is only too easy to misinterpret, after the years, the "culturalization" of the world as necessarily involving this "cultural relativism" with which the idea of culture seems today inextricably linked. The intellectual ideology of culture was launched as a militant, uncompromising, and self-confident manifesto of universally binding principles of social organization and individual conduct. It expressed not only the exuberant administrative vigor of the time, but also a resounding certainty as to the direction of anticipated social change. Indeed, forms of life conceived as obstacles to change and thus condemned to destruction had been relativized; the form of life that was called to replace them was seen, however, as universal, inscribed in the essence and the destination of the human species as a whole.

The original, legislative, version of cultural ideology thrived under conditions of certainty. It was advanced as a solution to a protracted "Pyrrhonian crisis" of Western philosophy; as a decisive rejection of half-hearted, proto-pragmatist compromises like those suggested by Mercenne or Gassendi (cf. Popkin, 1979), and a refusal to accept the attitude of modesty (and, in general, admit the temporarily and spatially "local" nature of the European form of life) best exemplified by the sceptic reflections of Montaigne. Intellectual legislators entertained no doubts as to representing history and reason; and authority of both history and reason stemmed from the fact that – unlike the parochial errors they were bound to leave behind – they were grounded in universal traits of human species and thus suffered no competitors.

It is tempting to connect this remarkable upsurge of certainty, coming in the wake of the early-modern crisis of self-confidence, with the formidable advances of the absolute state in neutralizing and subordinating "traditional" seats of power; with the spectacular penetration by purposefully acting administrators into the areas of social and individual life previously left to their own "natural" flow; with the powerful strides of the state power away from the "gamekeeping" and toward the "gardening" practice of authority; with – last but not least – the rapid growth of West-European economic and military superiority over the rest of the world. Limits to new, modern powers were prominent only by their ability to be broken; the capacity of such powers to impose one chosen pattern over everything and everybody did seem a matter of time, will, and technique. As long as the practical capacity of ecumenical ascendancy was believed to be boundless, there was no clear reason why the absolute character of knowledge that underpinned such practice should have been questioned.

Certainly, this intellectual reflection of the apparent infinity of power was to become the major characteristic of this peculiar West-European mental climate known as "modernity." I take here the concept of "modernity" to stand for a perception of the world, rather than (as it has been misleadingly intimated) the world itself; a perception locally grounded in a way that implied its universality and concealed its particularism. It had been the decisive feature of modernity so understood that it relativized its (past and contemporary) adversaries and thereby constituted relativity itself as an adversary; as a spoke in the wheel of progress, a demon to be exorcized, a sickness to be cured.

The spirit of modernity inspired ever renewed, though never conclusive, attempts to pinpoint the universally binding, apodictically correct resolutions to the questions of truth, judgment, and taste. It is all too easy to pronounce with the benefit of hindsight the failure, or even misdirectedness, of such trials. What, however, constituted the formative features of cultural ideology in its "legislative," optimistic, and audacious, modern phase, was not so much the success of the enterprise, as the possibility of its continuation, and of the absorption of successive drawbacks with no irreparable harm to the ongoing discourse. The remarkable resilience of purpose so typical of modern mentality was grounded in the unshakable belief that the efforts have history and invincible reason on their side and that the ultimate success was not just attainable in principle, but a foregone conclusion. The conviction had in turn all the backing of social, economic, and political realities. Paradoxically, though, modernity militated against the pragmatist compromise, it was in the end the pragmatic argument from the ever more evident superiority of the Western mode of life and thought that kept lending credibility to the hopes of finding the clinching proof for the species-wide validity of the Western science, morality, and aesthetics; or for the form in which they had been conceptually sublimated.

The other side of philosophical certainty was cultural self-confidence. It was the latter that gave the unreflective and unyielding resolution to that Europe's missionary zeal, for which the colonial episode of modernity was so notorious. The full history of the relentless suppression of locality- and class-related forms of life at home remains still to be written, though many long-forgotten alternative narratives have been unearthed in recent years. Extirpation of local and class autonomy was waged doggedly and unswervingly under the banner of objectively superior cultural values, at war with not-fully-human, erroneous, retarded, or superstitious forms of life and thought. Again, it was the apparent irreversibility of early-modern power struggles, the ostensible finality of the established structure of societal and world-wide domination that offered a truly supracultural, quasi-natural sanction to the unflinching dedication of cultural crusaders. No room was left for second thoughts, hesitation, scruples.

The conviction of the objective superiority of the social order formed in the northwestern tip of the European peninsula was not partisan in terms of European politics. It united the intellectuals regardless of their political allegiance, or declared class loyalty. Cultural ideology was shared, as was its underlying premise that the human world has been always man-made, that the time has arrived to make it in a conscious, reasonable manner, and that the way contemporary society has been organized opens the way to do it. To put it bluntly, the intellectuals' self-identification with what they articulated as the

"Western values" could (and did) remain unfaltering as long as the expectation that the Western sociopolitical system would be hospitable to knowledge-based (i.e., "rational") sociopolitical blueprints, could be seen as plausible. This expectation suffered many blows, and finally yielded to the accumulated pressure of adversary evidence; its slow and painful demise was only partly concealed by occasional, always short-lived, resurrections.

The deepest cause of the gradual dissolution of modern self-confidence can be, arguably, traced back to the slow but steady disengagement between the intellectuals, as collective guardians of societal values, and the modern state. Much in the same way as Marx took the last desperate attempt of yesterday's free producers to arrest the industrial steamroller for the prodromal symptom of the future anticapitalist militancy of industrial proletariat, *les philosophes* of the sanguine and expectant Enlightenment era took the young modern state's longing for guidance and legitimation for the promise of an imminent kingdom of reason. Both mistakes proved to be pregnant with frustration. Post-Marxian socialists and post-Enlightenment intellectuals alike are still reeling in the face of the world reluctant to conform to the model in terms of which they originally defined their role and function. Rather than admit their error, they would explain away the gap pointing to the world betraying its promise, taking a wrong turn, or otherwise failing to live up to its potential.

The openness of the early-modern state to the intellectual guidance was genuine enough. The territory that state was to invade was, for all practical intents and purposes, a virgin land, unexplored and uncharted. In a situation of acute uncertainty one had to rely on the loyalty of the crew. Turning the crew away from their old allegiances and realigning them aroung the new ones called for mobilization: dissemination of ideas simultaneously discrediting old creed and showing the new one worthy; and for a new kind of expertise, required by the gigantic task of massive conversion. With the intellectuals ready to satisfy both needs, the state seemed to depend on them for its survival. Because of that dependency, it also seemed a pliable and grateful object of intellectual legislation.

Dependency proved, however, short-lived. Political technology developed by the modern state was soon to render legitimizing services of the intellectuals increasingly redundant; or reduce them to a subordinate role, thus revealing the reversal of the original dependency.

The twin technique of panoptical power and seduction (with the balance between them gradually shifting into the direction of the latter) were increasingly put in charge of the reproduction of social order. With their efficiency and effectivity growing, the role of legitimation shrank. In a fully developed modern state, effectivity of state power, and indeed its performance in the systemic reproduction, may be maintained and perfected regardless of the scope and intensity of social commitment to the "ruling values" – or to any values for this matter. The "legal rationality," which Weber (1948) counted among historical forms of legitimation, in fact sounded the death knell to the legitimation era; as if to emphasize the fact by selecting "value rationality" as its opposition, it proclaimed the modern freedom of the state from ideology; to wit, from the ideologywriters. The latter would try to console themselves through presenting the demotion of legitimation as "legitimation crisis;" hoping against hope that the state can go on doing without legitimation only at its peril.

To describe the consequences of new political technology as the dispossession of the intellectuals needs, however, two important qualifications must be made.

First, the fading of the "legislative" role has not been connected with material deprivations. If anything, the opposite has been the case. The "general intellectuals" of yore have spawned numerous, still ramifying and growing in size, educated professions who command large income and – by all standards – privileged social standing. The failure of the bid for power has been compensated, so to speak, in a different currency – that of material gain. However dismissive (and, on occasion, hostile) of the "legislative" ambitions of the intellectuals, the modern state presided over an unprecedented growth of "experts" – this thoroughly modern phenomenon, transforming on a massive scale, the esoteric, minority knowledge into the bureaucratic power. The experts did become an indispensable part of the system's reproductive mechanism, however strongly their role differed from one sketched, and worked toward, by *les philosophes*. Technologies of panoptic control and of seduction proved particularly fertile as a breeding ground for the ever new, and ever more numerous, ranks of experts and fields of expertise. Among the expert-intensive techniques, one spots immediately those central to panoptic control, like surveillance, "correction," welfare supervision, "medicalization," or "psychiatrization," as well as the servicing of the general legal/penal system; or the many professions called into service and prominence due to the growing importance of needs-creation and entertainment as a paramount network of social control. Many more areas particularly hospitable to experts can be seen, however, as ultimately related to the modern techniques of power, though in a somewhat less obvious way. To name just one example: the modern weapons, ostensibly destined for an external enemy in some ill-defined future, while at present serving as a most powerful lever lifting the state out of the reach of an effective political control (and thus reinforcing its independence from the legitimizing discourse).

Second, while rendering the "legislative" function of the intellectuals irrelevant, the modern state disposed of any reason why the intellectual discourse should be subject to political control or otherwise externally limited or regulated. Having reached the nadir of their political relevance, modern intellectuals enjoy freedom of thought and expression they could not dream of at the time the words mattered politically. This is an autonomy of no practical consequence outside the self-enclosed world of intellectual discourse; and yet this is an autonomy all the same, a most precious and cherished consolation for the eviction from the house of power. The House of Solomon is now placed in a prosperous suburb, far away from ministerial buildings and military headquarters, where it can enjoy in peace, undisturbed, the elegant life of mind complete with a not inconsiderable material comfort. Intellectual freedom is not something to be treated lightly. It offers a unique chance to make the pursuit of the matters of intellectual concern into a total, self-contained, and self-sufficient form of life; and it offers the practitioners of such a form of life the gratifying feeling of being in full and exclusive control of the life-process and its products: truth, judgment, taste. Given the memory of the intimate link between political engagement and intellectual unfreedom – the autonomy of intellectual discourse turns into a highly attractive value in its own right; an attainment to be taken pride of, used to the full, staunchly defended. Defended against the governments which from time to time make half-hearted attempts to cut what they see as useless expenditure; and against the rebels from its own ranks who jeopardize the comforts of freedom, drawing the dusty skeleton of political commitment out of the old family cupboard.

Political dispossession of the intellectuals has not been, therefore, a disaster pure and simple. It has brought in its wake unexpected bonuses, some of them undoubtedly attractive, and all endowed with the quality of rendering themselves desirable and indispensable through protracted use and habituation. For this reason, it does not necessarily breed discontent. On the other hand, however, it certainly does not add life to the old legislative ambitions. To remain eligible for the bonuses, contemporary intellectuals must stick unswervingly to the Weberian injunction of keeping the poetry of values away from the prose of bureaucratically useful expertise.

Among the areas of social life that lost their significance for the reproduction of social order and hence have been freed from the direct supervision by the state, was one that the intellectuals considered as their domain of right; they hoped to be the direct and only beneficiaries of the withdrawal of political control and the new disinterestedness of the state. This special area was, of course, one of culture – now reduced to things of no concern to political powers. Here, as elsewhere, the overstretched, global ambitions entailed by the original concepts have been realistically tapered so that they will never trespass on the grounds reserved for the administrative interference of the state. In its new, more modest boundaries, however, culture seemed a natural domain of the intellectual, direct and unshared, rule. It is in this domain, therefore, that the legislative ambitions of the intellectuals have suffered the final and decisive blow.

As the interest of the state in culture faded (i. e., the relevance of culture to the reproduction of political power diminished), culture was coming within the orbit of another power the intellectuals could not measure with – the market. Literature, visual arts, music – indeed, the whole sphere of humanities – was gradually freed from the burden of ideological message to carry, and ever more solidly set inside the market-led consumption as entertainment. More and more were the culture of consumer society subordinated to the function of producing and reproducing skillful and eager consumers, rather than obedient and willing subjects of the state; in its new role, it had to conform to the needs and rules as defined, in practice if not in theory, by the consumer market.

Publishers, art galleries, record companies, managers of the mass communication media wrestled the hoped-for cultural domination from philosophers, literary theorists, musicologists, aestheticians. Offended and outraged, the latter responded with the accusations typical of the language used over the ages by the rightful gamekeepers against poachers (i.e., imposter gamekeepers). The new rulers of cultural domain were accused of demeaning the quality of the "cultural objects" by being brash, undiscerning, crude, and on the whole not up to the task that required the degree of sophistication they did not possess, and of care they were not capable of. Most interestingly, the new managers were accused of the very action the accusers considered the major cultural mission of their own at the time they seemed to be holding the political assignment of cultural leadership: of extirpating the autonomous seats of culture, the "natural," "spontaneous," cultural processes, and the very diversity of cultures that such natural processes may support. The new managers were accused of imposing one, "middle-brow," homogenized standard upon the original richness of diversified cultural traditions; of substituting factory-produced "popular" culture for community-sustained "folk" culture. Cultural uniformity lost its attractiveness once it had become clear that someone else – forces beyond the intellectuals' control – was to set its standards and preside over its implementation.

It is arguable whether market domination of culture does indeed promote cultural uniformity, middle-, low-, or any other brow. There is plenty of evidence that the opposite is the case. The market seems to thrive on cultural diversity; there is hardly a cultural idiosyncrasy the market cannot take into its stride and make into another tributary of its power. Neither is it evident that cultural uniformity is "in the interest" of the market forces; again, the opposite seems to be the case. It is plausible that in the new domination of the market forces culture has recovered a mechanism of the reproduction of diversity once located in autonomous communities and later ostensibly lost for a time in the era of politically sponsored cultural crusades and enlightened proselytism.

Whatever is the case, and whatever are the reasons for such a remarkable turn-around, the intellectuals of our times tend to deploy the "cultural vision" of the world in such a way that is almost totally opposite to the context in which this vision had been first shaped. The overwhelming tendency today is to see culture as the ground of perpetual, irreducible (and, in most cases, desirable and worth conscious preservation) diversity of human kind. As before, culture is understood as the process of "humanization"; but it is emphasized now that there is an infinite variety of ways in which humans may be, and are, humanized; and it is strongly denied that one way is intrinsically better than another, or that one can prove its superiority over another, or that one should be substituted for another. Variety and coexistence have become "cultural values" – ones the intellectuals are most zealously committed to defending.

There are numerous symptoms of this tendency, which exerts a truly formidable influence on the direction taken by contemporary social theory. Among the symptoms, the passage from the "negative" to the "positive" concept of ideology is arguably the most significant, being an emphatic rejection of the earlier claim to the "legislative" role of philosophers, and of the supracommunal, extraterritorial intellectuals in general, in questions of truth, judgment, and taste; if the "legislative" role is retained by the new vision, it is confined to the intracommunal territory, to legislation from "the inside" of a tradition, always acutely aware, of the limits of its application and relativism of its validity claims. In the intercommunal space, no room is left for the "legislative" ambition. Either the very possibility of extraterritorial grounds of reason is denied, or the impotence of reason in the face of power-supported traditions is recognized; in both cases, the effort to invalidate alternative traditions, forms of life, positive ideologies, cultures, etc. as erroneous, biased, or otherwise inferior, has been all but abandoned.

The same tendency of the intellectual perception of the world, and of the way the position of the intellectuals is defined within the world so perceived, may result, and does result, in a variety of strategies. This variety often prevents the observers of the contemporary intellectual scene from spotting the shared outlook from which all strategies, however diverse, derive and from which they draw their meaning.

Leaving aside academic philosophy as a technical discipline, which conceivably can go on indefinitely reproducing its own institutionalized discourse, by and large unaffected by the changing world in the absence of all interface with social praxis – one can attempt to synthesize a few basic types to which all strategies can be in the end reduced.

One strategy is perhaps best encapsulated by the melancholic admission of Wittgenstein: Philosophy leaves everything as it is. Practical impotence of value, truth, or judgment discourses is not just overlooked and not merely tacitly accepted or reflected upon as an unpleasant possibility, as an eventuality one would rather avoid or at any rate one would rather not look in the face (there would be nothing particularly novel about such an attitude) but brought into the very center of reflection; more than that, made into a new source of philosophical courage and determination. From Adorno (or, perhaps, Nietzsche?) to Rorty philosophers demand the continuation of legislation function for the sake of the importance intrinsically carried by concern with reason, ethical norms, aesthetic standards; that importance does not diminish, so they say – on the contrary, it attains particularly huge proportions for the fact that there is no one to legislate for, and that the legislative debate is in all probability bound to remain a self-contained, private affair of the legislators. This strategy abandons the intention of proselytizing; it puts paid to the hope entertained by the enlighteners that truth, if only discovered, will out and vanquish ignorance and error. In no way, however, the resignation detracts from the resolution to go on with the task given reality by the centuries of Western intellectual tradition.

There is, of course, an inner differentiation among the followers of this strategy, as there is a not insignificant difference between Adorno and Rorty. On one extreme, there is a genuine feeling of defeat, despair, and desperation;

the fact that the hopes of *les philosophes* have been dashed is regretted and bewailed, and the culprits are sought; the capitalist rule, bourgeois philistinism, or ruthless market forces are alternatively selected and condemned as villains of the sad piece. Step by step, social reality itself comes to be seen as doomed and is duly condemned. As if following August Bebel's commandment "Beware the praise of your enemies," practical success of philosophical critique is detracted in advance as a sign of blunder or lack of fortitude, which is to be avoided at all costs. Even in their surrender (particularly in their surrender?) philosophers remain incessantly and painfully conscious of the practical connection of the cultural ideal. Its impotence is as much a constituting factor of their discourse as its assumed all-conquering potency was of the discourse of their Enlightenment ancestors. Impotence itself becomes now potency; the cultural ideal stays pure and truly worthy as long as it is not contaminated by intrinsically impure reality; it stays pure and worthy because it steers clear of practical success. And yet, in a curious twist of mind, this pure, ethereal, cultural ideal is believed to be reality's best chance.

On the other extreme (best exemplified by numerous "protreptic" statements by Rorty, cf. Bernstein, [1985]), torments and agony Adorno-type are replaced with a simple "so what?" Indeed, the hope of converting the world to better standards of truth, judgment, or taste was at best naive; indeed, it would be naive in the extreme to hold it still today. Yet the worst naivety was to suppose that the validity of the "civilizing" enterprise of cultural discourse was at any time dependent on realism or irrealism of that hope; on the feasibility of proselytizing success. Now that we know that the massive conversion of the world to our standards is not on, we can better concentrate on the task at hand. And the task at hand is to keep the unique values of the Western civilization alive, if only as the content and the pragmatics of philosophical discourse; to continue a cultural tradition out of conviction of its intrinsic worth, all the more zealously for the realization that it is indeed a "local" tradition and in all probability would at best remain so. Insiders as we are, we need not wax humble or cynical as we admit the "locality" of tradition we guard: It is not just a local tradition, it is *our* local tradition, and we would go on praising its virtues even if the rest of the world refuses to join in the accolade.

Again, like in the case discussed before, culture as a basically converting, proselytizing action remains very much a subliminal ground of the strategy. In the face of the improbability of practical conversion, the emphasis shifts however to the gospel itself: yet the very insistence on its superiority over other evangelical traditions draws its sense and its importance solely from the original missionary context of cultural discourse.

What makes the two extreme points plotted on the same continuum of attitudes is their refusal to abandon the legislative mode of intellectual discourse. Legislation now lacks a vehicle of enforcement; old vehicles have been either scrapped or captured by powers impervious to the intellectual counsel, if not downright hostile; that circumstance is however denied the force of an argument in favor of renouncing the legislative mission. One could say that the legislative mode of the new strategy differs from its older version first and foremost by the way it is grounded and legitimized (or, rather, by the way in which the precept of legitimation is declared redundant).

Another strategy is, in a sense, more radical: It entails a formidable redefinition of the intellectual role and social position, to a point where the metaphor of the "legislator" ceases to be an adequate description of the latter. Another metaphor is called for instead – that of the "interpreter."

Empirically evident relativity of knowledge, dependence of truth judgment, and taste on overt or tacit assumptions embedded in communally based traditions was a vexing problem for the legislatively oriented cultural discourse; a difficulty to be resolved theoretically *and* removed practically. For the "interpretive" strategy, relativity is not just a transitory state, but an apodictically given existential condition of knowledge. Something not to be frowned upon and objected against, but to be drawn conclusion from and adjusted to. The "interpretive" strategy gestates an ontology that legitimizes it in terms of the intellectual mode: an ontology within which language only is accredited with the attribute of reality. The world within this ontology is an intersubjective world of communication, where "work," like in Schutz (Schutz and Luckmann, [1974]), consists in making irreversible changes in the conversationalists' respective cognitive maps, stocks of knowledge, or distributions of relevances. Within such a world, knowledge has no extralinguistical standards of correctness and can be grasped only inside the communicatively supported, shared stock of knowledge of the members. Pluralism is an irremovable feature of such a world. The most salient practical problem in such a world – one with which ordinary competence of otherwise knowledgeable members cannot cope without assistance – is communication between systems of knowledge enclosed within their respective stocks of knowledge and communal systems of relevance. Here interpretation, in other situations accomplished by members matter-of-factly and on the whole adequately, calls for special skills not normally available in daily life.

Interpretation between systems of knowledge is recognized, therefore, as the task of experts armed with specialist knowledge, but also endowed, for one reason or another, with a unique capacity to lift themselves above the communication networks within which respective systems are located without losing touch with that "inside" of systems where knowledge is had unproblematically and enjoys an "evident" sense. Interpretation must make the interpreted knowledge sensible to those who are not "inside"; but having no extraterritorial references to appeal to it has to resort to the "inside" itself as its only resource.

Social-scientific and philosophical approaches to culture converged upon such breathtakingly paradoxical strategy in the course of several decades and from different sides. One can point out many tributaries to the current. Simmel's concept of the intellectual as essentially a stranger; Mannheim's (cf. Bauman, 1978) association between true knowledge and homelessness, the state of being "freischwebend;" Kroeber's, Kluckhohn's, Sapir's, or Benedict's (cf. Bauman, 1973) ideas of "ethos," "style," "pattern," which make for the uniqueness of each culture and offer the only acceptable criteria for its understanding, establishing simultaneously their ontological equality; Frank Cushing's personal exploration of the possibility of making Zuni understandable to the non-Zuni only by becoming *plus Zuni que les Zunis*; Clifford Geertz' precept of "thick description" – an intellectual immersion in ever deeper layers of localized meanings too routine for the locals to be articulated. The themes of "outsidedness" turned over and promoted primarily by cultural anthropology, converged in the present array of hermeneutic strategies taking the essentially philosophical sources (Heidegger, late Wittgenstein, Gadamer) as their discursive home.

The redefinition of the study of culture as an essentially hermeneutic enterprise does not only recognize relativity of all knowledge and perpetuity of cultural pluralism. On the way, it also revises the idea of culture. The most striking of all revisions is the novel "impersonality" of culture, elimination from the model of culture of the "author" – be it the legislator or the educator. The vision of culture as, essentially, an activity performed by a part of the population and aimed at another part, is replaced with a vision of a spontaneous process devoid of administrative or managerial centers, free of an overall design, and perpetuated by diffusely deployed powers. Language stands out as a most seminal epitome of such spontaneity and impersonality of culture. Alongside with language, "traditions," "universes of meaning," or meaning, or "forms of life" replace the educators and the educated as major categories of cultural discourse.

A case can be made that the total disappearance of the issues of politics and domination from the vision implied by the "interpretive" strategy has more than an accidental connection with the currently experienced dislocations in the social function of the intellectuals, and particularly in their relation to the effective powers that be; from the perspective of the present-day intellectuals, culture does not appear as something to be "made" or "remade" as an object for practice; it is indeed a reality in its own right and beyond control, an object for study, something to be mastered only cognitively, as a meaning, and not practically, as a task.

When related processually, rather than juxtaposed laterally, "legislative" and "interpretive" strategies can be recast as, respectively, "modern" and "postmodern." Indeed, the recently fashionable opposition between "postmodernity" and "modernity" makes most sense as an attempt to grasp the historical tendency of last centuries, and the most crucial discontinuities of recent history, from the perspective of the changing social position and function of the intellectuals (it is because of this specific vantage point from which it has been made that this opposition is not simply restating the propositions entailed in other, ostensibly similar, oppositions). The postmodernity/modernity opposition focuses on the waning of certainty and objectivity grounded in the unquestioned hierarchy of values, and ultimately in the unquestionable structure of domination; and on the passage to a situation characterized by a coexistence or armistice between values and a lack of the overall structure of domination, which makes the questions of objective standards impracticable and hence theoretically futile. In this opposition, "modernity" is seen in a new way, redefined retrospectively by the novel experience encapsulated in the idea of "postmodernity." Modernity is reconstructed ex-post-facto as an era possessing the selfsame features the present time feels most poignantly as missing, namely the universal criteria of truth, judgment, and taste seemingly controlled and operated by the intellectuals. As all reconstructions, this one tells more about the reconstructors than about the reconstructed epoch, and in this respect it is highly illuminating.

The prevalence of interpretive strategy, sometimes problematized as the advent of postmodernity, signifies a most radical departure in the cultural discourse since the introduction of the concept of culture and the establishment of the culture-oriented vision of society. Indeed, the radicality of shift has induced some analysts, notably George Steiner, to speak of a "postculture," on the assumption that the cultural situation is inextricably associated with a clear notion of superiority and inferiority in the realm of values, and that the current situation of the West, when such notion is questioned or ridiculed, cannot be described as "cultural" and ushers us into heretofore uncharted waters.

It is the central suggestion of this chapter that the contemporary reorientation of cultural discourse can be best understood as a reflection on the changing experience of intellectuals, as they seek to reestablish their social function on a new ground in a world ill-fit for their traditional role.

References

Bauman, Zygmunt (1973). *Culture as Praxis*. London: Routledge & Kegan Paul.

Bauman, Zygmunt (1978). *Hermeneutics and Social Science, Approaches to Understanding*. London: Hutchinson.

Bauman, Zygmunt (1987). *Legislators and Interpreters: On Modernity, Postmodernity, and the Intellectuals*. Oxford: Polity Press.

Bernstein, Richard (1985). *Philosophical Profiles; Essays in Pragmatic Mode*. Oxford: Polity Press.

Cochin, Augustin (1978). *Les sociétés de pensée et la democratie moderne*. Paris: Gallimard.

Febvre, Lucien et al. (1930). *Civilisation, le mot et l'idée*. Paris: La Renaissance de Livre.

Foucault, Michel (1980). *Power/Knowledge*. Brighton: Harvester Press.

Furet, François (1978). *Penser la Révolution Française*. Paris: Gallimard.

Gramsci, Antonio (1957). *The Modern Prince and Other Writings*. London: Lawrence & Wishart.

Habermas, Jürgen (1974). *Theory and Practice*. London: Heinemann.

Popkin, Richard H. (1979). *The History of Scepticism from Erasmus to Spinoza*. Berkeley: University of California Press.

Schutz, Alfred and Luckmann, Thomas (1974). *The Structures of the Life World*. London: Heinemann.

Simmel, Georg (1968). *The Conflict in Modern Culture and Other Essays.* New York: Teachers College Press.
Weber, Max (1948). *From Max Weber*, ed. H.H. Gerth and C. Wright Mills. London: Routledge & Kegan Paul.

The Authors

Bauman, Zygmunt taught successively at the Universities of Warsaw, Tel-Aviv and Leeds, where he is at present Professor of Sociology. Recent books: Hermeneutics and Social Science (1978); Memories of Class (1982); Legislators and Interpreters (1987); Freedom (1988).

Bleicher, Josef, PhD University of Leeds 1981, 1978 Lecturer in Sociology at the Glasgow College of Technology, 1985 Reader in Sociology. Main emphasis of research: social identity. Recent publications: Contemporary Hermeneutics, London 1980; The Hermeneutic Imagination, London 1982.

Boudon, Raymond is Professor at the University of Paris-Sorbonne and Director of the Groupe d'Etude des Méthodes de l'Analyse Sociologique. He is a foreign member of the American Academy of Arts and Sciences, of the International Academy of Education and the Academia Europaea. He has been a fellow of the Center for Advanced Study in the Behavioral Sciences at Stanford; invited professor at Harvard, Chicago, Geneva, Stockholm; he has given the Hobhouse Lecture at the London School of Economics (1981), the Lazarsfeld Lecture at Columbia University (1982), the Fulvio Guerrini Lecture at the University of Turin (1984), the Patten Lecture at the Indiana University (1985), the Lurcy Lecture at the University of Chicago (1986). He is the author of Education, Opportunity and Social Inequality; The Unintended Consequences of Social Action; The Logic of Social Action; Theories of Social Change; Dictionary of Sociology (forthcoming); The Analysis of Ideology (forthcoming). He is the editor of the Année Sociologique and of the series "Sociologies" at the Presses Universitaires de France.

Eder, Klaus, *1946, Dr. rer. soc., is directing social research at the Münchner Projektgruppe für Sozialforschung e. V. and Associate Professor of Sociology at the University of Düsseldorf. Important publications: Die Entstehung staatlich organisierter Gesellschaften. Ein Beitrag zu einer Theorie sozialer Evolution, Frankfurt 1976; Geschichte als Lernprozeß? Zur Pathogenese politischer Modernität in Deutschland, Frankfurt 1985; Die Vergesellschaftung der Natur. Studien zur sozialen Evolution der praktischen Vernunft, Frankfurt 1988. Moreover articles on the sociology of law and on the sociology of social movements.

Eisenstadt, Shmuel N., *1923 at Warsaw, M.A. 1944 at The Hebrew University of Jerusalem, PhD 1947, 1949–57 Lecturer at The Hebrew University of Jerusalem, 1957–59 Associate Professor, 1959 Professor of Sociology in Jerusalem; since 1958 several times visiting professor in Europe and the USA.

Publications i.a.: The Absorption of Immigrants (1955, 1978); From Generation to Generation (1956, 1970); The Political Systems of Empires (1963, 1969); Essays on Comparative Institutions (1965); Modernization: Protest and Change (1966); Israeli Society (1968); Social Differentiation and Stratification (1971); Tradition, Change and Modernity (1973); (together with M. Curelaru) The Form of Sociology: Paradigms and Crises (1976); Revolution and the Transformation of Societies (1978); The Transformation of Israeli Society (1985); Center Formation, Protest Movements & Class Structure in Europe & the United States (1987); European Civilization in a Comparative Perspective (1987).

Featherstone, Mike, is Senior Lecture in Sociology at Teesside Polytechnic. He is founding-editor of Theory, Culture & Society and chair person of the Centre for the Study of Adult Life. He had published articles on sociological theory, the sociology of culture, and the sociology of ageing and co-authored the book Surviving Middle Age (1982).

Gallino, Luciano is Professor at the Dipartimento di Scienze Sociali, Università degli Studi di Torino. Recent Publications: La società. Un' introduzione sistemica alla sociologia (1981); L'attore sociale. Biologia, cultura e intelligenza artificiale (1987); Della ingovernabilità (1987).

Giesen, Bernhard, *1948, studied sociology, history and philosophy; 1974 PhD and Assistant Lecturer at the WiSo Faculty of the University of Augsburg, 1976 Lecturer at the Westfälische Wilhelms-Universität Münster, at present times Professor of Sociology at the University of Gießen. Main publications: Probleme einer Theorie struktureller Inkonsistenz (1974); (together with M. Schmid) Wissenschaftstheorie (1976); Makrosoziologie (1980); (together with J. Alexander, R. Münch, N. Smelser) The Micro-Macro Link (1987). Main fields of research: Theory of social change and modernity; nationalism; sociology of culture.

Haferkamp, Hans studied sociology, economics, statistics, social education and social work; PhD in Bielefeld 1972. 1974–1987 Professor of Sociology at the University of Bremen. Recent main publications: Herrschaft und Strafrecht (1980); Soziologie der Herrschaft (1983); Soziales Handeln. Theorie sozialen Verhaltens und sinnhaften Handelns, geplanter Handlungszusammenhänge und sozialer Strukturen (forthcoming).

Kilminster, Richard, BA University of Essex 1970, MA University of Leicester 1971, PhD University of Leeds 1976, Lecturer in Sociology at the University of Leeds. Author of Praxis and Method (1979) and numerous articles on the sociology of knowledge and on Norbert Elias. At present researching a book on contemporary sociological theory in historical perspective (forthcoming, 1990).

Lindenberg, Siegwart, Professor of Theoretical Sociology at the Rijksuniversiteit in Groningen Netherlands. Mains fields of research: methodology of structural-individualistic sociology, construction and empirical testing of a theory of purposive behavior, construction and empirical testing of theories of genesis and change of solidarity and authority structures. Publications in German, Dutch and American volumes and journals. In 1989 the volume "Zur neuen Soziologie: Methodologische Essays" will be published.

Mongardini, Carlo, Professor of Sociology at the Faculty of Political Sciences at the University of Rome. Research fields: History of Sociology, Sociological Theory, Political Sociology. Publications i.a.: Ideologia e società (Rom 1969); L'epoca della società (Rom 1970); Tradizione e innovazione nel Sud (Rom 1976); Studi sull'ideologia (Rom 1978); Le condizioni del consenso (Rom 1980); Epistemologia e sociologia (Mailand 1985).

Münch, Richard, *1945, Professor of Sociology at the University of Düsseldorf. Publications i. a.: Gesellschaftstheorie und Ideologiekritik (1973); Legitimität und politische Macht (1976); Theorie des Handelns (1982); Die Struktur der Moderne (1984); Die Kultur der Moderne (1986); Theory of Action (1987); Understanding Modernity (1988).

Schmid, Michael, *1943, Professor of Sociology and Philosophy of Sciences at the University of Augsburg. Publications i. a.: Leerformeln und Ideologiekritik (1972); (together with B. Giesen) Wissenschaftstheorie (1976); Handlungsrationalität. Kritik einer dogmatischen Handlungswissenschaft (1979); Theorie sozialen Wandels (1982).

Segerstråle, Ullica, M.S. in Organic Chemistry, M.A. in Sociology and Communications, PhD in Sociology at Harvard University, Assistant Professor of Sociology at Smith College, Acting Professor and Chair of Sociology at the Swedish-speaking University Åbo Akademi in Finland, since 1988 Assistant Professor of Sociology at Illinois Institute of Technology, Chicago. Publications: She has contributed to journals and anthologies in the general fields of sociology of science, and social theory and metatheory, particularly focusing on moral and scientific issues in academic conflict. She is currently working on a book on the sociobiology controversy.

Tenbruck, Friedrich H., *1919, studied philosophy, history, and "Germanistik" at various German universities and completed his doctorate in 1944 at the University of Marburg. Following postdoctoral studies in the social sciences as a Fellow at the University of Virginia, he was a member of several social research institutes in Germany, a guest professor in several countries, and Theodor Heuss Professor in the Graduate Faculty of the New School for Social Research, N.Y. Since 1967 Professor of Sociology at the University of Tübingen. Publications i. a.: Jugend und Gesellschaft, Freiburg (1962); Zur

Kritik der planenden Vernunft, Freiburg/München (1972); Die unbewältigten Sozialwissenschaften oder Die Abschaffung des Menschen, Graz/Wien/Köln (1984); Geschichte und Gesellschaft, Berlin (1986); Die kulturellen Grundlagen der Gesellschaft. Der Fall der Moderne, Opladen (1989).

Weiß, Johannes, *1941, is currently Professor in the Social Science Department of the University of Kassel, specializing in sociological theory and philosophy on the social sciences; co-editor of Soziologische Revue. Among his major publications are: Weltverlust und Subjektivität. Zur Kritik der Institutionenlehre Arnold Gehlens (1971); Max Webers Grundlegung der Soziologie (1975); Das Werk Max Webers in der marxistischen Rezeption und Kritik (1981) (engl. translation: Weber and the Marxist World (1986)). His additional areas of interest are cultural sociology and social philosophy. He is presently involved in research projects on representation and deputyship and on social causality.

Index

action(s), (social), 6ff., 9, 16, 20f., 22ff., 26ff., 32ff., 38ff., 45, 50ff., 67ff., 71ff., 102f., 109f., 113ff., 175, 177ff., 192, 195, 203, 205, 207ff., 218f., 221, 225, 233, 236, 239, 245ff., 253, 261, 286f., 294, 298, 320
action space, 39ff., 50f., 61, 64, 205, 208ff.
action theory, 102, 176ff., 203, 214, 217, 219, 226
adaptation, 21, 47, 74, 109
aestheticization of life, 150, 154, 160, 164, 166
aesthetics, 70, 156ff., 164, 322
anthropology, 6ff., 27f., 116, 175, 178, 330
association(s), 17, 32f., 40, 72f., 110, 206, 209, 213, 217, 232
authority, 25, 29ff., 40, 50ff., 70f., 77, 90, 104, 106, 159, 248, 253f., 258, 260, 280, 290f., 320f.
avant-garde, 72, 81, 149, 155f.

behavior, (social), 6ff., 10, 20, 23, 29f., 50ff., 103, 112, 116, 129, 164, 176ff., 201f., 204ff., 218, 221ff., 250ff., 273f., 285, 320
behavioral/behaviorist(ic) approach, 8, 21f., 175, 187, 194
body, 157, 164, 203ff.
bourgeoisie, petite, 129, 137, 154, 162, 294

capital, (cultural, economic, moral, symbolic), 129, 132, 153, 155, 162, 253ff.
choice, (concept of), 175ff., 221, 292
civilization(s), 10, 91, 97, 110, 149, 223, 328
civilizing process(es), 112, 151
class(es), (social), (concept of), 7, 93, 105, 107, 125ff., 194, 235f., 269, 271, 282, 294, 313, 322
– bourgeois, 125, 127, 137, 153
– lower, 129f., 137, 140f.
– (new) middle, 125, 129f., 132, 137, 153, 161ff., 231
– upper, 137, 140f., 231
– working, 32, 129, 133, 236, 294
class culture(s), 119, 140
class formation, 126, 130, 134
class membership, 79, 126
class position, 128, 130
class society, 93, 125f.
classification, 125ff., 129
closure, 118, 130, 303
collective consciousness, 89, 94f., 97
communication, 40, 51ff., 72, 78, 81, 133, 156, 211, 246, 248, 256, 305f., 326, 329
community, 40, 42f., 51ff., 75ff., 91, 97, 109, 120, 165, 206ff., 219, 224f., 229, 233, 248, 251, 258, 305f., 316f., 326
– lay, 246, 248, 252, 254f., 260
– scientific, 38ff., 96, 248f., 252, 256, 258, 260, 277ff.
competence, 127, 130ff., 138
conflict(s), 17, 90, 104ff., 128, 156, 165, 179, 182, 207f., 217, 223, 238, 291, 302
consensus, 89, 92, 94, 105f., 245, 291
control, 19, 24, 47, 69, 76f., 104, 109, 130, 164, 221, 290f., 316f., 324ff.
countervalue(s), 114f., 223
crisis/crises, 5, 89ff.
counterculture(s), 32, 114, 158, 163
cultural patterns, 7, 26f., 110
culture, high(er), 130, 134, 157, 163, 233
– immaterial, 22, 24
– material, 20, 22, 24
– modern, 17, 29ff., 71f., 74, 80, 98, 108f., 126, 138, 147
– political, 120, 131
– popular, 72, 163, 233
– postmodern, 147, 151ff.
– premodern, 23, 37
– Western, 18, 38f., 89, 96f.

dedifferentiation, 105f.
definition of the situation, 6, 16, 50ff., 176, 179, 182, 186, 190, 194, 211
determinist, cultural, 27, 102
– social, 27, 102

differentiation, 67ff., 78ff., 92, 101ff., 131, 315, 317
discourse, 5, 16, 18, 41, 52ff., 57, 60, 63, 66, 72, 125ff., 140, 148, 155, 160, 245ff., 305, 324f., 327f., 331
disintegration, 118, 230, 235f.
division of labor, 25, 72, 90, 126, 299, 303
domination, 26, 96, 109, 159, 316f., 322, 326, 330f.

effects, (communication, disposition, epistemological, position), 272ff.
Enlightenment, 43, 137, 231, 259, 270, 320, 323, 328
equality, (social), 75, 78ff., 117, 126ff., 296
ethics, 261, 293
evolution, 67, 77, 82, 107, 128, 202, 221
evolutionary scheme/theory, 106, 108, 120
exclusion, 80, 118, 120
expectation(s), 17, 69, 75, 77, 80, 102ff., 178, 180, 185, 187, 221ff.
expert(s), 245f., 248f., 257f., 260, 317, 324

frame(s), 187, 189, 191f., 195, 206, 211f.
framing, 176, 184, 186f., 190ff., 235
function(s), (concept of), 8f., 40, 67, 106, 108, 117, 127f., 144, 181ff., 205f., 210, 213, 223f., 261, 317, 323, 331

game, concept of, 218, 220ff.
goal(s), 40f., 109, 176, 182, 188, 190ff., 203ff., 218f., 221

habit(us), 119, 163
hierarchy, 72, 127, 154, 156f., 161, 163, 233

idea(s), 18, 22, 24ff., 42f., 45, 56ff., 72, 74, 80, 102, 136, 147, 219, 237f., 270ff., 291f., 319, 323
idealist approach, 7f., 93, 175, 177ff., 302
ideology, 5f., 17, 22, 30, 67, 97, 148, 217, 231, 235, 239, 245, 269ff., 295, 313ff.
inclusion, 78, 80, 118ff.
individualization, 79, 115, 127, 132
inequality, (social), 75ff., 90, 94, 125ff., 235, 277, 280
institution(s), 7, 19, 24f., 31, 33, 67, 70ff., 105, 116, 119, 156ff., 183, 223f., 229, 238, 284f., 291, 298
institutionalization, 10, 71f., 80f., 128, 247f., 261, 315
integration, 67, 71, 76f., 93f., 103ff., 217, 229, 234, 237
intellectuals, 25f., 28, 30ff., 43, 109, 154, 156, 158ff., 233, 236ff., 257, 259, 297, 313ff.
interaction(s), (social), 25f., 31ff., 41, 50, 58, 61, 64, 67ff., 75ff., 102, 108, 110, 114, 116f., 133, 178, 189, 192, 195, 206, 219ff., 298
interactionists, (symbolic), 6, 106, 109f., 118
interest(s), 10, 21, 24, 28, 30, 44f., 67, 73f., 78f., 90, 95, 102, 111, 139, 182, 192, 201, 206ff., 230, 232, 236f., 239, 245, 247ff., 269, 271, 277, 282, 313
– ideal(istic), 24, 237f.
– material(istic), 24, 102f., 139, 232, 236ff.

knowledge, 6, 9, 17ff., 23ff., 37ff., 50ff., 68, 71, 75, 92, 94f., 129, 135, 137, 148, 150ff., 159f., 226, 245f., 248f., 252, 258f., 275, 284, 289f., 292, 296ff., 313f., 319ff.

learning (processes), 39ff., 50ff., 92, 140, 176, 179, 191f., 195, 210, 314f., 319
life-style(s), 29f., 32, 44, 108, 117, 129, 154, 162f., 164, 166
life-world, 31, 39f., 44, 56ff., 75ff., 109f., 120, 133f., 150, 237, 245ff.

magic, 25, 224, 275ff.
market(s), 40, 44, 46, 51, 53f., 58, 79, 81f., 132, 154f., 159, 162, 261, 294f., 325f., 328
materialist approach, 7f., 94, 175, 177f., 183, 302
meaning(s), 8f., 15f., 20, 22f., 47, 50ff., 67f., 70f., 73f., 80f., 96, 151, 175, 192ff., 212, 221, 234, 237f., 249, 252, 255f., 269ff., 291f., 314, 330
meta-problems/theory, 5, 152, 248, 250, 257, 260f.
mind, 6, 8, 201f., 206ff., 217
modernism, 149, 156
modernity, 5, 72, 92ff., 108ff., 130, 137, 147ff., 230, 294, 317, 321f., 330f.

modernization, 5, 97, 107, 112, 127, 134, 161
moral(s), 24f., 91f., 130
morality, 70f., 73f., 91, 94, 129, 134, 137, 140, 150, 156, 158f., 252, 254, 301, 322
movement(s), 26, 32, 115, 149, 152, 154, 167, 231f., 234f., 273ff.
– (new) social, 73, 111, 114f., 117, 120, 129, 132, 295

nationalism, 229ff.
nature, human, 127, 166, 177, 251, 259
nature-culture distinction, 221, 316
nature-nurture controversy/distinction, 248ff., 314, 316
negotiation(s), 6f., 9, 105f., 112, 164, 218ff., 249, 259ff.
norm(s), 6, 8f., 22f., 27f., 31, 39ff., 43f., 51, 56, 59, 67, 69ff., 102ff., 113, 115ff., 135, 182, 191ff., 201, 246, 248, 261, 314, 327

order, (social), 9, 16f., 24f., 78, 82, 91, 94ff., 126, 129, 132, 212, 315ff.

personality, 7ff., 43f., 50ff., 177f., 219f., 222ff.
philosophy, 24, 40, 93, 98, 148, 152, 155, 158f., 256, 289ff.
pluralism, 29f., 159, 330
position(s), (social), 22, 71, 75ff., 126f., 130, 134, 137ff., 162, 190, 205, 209ff., 232, 261, 272ff., 329f.
positivist(ic), approach, 8, 92f., 252, 260
postmodernism, 147, 149ff.
postmodernity, 147ff., 330f.
postmodernization, 147ff.
power, 6f., 25f., 40, 43, 56, 59, 69f., 77, 79, 90, 92, 105f., 111f., 130, 140, 147, 151, 153, 158, 161f., 165ff., 211, 225, 230ff., 245, 258, 261, 273, 289, 294, 296f., 303, 313, 316ff.
praxis, 76, 136f., 313
prestige, 19, 25, 77, 91, 155, 190, 237, 289, 292, 301, 303
professionalization, 19, 296

rational choice, 6f., 176, 190f., 194f.
– approach/theory, 7, 10, 180, 182, 187, 194
rationality, 42f., 45f., 73, 91f., 95ff., 150, 181ff., 223, 245, 247, 269ff., 320, 323
rationalization, 92f., 95, 128, 130, 135, 179, 182, 245, 297
reason, 42, 44, 182f., 191f., 314, 320f., 327
reification, 7, 19, 21
religion, 6, 9, 16, 18, 24f., 72, 93, 136, 152, 194f., 256
representation(s), 20, 23, 125, 128, 139, 202, 205f., 209ff., 219f., 221, 223, 225, 236, 302, 313
reproduction, 80, 82, 126, 128, 133, 135, 140f., 153, 204ff., 221, 313f., 316ff.
role(s), (concept of), 17f., 22f., 25, 28f., 31, 39, 50, 58f., 64, 93f., 118, 164, 178, 182, 190ff., 208, 261, 274, 313f., 323ff.
role inclusion, 103, 107, 110, 113, 118ff.
rule(s), 7ff., 39, 43f., 69ff., 74ff., 80, 136, 177ff., 221ff., 258, 260, 275, 304, 320, 325

sanction(s), 24, 69, 77f., 81
scarcity, 82, 176, 179f., 182, 192, 194
science(s), 5ff., 16ff., 25ff., 46, 72f., 81, 89, 91ff., 96, 108, 110, 150, 152, 160, 162, 245ff., 277, 286, 290ff., 322
– modern, 37ff., 40ff., 72, 81, 96
– natural, 8, 19, 245, 247ff., 277
selection(s), 23, 67, 82, 104, 107, 111, 185, 187, 250
social change(s), 16f., 44, 102, 252, 269, 294, 296, 321
social fact(s), 7, 23, 26f., 32, 104, 125, 238
socialization, 23, 70, 78, 178, 190f., 193, 211, 217, 224, 252, 261, 286
society, concept of, 16ff., 91ff., 217ff., 294f., 301
– contemporary, 101, 107, 109, 112, 114f., 117, 120, 210, 322
– mass, 119, 233
– modern, 5, 16f., 29f., 72f., 74, 94, 97, 107f., 112f., 118ff., 125ff., 225
– primitive, 21, 25, 27f., 68, 126
– traditional, 41, 74, 126ff., 211, 295
– Western, 103, 117f., 120
sociobiology, 248ff.
sociology, postmodern, 97, 151ff.
solidarity, 72f., 75, 133, 235, 297
specialists, 77, 153ff., 289ff.

status, (social), 79ff., 129ff., 159, 181, 190, 193, 210, 236, 277, 289ff., 318
stratification, 72, 117, 134, 274
(structural-)functional school/approach, 5f., 8, 284ff.
structuralism, 6ff., 68, 148, 291
structuration, 147, 219
subculture(s), 44, 58, 60, 71, 105, 114, 119f., 133, 135f.
subsystem(s), 71, 103, 109, 120, 202, 205ff., 245, 261
symbol(ic) production, 7, 151, 153f., 156, 158f., 161ff.
systems world, 245, 261

technology, 38, 41f., 43, 73, 95, 109, 211f., 245
theory of ideology, 269ff.
theory of society, 18f., 28, 33, 91f., 94f.
tradition(s), 5, 9, 15, 19, 23, 27, 40, 69f., 72f., 77, 81, 116, 120, 150, 155, 160, 238, 270, 278, 291ff., 326ff.

universalism, 39, 137, 140

value(s), 6, 22f., 25, 27f., 31, 70, 90, 96, 102ff., 114f., 132f., 135, 138, 154, 165f., 177f., 180f., 188, 190f., 193f., 207ff., 218ff., 233, 246, 248, 251, 254f., 260, 275, 278, 289, 297, 299, 303, 306, 313f., 320, 322ff.
value change, 32, 113, 115
value generalization, 107, 113, 115ff.
value-orientation, 69f., 73f., 76ff., 175
value theory, (of action), 177, 182, 191f., 195
variation(s), 18, 71ff., 111

Bei Fragen zur Produktsicherheit wenden Sie sich bitte an:
If you have any questions regarding product safety,
please contact:

Walter de Gruyter GmbH
Genthiner Straße 13
10785 Berlin
productsafety@degruyterbrill.com